Hedley Thomas, *The Australian*'s national investigative journalist, author and true-c

His first job in newspapers was as a c *Bulletin* in 1984. Hedley worked as a journalist covering tumultuous news events in London, Europe and Hong Kong for eight years. He and his wife, Ruth, have lived in Brisbane since 1999.

His investigations since 2017 have attempted to solve cold case murders of Australian women. His podcasts in order of release since 2018 are *The Teacher's Pet*, *The Night Driver*, *Shandee's Story*, *The Teacher's Trial*, *Shandee's Legacy* and *The Teacher's Accuser*. Hedley's first book, *Sick to Death*, was published in 2007.

Hedley has won eight Walkley Awards including two Gold Walkleys. For his reporting in 2022, he received the Graham Perkin Australian Journalist of the Year Award.

This book contains descriptions of sexual assault and domestic violence. These passages may be triggering for some readers. Reader discretion is advised.

HEDLEY THOMAS

with Epilogue by Matthew Condon

The Teacher's Pet

MACMILLAN
Pan Macmillan Australia

Some of the people in this book have had their names changed to protect their identities.

First published 2023 in Macmillan by Pan Macmillan Australia Pty Ltd
1 Market Street, Sydney, New South Wales, Australia, 2000

A catalogue record for this book is available from the National Library of Australia

Typeset in 11.8/15.75 pt Minion Pro by Midland Typesetters

Printed by IVE

Image on page 4 of picture section reproduced by permission of the Australian Broadcasting Corporation – Library Sales © 1975 ABC.

The author and the publisher have made every effort to contact copyright holders for material used in this book. Any person or organisation that may have been overlooked should contact the publisher.

For my father, Hedley, my mother, Diana, and my loving family, Ruth, Alexander and Sarah.

And for Lyn.

Contents

Author's Note

Some of the people in this book have had their names changed for legal reasons and to protect their identities.

Pseudonyms are used for the former Cromer High student and babysitter who became Chris Dawson's second wife, as well as her parents, her stepfather, her younger sister and her daughter with Chris. Their names have been changed, respectively, to Jenny Carlson, Graham Carlson, Ann Carlson, Ron, Naomi Carlson and Mikaela Carlson.

The name of Lyn's youngest daughter has been changed to Amy.

The name of a woman who was a teenager when she went to Forest High in the early 1980s has been changed to Alice.

The name of a man who was a teenager when he went to Cromer High in the early 1980s has been changed to Rhys.

The name of a woman who was a teenager in January 1982 when she worked at Northbridge Baths has been changed to Janet.

The name of a man who was a teenager at Asquith Boys High in the 1980s has been changed to Adrian.

Part 1
Gathering

Chapter 1

Bowen Hills

27 October 2017

Dear Greg,

Please let me reintroduce myself. It has been some years since our last contact. My name is Hedley Thomas and I wrote some lengthy articles about your sister Lyn in 2001.

This happened after I met and interviewed Pat at her home in Sydney, as well as Detective Loone at the police station he was then working from.

Detective Loone was good enough at the time to give me access to his police and coronial files, and on my return to Brisbane I developed a feature article, headlined 'Looking for Lyn', and published in *The Courier-Mail*.

The dignified efforts of you, Pat, your mother until her passing, and Lyn's other relatives and friends to find Lyn, and to achieve justice, have been unstinting over so many years.

It is one of the reasons Lyn's story has always stayed with me.

It is late in the afternoon on the last Friday of October in 2017 and the office of *The Australian* in Brisbane is quietening down near the end of the week's news cycle.

I've started drafting an email at my computer in the corner, affording a view across a dozen work desks in a messy office enclosed

3

with glass in the heart of a building I've known well, on and off, over the previous three decades.

There's no natural light in this part of the edifice in Bowen Hills where, as a 21-year-old, I'd watch in awe as hot, thundering printing presses magically produced first editions of the newspaper.

With reporter friends, I'd come here at midnight to grab a newly printed paper and we'd marvel at how our stories had been used.

The presses are long gone, replaced by smaller versions far from here printing fewer papers with earlier deadlines.

I get up and walk past files of months-old newspapers. Around shelves of unread books sent by hopeful publishers and sometimes the authors themselves. They seek the oxygen of publicity and a favourable review.

Constant chatter from talking heads, reporting and commenting on the day's news, bears down from TV screens on wall mountings above framed front pages. Some of the Queensland office's biggest scoops are hung up there.

My friend Michael McKenna, a dogged reporter and a much-admired chief of our Queensland bureau, sits fidgeting at his cluttered desk – separated from the rest of us by a door he pulls shut – as I start to explain a story I haven't picked up for 16 and a half years. A cold case.

I tell him about a woman in her early 30s, a nurse, called Lynette Joy Dawson. How she lived with her rugby league star husband Chris, a schoolteacher who played for the Newtown Jets with his twin brother, Paul.

'Lyn has a brother, Greg Simms. And a sister, Pat Jenkins. Lyn and Chris had two little girls. They lived in a picturesque place called Bayview on Sydney's Northern Beaches,' I tell Michael.

'Dawson is infatuated by a teenager from his school. He gets her into the family home as a babysitter to the two Dawson daughters. Dawson is having sex with the girl there.

'Lyn finds out. It's an impossible situation.'

Impossible, until the day Lyn suddenly vanishes and Chris Dawson's problems melt away.

It is as if the universe swallowed the lively, warm and loving woman, serendipitously delivering Dawson uncontested custody of the children, ownership of the marital home and the sexual freedom of a single man.

Lyn vanished on 9 January 1982. Michael and I were teenagers on school holidays, he in Brisbane and me at Main Beach on the Gold Coast.

Michael is a coiled spring of energy and contagious curiosity. I can see he's intrigued.

I go on to tell him that the teenager marries Mr Dawson, who was twice her age when he zeroed in on her in the playground of Cromer High. They have a child in 1985 but within five years they'll separate, then go through a divorce.

'And nobody hears from Lyn again.'

He's hooked now.

Michael is a reporting bloodhound. His intuitive news sense – the difference between adequate reporters and great ones – is acute. His commitment to breaking yarns and uncovering powerful facts, from political and corruption scandals from Canberra and Brisbane, to digging deep into some of Queensland's most heinous crimes, to shining a light into dark corners of remote Indigenous communities in the hope that highlighting the plight of many abused women and children will make a positive difference to their lives, has inspired all with whom he has worked. On this balmy Friday afternoon, I'm trying to make a sales pitch and get a concrete commitment. I'm telling Michael why it would be a good idea for me to drop other stories I'm working on to concentrate on just one. Lyn's case.

And not for just a week or a fortnight. At a time in journalism when job-shedding and the farewelling of our friends and colleagues from once-boisterous, busy newsrooms have become depressingly repetitive – an era of digital click-bait, in which the demands of bean counters to squeeze more from less have put heavy burdens on editors and everyone down the chain – I need Michael's blessing to give me free rein on one story for perhaps six months.

'I think it can be solved. If I do it as a podcast.'

It's an enormous ask. I've never done a podcast before. Audio and narration are a new medium for a reporter who started when the clatter of typewriters filled newsrooms.

In the true crime podcast space, I've only heard a few: American broadcaster Sarah Koenig's 2014 podcast *Serial* about Adnan Syed, a convicted killer who denied slaying his former girlfriend Hae Min Lee in Baltimore in 1999, was the first.

Newspaper journalists are, in the main, soloists who recoil from the long arm of management. We persuade ourselves that we're doing our best when left well alone to go away and dig and dig. It presents impossible challenges for editors, who must fill the newspaper every day.

Michael's unenviable job includes balancing the endless daily needs of the paper with the independent spirit of quixotic journalists spouting grand ideas and big promises with rubbery deadlines.

He wants to know about the progress of the other stories I've been working on. Nothing has been converted to newsprint yet.

The truth is that since my father died earlier in the year, none of the stories I would once have tackled with relish have felt worthy.

My father's strong interest in my reporting – his encouragement and feedback – were powerful motivators. I was named after him, so my byline was also his.

I gave Michael a pessimistic update on two of my incomplete investigations.

There's a rape survivor and her allegations of being brutally violated as a teenager by a young man, many years before his bid for political high office. It's a fraught case of word against word – a 'she said, he said', I tell Michael, adding that the woman in her 40s is in physical and psychological torment.

She's sent me hostile text messages despite our first round of interviews having gone smoothly. She's stopped returning my calls. I doubt we can get the investigation back on track.

Then there's the untold story of a hard-working single father who has written thousands of words to me and the Office of the Director of Public Prosecutions (DPP) about his certainty that the death of his son was not a suicide – as determined by the magistrate in charge of a coronial inquest – but a coldblooded murder.

This gentleman is convinced his son's former partner is a cruel, sociopathic killer.

His son was a drug dealer known to police for crimes including armed robbery. I tell Michael that some newly discovered facts from the father's careful analysis of evidence from an inquest do raise suspicions of foul play. His theory isn't completely far-fetched but I've held something back while explaining my reluctance to develop this case.

When there are countless unsolved and suspected murders of the innocent and defenceless, waiting to be investigated, reported and potentially resolved, I'm struggling to commit to the case of a thug who terrorised bank tellers and sold hard drugs to vulnerable young users.

The dead man's father knows it.

'You turn a deaf ear to this dear Hedley, and your dear grandchildren will pay for it with the way this evil system is run,' he writes to me. 'I am like a little David against a giant Goliath. But I stand for truth, justice, honesty, integrity, equity and everything decent.'

His handwritten letters are strewn across my desk. They remind me of my failure to properly run his claims to ground. Avoidance looms large.

'Lyn's story is special. I've known this for 16 years,' I tell Michael. There's an urgent plea in my pitch.

If I can secure Michael's backing, it will be easier to convince editors in the Sydney head office of the need for a lengthy, costly investigation. And that it needs to be done through this unfamiliar new form of journalistic storytelling: the podcast.

As Michael hears me out, my colleagues Trent Dalton, Sarah Elks and Jamie Walker file their stories for the fast-looming weekend edition. I'm ending another week without a yarn. At times like this it's hard to shake the uneasy sense that you're an impostor on the brink of being exposed.

No matter how many stories you've broken or reported, journalistic insecurities bubble just below the surface. Regular bylines quell the unease, a journalist's measure of self-worth.

Going without for a few days elicits despair and an irrational, gnawing fear that faceless readers and colleagues are noting your absence from the paper. Keeping score.

Nine hundred kilometres away in Sydney, subeditors are deftly removing typos from the reporters' copy which is arriving on, but mostly after, the tight deadline. Sentences are being snappily rewritten and headlines and photographs placed. If it all works as intended, they'll draw the reader into the story. Somebody in the business will count the clicks. Keeping score.

'I agree, it sounds remarkable,' Michael tells me. 'Do you think you can crack it?'

'Yes, Mickey. Absolutely.' I'm overselling now. I need a green light. He agrees.

The thrill of an exciting new challenge has given me a happy charge. It must be adrenaline. I've now got the most valuable commodity in investigative journalism: time.

I return to my desk to continue drafting the email to Greg Simms, Lyn's brother, a former police officer with whom I've had sporadic email contact since I first looked at Lyn's case in 2001.

I have begun re-reading the media files and refreshing my memory as I would like to make Lyn the subject of a significant new investigation and a multimedia project in *The Australian* and *The Weekend Australian*.

If it goes to plan it would be a powerful documentary podcast series spanning two to three months with numerous interviews and related articles. It would be widely promoted, and it would strive to tell Lyn's story in exhaustive detail in a way that has not been attempted before. This would be a significant undertaking. It would depend on the cooperation and blessing of Lyn's (Simms) family, friends and police.

We may only hope that it would finally produce a result. In this regard, you may have heard of the Bowraville podcast series which was produced by my colleague at *The Australian*, Dan Box.

After many years of inaction and prevarication by prosecutors, Dan's podcast series made such a powerful impact that it led to a new top-level review, and charges against the suspected murderer.

Several years ago, I spoke to Rebecca Hazel as she contacted me while she was researching a book about Lyn, and wanted to talk to me about the article I had written. I called Rebecca today to ask what happened to her book. We spoke at length, and I confided my idea.

The upshot was that we think there is a reasonable chance we can collaborate on the project and hopefully publish her book. It's early days, of course, but sometimes a good idea runs quickly with goodwill and motivation.

Greg, can you please let me know your views as I would like to come to Sydney to talk to you and Pat about logistics as soon as possible.

I would like to catch up with Rebecca in Sydney, however, she is interstate at present and may not return to Sydney until Thursday.

Finally, can I just ask that you keep the proposal quiet for as long as possible, so that we are not disrupted or copied by opportunists.

Thanks for reading this far, Greg. I hope you have a great weekend.

Best Regards

Hedley

I read the email over and over. It's vital to get the tone right and leave no room for misunderstandings.

Even though there's never been any trace of a body, I'd long held the view that Chris Dawson had probably got away with Lyn's murder. I didn't want to come straight out with this assertion in writing, even though Greg needed no convincing.

I held out to Greg the promise of a breakthrough – *we may only hope that it would finally produce a result* – and emphasised my keenness to start immediately. I was anxious to build momentum.

I had personal motives too but Greg didn't need to hear about my father, who grew up on the Northern Beaches. His mother had disappeared from that place, from her two children, when she was in her 30s, just a little older than Lyn.

Like Lyn, my grandmother was never seen by her children or friends and loved ones again.

Like Lyn, she was ephemeral and shrouded in mystery. We scarcely talked about her when Dad was alive because I knew how much it pained him.

I remember my mother telling my sisters and me when we were small children that Dad would walk around street corners and through shopping centres and other busy public places, scanning the crowd for his mother's pretty face. He looked for her for many years until he finally accepted he would never see her again.

I knew that Dad always hero-worshipped his father, who had died a year after I was born, but my mother couldn't stand him. I knew that two of my grandmother's siblings had died by suicide in the years before Dad's mother disappeared; that my grandmother probably had depression and my grandfather was not suspected by police of wrongdoing after her disappearance in October 1956.

Mum told me she had heard that searchers found my grand-mother's nightdress on the sand near the waves at Dee Why. It was believed that she had walked into the ocean and kept swimming until she drowned. I had never seen any corroborative documentation. My love for my father was such that I did not want to add to his lifetime of pain by asking about it.

There was much to do. I felt enormously privileged and excited but also daunted by the assignment into which I'd just manouevered myself.

Thousands of pages of inquest transcript evidence, which I hoped to prise from courts and cops, needed to be read and re-read for clues and new angles. Dozens of people mentioned in those pages, in the pages of witness statements or by Lyn's relatives on the family grape-vine would need to be located and persuaded to talk to me.

Neighbours, friends, former footballers and schoolteacher colleagues of Chris Dawson. Reporters who had followed the story in the distant past. Anyone ever quoted in any of the numerous articles about Lyn's case. Women who went to nursing college with Lyn or worked with her in the hospitals or at a childcare centre on the Northern Beaches. Did any of them have jottings or old cassette tapes from their interviews with police two decades ago? All were on my list for follow-up.

Even some of my own friends and teachers from high school might be relevant. Chris started teaching physical education at my old school in Southport in January 1985, weeks after I had graduated to start work as a 17-year-old copyboy at the local newspaper, the *Gold Coast Bulletin*. The high school connection was another strange coincidence. What were the chances?

As a cadet sports reporter in 1985 and 1986, I enthusiastically reported on schoolboy rugby league contests in which my old school, Keebra Park State High, reigned supreme. I must have met or at least seen Dawson at that time. I was filling the back pages with laudatory pieces about my former school team where he was a prominent teacher and an assistant coach.

I press send at 5.23 pm and the email goes to Greg Simms at his home near Newcastle.

It had been almost 36 years since Lyn vanished from the lives of all who knew and loved her, most painfully her two young daughters. Chris had always strenuously asserted his innocence of any foul play. He had remarried, divorced and married again.

With the sending of that email, the clock was now running down on Dawson's comfortable life near the beach in Coolum on the Sunshine Coast, about a 90-minute drive from my home in Brookfield, just beyond the suburban sprawl of Brisbane's leafy western suburbs.

The idea sketched out in a Brisbane newsroom one Friday afternoon would take on a heartbeat of its own as my investigation went back on its trail of a schoolteacher who got away with murder for four decades.

In 2018, it would grow into the global juggernaut of *The Teacher's Pet*. As the 16th and final episode was about to drop in December that year, New South Wales Homicide detectives went to Queensland to arrest Christopher Michael Dawson for Lyn's murder. This was then followed by three and a half years of tortuous legal proceedings, in which Dawson and his legal team tried everything to show that he was an innocent man.

In a bid to permanently halt the planned prosecution, the Dawson camp mapped out a strategy to put me and the podcast on trial. The courtroom battles through 2020, 2021 and 2022, where his legal team waged this fight, were subject to reporting bans at the time; the judges, the lawyers for Dawson and the DPP were concerned that more prejudicial publicity would make it more difficult for him to get a fair trial.

When I wrote to Greg Simms on that Friday afternoon in October 2017, none of us comprehended that we had awoken something wild and dangerous, bound up in decades of hurt and mystery. Neither Chris Dawson nor I could have known that only one of us would survive it.

Chapter 2

Newspaper Stories

Late February to mid-March 2001

The library serving the journalists of *The Courier-Mail* and *The Australian* is a place of quiet refuge.

It is sometimes a location to briefly hide from a newsroom's harried chief of staff, searching desperately for a reporter to deliver on an editor's impossible idea for page one.

It promises an interlude for uninterrupted browsing of the day's newspapers, couriered here from all parts of Queensland and Australia then arranged by the helpful library staff into separate bound folders, with the newest editions on top for easy leafing. I was regularly drawn to this less frantic part of the building. The library holds the historical records of the people, the tragic and happy events, the natural and man-made disasters, the political scandals and the essential but boring details of tides and the weather going back to a newspaper's inception.

'Newspapers, after all, are the first drafts of history, or pretend they are,' *The Washington Post* declared on its editorial page in October 1944.

Its former publisher Philip L. Graham is usually credited with the line. I believe it to be true.

When I worked for *The Courier-Mail*, its daily editorial page ran a quote which became seared in my mind and guided my journalistic compass: 'Our liberty depends on the freedom of the press, and that cannot be limited without being lost.' It was written by Thomas Jefferson in 1786, some 15 years before he became the third president of the United States.

In the newspaper's library the slightly musty smell of a century of Australia's and Queensland's history – albeit first drafts – wafts from the newsprint, old encyclopedias and almanacs.

One day during a tour of the building I brought the then Chief Justice of Queensland Paul de Jersey to the library, opened a filing cabinet and pulled a large, sealed envelope which held a draft of his obituary, fact-checked and ready to be published for when he popped his clogs. He looked surprised and thrilled.

Another time, I hid my notebook among thousands of the library's books after being warned one of my stories about alleged corruption would likely attract a search warrant as police tried to discover my confidential sources. The notebook stayed safely concealed for several years.

This was a time when journalists were using fax machines to send and receive documents, not email. Attachments sometimes described minor obsessions between lovers, not PDFs. Google was in its infancy. Newspapers with modest websites gave their stories away online because print editions were still widely favoured.

But in early March 2001, I went to the library for something more mundane. I wanted to catch up with news and features published in the metropolitan daily newspapers in Sydney and Melbourne. A 2001 story in Sydney's *The Daily Telegraph* grabbed my attention. This was the first time I heard about a couple called Chris and Lyn Dawson.

The story appeared under the byline of *The Tele*'s highly regarded reporter Charles Miranda.

Police have stepped up the hunt for the body of a woman missing for 19 years as a chief prosecutor decides if her fate was murder.

The 1982 disappearance of Lynette Joy Dawson was publicly forgotten until a police prosecutor told an inquest this week that she was dead.

The inquest was told her husband and former League star Chris Dawson was a violent controller who had allegedly once throttled her and planned to hire a hitman to kill her months before she disappeared.

On Wednesday, Glebe Coroners Court heard Dawson had begun a sexual affair with babysitter Jenny Carlson more than a year before his wife disappeared.

Ms Carlson, who attended the hearing, was allegedly told by Dawson about the hitman plan, which he later abandoned because 'innocent people would get hurt'.

Sydney detective Damian Loone said new information received this week about the possible whereabouts of Mrs Dawson's buried body was being actively pursued.

Senior Constable Loone, who has been working the case for more than three years, said the investigation, named Operation Luzon, would continue regardless of whether the NSW Director of Public Prosecutions decided if any charges could or should be laid.

'We will keep searching and I'm not giving up,' he said yesterday.

The DPP is examining more than 30 witness statements totalling hundreds of pages and a cut woman's cardigan, believed to be Mrs Dawson's, to decide whether a prima facie case exists.

One statement presented to the DPP states Mrs Dawson spoke to her mother the day before she disappeared. Sounding groggy, she told her mother: 'Chris has made me a lovely drink.'

The court had earlier heard Mrs Dawson did not normally drink alcohol but in 1981 Dawson regularly gave it to her to make her sleepy so he could pursue his sexual relations with his 16-year-old babysitter.

I found the story riveting.

Charles Miranda's report was a follow-up to one published on page 9 of *The Daily Telegraph* on 1 March, the day after State Coroner Jan Stevenson found that a jury could reasonably conclude that Lyn was killed by '*a known person*' and that the DPP should consider prosecuting that 'known person' for murder.

The euphemisms could not disguise the identity of the 'known person': Christopher Michael Dawson.

> There was not a spare seat in Glebe's Court 1 as for more than two hours, evidence was heard yesterday of gifts of sex, love, murder, violence and archaeological digs.
>
> But Coroner Jan Stevenson yesterday terminated the reopened hearing into Mrs Dawson's disappearance 19 years ago after declaring an indictable offence had been found and the Director of Public Prosecutions should be informed. The DPP will decide who should face charges, if any.

Miranda's story included a quote from Peter Dawson, a solicitor who represented his younger brother Chris at the hearing.

Chris was conspicuous by his absence.

> An emotional Peter Dawson told the court the evidence was smoke and mirrors, rubbish and remained untested.
>
> 'We're talking about my sister-in-law, Your Worship. I loved that woman something shocking – I still do,' he said.

Near the end of his follow-up report, Charles Miranda disclosed that Chris Dawson 'has taken leave from his physical education teaching job at St Ursula's Girls College in Yeppoon'.

> His school's principal, Margaret Ramsay, however, said Dawson had made her aware of the issue ahead of the inquest.
>
> Mrs Ramsay said she had received no direction from the Catholic Education Office as to his future.
>
> 'The college is committed to respecting legal process and upholding the presumption a person is innocent until proven guilty,' she said.

After reading both of Charles Miranda's reports, I wanted to delve more deeply.

As a features writer for *The Courier-Mail*, I strove to write pieces of a couple of thousand words for the weekend section called *Inside Mail*. It was edited by Graham Lloyd, whose laid-back management style and remarkable brain suited me. He trusted my instincts to come up with an idea for a feature and then he let me get on with it until I sought his guidance. When he gave it, he was always right. Graphic designer Vanessa Hunter did the arresting artwork. Her brilliant eye meant the artwork and layouts she commissioned and designed gave the pages of *Inside Mail* an edge usually reserved for high-end magazines.

Reporters and readers were spoiled by a newspaper in its prime, led by a visionary editor-in-chief, Chris Mitchell, who had spared no expense in hiring some of the country's most talented journalists. Their dedication to producing quality sections inspired me and our colleagues to deliver our best.

I told them my idea. I'd try to talk to more people involved in this intriguing case, travel to Sydney, profile Chris, Lyn and the young woman who was the family's adolescent babysitter when she started having sex with her PE teacher. I wanted to talk to the police officer, Damian Loone, and his only suspect, Chris, as well as his second wife, the former high school student. If Chris didn't want to talk, I needed to hear from someone who backed him. For Lyn's profile, a member of her family would be essential.

I felt sure I could write a weekend feature which would be detailed, moving and, I hoped, as riveting as the news stories by Charles Miranda.

I started with an online property ownership search which showed where Chris Dawson and his third wife, Susan Constance Dawson, lived near Yeppoon, a town about an eight-hour drive north of Brisbane.

Some brief letters had been emailed by readers responding to Charles Miranda's reports, which had also been published, albeit less prominently, in *The Courier-Mail*. The letters were in an internal production folder. I printed them out.

One was dated 1 March.

I happened to pick up a copy of *The Courier-Mail* and noticed a familiar face, a high school teacher of mine, at one stage being accused of hiring a hitman to kill his wife in 1982.

It also made mention of his twin brother who teaches at my sister's school, also one of my ex teachers. The article was very biased in the way it was written. And misleading to anyone who may have read it.

Both men are incredibly kind people to those who know them. And you made both of them sound like perverted maniacs.

If you were being harassed by the media, wouldn't you feel a little pissed off? Doesn't the media believe in *innocence* before proven guilty?

I called the landline number on the letter and explained that I planned to write a longer piece and wanted to hear the other side of the story.

Susan, who was 18 and studying pharmacy at the University of Queensland, painted a picture of a gentle, kind man whom she came to know at Coombabah State High on the Gold Coast, where he had gone after two years of teaching at Keebra Park.

'I had Chris Dawson in Year 8. Every week he would stand up to tell us jokes,' she told me. 'The next year, we had Paul Dawson. You could talk to him very freely and he was a nice guy. They were genuinely very nice people. Chris Dawson's wife worked as a teacher.

'I had never heard anything bad said about them at all. They were very cool. Their attitude to us was really free and they were very up-to-date with what we were thinking.

'I read that they shared girls, I thought, "Woah, we are not talking about the same person here."'

I asked the good-natured and loyal former student what she would say to Chris Dawson now in light of the evidence in the inquest and the coroner's recommendation to the NSW Director of Public Prosecutions that consideration be given to prosecuting her former teacher for murder.

'I would just go up to him and say, "I don't believe a word of it and I can't accept what's being said." Any person you meet would defend them because they are really nice.'

Another letter, this one sent by fax machine and headed 'ANOTHER REPUTATION RUINED', came from Nancileigh, the 2000 school captain of St Ursula's.

When I went to its website, it proclaimed, 'We are a Christian school and the joy of the Risen Lord must find its home in us. So, lessons in religious and moral education, and in raising awareness of current social issues, help, not only the students but also the entire college community to realise that we are striving to build a faith community.'

'I am sickened by the fact that yet again an innocent man is accused of committing a nefarious crime,' Nancileigh wrote, continuing:

> I have known Mr Dawson for a period of two years. Within this time, I have found him to be a caring, giving and magnanimous man who would do anything for anyone.
>
> He is a well respected teacher at St Ursula's College, he is known to be someone who can be trusted and who always has time for his students. I know he will always be someone that I look up to.
>
> This is why I find it outrageous that he has been accused of allegedly planning to hire a hitman to kill his wife. There is no way in the world that Mr Dawson would do this.
>
> It seems to me that his second wife is just looking for attention or something and has made this complete story up.
>
> When this has all blown over and it is seen that Mr Dawson never had any intention of hiring a hitman to kill his first wife, I hope the public realises that the lives and reputations of innocent people have been ruined by others lying.
>
> I would like to finish by saying that if there were more people like Mr Dawson in this world, the world would be a better place.

The spirited defences of Chris Dawson were surprising. Two young women were describing the apparently unimpeachable character of a teacher who sounded nothing like the student-grooming, narcissistic wife-killer depicted at the inquest. It was like Jekyll and Hyde.

I printed a snippet which I found online from an early 2001 newsletter called *Sporting News, St Ursula's College*.

Welcome to the new school year and hoping your daughters will
have an enjoyable 2001. All girls are presently swimming in PE
classes and after the carnival they will be running cross country and
swimming. By the end of term, we'll have some very fit young ladies.
Mr Chris Dawson, Sports co-ordinator.

After a couple of calls to police stations on the Northern Beaches, I had
a phone number for Damian Loone, who was happy to help. When I
asked him who I could talk to in Sydney, he nominated Pat Jenkins first.

'The sister of the first wife is closest. She's onside with police,'
Loone told me. 'The ex-wife lives locally in Dee Why and is willing to
speak too. It's a very controversial brief. Because it's before the DPP,
I have to be very careful about what I say.'

I told him I'd like to come to Sydney to try to cover the story in
more detail. Loone recommended the Brookvale Travelodge.

When I called Charles Miranda, he told me the twin brothers,
Chris and Paul Dawson, were bizarrely close. 'There's a Jeremy Irons
movie with twin brothers obsessed with themselves. And this is how
he was. Chris lived two doors down. They were into group sex.

'The court has informed the Queensland Department of Education for an investigation into [Chris] having underaged sex with the
girl he married. A whole bunch of statements were tendered that we
did not get access to.'

I didn't tell him that Loone had just told me he had a more senior
officer's permission for me to read these statements, if I came to the
Dee Why police station. Loone was offering to show me the police brief
of evidence which had persuaded the coroner that Lynette Joy Dawson
had been dead since January 1982 – and that 19 years later, the case
against her husband was strong enough for a murder prosecution.

My next call was answered by Pat Jenkins, Lyn's older sister.
Before spending the company's money, I needed to be confident of
the family's cooperation.

I needn't have been concerned. In this first conversation, and in
the hundreds we've had since early 2001, Pat has been a model of
openness and honesty.

'I have two darling nieces that I really love and we always had to . . .' Pat started to tell me when we spoke for the first time.

She was trying to explain how hard it had been to balance the relationship that she and the rest of the immediate Simms family – her parents and her two brothers – wanted to maintain with Lyn's two daughters, who remained close to their dad.

'They were brought up believing their mother had walked out on them and didn't love them. We could never say anything else,' Pat told me.

Two decades after their mother's disappearance, Lyn's two daughters faced the prospect of also losing their father, who had raised them.

'One is in the United States on a working holiday. I thought that she should know and I have emailed her previously, telling her that I would tell her as much or as little as she wanted. Her sister is still with her dad. She's the younger one.

'We want justice to be done.'

Although we had not yet met, Pat Jenkins answered my questions and passed on her home address for the proposed face-to-face interview. I wanted it to occur in the afternoon at the start of the following week, Monday 5 March.

It was an auspicious date: Ruth and I were wed on that day in Hong Kong. In our six years of marriage, we had already travelled widely and witnessed historic change in one of the most exciting cities in the world. As journalists for the *South China Morning Post*, we reported on the 1997 handover of the British colony to China. When Ruth gave birth to our son, Alexander, the following year, we knew that it was time to put down longer-term roots back in Brisbane.

We fell in love with one of the first houses we saw in Brookfield. At the open-house inspection Ruth, trying not to show how much she wanted the house lest the agent notice, breastfed five-month-old Alexander in a downstairs bedroom, his room for the next 22 years.

As I made plans to meet Pat Jenkins and Damian Loone in Sydney on 5 March 2001, Ruth was heavily pregnant with our daughter, Sarah, due in six weeks. An outstanding journalist and gifted writer who wanted to put her career on hold as we grew our family, she didn't bat an eyelid that I would be away for our wedding anniversary.

We talked about the case before I flew to Sydney. We were the same age as Chris and Lyn when she disappeared. I tried to imagine the heartache of Lyn's two young adult daughters having been raised, according to what Lyn's sister Pat Jenkins had just told me: *believing their mother had walked out on them and didn't love them.*

I thought about how my father had dealt with this concept, how he had looked for his mother's face in crowds for so many years. Did that mean he doubted the story of her having walked into the ocean at Dee Why, swum out and drowned?

And if he doubted that story, would it follow that he perhaps believed that his mother had walked out and didn't love them?

The love Ruth and I felt for our toddler son and his soon-to-be-born sister was profound and, I expect, influenced my determination to pursue the case.

But there was more to it. The shadow of my grandmother hovered over everything. Her fate was a taboo subject. I wouldn't raise it with Dad, nor would I delve into it directly by, for example, seeking long-archived police or coronial records. By exploring Lyn's case, I hoped to somehow understand or learn about my grandmother and her disappearance.

Before I met her, Pat told me that as a result of the evidence she had been exposed to during Damian Loone's investigations, she believed that Chris and his brother Paul 'were totally out of control and behaving like schoolboys' when Lyn disappeared.

Pat spoke without bitterness about the schoolgirl, Jenny Carlson, who became Chris's second wife and stepmother to Lyn's girls.

'When Jenny left Chris, she came down here. My mother, because of all the memories, couldn't bear to see Jenny. Jenny just wanted to see her and tell her things that were on her mind. My brother and his wife saw her.

'She told them some quite unsettling things. Nothing was done.'

I didn't yet understand how the case of a missing person had got to this stage – a murder investigation with a possible pending prosecution – if, as Pat had just told me, 'nothing was done' when Jenny left Chris in 1990 and divulged 'some quite unsettling things'.

Pat explained that in 1998, Detective Senior Constable Damian Loone 'put something on the front page of the local paper and people came out of the woodwork'.

She circled back to some of the hurt Chris had inflicted upon her father, Len, who had died two months earlier, and her mother, Helena. Pat believed that Chris used Lyn's two daughters as bargaining chips, and would withhold them when it appeared his in-laws were being difficult. 'He used to drop the girls off occasionally to visit my mother. The two grandchildren meant so much to her.'

Visits to the grandparents became more rare when Chris and Jenny moved their young family to the Gold Coast at the end of 1984.

When Lyn vanished, Pat was geographically isolated from her sister and her parents.

'I was living 600 kilometres away in the country with a new child and family. I didn't see much of Lyn through that period. We had a phone call before she went missing.

'I rang her a couple of times when Chris had gone just before Christmas and we didn't know if he was coming back. We didn't even know he had gone off with someone; that's how naive we were.'

Seventeen-year-old Jenny was the 'someone' with whom Chris had left, abandoning his wife and daughters shortly before Christmas Day 1981.

'Chris said to Lyn, "Jenny's having problems, do you mind if she stays here a while?" Lyn said okay. The police said they were already having an affair by that stage.'

Having finished the phone interview with Pat, I telephoned a home in Yeppoon. I identified myself to the woman, whom I believed to be Chris Dawson's third wife, Susan, and explained that I was seeking an interview with him for a lengthy feature article.

She was perfectly civil. 'That all sounds good but all I want to say at the moment is "no comment."'

Before I left for Sydney, a photocopy of another letter intended for publication in *The Courier-Mail* fell onto my desk.

Denise of Acacia Ridge on Brisbane's southside wrote:

> The position of teacher is a position of trust, demanding inherent moral and legal accountability on behalf of school board and individual teachers. Parents are entitled to expect teachers will not morally or sexually exploit their precious children entrusted to the school's care.
>
> In this case, Mr Dawson admits to shamefully exploiting his naive vulnerable former student with whom he became 'infatuated' by forming a sexual relationship with her, and like a lovesick teenager 'left the love letters in her school port'.
>
> Mr Dawson is also under investigation by the DPP concerning his possible role in his ex-wife's death.

She then castigated St Ursula's for placing 'the lives of innocent school children at risk by condoning the practice of allowing an adult who has previously abused his position of trust unrestricted, unsupervised legal access to schoolchildren'.

'May God protect these children from the perverted amongst us when those who should will not.'

Chapter 3

Northern Beaches

Dee Why Police Station, Sydney
5 March 2001

As a little boy living in landlocked Canberra, it was always thrilling to visit Sydney's Northern Beaches with my father. We would stay with his sister, my Aunty Judith, in her unit in a walk-up building on the beach at Narrabeen.

Dad was a powerful swimmer, a New South Wales schoolboy champion who was impossible to beat in the North Sydney Olympic Pool where his father, Hedley Darlington Thomas, mother, Gladys, and younger sister, Judith, would go to watch and cheer.

The story I grew up hearing from Mum was that the legendary coach Forbes Carlile saw a future Olympian in the clean-cut, strongly built young Hedley. Dad, however, was determined to become a pilot.

Aunty Judith fondly recalls him being dunked head-first into a barrel of ice-cold water by his South Coast Aero Club mates after receiving his pilot's licence aged 16.

Judith would fly to Perth to see Dad graduate as an officer in the Royal Australian Air Force, and in later years, they spent many hours together 'as he dictated, and I typed, his groundbreaking manual for helicopters'.

Dad's near-death experience in a jet aircraft left him with a badly broken back and the RAAF's best medical advice was that it was too dangerous for him to return to supersonic aircraft.

He transferred to helicopters instead and during the Vietnam War was formally recognised for bravery after flying into the jungle and enemy-fire to drop off Australian and American soldiers and collect them and the wounded.

Dad told his grandson James Frizelle about winching a special forces patrol from the jungle in 1969 when he had days to go to finish his year and time in Vietnam. I was a toddler.

As the helicopter hovered 'we were being shot at pretty severely, and you'd see the tracers going by and the smoke trails from the rocket propelled grenades which the Viet Cong were firing at us. The noise was just tremendous from everybody shooting'. The winch operator was giving Dad directions, 'Steady, hold it steady. Left three feet. Stop. Down. Hold'.

'And suddenly he's not speaking. [He] was so frightened, he just shut up. I thought, "This is it."' Dad 'started to speak very softly' to the crewman. Reassuringly. Any second one of the enemy's rockets could have killed everyone.

'He came back on the intercom and started talking again. We got all the guys up and headed away. That was probably the scariest time.'

My father's love of the ocean was contagious. At Narrabeen, Dad showed me how to bodysurf and I graduated from being like a pilot fish, hanging grimly to his neck, to venturing on my own past the shore break and sandbars to the second line of waves.

Dad taught me how to spot a dangerous rip which might sweep me out to sea and he explained what I should do if caught in one. The importance of remaining calm and gritting teeth while being stung by blue bottles was another important lesson. Dad was dogmatic about the critical importance of swimming between the flags, and of always checking your position in the water relative to the flags and the patrol area for the surf lifesavers.

I've wondered since if this was because Dad couldn't accept that his mother had swum out with no intention of returning. Did he believe that the young woman had innocently gone bathing outside the flags, been caught in a notorious rip and was swept far out to sea?

I arrived at Dee Why around lunchtime on Monday 5 March 2001. Fond memories of childhood holidays in this beautiful part of Australia flooded back as soon as I got out of the car.

There's a distinctive scent – the bittersweet Pacific Ocean salt and washed-up kelp going off in the sunshine – and it's unlike anything I've experienced along Queensland's coastline. For me, with only good experiences in this place, it's a reassuring scent laden with reminiscences. Others find the smell repugnant – a reminder of their childhood exploitation and abuse.

At the front desk of the Dee Why police station, I met Detective Senior Constable Damian Loone. Immediately likeable, candid and easygoing, he led me to what appeared to be a disused office with a desk and a cardboard box.

'I'm a twin myself,' Loone told me.

He pulled out a file, the police brief of evidence in the matter of Lynette Joy Dawson, and told me I could read all of it and take notes from the dozens of statements and other pages of evidence but no photocopies.

When Detective Loone left me to it, I could scarcely believe my good luck. Many times in the past I'd been assured by a contact, government official or confidential informant of help for what sounded like a brilliant story only to be let down when it came time to see the evidence.

The excuses varied. They were threatened or they suddenly became ill or somebody took away their access to the material.

In newsrooms, the risky act of promoting a yarn to the chief of staff and news editor before it had fallen into our hands was called 'selling off the plan'. Experience of multiple disappointments with people whose promises rang hollow when it came time to deliver had taught me to be careful.

But Loone was solid.

I started with a 10-page summary of the case written by a police prosecutor Detective Senior Constable Matt Fordham headed: *Lynnette Joy DAWSON Suspected Death 1137/99.*

Loone helpfully reminded me that there was a typo – it should be 'Lynette', not 'Lynnette', and that, contrary to the section *Background of Lynette Dawson*, she grew up in a family of four children, not five.

On the second last page of Officer Fordham's summary, which was his opening address to the Coroner Jan Stevenson, details about police searches for Lyn's body were described: 'Detective LOONE has caused certain areas of the property at No. 2 Gilwinga Drive to be scientifically examined with the aid of Ground Penetrating Radar on 7 April 1999, and has dug up some areas of the gardens surrounding the home's in-ground swimming pool. Several items were found in areas where the radar suggested that the earth had been disturbed.'

The next seven lines of type were obscured. Someone had wanted to black these out but hadn't done a great job. By peering closely and squinting, the words were still legible and I got the gist.

A Popper brand juice container had been found by Loone during a dig of the earth around the swimming pool of the house where Lyn and Chris lived, along with fragments of what appeared to be a woman's cardigan.

'The cardigan was in several pieces and a scientific examination has revealed at least 22 cut marks on its material,' the blacked-out type stated. 'Significantly, the sleeve of the cardigan indicates that there appears to be cuts consistent with the wearer of the cardigan trying to fend off an attack.

'Preliminary examination of stains on the cardigan indicated the possible presence of blood however further testing with new DNA techniques is being conducted by the police to attempt to determine the identity of the source of any blood that may be on the cardigan.'

The obscuring ink ended there.

The next visible paragraph stated, 'Further areas at No. 6 Gilwinga Drive, the home of Paul DAWSON, have also been examined by the police, as well as areas of bushland surrounding the properties with the aid of specially trained cadaver dogs. No deceased body has been located.'

Detective Loone had told me, 'Paul is now at Main Beach.'

I silently clocked the connection. It was where I lived as a teenager with my mother and three sisters in the years following

Mum and Dad's divorce and our move from Canberra to Queensland's Gold Coast.

I must have asked Loone about Chris and Paul Dawson's older solicitor brother, who acted for them in the coronial proceeding, an unusual legal arrangement.

In my notebook I wrote: *Peter still in Sydney. Conflict of interest. Nothing for Jenny to gain.*

For several hours, I read and wrote, read and wrote, saving some time and space with the rough shorthand I'd picked up at TAFE as a copyboy.

Transcribing the witness statements – and noting the private home addresses and telephone numbers in case I needed to follow anything up with them directly – transported me to the Northern Beaches in the early eighties and a school called Cromer High, where a strapping teacher with a roving eye and renown as a rugby league star for the Newtown Jets groomed a teenager.

Hers was the first statement I read and started to reproduce in my notebook. It was dated 18 September 1998 and ran to 27 pages, with each one signed and witnessed. This is some of what I read as Damian Loone got on with his job elsewhere.

I am a divorced woman, having reverted from my married name of DAWSON to my maiden name. I first attended Cromer High School in Year 7 in 1976 and remained there until Year 12, leaving in November 1981.

During the years following my parents' divorce, family life was difficult, with all of us crowded in a small unit. I would regularly visit my father who was living by himself in a one-bedroom unit in Bondi.

In Year 11, in 1980, Chris DAWSON became my sports coaching class (teacher). He later told me that he had deliberately chosen this class because I was in it as he had noticed me and taken a liking to me the previous year. Chris took my class for a couple of hours each week for a number of sporting activities.

Almost from the beginning he started paying particular attention to me. He appeared to single me out by speaking and being involved in what I was doing.

This situation continued up to about the middle of that year. I did not have any association with him outside school time and nothing more serious had occurred outside the activities of student and teacher.

At this time I was having problems at home. My stepfather was physically and emotionally abusive to my mother and my home life was unhappy and unsettled. This had been going on for some time.

As a result I felt I needed to speak to someone about this situation and because of the attention Chris DAWSON had paid to me, I felt I could talk to him about my problems. He just seemed to be a caring type of person.

I approached him at school and outlined to him my problems at home. As a result I formed a relationship on a counselling basis, where he would listen to my problems at home.

Following that he then asked me to babysit for him and his wife at 2 Gilwinga Drive, Bayview. I therefore became acquainted and friendly with his wife, Lyn, and his two children, Shanelle and Amy, who were then aged three and one respectively.

I babysat at his home on numerous occasions at the weekend. He would pick me up at my home on a Saturday afternoon and drive me to his home at 2 Gilwinga Drive, Bayview.

Quite often I would stay the night in a spare bedroom at their home and he would drive me home Sunday afternoon. The babysitting duties became a weekly routine, even when Lyn and Chris stayed at home.

Over this time, I virtually became a member of the family and also became acquainted with Chris's brother Paul and his wife, Marilyn, and their three children, who lived down the street at 6 Gilwinga Drive. Paul was an identical twin brother to Chris and was also a teacher at Forest High School.

Jenny described Friday nights at The Time and Tide Hotel where she and other high school students would go drinking with some of the teachers after class.

Initially Chris did not come there but later he attended and would talk with me all evening.

He then started taking me for driving lessons in his car. He would pick me up from my home in the evening and accompany me for driving lessons. On one of these occasions we drove down and parked at Dee Why Beach. I recall he said, 'You make me feel like an older Rhys,' referring to a classmate of mine called Rhys.

It was on this occasion that he first kissed me.

On one occasion we went to his parents' house at Maroubra when his parents were away and this was the occasion when we first had sex together. This was towards the end of 1980.

After this Chris would then pick me up on a regular basis in his car on a Friday evening and we would end up parked somewhere and we would have sex. This sexual relationship continued into 1981. I would still babysit at his home and he would pick me up and take me out in his car. At this point in time, we were only having sex in his car.

Her account of the drunkenness and violence of her stepfather, Ron, rang true. She described an incident in October 1981 when Ron 'struck my mother and manhandled me as well when I intervened'.

'I told my father of this incident and he insisted I leave my mother's place. I recall attending Chatswood police station with my father and having photographs taken of bruises on my body.'

Jenny did not want to go to her father's place, far from Cromer High. She 'did not want any further disruption to my studies'.

As a result Chris DAWSON offered to allow me to stay at his home for an indefinite period. Lyn seemed sympathetic to my plight and I therefore moved into their place.

There were therefore occasions when Chris and I were alone together in the house and able to continue our sexual relationship. Our relationship was fairly strong. Since 1980, Chris had asked me to marry him on a number of occasions but I declined every time.

I was stunned by Chris Dawson's audacity. His grooming of a student half his age – a troubled teenager he'd introduced to his wife as someone needing their help – whom he then bedded in the family home as his wife and children slept metres away, in the family car at the beach or wherever the opportunity presented.

In late 1981, according to the statement, Lyn realised what had been going on and she said to Jenny, 'You've been taking liberties with my husband.'

The schoolgirl was told to leave the house. She moved into Paul and Marilyn's house a little farther down Gilwinga Drive.

My eyes must have widened as I leafed the pages of the statement and wrote it all down with the sort of precision I'd need to be able to quote directly from my notebook.

By November 1981, I read, Chris was forging ahead with his plans to leave Lyn and move into a rental with Jenny. He put down a $500 bond for a flat in North Manly. Around the same time, he telephoned his solicitor brother, Peter.

> I was present in the house when I heard Chris say, 'Do I forfeit the property?', or words similar to this. After he finished the conversation, Chris said, 'Yes, I would lose the house. If I leave, she gets the house. I'm better off staying in the house.'
>
> On one occasion, I cannot recall whether it was 1980 or 1981, after I was going out with him in his car, we drove somewhere, maybe out the western side of Sydney and whilst I waited in the car, he went up some stairs into a hotel.
>
> When he returned he said something like, 'I was going to get a hitman to kill Lyn but I couldn't because innocent people would get hurt.'

She described the awkward living arrangement at Paul and Marilyn's house. Paul's daily betrayal of his sister-in-law struck me as unforgivable. Lyn did not know her husband's twin brother was sheltering Chris's girlfriend just down the road. Marilyn and Lyn were friends.

For several weeks, Jenny slept in the bed of one of Paul and Marilyn's three daughters. When the child fretted that Santa Claus would not be able to find her at Christmas if she was not in her own bed, Jenny was shifted to the study.

> In addition, there was some pretence to their children that I had actually left the house and to support this, I would be awoken early each day, and walk outside into the bush near the cul-de-sac where I would stay until the children were driven to school.
>
> Obviously this type of situation could not continue and therefore Chris decided that he would leave his wife and children and go together to Queensland.
>
> A few days later, during the daytime, on 23 December 1981 we packed possessions and clothing in Chris's car and drove off from 2 Gilwinga Drive, Bayview.
>
> Our plans at that point were to make a life for ourselves in Queensland with Chris leaving his wife and children at Bayview. There was no one there when we left. I still have a photograph of me standing by Chris's car just before we left.

I tried to picture them. A girl from a broken home and her high school teacher, completely infatuated with each other. A few suitcases and a family car being driven north up the Pacific Highway a couple of days before Christmas, not for a brief holiday or a dirty weekend but for good.

> We drove through the night and eventually stopped at Murwillumbah. By this time I was feeling horrible. I had hives and I was scratching all over my body. This undoubtedly was brought on by the stress of the situation.
>
> I told him I missed my family and I did not want to go through with this. As a result we turned around and headed back to Sydney, again driving through the night. We arrived at Paul and Marilyn's place in the early hours of Christmas Day morning. When the kids got up in the morning, Chris and I hid in the wardrobe until they had finished unwrapping their presents.

Thanks to Paul Dawson's teaching job at Forest High School, he had keys to the premises.

'Chris and I stayed the night in the school gym. On Boxing Day morning I told Chris I wanted to go home. He then dropped me off at my mother's house . . .'

Her plan to stay in her own home soon unravelled. She called Chris, according to her statement, and he drove her to her sister's flat in Neutral Bay for a stay of about a week. Chris visited her there regularly.

Jenny was effectively homeless, moving between temporary accommodations and unsure where she would be able to live for the longer-term.

'I wanted to break off our relationship because it was making me unhappy. He kept insisting that he loved me and wanted to keep the relationship going.'

I ploughed through this statement of wretched tragedy described by a woman who at 34 was twice the age of her teenage self when she became hopelessly entangled in a relationship and then a possible murder. Nothing of this detail had emerged in the newspaper reports of the inquest.

I didn't understand why I'd been given access to all of these documents but I knew I needed to keep transcribing as fast as possible before someone changed his or her mind.

On New Year's Day or perhaps 2 January – Jenny wasn't sure which – she called her father, Graham Carlson, to ask if she could go with her sisters and some of their friends to the family caravan at South West Rocks. It seemed a bit out of place after her decision, without reference to her father, to up and leave her home, friends and family the week before to start a new life with Chris in Queensland.

> Before I left to go to South West Rocks, Chris begged me to ring reverse charges every day to his home. He said, 'I'll die if I don't speak to you every day.'
>
> When I telephoned him, he asked what I was doing and we would talk about my activities at South West Rocks. He kept

insisting he missed me and to keep on ringing him every day . . .
About 9 or 10 January 1982, as I recall I had been up there about
a week, I telephoned him in the usual manner. He said, 'Lyn's gone,
she's not coming back.'

These six words carried powerful force when I read them then, and
on every subsequent occasion.

The first part – about Lyn having gone – could be understood in
an innocent context. Lyn wanting to go away on her own to think for
a while, having become fed up with her husband's conduct, would
make sense. But the next four words – 'she's not coming back' – make
it plain that this is permanent. It's over. Lyn's gone for good.

I checked the date of the statement – 16 years and 9 months after
the conversation was said to have occurred. Lyn still hadn't – and
hasn't – come back.

'He then said, "I need you now. Come and live with me and the
girls at Bayview." He then arranged to come up and pick me up from
South West Rocks straight away.'

Jenny and her younger sister Naomi drove back to Bayview. There
was no longer any question about where she would live.

Initially on returning to Chris's home, it was a period of settling
in and becoming accustomed to my new role as Chris's de facto
wife and mother to his two children.

For the remainder of January 1982, Chris was on holiday from
school before returning to Cromer High School for the start of
the school year. I took on the role as housekeeper and de facto
wife to Chris.

Before Chris went back to school, I tried to enrol in a childcare
course but was unable to gain entry and then attended a
secretarial course at Gore Hill, North Sydney before abandoning
it after only three days. Following that I remained at home looking
after the household . . .

I do recall in that early period that Chris and I went to the
Women's Refuge at Dee Why where we spoke with Barbara

KILPATRICK whom I had known previously through my mother.
I cannot recall what caused Chris and I to go there. I do remember
that Barbara made it quite clear to Chris that he and I should part
and that he should just let go of me.

Although Chris and I gave the impression to Barbara that
we would do this, once we left Chris said something like, 'We'll
show her. We'll make a go of it. We're not going to let this die a
natural death.'

At that time I was still besotted with him. To me he was the only
person who really cared about me. I was not on speaking terms
with my father because of my relationship with Chris and because
of my stepfather's attitude, I had problems communicating with my
mother.

I was completely isolated from my own family and therefore
had only Chris and his brother Paul's family as support.

When Jenny pulled together this police statement in the same police
station in which I was sitting, she was about 15 months older than
Lyn was when she disappeared. Jenny's daughter with Chris was 13.

I wondered how Jenny, as an adult woman and mother, reconciled her role in whatever befell Lyn. Jenny's description of Lyn from
having known her 18 months was warm and fond.

She was a devoted mother, especially with the older child,
Shanelle. She was an affectionate wife and obviously in love with
Chris. She loved her house and had a real talent for interior design
and making the place look great. She was houseproud and paid
detailed attention as to how the place looked.

She was a nursing sister with high qualifications but only
worked part-time at the Warriewood Square Occasional Care
Centre. Lyn appeared close to her mother and visited her quite
often. All these activities kept Lyn fully occupied especially as their
house had only been built in 1976 . . .

In contrast to Lyn being devoted to Chris, Chris's attitude to
Lyn appeared very cool. When Lyn tried to hug him he would recoil

away and shrug her off. He would sing songs with hurtful lyrics or double meanings in order to antagonise her. He did not appear to have any warmth towards her. Lyn obviously adored Chris right to the time she went missing. She did not appear to blame Chris for our relationship.

I remember on one occasion after I had moved into their house, Lyn came and found me sitting on Chris's lap, playing with the kids. She said to Chris, 'What's going on?' And he said, 'It's nothing, we're just playing with the children.'

That was the only occasion that I heard Lyn confront Chris about our relationship.

Jenny's statement returned to South West Rocks and the start of January 1982 when, she said, she wanted 'to clear my head, I wanted to break off our relationship'.

'I was unsure whether he was going to leave Lyn and the kids at the house and get his own place. Nothing definite seemed to have been worked out ... As far as Chris was concerned, the relationship which he wanted to continue was obviously at a crisis point. He indicated to me that he feared that I might break off the relationship which is what I wanted to do.'

For the days she was up there and away from him, 'this desire to break off the relationship became stronger'.

'I think this was because I was physically out of his reach and therefore less under his influence. Whether he was able to detect this in my manner and therefore [it] caused him to drive up and collect me, I cannot say.'

The narrative weaved through the pages of this typed statement on official New South Wales Police stationery was spellbinding, and I'd read only half of it to this point. Circumstantial threads were pulled together and tied into what appeared to me to be a knotty problem for Christopher Michael Dawson.

For the next few pages, Jenny described her observations of the house. Lyn's house. She noticed 'that there did not appear to be any of Lyn's clothing missing'.

'There were no gaps in her clothing drawers and wardrobe. They were chock-a-block. I remember her underwear drawer was full and nothing obviously missing.

'Numerous items of her jewellery, including two expensive diamond rings, were left behind in her jewellery container. However I did not find her gold band wedding ring and neither did I locate her nursing badge.'

Jenny described the swimming pool – how there was a narrow strip of pavers around the perimeter, and then grass which was planted in 1982 over the surrounding dirt, then pavers to replace the grass, which hadn't worked out.

Jenny also recalled occasions from the weeks in which she had been living in the house with Lyn and Chris from October 1981. She said that Chris would pour his wife drinks, although she was not a drinker.

'I believe that they were a spirit drink of some kind. The reason for doing this was in order to make Lyn sleepy so she would go off to bed and leave us alone together.'

Jenny next dealt with what she called the 'extremely close' relationship between the twin brothers, Chris and Paul.

They both did similar activities. They were both high school PE teachers at the same time, both played first-grade rugby league for Newtown at the same time, both played A-grade for Belrose Rugby League at the same time, for Gosford Rugby League at the same time, undertook their correspondence degrees at the same time.

They did their casual garbage jobs at the same time, they exercised together and they were constantly in each other's company. They had a constant desire to be with each other. They seemed to have an extraordinary closeness.

Paul seemed to be a more calm person whereas I did see Chris lose his temper. In football terms, Chris was known as 'Cranky Chris', and Paul as 'Passive Paul'.

I was aware that whilst Paul was teaching at Forest High School, he had affairs with female students there. I was present when Paul and Chris would talk about which student Paul would choose.

She named a girl from Forest High, a babysitter in Paul and Marilyn's home and a sexual conquest, who joined Jenny, Paul and Chris on a trip to the country town of Armidale for a week when the teacher brothers 'had to complete their week's residential part of their degree course'.

It sounded incredible when I read it, and all these years later it's still hard to fathom. Two married high school teachers taking two teenage schoolgirls away for a week of sex in an otherwise boring week of academic study.

After Jenny moved in Chris offered explanations for Lyn's absence. One time, he told her, 'I think she's gone off with those religious people who came to see her at the house.'

> On one occasion, I cannot recall when, the telephone rang in the kitchen and Chris answered it. Chris did not say very much on the telephone but after he put the telephone down, he said, 'That was Lyn. She says, "I'm having a holiday now. I'm with friends and I'm alright."'
>
> On another occasion, Chris said to me, 'I heard she's gone to New Zealand.' This may have been when I pressed him as to 'Where is Lyn, why should I have to look after the kids?'

Over time, according to the statement, Jenny became more involved in looking after the two girls. Her relationship with Chris, she stated, 'remained stable and healthy and we became committed to each other', culminating in a wedding on 15 January 1984 at the home – Lyn's old home – and a honeymoon in Western Samoa. Later that year, she became pregnant.

Chris, Paul and Marilyn wanted to move from Bayview to the Central Coast, and they looked at land around the idyllic seaside location of Kincumber. When Marilyn changed her mind about the Central Coast, they settled instead on acreages in bushland on the Gold Coast.

Jenny set out how Chris started a teaching job in early 1985 at Keebra Park High School and Paul at Coombabah High School. My sister Rebecca attended Coombabah when Paul and, later, Chris taught there. Rebecca remembered Chris and Paul, saying they were 'odd'.

The Dawson twins had once again decided that they needed to live close to each other. Their houses were completed within a month of each other in mid-1985.

They were living near an iconic new theme park called Dream-world, the brainchild of the father of my friend from Keebra Park, Carolyn Longhurst.

'At this time we had three girls in our family, as did Paul and Marilyn. We both had Dalmatian dogs from the same litter, both had swimming pools and tennis courts on our respective properties,' Jenny said in her statement.

While she remained at home looking after the house and the three children, her relationship with Chris, and with Lyn's two daughters, began to fray. Jenny said she 'could not treat Chris's children the same as my own child and [Chris] could not accept that'.

In early 1987, Jenny started taking her toddler daughter to a local playgroup, where she met other young mums.

'Chris forbade me to continue to attend this playgroup but as Mikaela needed the contact of other children I defied him and continued to take her there. This was my first taste of freedom away from the family home and it opened up a different lifestyle for me.'

As her marriage frayed, Jenny and her daughter found comfort and friendship at Dreamworld. She met a woman who was part of one of the stage shows, Toni Melrose, and they started going to lunch together, doing aerobics and playing in an indoor cricket team.

> Chris resented the time I spent with Toni. During 1989, I went to a lingerie party with Toni and purchased a pair of G-string underwear. I brought them home and put them on for Chris. He said, 'You're only going to wear them for me, aren't you?'
>
> I then said, 'I'll wear them when I like' at which time he grabbed me by the neck and started choking me. I did not lose consciousness or anything and he released his grip within a second

or two. I think this may have been the occasion when I said to him, 'You got rid of your first wife, you could easily get rid of me.'

He stood stock-still and said, 'Don't say things like that.'

Jenny went to see a solicitor around this time for advice about her rights in the event of a divorce. She knew she wanted to leave her husband. On 14 January 1990, she went to Sydney with her daughter to see friends and family and try to make a decision about whether to move back to the Northern Beaches. It was the day before her wedding anniversary.

A fortnight later, Jenny and her daughter returned to the relatively new home she had built with Chris, backing onto bushland on a western fringe of the Gold Coast. Her mind was now made up. Jenny just needed to pack.

On 1 February, they drove away for good. Chris tried to persuade her to stay, though he did not 'physically try and stop me'.

On the penultimate page of her police statement, Jenny noted the regular visits that would be made back to 2 Gilwinga Drive by Chris, and his chats to the new owners about further buildings on the property, including a rumpus room extension and a four-car garage.

In relation to the disappearance of Lyn, I now recall that about 1982 Chris saying words similar to 'She's an adult. She's entitled to leave if she wants to. It's her business. If she doesn't want to be found, I'm not going to worry.'

There was very little said by Chris or in fact his two children in regard to Lyn's disappearance over the years. I always assumed during all the years I lived with Chris that Lyn had left of her own accord and never questioned Chris about it.

Chapter 4

Terrible Twins

I wrote shorthand for hours. My hand ached.

There were statements and documents from Jenny's father, Graham Carlson, and Jenny's sister, Naomi Carlson, as well as school friends.

I read statements from Lyn's siblings – Pat Jenkins, Phil Simms and the youngest of the four, Greg Simms – as well as from Greg's wife, Merilyn.

Lyn's friends and work colleagues Barbara Cruise, Sue Strath, Annette Leary and Anna Grantham were in the brief of evidence.

Barbara Cruise's statement included an observation that in the aftermath of Lyn's disappearance, Chris didn't appear to suffer in the least. In Barbara's view, he prospered: 'He got all the money, whatever money they might have had. He got the children. He got the house. And he got the girlfriend. He didn't dip out in any way, shape or form. And it would appear that he did it without anyone questioning him.'

It was impossible to ignore the inference that this was his objective all along, providing multiple motives for foul play.

Nine years after Lyn's disappearance, there was some questioning of him. Two detectives from the Homicide Squad in New South Wales travelled to Queensland to do a videotaped interview with Chris Dawson in 1991. There was a detailed account of his answers, and I summarised it.

The last night they spent together, Friday 8 January 1982, was 'supposed to be a sexy celebration', Chris later said. Lyn was drinking wine after their marriage counselling earlier that day.

The next morning, he said, Lyn went out shopping – and he never saw her again. He said he had four telephone calls from her. The last call, Chris said, was within a fortnight of her leaving on her shopping outing on Saturday 9 January.

'The whole purpose of Jenny raising the allegations is to slur my character with the upcoming custody battle which has turned extremely nasty and bitter.

'And Jenny doesn't know that I lay awake crying my heart out hoping for some contact from Lyn, the nights that I spent extremely concerned about Lyn's whereabouts.

'I guess that perhaps she had a nervous breakdown.'

There were interviews with his twin brother, Paul, and Paul's wife, Marilyn, at the Surfers Paradise police station in 1999. Transcripts of their conversations were included in the bundle.

There was also a very lengthy statement from Damian Loone, who didn't start investigating until 1998, separate to the 1991 work by homicide detectives.

'One female student has stated that she had sex with Chris Dawson as a birthday present at the request from Paul Dawson,' Loone stated. 'Later, both Chris and Paul Dawson engaged in a sexual encounter with this female.'

This witness told police that, as a teenage student who believed Paul Dawson cared for her, she agreed to group sex with him, other teachers and football teammates at Forest High.

Her statement was an account of a girl's exploitation by her teacher, a man whom she believed she loved and who told her he loved her. He shared and debased her with his mates for sport, she said, adding that she was 15 when they started having sex.

As Year 12 master, Paul Dawson, according to this former student, sent a note to her to leave class and go to his office to perform oral sex, which she said she duly did. On other occasions, she was told to have sex with two other teachers on their lunchbreak.

'Paul would organise for me to go to my place which was close by and he would organise with those teachers to come to my place. At that time of day my parents were not home. When those teachers arrived I would perform for them . . .'

At the time she prepared this statement, the woman was 33, married and raising a small child. She tried to explain why she went along with the sexual encounters: 'I consented only because I was told by Paul that there was nothing wrong with what I was doing. And Paul had told me frequently that he was in love with me and I believed him.'

Loone told me later that the woman did not want to proceed with any action against Paul Dawson or the other teachers; however, her statement was not withdrawn.

Loone did not leave those who read his own lengthy statement in any doubt. He suspected that Chris Dawson 'with counselling and assistance of others' murdered Lyn.

> This belief is supported circumstantially by close examination of events leading up to Lynette Dawson's disappearance, together with the extraordinary situation of there not being any contact whatsoever with her mother, father, brothers, sister, friends and two very young daughters.
>
> It is extraordinary that we are asked to accept that despite not contacting any of those persons, she does in fact contact the one person who she is in conflict with, being her husband Christopher Michael Dawson.
>
> I believe that Lynette Joy Dawson was murdered and her body disposed of between the hours of 9 pm Friday 8 January 1982 and 8 am Saturday 9 January 1982.

In my notebook, under a heading *Loone: to me* to distinguish the couple of jottings to follow as coming from a brief chat we had in the police station, I wrote down the officer's words:

Gut feeling is that CD hired a hitman to take her away and kill her. He couldn't have done it himself.

He had about a 12 hour timeframe to do it.

I'll keep looking for her. 20 years ago she was a missing person; wasn't a priority.

Media has brought people out of the woodwork. Had a lot of positive feedback from former friends who say the affair was very obvious.

For the coroner to terminate and refer it to the DPP, it's a very big step.

My notebook jottings in 2001 included a quote from Marilyn about Paul's attributes and brotherly loyalty. Of the two brothers, according to the 1999 police interview with Marilyn, Paul has the 'more dominant personality, has more common sense, and I believe my husband loves his brother and protects him in any way that he has to.

'I don't believe that Chris could do anything to harm his wife Lyn, and I don't believe that my husband could hide that from me. We are good honest citizens.'

Paul Dawson was asked during his police interview about the former student who had given police a detailed account of months of sexual encounters with Paul, starting when she was 15 and including intercourse at the school.

He acknowledged that there was a sexual relationship but their stories parted company when it came to the timing; Paul said it began after she had left school. If true, this would mean he had not committed a criminal offence.

'We used to talk a lot at school, she got on very well with myself and other teachers at school. After school, she kept in contact with us, with me, and we saw each other after she left school.'

I remembered the Surfers Paradise police station well from my days as a cadet reporter on police rounds, when I would sit to hear a senior cop lie about crime clearance rates. Years later, he was exposed as corrupt, having pocketed thousands of dollars in protection money from the operators of illegal brothels and gambling joints. The Surfers Paradise police station had seen many liars.

Paul Dawson was asked about the possibility his beloved brother Chris had been involved in foul play; that he'd killed Lyn or had her killed.

'It wouldn't have happened. I know. I mean, he's my twin brother.'

Officer Fordham had a heading, *The Facts – Timeline of Events*, around the halfway point of his lengthy submission. It started with accounts from Jenny of the mixing of alcoholic drinks by Chris for Lyn. 'Not being a usual drinker of alcohol, this would make Lynette sleepy, and when she went to bed, this allowed Chris to pursue his relationship with Jenny inside the matrimonial home.'

The night before Lyn disappeared, Fordham's submission stated, her mother telephoned the house at Gilwinga Drive, intending to speak with Lyn.

He described what he said was Chris Dawson's reluctance to allow Lyn to come to the phone until her mother insisted. She sounded 'very groggy' to Helena.

'Lynette said, "Chris has made me a lovely drink."'

It was the last time Helena spoke to her daughter. They had made a plan to meet the following day at a place known as Northbridge Baths, a popular destination for swimmers and families. Chris and Paul worked there as part-time lifeguards.

I pictured the scene. A doting grandmother on a hot Saturday afternoon in January, chatting to her son-in-law and the two little girls while waiting for her daughter to arrive. She never would.

Matt Fordham continued. 'Chris asked her if she has heard from Lynette. Lynette's mother recalled that Chris appeared agitated. Only after the arrival of Lynette's mother at the pool does Chris apparently receive a call at the pool's kiosk supposedly from Lynette when she informs him for the first time of her intention to have a break.'

The police prosecutor dealt over several pages with other, in his view, improbable scenarios: that Lyn had left voluntarily; that she had met with misadventure unrelated to Chris; or that she was killed by a person or persons not previously known to her and unconnected to Chris. He ruled each of these scenarios out and cut to the chase with a final written and oratory flourish:

'The most plausible explanation for Lynette's disappearance is that a known person is responsible for the disappearance of Lynette DAWSON. I note, Your Worship, that Chris Dawson had contemplated arranging a hitman to kill his wife, and told Jenny CARLSON the day after the disappearance that Lynette "will not be coming back".

'The implications of such a finding are quite severe, however in my submission, the overwhelming weight of evidence against a known person will allow Your Worship to make such a finding.'

I packed up and walked outside Dee Why police station. Into the late afternoon light and the briny smell of the nearby Pacific Ocean. Those familiar smells were reassuring after the hours spent reading statement after statement in a case filled with darkness.

It looked fairly obvious. In my mind, the lack of resolution in the 19 years to that day in March 2001 was ludicrous. It was already affecting me in a way very few stories ever had. Soon I would be worrying about how I could do justice to the case when it came time to sit at my desk in Brisbane and write a couple of thousand words for the weekend's feature pages.

I hurried from Dee Why to the house of Pat Jenkins, a 20-minute drive. A face-to-face interview with Lyn's sister, coming immediately after the dozens of pages of notes already transcribed in my notebook, would help to tie things off.

A friendly woman with an easy smile which lit up her eyes, Pat welcomed me warmly. She seemed humbly surprised that a reporter from Queensland would go to the time and trouble of travelling to Sydney for a story about her younger sister. Pat served a supper snack and a cup of tea as she started to tell me about her family's great affection for her former brother-in-law, Chris Dawson.

'He was a special part of our family, always polite and he loved his two girls. And my mother had believed in him implicitly.'

I asked Pat why her side of the family did not raise suspicions in the years before Jenny went to police in 1990.

'If we had thought Chris had done something, then there was no way Lyn was coming back,' Pat told me. 'If she had left, we still had hope that she would come back. What else were we to believe? Your emotions sort of take over your rational thoughts.'

Pat's explanation made sense. Avoidance of the most probable scenario – Lyn was dead, whether by her own hand, an accident or foul play – allowed the hope that by some miracle she'd come home, throw her arms around her daughters and put her absence down to a brain injury and memory loss.

'Mum just always wants Lyn to come back and we thought that perhaps she'd had a mental breakdown – that was the only possibility which we thought could explain why she would leave all the things she loved so much.

'She was really affectionate. So warm. Overly generous. She was funny and a little cheeky. I think Chris was the centre of her world.'

Pat and her brothers had sought to shield their mother from some of the evidence. The woman was in her 80s and for so long she had believed in Chris.

'She is so innocent and honest and naive and gullible,' Pat said. 'She feels terribly deceived about the rings. She always thought that Lyn had her rings because she asked Chris and he told her yes.'

It would be years before I appreciated the significance of what Pat was disclosing to me about Lyn's jewellery, and how her rings were recycled for Jenny to wear, gifts from Chris to mark their engagement and wedding. Helena had been comforted for years by the thought that should Lyn need money while on her inexplicable break from her family, she would be able to sell her rings. In truth, they had never left the house at Bayview.

Pat spoke fondly of Damian Loone and his efforts over the previous three years from 1998 to put his brief of evidence before a coroner. 'He's like a dog with a bone. He just doesn't give up.'

'Damian had told us things before we heard them to try to prepare us for the shock. He told us about some of the awful things, like the digs and the colleague talking about the bruising on Lyn's neck. We didn't know any of it.

'Peter Dawson was flinging himself around in the court, throwing papers and being very emotional.'

Lyn's older sister expressed disdain for the woman who got the ball rolling with police in 1990. 'There was Jenny in my sister's house with her husband, her kids, and all of her things – even their wedding presents.'

We talked for a couple of hours and the longer I stayed, the more I liked Pat Jenkins. She sounded strong and purposeful after a long period of grief, weakness and indecision.

'It's been 19 years. We want to know the truth.'

I left her home in Sydney tired but relieved at how much had been accomplished in one long day. I would return to Brisbane carrying a notebook full of details, evidence; almost everything I needed for a powerful telling of a remarkable story.

A fuse was unknowingly lit in the Dee Why police station on that day in March 2001. It would take 21 years for its wick to burn to the end.

Chapter 5

Newtown Criminals

Back at my desk in Brisbane, I wrote further questions I wanted answered as well as a few observations of my own beneath a heading – *Issues re Damian.*

One of them was: *Protection of statements, were they exhibits?*

Evidence of (the former student who described shocking grooming and sexual exploitation, and whose identity I would not disclose). Antics of teachers with students.

What about the molestation claims? What about criminal carnal knowledge? Are other teachers being interviewed?

Would you like to talk to Chris?

Where do you believe Lyn Dawson's remains are?

I telephoned the police prosecutor, Matt Fordham, who suggested that the brief of evidence I had devoured at Dee Why police station the previous day should not be accessible to media as the coroner had terminated the inquest to refer the case to the Director of Public Prosecutions.

'It's as though the inquest never took place as far as access to documents go,' he told me.

It dawned on me that I'd been permitted to read hundreds of pages because Matt Fordham didn't know that the cops at Dee Why police station had done something highly unusual.

'If it was to be printed that Damian showed you the brief, he would be in strife,' Fordham told me.

I asked if there had been any suppression orders relating to individuals named in the two volumes of evidence comprising the brief.

'No, I applied re Jenny Carlson, but it wasn't granted.'

The next call was to Alexandra Wake, a former journalist working as a media manager for the Queensland Government, having previously been in the Education Minister's office as a senior adviser.

Putting aside the allegations of foul play, the evidence concerning Chris and Paul Dawson was damning. Chris was acknowledging a relationship with a student whom he later married; Paul was accused by a student of having passed her around other teachers for sex after his own needs were satisfied, and there was a live question over whether her claims were more or less credible than Paul's version, which admitted to the relationship but denied the timing.

I suspected that Queensland authorities, which had granted registration to Chris and Paul Dawson to teach, were possibly ignorant of these claims in Sydney, despite Charles Miranda having mentioned a referral.

Alex told me that Queensland's Board of Teacher Registration would not have screened teachers who had already been in the system for a number of years. New applicants were screened for police records and other red flags but there was, she explained, a 'big loophole' when it came to retrospective checks. Neither Chris nor Paul Dawson had criminal records.

We talked about the alleged circumstances in this case and I told Alex some of what I had read in the police brief.

She replied, 'The process is that the New South Wales authorities should have alerted the Queensland authorities and they should have alerted the Board of Teacher Registration.'

Alex didn't know whether any alert had happened but my call to her meant there was no chance it would be overlooked now.

I strongly doubted that either Chris or Paul Dawson would want to make any comment for the story. Their solicitor brother said from Sydney: 'Please note that the only statement being made by the Dawson family is that we believe Lyn Dawson is alive and that we hope she contacts us. But thanks for your interest.'

The feature-length story published under my byline in *The Courier-Mail* that Saturday, headlined 'Looking For Lyn', was the cover story of the *Inside Mail* section on 10 March 2001.

Vanessa Hunter's arresting page design and the selection of a striking photograph of an adoring young woman, Lyn, looking lovingly up at Chris, a dashing and handsome man in a dinner suit, would have captured every reader's attention.

I fact-checked the piece with a red pen, circling, underlining and inserting ticks and crosses where needed. The story was vitally important. It would be unforgivable to screw it up with factual errors.

The newspaper's chief of staff, Paul Whittaker, my close friend and brother-in-law, knew about the pending feature. Paul asked for an accompanying news story to heighten the impact. It was written by my colleague Malcolm Cole, a state politics reporter, and me. It started like this:

> Two Queensland schoolteachers face an Education Department investigation following claims to a Sydney Coroner's Court that they had sexual relationships with students.
>
> Education Minister Anna Bligh yesterday ordered the department investigate the allegations, made against twin brothers Paul and Chris Dawson, who 19 years ago were physical education teachers in NSW when the alleged events took place. Both now work in Queensland.
>
> Paul and Chris Dawson, both of whom are former top rugby league footballers who taught at public high schools in Sydney, are accused of seducing the girls in and out of school.

After establishing that the Education Department in Queensland was 'unaware of the allegations and had not received any official notification from the New South Wales Police or the DPP', Malcolm Cole went to the Education Minister, Anna Bligh, for comment.

Her concerns were faithfully quoted. 'I take these matters seriously. I've asked the Director-General to ensure these allegations are investigated, and to take any necessary action.'

The stories were widely read. My father remarked upon them approvingly over the weekend without mentioning his mother's disappearance.

I raised the Dawson case with a journalist friend Darren Goodsir, with whom Ruth and I had worked closely at the *South China Morning Post* in Hong Kong. Darren had returned to Sydney and been the media manager for the commissioner of police then joined the *Sydney Morning Herald*. When I sent Darren the story in 2001, I told him I wanted to write a book about the case. 'Like all good books, the deeper you dig, the better it gets,' Darren said.

The following Tuesday, I received a fax from David Middleton, a highly regarded and longtime rugby league writer, of a 1974 article from an old copy of *Rugby League World*. The Dawson twins were profiled for having crossed from rugby union to rugby league.

In a cover note to me, David wrote: 'One interesting point you may not be aware of regarding the Newtown side of that era. A lock forward around that time was Gary Sullivan, who was in the last decade one of Australia's most wanted criminals. He was involved in an armed robbery and later escaped from prison. He was recaptured about five years ago.

'Five-eighth in the mid-1970s was Paul Hayward, jailed for heroin trafficking in Bangkok . . .'

Paul Hayward's friend and brother-in-law was Arthur 'Neddy' Smith, a sociopathic serial killer and rapist.

None of these connections made Chris Dawson a murderer but I appreciated Middleton's point: there were dangerous criminals in and around the Newtown Jets when the Dawsons played there, and a footballer who wanted to get rid of his wife would know where to go for help.

Chapter 6

Bullets

THE AGE
25 October 2002 – 10.00 am

Journalist shaken after attack on home

Queensland journalist Hedley Thomas fought back tears yesterday as he revealed how his wife was almost shot in an overnight attack on their home.

Mr Thomas, an investigative journalist for *The Courier-Mail*, said he had received a death threat a year ago and believed someone intended to kill him when several shots were fired at his family's Brisbane home with a high-powered weapon.

Three bullets were found at the home in the western suburb of Brookfield, including one that pierced the wall of the children's toy room. Mr Thomas said another had come within centimetres of his wife, Ruth Mathewson, and showered the couple with glass after it broke a window above her pillow.

The couple were lying in bed with a bedside lamp on when the shots were fired about 10.20 on Wednesday night. They heard a 'tremendous cracking noise' and, when they went downstairs to investigate, found a bullet hole in the garage door.

'The person fired indiscriminately at our house with reckless disregard for who was inside,' Mr Thomas said.

He said his 18-month-old daughter, Sarah, had woken up screaming but three-year-old son Alexander had slept through.

The couple are considering police protection after being moved to a safe house.

'We believe that this was an attack, with deliberate intent to cause us serious injury or death,' Mr Thomas said.

'It was an attack not just on me as a journalist but on *The Courier-Mail*, on press freedom, on journalists everywhere.'

Mr Thomas won a Walkley Award in 1999 for Australia's best investigative report, a story he co-wrote about Queensland politicians' involvement in an illegal online gambling site. His most recent exposé focused on property marketeers who have been ripping off hundreds of thousands of dollars from investors.

Courier-Mail editor David Fagan said security was being assessed at the newspaper.

Mr Thomas declined to speculate on a suspect or motive for the attack.

'A year ago, my wife received a death threat at our home,' he said. 'We still don't know what story that was related to. At this stage, I remain strong-willed about being a journalist.'

Ruth and I had just gone to bed.

The shooter came by car and stood outside our house, pointed a gun and fired four times.

The blasts woke up the neighbours.

The final bullet was never recovered; police ballistics experts speculated that the kick-back from the weapon after each firing resulted in the fourth projectile going over the roof.

The first three bullets blasted into the house, smashing the children's toy room downstairs and our bedroom window directly above. Ruth felt the smithereens of glass on her face and arms but neither of us comprehended in the immediate aftermath that it was from a shooting.

A minute or two later, as I rushed downstairs and outside, our next-door neighbour told me we'd been shot at. From a window, she'd caught a glimpse of the car speeding off.

Police sped to the semi-rural neck of the woods. My sister Kate and brother-in-law Paul Whittaker rushed to Brookfield along with the newspaper's editor, David Fagan, and his wife, Madonna King. Media crews were not far behind.

Ruth and I were dazed. Who had done this? Why?

We left the house with the children that night and went to a hotel room in the city. Over the next couple of days, we spoke at length to detectives to try to develop a list of suspects based on the cases I'd been investigating and the stories I was writing.

The list grew as I scrolled through the online database of articles published under my byline. Messages of support from friends and complete strangers poured in. Journalists in Australia were routinely sued but rarely targeted in violent reprisal.

Ruth and I decided to go away for two to three weeks to remove ourselves and the children from the stress. We went to Tasmania and tried to make sense of what had happened while tradies got to work on the house so that when we returned – if we returned – there would be no bullet holes; no broken glass; no shattered ensuite bathroom tile from the projectile which had narrowly missed us when it passed through the window above our heads and kept going.

The Commissioner of Police, Bob Atkinson, called me in Tasmania with updates on the investigation. A partial DNA profile was obtained from the gun, which was found by children playing in a nearby creek. The shooter must have thrown it while speeding away.

On our return to Queensland, we moved home and tried to go on as if nothing had happened. It was impossible. I seethed over the attack upon my home and family. I started to drink heavily. I was back at work, back at my desk, and receiving calls and emails from people who wanted me to investigate their particular grievance because, as several put it, the attack upon me meant that my journalism had really got under a baddie's skin. So I must be a high achiever; I'd get results for them, whatever the cost to me and my family.

I understood the shallow logic but raged internally at what felt like the disregard of these strangers who knew nothing of the trauma with which Ruth and I were dealing privately.

Mum and Dad were shocked by what had happened and the risk to their flesh and blood. My father came to visit. He took me aside on the paved path behind the house and confided that he stayed in contact with retired Australian special forces officers with whom he had served some 35 years earlier in the Vietnam War. He asked if I had any leads about who was behind the shooting. I immediately understood and appreciated the gesture. I told him we had no leads, only speculations.

He implored me to hang in because it would slowly get better. 'Remember one thing, pal. It's always darkest before the dawn,' Dad told me.

He knew things on the home front were bad. And he didn't know the half of it.

Alcohol was my temporary balm, though it corroded our marriage. Ruth was a rock of support and stability while trying with all her energy and willpower to keep the children calm and happy. I yearned for the carefree lives we led before the shooting, when I didn't feel the urge to stalk outside the property at night; to note every car that rolled down our street; to worry that if the shooter came again, Ruth or one of the children would be hurt.

There was something else. Every time anyone asked me a perfectly reasonable question related to the shooting, my eyes filled with tears. They streamed down my cheeks. It was automatic, unstoppable and would sometimes culminate in quiet sobs where I would be fighting the emotion, unable to talk or explain what was going on. It happened in a meeting Ruth and I had on the executive floor of the News Limited Building in Sydney with Lachlan Murdoch and John Hartigan, who were running the company.

A week later, as Ruth was driving us back from the mid-December wedding of our friends John Lehmann and Megan Turner in the hills behind Noosa, I raged about her missing a turn. It was a nothing event but in my drunken state, it escalated. I tried to open the door to jump out of the moving Jeep Grand Cherokee as Paul Whittaker, a passenger in the back, looked on horrified. Fortunately, Ruth had the presence of mind to child-lock the doors and the tensions gradually eased.

We were close to rock-bottom when a psychologist organised by John Hartigan took me under her wing. She explained why I was angry and described the function of my brain which, she said, was dumping chemicals every time someone asked me about the shooting. Hence the uncontrolled tears.

She told me about the cops and firefighters and ambulance officers whose lives, careers and families had been defined and severely damaged by PTSD arising from the trauma they'd witnessed. A trail of broken marriages and family dysfunction.

'You can avoid this,' she promised me.

It sounded too good to be true. Having become sad, angry and pessimistic, I couldn't see how things could be easily turned around. Ruth pushed me to follow the advice.

The first step, she told me, was to cease drinking immediately. The alcohol exacerbated sorrow. It had to end.

Knowing that I was drinking far too much, and more than even Ruth knew, I was privately relieved at the direction to stop. I surprised myself by adhering to it.

The second step was to raise my heart rate with exercise for at least 30 minutes every day. Endorphins, she told me, are the brain's natural antidepressant and they'll release and flood your grey tissue when you're exercising hard.

I started swimming laps of the Centenary Pool at Spring Hill before work and on weekends. And it was true; the longer I swam, the more positive I felt. The line on the bottom of the pool became my therapy friend. Underwater, I could shout profanities at the unknown shooter and nobody would hear; I could cry with my head in the chlorinated water and nobody would see.

Swimming saved our marriage and our beautiful family from ruin. I counted my lucky stars for the tough-love help of a psychologist and I continued reporting at *The Courier-Mail*.

Four months after the shooting, Pat Jenkins was back in touch by email to tell me 'there is to be a second coronial inquiry into the death of my sister, Lyn Dawson'.

Pat and I had talked about the case since the NSW Director of Public Prosecutions, Nicholas Cowdery, had decided in late 2001 that Dawson would not be prosecuted as, in his view, there was no reasonable chance of a conviction.

It was unusual to hold a second inquest two years after the first one. The thinking behind it was that if the witnesses from whom the detective Damian Loone had taken statements were cross-examined under oath, the case would be more persuasive to the DPP. Jan Stevenson, the coroner who ran the 2001 inquest, had made her decision to recommend a prosecution largely on the basis of her close examination of the police brief of evidence.

The only witness cross-examined was Damian Loone.

Pat emailed me again on 21 February 2003, with what she believed to be more positive news.

Inquiry still set for next week. Have been told a second week has been set aside in case.

There is to be a feature article in *The Telegraph* tomorrow. Publicity often gets action, so that is all to the good.

I don't expect the Dawsons to attend the inquiry, except solicitor brother Peter, who seems to have been thrown into the deep end again.

Dwindling contact with my niece in Queensland – very defensive of her father and believes it a conspiracy. This inquiry can only alienate her more. In contact with little gypsy niece in USA, and just trust our caring for each other can weather this storm.

The second inquest was conducted by Carl Milovanovich, a straight-talking deputy state coroner. I was following it at the time, keeping tabs from a distance.

At its conclusion, he too recommended that the DPP consider a murder prosecution of Chris Dawson.

'Such a strong result,' Pat wrote to me in March 2003. 'As we have accepted Lyn's death, coroner's finding was the best possible outcome.

'The case was overwhelming emotionally. Now waiting for the DPP to come to a decision. It took nine months last time. It is a difficult time with such an issue unresolved and wondering which way it is going to go.'

Pat added that a lawyer from the Queensland Department of Education had attended for two days of the public hearings and had said action would be taken, 'but not until Lyn's case has reached a conclusion'.

The coroner's recommendation was still under consideration by the DPP with a decision pending in late March when I spoke to Deb Fleming, then the ABC's executive producer of the acclaimed weekly program *Australian Story*. We had collaborated on several stories in the past.

I told Deb about Lyn's case, gave her a copy of my 2001 feature article, 'Looking For Lyn', and dug through my old notebook to find the names and telephone numbers of witnesses who were Lyn's friends from the childcare centre: Barbara Cruise, Sue Strath, Annette Leary and Anna Grantham, as well as Pat Jenkins and Detective Damian Loone.

Deb put producer Wendy Page and researcher Mara Blazic onto the assignment. The program, when it finally aired in early August 2003, was exceptional. Pat Jenkins and Greg Simms, Lyn's friends, Loone and other key figures made a powerful impression on the viewing audience. Pat regretted that her mother didn't see it. The heartbroken woman had died six months after the first inquest.

Deb Fleming told me it was one of their most successful programs.

Ruth and I were teary throughout our viewing of it at home. A number of witnesses who saw it came forward to talk to Loone for the first time, strengthening his brief of evidence.

But in the days after *Australian Story*'s airing, Pat received more distressing news: Nicholas Cowdery was unmoved by the findings of the second inquest and the testimony of the witnesses.

There would be no prosecution.

Chapter 7

Rebecca

By 2012, Lyn's case had been out of the news for years. I had occasional calls and email contact with Pat Jenkins and Greg Simms. There had been no breakthroughs or cause for optimism as far as they were concerned. The DPP would not budge.

When Greg last wrote to me in August 2011, he'd lamented, 'We are still unable to get the NSW Director of Public Prosecutions to prosecute the matter. They cite there is not enough evidence.'

Greg wrote that he was seeking my help through any connections in Queensland I might have to investigate some information he had received from a woman.

'The psychic advised me by email that a gentleman, asked to arrange a "hit" man on my sister, drank at The Mona Vale Hotel on Sydney's Northern Beaches.

'She indicated that the person is a petty criminal with underworld links, he is not a very large build with sandy thinning hair, feels he is bald or close to it now. He has a craggy face and squints a lot. Who knows what he looks like after nine years in the Queensland sun. From a rough guess I would say he would be in his late 60s or early 70s.'

Greg named the individual and the football club with which he had been associated prior to his move to the town of Beenleigh, about halfway between the Gold Coast and Brisbane. Greg added that the man was a heavy drinker who would not be too hard to find in one of the pubs or taverns around Beenleigh.

As a longtime sceptic, Greg's request struck me as odd and the information, far-fetched. I told him that, while my mother would beg to differ, 'I don't believe that information from psychics has a credible basis.'

Greg replied. 'Sorry you can't help us. Had dreams you could find him and break the case wide open! Maybe I should get your mother on the case!'

Greg was desperate. He was a police officer when Lyn disappeared, and he was still serving when Jenny shared her suspicions and secrets on leaving Chris in 1990. Greg knew that people wondered why him being a copper for 27 years had not helped his sister.

'Dawson was the next of kin and in control and investigating officers don't want suggestions from a relative,' he wrote.

He promised to pass on my regards to Pat, and he answered my question about Lyn's daughters. I had not met them nor seen photographs but they were on my mind whenever Lyn's case arose.

'We have had nothing to do with the youngest daughter. She announced at my mother's funeral that she wanted nothing to do with our family. We were accused of persecuting her father. The eldest has flittered from the US to Australia and England. I believe she is staying overseas for a reason. But who knows?

'The younger daughter looks like a Dawson, the older one looks like Lyn. It makes us wonder what she is thinking.'

Although I had contemplated writing a book about the case in 2001, nothing had happened. The arrival of our baby daughter Sarah in May 2001 with all the excitement a newborn brings, and then the fallout of the shooting 18 months later, weakened my resolve to write a book. The idea went on indefinite hold.

Five years later, I wrote a book about another scandal involving a dangerous surgeon called Dr Jayant Patel, whose incompetence had harmed his patients in a regional Queensland hospital and led to him being convicted of three counts of manslaughter. The verdict was quashed by the High Court on appeal. There was no retrial. Patel was also convicted and jailed in Brisbane for fraud.

A Google search I had done at my desk in 2005 exposed him as a public menace who had been severely disciplined and barred from doing certain surgeries in the United States because of his negligence and the harm he inflicted upon patients.

His career in Oregon was finished but Dr Patel wanted to keep working. He lied about his past when he applied to work at the Bundaberg Base Hospital and nobody in the Queensland Health system checked his background before giving him a job as the sugar town's Director of Surgery. I moved to *The Australian* newspaper, the national daily, as the book was being published in 2007, stayed a year, then went to what journalists call 'the dark side', as a general manager of communications at a resources company, which came with a higher salary, corporate credit card, travel in business class and, from time to time, on private jets. But the hours were longer and the stress levels higher. The work was tedious compared with the excitement and unpredictability of investigative journalism.

By 2010, I was yearning for journalism again. Two years in public relations was more than enough. With a hefty pay cut, I was back at *The Australian*.

In late April 2012, I received an email from a woman called Rebecca Hazel. She described a project which made me immediately envious: 'I am a writer researching a book on the disappearance and presumed murder of Lynette Dawson. I read an article you wrote for *The Courier-Mail*, 10 March 2001, "Looking for Lyn" and I was hoping you might be willing to chat with me about the case? I thought it was an excellent article and I thought you might have insights that would be most helpful to me.'

I called her the same afternoon and we spoke at length about Lyn's disappearance. Rebecca told me she didn't have a publisher but she was pressing on regardless.

It had been a difficult day. I had spent a couple of hours that morning talking to a friend whose wife Allison, a friend of Ruth's, had been missing for ten days. Gerard Baden-Clay and I were not close but we knew each other from the Brookfield community, school fundraisers and occasional catch-ups. Gerard asked me to come to see him at his parents' house on the morning of 30 April to talk about

Allison, who was 43 and a doting wife and mother of three little girls. Police, official volunteers and hundreds of people in the Brookfield community had been searching for her, and police divers had even waded into the creek and swimming hole behind our home.

Gerard was strangely reluctant to take advantage of the public interest in the case; I told him he needed to make daily appeals through the media for anyone with information about Allison to come forward. He told me his lawyers wanted him to lay low. My suspicions about Gerard only grew.

At noon, I left him with his parents and two of his daughters and drove north along Rafting Ground Road towards the Brookfield Showgrounds, turning on ABC radio news to catch the update – a woman's body had just been found in Kholo Creek. Three little girls, one of whom was a schoolfriend of our daughter Sarah, had lost their adoring mum. Homicide Squad detectives, rightly, had Gerard in their crosshairs, although I did not know about their strong suspicions at the time.

When I spoke to Rebecca Hazel several hours later, Ruth and I were in shock about Allison's fate. I blurted out my suspicions around Gerard Baden-Clay, and we talked about Chris, Lyn and Allison. Two women probably slain. Five children irrevocably damaged.

Rebecca emailed me again that evening to thank me for calling.

'I can hear the genuine interest you have in her disappearance and I would very much welcome your input, even your file on her if you can locate it, as time goes by. I will let you know how I progress and look forward to further discussions with you.'

The next day, I found a number of stories from 2001 and 2003 in *The Courier-Mail*'s database and copy-pasted them in a reply.

'I think your book is a very worthwhile exercise as well as a likely cracking read. Lyn, and her family, deserve a result and perhaps the book will provide the breakthrough.

'When you know you've got a book, I'll dig out the file – it's hard to reach in a part of the roof that gives me vertigo and shortens my life expectancy.'

Rebecca was optimistic. I liked her over the phone. She sounded caring, intelligent and earnest but not pushy.

She wrote: 'I hope I can do Lyn justice. Will stay in touch.'

A killer appeared in my dreams that night.

Gerard sat opposite me at his parents' home. Clouds of black wasps poured from his mouth as he stressed his innocence.

Six weeks after telling me that his newly grown beard would be shaved as soon as Allison returned home, the friendly, community-minded real estate agent, chamber of commerce executive member, church-goer and school fundraiser was charged with murder and interfering with a corpse.

He had grown the facial hair to disguise the deep finger-nail scratches inflicted by a dying Allison as she fought for her life.

Gerard had been having multiple secret affairs with other women. A lover had warned him that he had to choose – her or Allison. But in the event of a divorce, he would have been penniless. Instead, he killed her in cold blood, dumped her body in the mud and weeds around Kholo Creek, nine kilometres from their house near the Brookfield General Store and cuddled his girls as they willed their mother to return.

He was found guilty of Allison's murder two years later. Along with our friends and neighbours in the Brookfield community, we were sure the jury got it right. The vagaries of the criminal justice system were demonstrated over the next two years. His appeal to the Queensland Court of Appeal resulted in his conviction for murder being downgraded to manslaughter. This highly controversial decision was appealed by the Queensland DPP to the High Court, and in 2016 the murder conviction was restored.

The memory of Rebecca Hazel's fortuitous contact on that awful day stayed with me. In late October 2017, Rebecca was the first person I wanted to talk to about Lyn's case and my plan for a podcast. I found her emails from our fleeting contact and called her mobile number. Rebecca was at Sydney Airport for a flight to Melbourne but we talked at length and again when she landed. She told me her book was largely complete but she did not have a publisher. I raised the possibility that we could collaborate on a podcast as well as get her book published, perhaps by News Corp's sister company HarperCollins.

The rapport we had on the phone in 2012 was evident again in our impromptu conversations. I emailed Rebecca shortly after lunch that day in late October 2017:

> When I first wrote about Lyn Dawson in the early 2000s I recall being deeply moved by the tragedy of her sudden disappearance, the impact on her daughters, and the integrity and decency of her siblings. I have thought about the case many times since.
>
> I just mention this as a private aside. My father, who passed away in March, lost his mother when he was a young teenager, and her disappearance was never resolved. She had mental health challenges and walked away from their Sydney Northern Beaches home one night, never to be seen again.
>
> It was believed that she walked into the ocean, swam out and drowned. There were no suspicious circumstances, and I know my dad never stopped wondering whether his mother would return one day. I imagine Lyn's daughters have similar longings.
>
> It is a travesty that your book has not been published. I think that a forensically researched and professionally produced podcast series would be very much in the public interest.
>
> It would be undoubtedly enhanced by your research, contacts and knowledge. Please be assured that I am a stickler for upfront attribution and acknowledgment – I would not dream of ripping off your efforts.
>
> Please keep all of this in confidence as I would hate for someone to steal the idea and beat us to it.

Rebecca's husband, Harry, sent me several early chapters of her manuscript and I dived in, riveted by her descriptive writing about a subject I knew well. Her chapter about Lyn was elegant and I had texted her to say: 'I really couldn't put it down, it was gripping. It is a seriously great piece of descriptive writing. I hope they don't propose change to any of it. The observations are poignantly insightful. Greg and Pat will be honoured'.

Rebecca got back to me early the next morning, Saturday, and the signs were still encouraging: 'I too am very grateful that you found me. Your grandmother's story is terribly sad. For Lynette's siblings, the pain hasn't diminished and has continued through the next generation. I can see how your attachment to Lynette's disappearance would resonate with your own family's history. I'm impressed by your urgency to push ahead with this project and I look forward to getting together soon.

'I appreciate you forwarding me your email to Greg and I ask that you keep me in the loop at every stage. In turn, please be assured of my absolute discretion.'

Rebecca was on board. I repeatedly refreshed my email in the hope I would get a reply soon from Greg Simms. He got back to me before 10 am on Saturday.

Good Morning Hedley,

Nice to be able to be in contact again. Your article in 2001 was hard-hitting and we really appreciated what you did for our sister.

I have spoken with Pat in Sydney and we are happy to do what we can to help out. I have spoken to my brother Phil and sent him a copy of your email (as he was out shopping).

This will all be kept in the strictest confidence. I hope Phil wants to get involved in this along with Pat and myself.

Greg told me the brief of evidence, which I'd first read back in 2001, was with police prosecutors, pending another handover of the file to the Office of the DPP. It seemed that the authorities were playing the same broken record again.

I read Greg's email and was immediately thrilled. Forty-eight hours later, he emailed again with names and numbers for key people in the Simms family.

Greg related the recollection of a cousin, Jenny McDonald, who introduced herself to Chris Dawson at a party of mutual friends in Queensland.

'He made sure he kept a wide distance from her. On the other hand, his twin and his wife spoke with her. She still remembers when any reference came up about Lyn, they both used the past tense.'

I suspected Lyn had been dead since the night of 8 January 1982. Did Greg believe in a miracle in which Lyn left Bayview all those years ago and lived happily ever after?

Part 2

Momentum

Chapter 8

Alexander's Ladder

When our good friend and builder Jack Nash came to repair damage from the bullets fired into our house in late 2002, I asked him to create a storage space in the roof of the carport. It was soon filled with large plastic containers of notebooks, newspaper articles and folders from our years in journalism.

My 2001 file on Lyn Dawson went up there, along with dozens of folders about government corruption scandals, legal scams, property rip-offs, illegal gambling and dangerous doctors. The roof space in the carport was where old stories came to die.

Alexander, now just a fortnight shy of 19 and in his second year of a chemical engineering degree at the University of Queensland, was gaming in his room when I asked for his help. Fitter, lighter and far more agile on a ladder than me, he clambered into the roof space. Nobody had been up there in years. When it was built, I had every intention of revisiting old cases and reworking them with new story angles but there was always something fresh instead.

Mice and bats had taken up residence, their droppings carpeting the plywood. There were snake skins and thick cobwebs. And something must have died up there too.

Alexander needed to drag the many containers across the filthy timber and carefully place them onto the top of the ladder for me to put on the pavers. It was a sweltering hot and humid day out in the open. Under the tin of the carport roof it was an oven. On the ground, I opened a container and rifled through the contents to look for a manila folder. Then we'd do it again.

Although I hadn't seen it for many years, I could still picture the yellow cover with two words on the front in my handwriting – 'Lyn Dawson'. I couldn't remember the contents of it aside from my 2001 notebook but I knew that recovering this file would be integral to the podcast investigation.

For the first hour of Alexander's dirty work, we came up empty-handed, and the pavers beneath the carport were strewn with plastic containers, unused wedding gifts and mementos from reporting assignments which must have seemed important at the time.

'Dad, why are you going to so much effort for this one story? What's the big deal with it, anyway?' my exasperated teenage son asked through gritted teeth.

I gave him the bare facts about a mother having gone missing and her husband just getting on with his life and a relationship with his former high school student; of how he eventually came to be suspected by this young woman and police of having murdered his wife, and that there was overwhelmingly suspicious circumstantial evidence, yet he had never faced justice.

We spoke of Allison Baden-Clay's slaying an easy walk from our home. Her killer, her husband Gerard, had visited our home with his daughters, with whom Alexander and Sarah had gone to primary school. Alexander remembered. His bedroom overlooked a creek and deep swimming hole behind our home. Police divers searched the water for Allison's body in 2012.

I told him what I knew for sure: a powerfully important story was bound up in the missing file. If we found it, the information therein would be a big help for me in telling this story properly, in much more detail than I had tried to do in 2001. Maybe it would deliver justice for Lyn and her loved ones.

He went back up the ladder without complaint and stayed there until every container had come down. We got lucky with the last container in the darkest recesses of the roof space.

Prising the lid off, I went straight to the 'Lyn Dawson' folder – one of about 20. All had remained high and dry over the years. Leafing through it beneath the ladder and seeing my several dozen pages of notes from transcribing witness statements on that long day in the Dee Why police station, I felt a bolt of excitement and hope. Alexander got a bear hug and $20. He took an early shower to wash the dirt and cobwebs away then returned to his gaming.

I started making plans to fly to Newcastle to see Greg and his wife, Merilyn, then drive to Sydney to see Pat Jenkins for the first time since 2001, and hopefully meet Rebecca Hazel. There would be no recordings nor interviews on this visit. There would be time for that later. This trip was about building rapport and answering their questions.

But while sitting in Greg and Merilyn's lounge room on a Tuesday afternoon, just four days after raising my idea for a podcast investigation into Lyn's disappearance, I realised something had shifted.

Before I had booked a direct flight to Newcastle, Greg could not have been more co-operative. When I spoke to him from Brisbane on the phone, he told me that in his study he had a box of police investigation documents which would be a great help for what I wanted to do. In my mind, we agreed that I would take them with me after my visit to his home.

However, Merilyn made it clear on the day that I would not be taking any documents with me. She wanted to know how I was going to include Rebecca Hazel, who had been talking to the family for several years.

Merilyn's loyalty to Rebecca was not going to suddenly switch to me just because I had turned up on their doorstep with a plan for something called a podcast, 16 years after I'd written a lengthy article about Lyn's disappearance. Neither Merilyn nor Greg had ever heard a podcast episode. They were not interested in the audio format and couldn't imagine a podcast having more impact than traditional media. They asked their daughter Renee, who bore an uncanny physical likeness to Lyn, what a podcast was. The fact that I had never done one cannot have instilled confidence.

Merilyn, friendly but guarded, was equally firm when I asked whether I could briefly look at the police investigation documents that Greg had referred to, just to get a sense of what was there.

I was deeply disappointed. One of the reasons for my travel that day was to collect this vital material and start investigating. But there was no point disagreeing with Merilyn and Greg at this early stage. It could have ruined everything.

I did my best to explain, again, my bona fides and to reassure Merilyn that I wanted to work with Rebecca. I had already done work behind the scenes to try to set up a meeting for Rebecca with publishing executives.

Merilyn could be forgiven for being sceptical, for thinking it all sounded a bit too convenient. Rebecca and I had not even met yet here I was, promoting a professional partnership.

In 1990, as a young reporter trying to make sense of the craft, I read the acclaimed American author Janet Malcolm's book, *The Journalist and The Murderer*. Her publishers described it as 'a seminal work and examination of the psychopathology of journalism'.

Malcolm wrote, 'Every journalist who is not too stupid or full of himself to notice what is going on knows that what he does is morally indefensible. He is a kind of confidence man, preying on people's vanity, ignorance, or loneliness, gaining their trust and betraying them without remorse.'

It's a killer passage but, in my experience, it is a callous and untrue declaration. What journalists do in persuading people to talk is vital in any democracy. Of course, a journalist should work to gain the trust of people who are to be interviewed or written about but her pay-off line alleging betrayal without remorse is hyperbolic rubbish.

I was not preying on Lyn's family's desperation. They were not vain or ignorant or lonely but they were vulnerable in another way – they felt abandoned by the criminal justice system for its refusal to prosecute Christopher Michael Dawson.

They were left wondering why there had been no justice for Lyn despite the findings of State Coroner Jan Stevenson in 2001 and

Deputy State Coroner Carl Milovanovich in 2003 – that there was a reasonable prospect a jury could find Lyn's husband guilty of her murder.

Lyn's loved ones did not know that when I started the podcast investigation, my motives went beyond my sense of the injustice in this case. They did not know back then that my interest was also bound up in the unanswered mystery of my grandmother's disappearance. But we shared a well-grounded suspicion about prosecutorial failure and bungling, and I emphasised this in Merilyn and Greg's home.

I had previously investigated and reported closely on a swim coach's alleged sexual assaults on girl swimmers. One of those swimmers, Julie Gilbert, had shared with me her case files and a recording of the absurd explanation she was given by a top prosecutor for her decision to not prosecute. The so-called reasoning, when it was published in black and white in my reports, shocked and appalled lawyers and defence counsel.

Julie had disclosed something deeply personal when she gave her statement to police during their investigations. She told them she had experienced an orgasm during the allegedly indecent massage by her coach. As a 13-year-old at the time, she did not know what it was; when she was older she realised it was an orgasm. But her openness was seized on as a reason to justify not prosecuting her alleged abuser. The prosecutor's written advice stated 'this is quite unlike the situation that pertains when an adult male is assaulted and experiences orgasm as an involuntary and momentarily pleasant reflex'. The legal advice described the 'unlikelihood' of Julie's claim, adding 'it is difficult to accept that [she] could have been feeling sufficiently relaxed for orgasm to ensue'. Having dealt with Julie's allegations that her coach had massaged her groin and legs, the prosecutor addressed the allegation that Julie's breasts were also massaged, and wrote: 'It is legitimate to consider whether 12-year-old swimmers even had breasts, but that is the allegation.' Julie was aghast. I interviewed a leading psychiatrist, Dr Warwick Middleton, and a sexual assault expert, Dr Patricia Brennan, who described the advice as 'ignorant' and factually groundless. A top

Queensland lawyer, Russell Hanson QC, told me the reasoning from the NSW Office of the DPP was 'irrelevant, unprofessional and just plain silly'.

Bizarre conduct and strange decision-making at the highest levels of the Office of the DPP in Queensland and in New South Wales were laid bare in the official report of a Queensland Crime and Misconduct Commission inquiry: *The Volkers Case: Examining the conduct of the police and prosecution*, and in my investigations and reporting.

In this remarkable case, I had seen first-hand an egregious example of mishandling by prosecutors. It had left me under no misapprehension about their fallibility.

Another serious abomination which embroiled the NSW Office of the DPP came to a head in late 2017, at the end of a trial of two men over the death of 33-year-old Lynette Daley. The Indigenous mother of seven bled to death on a remote beach in 2011; her vagina had been mutilated by a bottle after repeated sexual assaults by the two men, one of whom was her boyfriend. They destroyed evidence, including a bloodied mattress.

Lynette Daley's family and friends were repeatedly told by prosecutors that they would not be putting the two men on trial as there was no reasonable prospect of conviction.

In contrast, then NSW State Coroner Michael Barnes, with whom I had a personal and professional relationship, had run an inquest into Lynette Daley's death. His findings raised powerful and evidence-based reasons for prosecution. Still, the DPP refused to even reconsider its decision.

The deadlock was broken by exceptional journalism. First, a hard-hitting series of stories in *The Daily Telegraph* by Janet Fife-Yeomans raised enormous public disquiet. Next, a searing ABC *4 Corners* investigation by Caro Meldrum-Hanna profiled the crime, the victim and her alleged killers. On TV screens in several hundred thousand living rooms across Australia, many viewers must have been disgusted with the DPP's timidity.

As the ABC's investigative reporter Caro Meldrum-Hanna put it, 'The NSW DPP has formally declined to prosecute on two separate occasions, despite the urgings of the investigating police and the recommendations of the NSW coroner.

'Ms Daley's family said they were deeply traumatised, shocked and confused with the NSW DPP's decisions.

'"They didn't care about her," her stepfather, Gordon Davis, said. "She was just a statistic with the DPP and with them. You know, 'It was just another Indigenous girl, we'll sweep it under the carpet' . . ."'

The report included damning rebukes of the prosecuting authority.

'The NSW DPP's refusal to prosecute is now drawing fierce criticism from several quarters, including legal and criminal law experts, who claim the justice system has grossly failed Ms Daley.'

Some of the experts who were quoted made the point that other prosecutions, which proceeded with less evidence, had resulted in convictions.

Under growing pressure to explain the reasoning of his independent office, Lloyd Babb SC, the Director of Public Prosecutions, agreed to seek an external review of the case from a leading criminal lawyer.

When his written opinion aligned with that of investigating police and of Michael Barnes in recommending a prosecution, a criminal trial of the two men was unavoidable.

The ABC reported on 6 September 2017:

Two men have been found guilty over the death of Lynette Daley, whose naked body was found bruised and bloodied after a boozy 2011 camping trip to a remote beach in northern New South Wales.

After listening to weeks of evidence and cross-examination, a jury at the Supreme Court in Coffs Harbour deliberated for just 32 minutes before convicting Adrian Attwater, who was Ms Daley's boyfriend, and Paul Maris.

Attwater was given a sentence of 19 years, and Maris got six years and nine months.

In a statement, Mr Babb publicly apologised: 'The question of whether there are reasonable prospects of conviction is a predictive exercise and one about which reasonable minds can differ. The case has now proceeded through the criminal justice system. Today, I publicly apologise to Ms Daley's family and the community for the delay.'

Case closed.

Dogged work by Michael Barnes, then by journalists, achieved this outcome. But for their efforts, nothing would have happened.

I let Michael know I was working on a podcast project and would be visiting Sydney. I told him about Lyn's case and its history. Michael, who had not been involved in the case at any stage and was in a new role as the NSW Ombudsman, told me that Carl Milovanovich, the coroner at the 2003 inquest, had recently retired.

In the past, he had made public statements to journalists. Perhaps he would talk to me for the podcast.

'He's a lovely man, warm and direct,' Rebecca Hazel assured me on a gloriously sunny day in early November. She had driven from her home on the Northern Beaches to Bondi's iconic Icebergs restaurant for our first face-to-face meeting.

The trust we had already placed in each other was unusual. Rebecca had emailed much of the manuscript for her proposed book and we'd talked for hours on the telephone.

In my mind, the stars lined up for a working relationship which would be good for everyone. With the exception of Chris Dawson. In a text message to Rebecca shortly before we met, I made my personal views all too obvious: 'It's regrettable that sexual assault charges were not brought by police on behalf of the other students over the brothers. What a pair of grubs.'

Before seeing Rebecca at Icebergs, I had caught up with Pat Jenkins at a cafe in Chatswood to explain my intentions for the podcast. Lyn's sister was happy to see me for the first time since 2001 and she welcomed a reinvestigation.

She handed me copies of some poignant letters written by her mother about Lyn. For eight years, the older woman had believed Chris's story that Lyn had left the house voluntarily. It was only when Jenny separated from Chris and reached out to the Simms family to share her concerns about Lyn's fate that the awful possibility of murder was seriously considered by the older woman.

Rebecca's friendship with Jenny Carlson, whom she met when they were working in a women's refuge, was key to our collaboration for a podcast. Both women wanted to see Rebecca's manuscript published.

I was confident that when the mutually beneficial opportunities were weighed by my ultimate employer, News Corp, and its publishing company, HarperCollins, there would be strong interest in taking Rebecca's beautifully written story for a book which could be released around the same time as my podcast.

It made perfect sense for Rebecca and myself to collaborate.

Over pasta and wine and our shared interest, Rebecca and I warmed up and found much common ground. We spoke about our families and the health challenges facing loved ones. We talked about the gentle arc of the narrative of her manuscript and the very different style I wanted to deploy in a podcast. We talked about the efforts over many years of Damian Loone, whom I had last seen in Dee Why police station in 2001.

Rebecca spoke particularly fondly of Jenny Carlson, her friend from the refuge and the catalyst for her proposed book.

We spoke of Lyn and the pain she must have endured while suspecting her husband was in love with the teenage family babysitter. Lyn had endured appalling betrayal and then forgiven Chris, before being erased from the lives of her loved ones and replaced by the schoolgirl she'd let into her home.

Neither of us could disguise our strong suspicion that Lyn was murdered in January 1982, either by Chris or by a contract killer. Where we differed was on the prospects of anyone facing justice.

I firmly believed that if the podcast went ahead with a powerful story which laid out all the facts, and questioned the Office of the DPP about its repeated failure to prosecute the case, we would see an outcome similar to that of the Lynette Daley case. I believed we would see an external review of the DPP's brief of evidence and a decision to prosecute Chris Dawson. It would be up to a jury to then consider his guilt or innocence.

Rebecca was pessimistic about it ever proceeding to trial. At that stage, she knew more about what some of the witnesses would say. The lawyer in her had landed on inconsistencies in testimony which would affect the credibility of people on whom the police sought to rely to justify Chris being a suspect in his wife's murder.

A number of witnesses, including Lyn's mother, were long-dead. Other witnesses were showing signs of mental and physical frailty.

Chris himself would not talk. When Rebecca wrote to seek an interview with him in May 2014, she received an email from his solicitor brother, Peter Dawson:

> There is no story or book in Lynette Dawson's decision to leave her husband and children. This is a decision made freely and consciously by many women including Lynette.
>
> Your interest in the matter can only be generated in the periodic media regurgitation of unsubstantiated and unsustainable allegations against Chris Dawson.
>
> Those allegations were made in the course of the incompetent, expensive and totally unnecessary forensic investigation of Lynette's decision, and have already caused great distress to Lynette's daughters and to the entire Dawson family.
>
> We have therefore no interest whatsoever in assisting you to perpetuate the myth that there is anything at all interesting about Lynette's decision.

Rebecca already disliked Peter Dawson but as a lawyer herself, she agreed with his advice to his brother – 'say nothing'.

She doubted there would be any formal justice for Lyn but hoped that telling her story would at least give her family some comfort.

We left Icebergs on good terms late in the afternoon. As I raced to the airport for the flight back to Brisbane, Rebecca sent an encouraging text: 'I think we might be able to do something very special.'

Chapter 9

Greg and Merilyn

Almost every investigative story in my career as a journalist has relied in part on original documentation. Alexander's success in finding my notebook and 'Lyn Dawson' folder was helpful as a starting point but if my podcast investigation was to make a significant difference, it would need much more than handwritten notes from old interviews and the partial transcript of police statements.

I was hopeful that Rebecca Hazel would be the bearer of further information and context. We spoke about the case almost daily through November 2017 as the prospects of her manuscript being published improved.

She told me Jenny had said she was happy to do the podcast with me as long as Rebecca would be at the interviews to lend support.

At a meeting in Sydney with Paul Whittaker, *The Australian*'s editor-in-chief, Rebecca and I talked about our proposed collaboration. We answered questions from Paul and James Kellow, the CEO of HarperCollins. They both indicated a lot of enthusiasm for the publication of Rebecca's manuscript in a joint enterprise with the podcast.

In Newcastle, Greg and Merilyn Simms organised a courier to deliver a brief of evidence from the 2001 inquest. It was a rare fluke that Greg even had a copy of the official police brief. Greg recalled that it was given to him by Andrew Bright, the barrister who had acted for the family.

Greg had not read the hundreds of pages of documents in years; he found the witness statements distressing. They were evidence of an accused killer's lies which Greg had believed for too long.

Rather than wait one more day, I drove to the courier's depot near Brisbane Airport, signed for the box and tore it open in the car. It would be several hours before I got home; the statements I read while parked on the side of the road were extraordinary.

It struck me that these were the same documents I had read in 2001 but this time, they were in my hands to keep and rely on in full, if need be. There were several other documents which I didn't recall seeing in 2001, and they related to legal correspondence and affidavits concerning Chris Dawson's divorce from Lyn in 1983, and his subsequent divorce from Jenny in 1991. It was a breakthrough, helping to clarify the chronology and tie up loose ends in the case.

One statement in particular from a woman called Julie Andrew, Lyn's friend and neighbour at Bayview, stood out for its detail and promise. I was confident I had not seen it with the other statements at Dee Why. Rebecca Hazel had not mentioned having any contact with Julie during research for the book. She had gone under the radar and it appeared from the transcript of the 2003 inquest that she had not appeared as a witness.

Julie Andrew gave her statement on 2 May 1999, describing having moved with her husband, Malcolm Downie, in 1979 into the house next door to that of Chris and Lyn Dawson.

> At the time I had two children close to the age of Lyn's two children. Being neighbours, Lyn and I became close friends.
>
> Our properties were not fenced at the time and Lyn would often walk over to my place through the bush where we would often sit down and have a cuppa and watched the children play.

Early in Julie Andrew's statement, she described an incident which must have had a significant impact upon her.

One day I was outside when I heard Lyn crying. I looked up towards Lyn's place and I saw Lyn leaning with her back against the trampoline. I saw Chris standing very close to her and they appeared to be arguing. I heard Lyn crying very loudly and I noticed that Lyn was very upset.

I heard Lyn say something like, 'Chris, how could you do it to us?'

I saw Chris shaking Lyn by the shoulders. I saw one of Lyn's children come out to where they were standing and Lyn picked the child up and hugged her to her chest.

Lyn was holding the baby and saying something like, 'What's Daddy doing to us?' Lyn was very upset and then walked back inside the house, sobbing.

Julie Andrew described having gone over to see Lyn later that afternoon.

'We spoke and Lyn told me that there were problems because Jenny was moving in. I advised Lyn to get rid of Jenny because I knew that Chris and Jenny were having a sexual relationship.'

According to Julie's account, 'Lyn didn't seem to want to accept what was happening', as Chris had reassured her that his relationship with the student was perfectly innocent.

'I would hear Jenny and Chris at home alone,' Julie's statement continued.

Jenny would sometimes be only wearing a G-string and would be topless around the pool. I knew that Jenny was only a schoolgirl at the time and I thought that this was inappropriate behaviour for a schoolteacher.

Lyn told me of an occasion when she left work early one day due to a headache and she caught a taxi home to her house. Lyn told me that she walked up the driveway to the house and then into her bedroom where she caught Chris and Jenny in a compromising position.

Somehow, Lyn told me that Chris had talked his way out of what was happening and Lyn seemed to believe Chris's story. This would have only been a couple of weeks prior to Lyn disappearing.

> Lyn DAWSON was a very houseproud person. She loved
> the house she and Chris were living in and would always be
> buying little trinkets to improve the house. Lyn was a wonderful
> homemaker and a wonderful and devoted mother to her two little
> girls. Lyn loved her mother and family and was a devoted daughter.
> Lyn was a beautiful mother and loved her husband and children
> very much.

Shortly after 9 January 1982, according to her statement, Julie became aware that Lyn was missing. Despite her being one of Lyn's close friends, she added, 'Chris has never spoken to me about Lyn, even just after she disappeared'.

> I do not believe Lyn DAWSON just up and vanished without a trace.
> Lyn would not have left her two girls as she loved them and adored
> them. Lyn would have told her mother what her intentions were and
> Lyn was not the type of person to let any person worry about her.
> I know Lyn was in an emotional state over Jenny but I can
> say that Lyn was not displaying any mental instability or mental
> problems.

Julie had divorced and remarried. And she had moved house several times. It took me some time to finally find her after a series of property searches and company director searches. I should have just gone to the White Pages. When we spoke on the telephone, Julie was direct and precise in her questions. What did I know of the case? Why did I want to investigate? What did I hope to achieve? After hearing me out, Julie paused and I thought I heard her sigh in relief. She told me that Lyn 'really cared for that girl, she wanted to help Jenny'.

Julie confirmed that she had not given evidence in front of Deputy State Coroner Carl Milovanovich when he ran the second inquest in 2003, perhaps because she was working at the time or away. She agreed to meet me in Sydney and answer my questions in an on-the-record interview for the podcast. Acquiring the cache of documents was a godsend. It ensured I heard about important witnesses like Julie.

The next windfall was foreshadowed in a text message from Greg Simms while we were talking about plans for my second visit to his house, this time with Rebecca Hazel and an audio producer, Eric George, for interviews for the podcast.

'We're on a learning curve with this podcast but it will be fine,' I assured him.

He wrote: 'Had a file on Lyn in our filing cabinet. Tapes there and a few other things. No need to reply. You can see them next week.'

On 22 November, Merilyn greeted us warmly with fresh banana cake and cups of tea. Her wariness at our first meeting appeared to have melted away.

Eric held the recording equipment and microphones. This was it – the first interview for the podcast. Eric nodded, said, 'Rolling', and the first interview started while Rebecca and Merilyn watched.

Greg looked and sounded nervous. We sat in comfortable chairs in the lounge room and my first question took Lyn's little brother back to happier days growing up near the seaside in a suburb called Clovelly.

'Okay, um . . . alright, so, Greg, I'd really love to hear about the family story, growing up at 53 Melrose.'

'Well, there were the four kids, Phil, Pat, Lyn and myself. Ah, there was ten years between the four of us. Phil, Phil being the eldest we were all . . . um, we were all swimmers, when we were, um . . . sorry, I'm getting nervous already.'

'That's alright, take your time.'

I tried to put Greg at ease by asking about his father, Len, who was nicknamed 'Schooner King' because of his fondness for an ale in a long glass. Len had served in the navy and this meant long periods away. By the time Greg was born, his father had left the service and started his second career, teaching mathematics at a nearby high school.

'Mum was the stay-at-home mother and she was the one who nurtured us through while he was away.

'When we were growing up, Clovelly, in a sense, was our world. We would be swimming all the time. Weekends, you'd swim, you'd go and see all your friends. Everybody knew each other. We used to walk to school from home which was probably about a 20-minute walk up to Clovelly Public School.'

A neighbour, old Mrs Thalberg, was a beneficiary of the community-minded values of Len and Helena. Their eldest, Phil, started the tradition of looking after Mrs Thalberg's lawn. Pat took over from Phil when he moved out, then it was Lyn's turn and, finally, Greg's.

'And it would be hard for me because I really loved swimming and you'd be out there clipping and mowing her front lawn and you'd see your mates walking down to the beach and you knew there was a good wave on.'

The childhood Greg described sounded idyllic with daily ocean swims and long walks around the bay in an era when youngsters rode their bikes, walked and took the bus to go places.

'I can always remember Lyn being down at the other end of the bay, they used to have an old swing set and slippery dip, and the girls used to congregate with their friends down there. I was a little bit of a hanger-on, I was four years younger than Lyn.'

Greg looked wistful and became noticeably calmer as he reminisced about Saturday walks with his mother and his two sisters to Coogee Beach, to an old aquarium where they'd compete in the swimming club.

'Lyn loved the beach – she was a water baby. At Clovelly Public School, she was the marching captain and sports captain of her group.

'I can always remember she was very strong. If she believed in something, she stood by her guns.'

I asked Greg if the strength he ascribed to Lyn was a family trait.

'No, she was more like Dad, whereas the other three of us were a bit more like Mum – we wouldn't stick up for our guns. We were more like the . . . um, what do you call it?'

Greg turned to Merilyn, sitting close and listening supportively, to help him complete the sentence. 'What do you call it?'

Merilyn whispered something and Greg, still nervous, continued.

'We were the peacemakers in the group. Whereas Lyn, if she believed in something, she would let people know. She wouldn't pull back.'

I tried to reconcile this quality in Lyn with the yielding, subservient woman described in the statements of people in the police brief of evidence.

Greg lauded his older sister as the family's organiser. 'Like birthday parties and things like that. She was always organising special events. When she went missing, she was organising Mum's 66th birthday party. That didn't go ahead.'

Twelve minutes into our first interview, Greg mentioned Chris for the first time. The talented young footballer was attending Sydney Boys High, and Lyn was at the nearby Sydney Girls. One day, during a sporting carnival at ES Marks Athletics Field in Moore Park, Greg was walking along in front of the stadium.

'I saw these two blokes walking towards me and I thought, 'Oh!' because I'd seen Chris before. I said, "Hi, Chris."'

Greg answered my question about his recollections of Chris and his relationship with Lyn when they were high school sweethearts. The mournful cry of a crow on the roof lent eerie atmosphere.

'Only good impressions that I can recall. Because once someone came into our family, we accepted them for what they were and they were a part of the family.

'Lyn was very happy. They were together. So it was just taken that he was part of the family. He was accepted as one of us. When we had family get-togethers, he was always there with Mum's brothers and sisters and Dad's siblings.'

'What about Chris's character in those early years? How would you describe his character?'

'I can only remember Chris's character as being very loving towards Lyn. They were always holding hands, cuddling each other. Always joking. There was nothing untoward in those early days that I can remember to put against him.

'I looked up to him as a big brother. I used to go to the football as a kid. To know someone who was actually playing was invigorating. Thrilling.

'I think his twin brother was a little bit better. They both played quite well together.'

I asked Merilyn for her impressions of Chris and Lyn from when she and Greg had begun dating in 1975. 'It was Easter, I was brought around to meet Greg's family. Once they got to know me and accepted me into the family, it was really good. They are very open, very loving, very accepting people who took things at face value.'

Being from the country, Merilyn, who was 19, had never met a professional footballer. She was a musician who had little to do with sport. Merilyn recalled 'being blown away by the size of Chris's thighs' in one of their first meetings, a dinner at Lyn and Chris's place in the Northern Beaches suburb of Cromer, and Chris being 'pretty chuffed' that Merilyn had noticed.

'Lyn was a really warm person and made you feel at ease straight away. She had the right nature for nursing. She was a very caring person. She was just a natural nurse and carer.

'The sense of humour was there and she was a great entertainer and always had everything beautifully presented. You just felt very much at home, in their home, and it was an easy relationship. The four of us got on extremely well. We always had a good time.

'At those early stages, he was a charmer. He knew all the right things to say. He was quite affectionate with Lyn.

'I can remember family gatherings at Greg's parents with the Simms side of the family. There was an Aunty Dolly and she was a real character and I can remember him cuddling her and having a lovely rapport with the family. Everybody liked Chris.'

Helena adored Chris. She took on a cleaning job at the University of New South Wales when she was in her mid-50s to save some money for Chris and Lyn's wedding.

When Greg and Merilyn were wed in the country town of Muswellbrook in late 1976, Chris performed the role of best man.

'He and Lyn had just been to Vanuatu not long before our wedding and they had actually been told not long before that they wouldn't be able to have children. And you know that was pretty damaging for both of them because that's what they really wanted.

'I remember even though it was a big wedding and all the rest of it but I did notice Chris being quite affectionate with Lyn when they were together and there's a beautiful photo of them dancing at our wedding. There was no announcement made but Lyn was actually pregnant at our wedding. It was a big surprise to everybody. They must have had that nice knowledge that they can, they're going to have a baby.

'We went to the hospital to see Lyn after Shanelle was born and she was a caesarean birth so Lyn was pretty sore but so excited and over the moon. And the glow and the look on her face to see this beautiful little girl. And Chris, too. Just adoring. We've got lovely memories of them sitting together with this dear little baby.

'She was just a natural mum. I used to describe her as an earth mum. It just came as normally as walking to her. The kids became her world.

'It was the one thing in her life that she really wanted above everything else was to be a mum. Lyn had a really lovely voice, a very gentle voice and a very calming voice. And I can still hear her talking to the babies in that lovely voice. Those girls were her absolute world.'

As most new mothers do, Lyn put on some weight. Merilyn recalled that Chris, chiselled and as fit as a trout, gave Lyn 'a hard time about that and she used to feel badly about it'.

'She would feel that she was fat, she was big and she wasn't. She never was. She's probably a size 14 at the most. And she used to say, "Oh, Chris says I'm too fat or I'm too big or I'm too this." She obviously felt that her image wasn't up to par, perhaps with maybe what Chris was hoping.

'She looked great as far as we were concerned. Paul used to give her a hard time too.'

Greg remembered that Chris wouldn't let Lyn spend money on alterations needed for a dress to wear to the wedding. Lyn borrowed a friend's dress instead.

Merilyn speculated that Lyn's pregnancy relieved her of a lot of pressure. Chris and his twin brother, Paul were exceptionally close and competitive. Paul was already a father of two little girls.

Merilyn and Greg became more relaxed as they filled in some of the significant milestones. They spoke of their surprise at Chris and Lyn's purchase of a steep, bushy and rocky block of land at Bayview for more than $30,000. It was isolated and Lyn didn't drive, making her completely reliant on Chris for transport.

'Why do you think Lyn didn't drive?' I asked.

Greg replied and for the first time, there was an edge to his answer. 'She wanted to. Because of the isolation. Chris didn't get around to teaching her. He certainly got around to teaching Jenny how to drive. He had Lyn where he wanted her.'

Merilyn added, 'Lyn would prefer to paint a bright picture, a happy picture, and we realise now in retrospect that she wanted to do that to save face, to make it appear everything was rosy and everything was going well. The twins were pretty revered in those days. They were put up there on a pretty high pedestal, and the general impressions of them were they were two very successful footballers, they had lovely wives, and that whole image was some-thing, I think, Lyn wanted to maintain. That image, she wanted to uphold.'

Greg chimed in. 'They [the twin brothers] were doing paid model-ling and TV ads, for clothing.'

'And any money they made from that, they put in an account together – it was called the twinnies account,' Merilyn said. 'That caused a little bit of unrest between both Marilyn and Lyn; they didn't like the idea the boys had this separate account they were not to have any access to.'

'Money seemed to be the order of the day. They were doing their part-time work here and there. I know they did a garbage run, both the boys.'

'The aerobics classes after school and at night.'

'And they both did tennis coaching at the weekend.'

'They were always off doing other things apart from their teaching.'

Greg observed that the brothers were exceptionally materialistic while funnelling funds into their 'twinnies account'.

Merilyn added, 'Lyn did tell me that she was not allowed access to a bankbook or bank account. She seemed to be cash-poor a lot and if Lyn needed something or wanted to get something, she would put it on Bankcard because she didn't have access to cash. And then Chris used to get very upset when the statement came in. Lyn told me that.

'My perception is Lyn was a very generous person. For birthdays and things like that she was always the first with a gift. She was a giver. Whereas the way I look at it probably more so now, Chris wanted to keep control of where the money was going to go.'

The home Lyn and Chris built and furnished was 'far more grand' than that of anyone else in Lyn's and Merilyn's immediate family. The decor was modern. Merilyn described cork flooring, a Spanish influence in the living room and kitchen and lots of decorative accessories; Greg remembered a large spa bath in the ensuite bathroom.

I asked Merilyn when she became aware that the image Lyn had wanted to uphold appeared to be blurring. She recalled the Dawson girls' fourth and second birthday parties in July 1981.

'They had a lot of the Dawson family there, and the Simms family. That particular day, Lyn was quite . . . well, she showed signs of stress because she was obviously busy trying to get a lot of food organised. There were a lot of children around and she wanted everything to be really nice. We just noticed that Chris was absent from helping her. He and Paul were sitting on the step outside the family room with Jenny in between them and she was upset about something and they spent a lot of time trying to console her. Lyn was trying to hold it all together that particular day but she was quite strained.

'I do think she was fighting for her marriage in the only way she knew she could without involving family or other people.'

The next time Merilyn saw Chris on 1 September 1981, it was her son Craig's first birthday party. Chris's infatuation with Jenny was intense at the time, although neither Greg nor Merilyn knew about it.

'He was very distant, clearly didn't want to be there that day, was very uncomfortable and made no effort to speak to anyone,' Merilyn said. Right around this time, Greg was transferred to the police station in Muswellbrook in the Hunter Valley, a short drive from Merilyn's home town of Aberdeen. Visits were rarer because of the distance, and long-distance telephone calls at the time were costly.

Pat Jenkins and her husband, Ron, had moved even farther away. They did not have the telephone on in their home and would go to the nearest town to make calls. Both couples were more isolated than Lyn was on the Northern Beaches. Helena was still in Sydney but it was a good hour and a half on public transport.

'And I rang Lyn because I was going through baby clothes that she'd lent us for our son and I said, "Lyn, I've got these baby clothes here that you've lent us. Would you like me to bundle them up and give them back to you? Because you might need them for number three?"

'And she sort of basically said, "Well, that's highly unlikely, Chris hasn't been near me for about six weeks." Which was highly unusual. And she said she questioned him as to whether there was anyone else in his life. And he said, "No, definitely not."'

In the conversation in October 1981, Merilyn heard Lyn's hurt at Chris's rejection of her. They were sleeping in the same bed but he wouldn't touch her; he was saving himself for Jenny.

'And she said, "Things are very strained, we're not getting on particularly well. And he wants to bring in Jenny to live here because there are problems in her own home." She was trying to study for her [Higher School Certificate] and Chris was quite determined she was coming, whether Lyn wanted her or not. And Lyn said to him,

"Don't you think we should sort out our own problems before we bring any more problems into the house?" And he didn't want to know anything about it. Jenny was coming, right or wrong . . . She really wanted things to work out. She was desperate for the marriage to keep going.'

I asked Greg, 'Do you recall Lyn having any other boyfriends before Chris?'

He replied, 'No. No, I don't. He was it. From high school to when she disappeared.'

Greg's deference to the most neutral version of events – that Lyn had 'disappeared' – was not incorrect but I found it surprising. I knew that Greg and Merilyn were certain that Lyn had been murdered by Chris but in their natural fairness, they chose not to declare it bluntly in our early interviews.

Greg's father, however, was suspicious from day one. 'When Lyn went missing, the first thing Dad said was, "The bastard has done her in."'

'When he first said it, we said, "Hey, you can't be that harsh." But as the years have gone on and we've heard other bits and pieces and we've been able to put the puzzle together, I think my father hit the nail on the head first-up. And that was as far as he was going to go with it.'

It was hard for me to comprehend. How could a loving father who strongly suspected his daughter had been murdered by his son-in-law let it go?

Merilyn offered this: 'Pa, he didn't drive. He had to rely on public transport. He wasn't particularly mobile himself. He would no more have picked up the phone to ring his own kids, let alone Chris, to question him about that. That just wasn't in his way, in his manner, in his personality. He would speak his mind within the family home but he wouldn't set about going and investigating himself because he'd leave that to Nanna, who did all she possibly could to try and find Lyn.'

It must have been a lonely quest. Helena couldn't talk to her husband about it as much as she would like because Len couldn't see the point most of the time. Lyn was gone. Unless there were new facts, Len didn't want to recycle old news.

'Once Pa had heard it once, he didn't want to discuss it further,' Merilyn said. 'And so he would say, "You've already said that", and leave it at that.

'When we came down, she would talk to us about it and I'm sure she used to speak to Pat when she saw her and Phil and Lynda. The pain that Nanna must have gone through, it must have been absolutely terrible as a mother to not know where her child was . . .

'So back to your original question – your instinct now is, "Why didn't Pa do something about this?" But Pa's hands were tied as well as Greg's, as well as everybody's, because she was classed as a missing person and we were not next of kin.'

Greg told me that he would be brushed off whenever he called the Missing Persons Unit to seek information. Legally, Lyn's husband – her next of kin – was the only person entitled to receive any information about Lyn from police. As police didn't suspect Chris of having murdered Lyn, he was the first and only point of contact. Lyn's family didn't press for this to change until after Chris and Jenny were wed in January 1984.

'And after he married, I rang up Missing Persons and they said, "No, Mr Dawson is still the next of kin." And I said, "Well, I'm putting you in the picture now that Mr Dawson is now remarried, my mother is now the next of kin, and any information will go through her or come through to me."

'And I didn't receive any information after that. So I don't know what happened.'

It was baffling to me that it took Chris six weeks to report Lyn's disappearance to police. Even guilty people handle formalities. Greg and Merilyn explained that it only happened as a result of Helena's insistence. By the time the police report was made, it had been about four weeks since, according to Chris, Lyn had last telephoned him. Although it seemed remarkable that family members were not more suspicious, I tried to allow for the circumstances. People were not as mindful of the probabilities around partner homicide back then. Chris was trusted. Lyn always strove to protect Chris's image; she had airbrushed and concealed from her family so much of what was going on.

'Greg, if there had been a murder investigation from the start rather than more than a decade later, what do you think would have happened? Within a day or so of Lyn disappearing?'

'Hedley, I don't think we'd be talking here now. He'd be in jail. Everyone would be younger, they'd remember more. There'd be more information available. The police would have more people to talk to, more assumptions to make. And if she had been buried somewhere, there'd be a fresh grave to be found or something.'

'Do you feel that the police force has let your family down, or let you down?'

'Yeah, to a certain extent when I look back now.'

Greg again blamed the 'set procedures', which related to how the system responded to missing persons in the 1980s. As a copper who had worked within the same system, Greg said he couldn't report Lyn missing at the time because this report had to come from her next of kin. Greg was a relatively junior police constable at the time. If he had gone to the police station and said, 'My sister is missing, and I believe her next of kin – her husband – has murdered her', there might have been a proper investigation but Greg didn't suspect Chris for years.

I shuddered at the realisation that hundreds of women who had suddenly gone missing from their family homes were in all probability murdered and that the system had helped their killers, who were able to cover their tracks as the trail went cold.

After January 1982, Chris never called Greg to talk about Lyn and where she might have gone.

Merilyn recalled, 'Even when he used to bring the girls to stay with Nanna and Pa, which they did occasionally, he would not come to the house. He would ring the house and the girls would pick up the phone and then they would be told to walk to a certain point, to a corner, to be picked up.

'We were so grateful that the girls did have time with Nanna and Pa. But I think it also suited his needs, gave him a break. He was able to be childfree and have some quality time with Jenny.'

I asked Merilyn whether she had an explanation for why Chris distanced himself from the Simms family at a time when they were confused and distressed.

'Well, I think he was a bit of a coward. Because Pa certainly would have questioned him. In the house, Pa certainly would have hauled him over the coals and questioned him in his own home. But he wouldn't have gone in pursuit of Chris. And Chris probably knew that if he stayed away, then he didn't have to answer any questions.

'And it's been the same since day one. If you truly believe that Lyn's gone of her own free will to wherever it is she's supposed to have gone, you would be out there looking for her, pleading with people, going everywhere. You would answer any questions that people asked you. But there's been none of that. And that's what we don't understand. And how we're so confused is why he refused to be questioned as time went on. It's always mystified us that if he's innocent, then why not come forward? Why not just answer the questions?'

Tentatively, I offered a theory about the Simms family's acceptance of Chris's story in those early years. 'I wondered whether another reason for the investigation going the way it did and the family's position being the way it was, was because of the delicacy of trying to continue to see the daughters, the little girls – and the risk that if you pushed things too far, that possibility would be withdrawn?'

Merilyn replied that this was 'very much uppermost, uppermost in Nanna and Pa's mind'.

'We were all very, very conscious of not asking the girls questions or pushing them in any direction. We just were so grateful that we still had some sort of contact with them, and especially Nanna. She didn't want to jeopardise the chance of getting to see the girls. That would have broken her heart, if she'd been completely denied access to the girls. I still believe, though, that she thought so much of Chris, she believed everything he said.'

One fateful day, several months after Lyn disappeared, Chris drove across the Harbour Bridge to the Simms family home at Clovelly with garbage bags of Lyn's clothing. Greg recalled that by this stage, they all knew that Jenny was living as Chris's partner in Lyn's house.

'Mum answered the door and I can remember him saying, "Helena, I've got some of Lyn's stuff here." Dad was on the verandah at the same time. And poor Mum was just standing there.'

Merilyn said, 'She was devastated. She was so lost, I think, just couldn't understand why Lyn hadn't made contact with her, because Chris had told her a couple of times that she would be ringing on certain days and then Nanna would stay in all day waiting for this particular phone call. And of course, it didn't ever come. She just couldn't believe that Lyn would go.'

Helena must have wondered why Chris was bringing what he didn't want of Lyn's belongings to her childhood home. Was Chris signalling to his mother-in-law that Lyn was never coming back? That he had given up on her, even if she did come back?

Merilyn continued. 'She was really pulled, I think, because she wanted to believe what Chris was telling her but she couldn't believe that Lyn would have gone. But he kept telling her things and she just took that as her only source of information about Lyn. She just took it all in good faith that that's what had happened.'

Greg added, 'He went away and kept coming in with all these plastic bags and Mum just directed him to put them in the hallway. And I looked up at him and I said, "Don't expect me to help you." I wasn't happy with him but there's nothing I could really do.

'Every time he came in, he had his head down and every now and then, he looked over to me. And you saw these big black eyes looking at you. In other words, he wasn't impressed. When the big black eyes were there, he was getting himself very uptight.'

The bags were left in the hallway for a while. Eventually, they were moved into Greg's old bedroom on the back verandah.

'They stayed there for quite some time, I think it was a couple of years. Merilyn and I were down there one time and Mum said, "I'd really like to move this stuff along. You know, I haven't had the heart to go through it all."'

'She said, "Could you help me do this? I just can't face having to do it on my own,"' Merilyn said. 'We were just about to leave but we put off leaving and we went through the bags.

'There was a blue velour dressing gown, which I actually took and wore for years.'

Since he was a small boy, Greg had a habit of going through the pockets of shirts, trousers and jeans. Sometimes he found coins; on a good day, a crumpled $1 or $2 note.

'Yeah. And in the pocket was a carbon copy from a real estate agent. Chris had wanted to put the house on the market, sell it and go to Queensland. And Lyn didn't want to. She had to sign up as well because the house was in both names. She wouldn't. And somehow this carbon copy of the real estate sale ended up in her dressing-gown pocket.'

Merilyn added, 'He hadn't actually put it on the market. He required her signature to allow that to go ahead. She may have been in a dressing gown when he presented her with the papers and she probably just folded it up, put it in the pocket, you know, and just not wanted to deal with it or she's hidden it in there. It had all been bundled up in these plastic bags.'

The local real estate agent's sale agreement for the house was dated 21 December 1981. It had been signed by Chris with a proposed asking price of $285,000. As the joint owner, Lyn would have had to agree for any sale to go ahead.

Greg said, 'And when we found it we just thought, "Oh, this is interesting that she's had the piece of paper."'

It was a striking piece of evidence. A detective with knowledge of the state of the marriage, the husband's obsession with a teenage baby-sitter with whom he wanted to start a new life and the omission of Lyn's signature on paperwork which would have allowed the lawful sale of the house and an exit strategy for Chris Dawson, would surely see this incomplete sale agreement as probative in a circumstantial case.

Greg told me they found other things in the garbage bags. 'In all Lyn's stuff, there were her nursing papers, her eye contact lenses . . . her glasses were in there.'

Chris had told them Lyn was wearing pink shorts on the morning of Saturday 9 January 1982 when, according to him, he took Lyn to the Mona Vale bus stop for her to go shopping.

Greg said, 'There were pink shorts in the bag. Dirty gardening gloves. Just everything of Lyn's was piled up. But no photos. Whether they were burned, I can only guess.'

Merilyn added, 'Jenny admitted to us many years later when she left Chris that she did a lot of that cleaning up and that bundling up. She just said, "I just wanted everything of Lyn's to be gone so there weren't reminders there."'

Merilyn recalled another unusual contact. They were at her parents' house in the country town of Aberdeen in September 1982. Lyn's girls were spending a week there, and Helena had come up from Clovelly.

'We got this very agitated phone call from Chris, who accused Helena of taking the girls away and having a secret meeting with Lyn somewhere, which of course didn't happen. And she tried very hard to say, "Well, I told you that we'd be away for a week. We're here at the farm at Aberdeen with Greg and Merilyn."

'And I had to sort of calm him down and say, "Chris, that's not it at all. There's been a misunderstanding with dates but the girls are absolutely fine. They're here."

I knew from reading the files and the statements in the police brief of evidence that Greg and Merilyn had met Jenny again in 1990. She was still a young woman – just 26 – but her life had changed dramatically since their first meeting in 1981.

On 1 February 1990, Jenny drove back with her daughter from the Gold Coast to the Northern Beaches to start again. She had asked a woman called Pam Eckford, a counsellor at the women's refuge, to call Helena.

Merilyn said, 'Helena wanted absolutely nothing to do with her because she still felt Jenny was responsible for the breakdown in the marriage. When Helena rang us and spoke to us about it, I sort of dwelt on it for a little while and then I said to Greg, "Look, I think she's got something to tell us and I think we need to listen. One of us needs to go down."

'You weren't interested at that point,' Merilyn added, glancing at Greg. 'And I said, "Look, as a family member but as a sort of neutral person, ask the rest of the family how they would feel if I went and listened to what she's got to say."

'So, yes, the permission was granted and we agreed to meet at a neutral place in the Central Coast, which we did. And Greg drove me down and he says, "No, I've got to come in, I have to, I can't just sit out here in the car."'

Greg said, 'I realised that, being there, I had to know what she was going to say and what was going on.'

'And we were there for several hours talking to her and she actually was a very frightened girl,' Merilyn said. 'She lived in fear of her own life and her daughter's.'

I asked Greg and Merilyn if they felt some underlying resentment towards Jenny. Helena believed her daughter had left her family home, heartbroken at having seen the obvious affection between the teenager and Chris.

Greg said, 'No, I didn't blame her.'

Merilyn added:

'We had moved on enough to realise that she was pretty much an innocent victim. We were that much older then. We had time to sit back and think about the fact that perhaps she had been groomed. She was only 17 years old . . .

'She saw moving in with Chris as being in a haven, somewhere she felt safe in the early days. And by that stage, we were starting to question as well. We felt we gave Chris the benefit of the doubt. His story, we had to believe what he was telling us because we had nothing else to go by. But there were starting to be little cracks. And you start to question things. I felt she had something to tell us and she could fill in some of those gaps. And as the discussion went on that day, I took a look at Greg and he just kept going whiter and whiter and whiter.

'A realisation was really starting to hit with him. "Well, yeah, Lyn, really, she's never coming back." None of us would admit it out loud that that's what we were thinking. But after hearing certain things – and none of the information was given to us in a vindictive fashion or a highly dramatised fashion, it was just telling a story . . .

'She had to make her escape because she told us that she was recognising things happening in her relationship that she witnessed happening between Chris and Lyn. When she was living in the house. The taunting, the singing, not allowing her to have access to bank accounts. Who she could be with. The socialising. Very controlled.'

I asked, 'Did you see her making amends or attempting to help you all by having that meeting and sharing with you things that she didn't need to share?'

'The counsellor told her it would do her a lot of good to talk about things,' Greg answered, 'and she wanted to get a lot of things off her chest in relation to her relationship with Chris and what happened with Lyn.'

'I think she was quite remorseful in a way for her treatment of your mum in particular,' Merilyn said. 'But she also said to us how much she regretted not being able to be a mother to Amy and Shanelle, not being able to give them the love that they needed.

'She said, "I was suddenly put into this child-minding role where I had to make clothes for the girls and dress them and do all this sort of thing while Chris could still carry on with his life."

'She was just so incredibly vulnerable and she saw this as an escape to get out of the situation at home. I don't bear any malice against her. I just think that she was very much a victim and she was moulded. Groomed.'

We talked about the events which followed these disclosures by Jenny in 1990. There was an investigation by homicide detectives which had faded away after Chris was interviewed on videotape in 1991. The videotape survived but the written statements given at that time by members of the Simms family were lost by police.

And then in 1998, another police investigation, this time by the detective Damian Loone, whose efforts resulted in two inquests run by different coroners, both of whom recommended that the NSW

Director of Public Prosecutions should consider running a case of alleged murder.

I asked, 'Do you believe the DPP has been unnecessarily tough in its rejection of the recommendations from two coroners that there be charges levelled and prosecutions?'

Greg sounded almost conspiratorial. 'This is just my interpretation – the file has got a little red dot on it there, and once you get a red dot on your file, they're not going to go any further with it unless they've got really good information. I know it's all circumstantial evidence but some of it's fairly strong.'

Merilyn said, 'The bottom line is we probably need a body. And that's the hardest thing to come to terms with after all these years. Where is she and how can we possibly find her and have that evidence? So you just, you wait. How much longer can we wait, though? We've lost Greg and Lyn's parents, aunts and uncles. But time is running out. We're all getting older too.'

I asked whether they knew what Lyn's daughters were told about their mother's disappearance by their father.

Merilyn replied. 'Yes. "Your mother has left because she doesn't love you anymore." Which is what the little girls told Nanna. They were sitting in the bath one night. So imagine how a mother would feel knowing that that's so far from the truth, it's ridiculous.'

Looking back, Greg added, there were clues to domestic violence, which he believed he should have been more concerned about before Lyn went missing.

'When I'd come down to Sydney, I might have a court case or something on, and Lyn always made an effort to gather the girls up and come over by public transport. And you would see a bruise on her arm or maybe on a leg.'

Greg recalled asking Lyn on a number of occasions, 'What have you been doing to yourself? What happened?'

'Lyn would just brush it off and say, "I walked into the doorknob" or "I walked into the benchtop", something like that . . .

'Lyn was the sort of person that would cover things up in respect to her marriage and all that. "Everything was perfect. Everything was good." She kept a lot to herself. She more or less tried to work it out herself, without involving anybody else in the family.'

Merilyn added, 'She wanted to try and convince people that she was in control and everything was alright. She was very big on making other people feel okay about things, and she'd protect her mother in particular. She wouldn't want to worry her about this sort of thing. In those days, you didn't openly talk about your personal relationships. Certainly you wouldn't discuss things with your parents . . .

'She adored him. You could tell by the way she looked at him and she was willing to trust him implicitly. In her eyes, he could do no wrong.'

Before Jenny moved into the house, Merilyn recalled Lyn telling her of an incident with other female students. Lyn regarded the inferences arising from it as improbable but with hindsight, they appear to be prescient.

Chris had gone swimming with some teenage girls in a private pool.

'And the neighbour complained to the principal, and the principal questioned Chris and he denied everything and Lyn went up and said, "I trust my husband implicitly. Our marriage is strong. There's no way he'd do anything like that."

'We were quite happy to accept what Lyn said. And at that stage, we didn't think Chris would ever do anything like that either.'

When we took a break, Merilyn showed me the contents of the file Greg had mentioned to me earlier. Everything was laid onto a dining table. There were audio cassettes – the official interviews Greg and Merilyn had done with Damian Loone in 1998.

I took out my iPhone and photographed dozens of newspaper clippings which Greg and Merilyn had collected over the decades. One in particular – a yellowing, slightly crumpled article – stood out. It was a television critic's review of an upcoming documentary called 'Heckle and Jeckle' on a program called *Chequerboard*, which was to screen on the ABC. The subject matter was to be twins and their closeness. The interviewees included the then famous rugby league footballers, Chris and Paul Dawson.

I read the article.

Reporter Robin Hughes talks with two sets of twins and their
parents to see if there is any truth in old proverbs or primitive
superstitions about twins. Chris and Paul Dawson of Sydney look
alike, think alike and live alike. At 25 years of age, to them the
words 'We', 'I' and 'Us' are interchangeable.

It was the first time I had heard of the program. Its potential significance was immediately obvious: the video and audio of the brothers,
if it still existed, would be invaluable in trying to profile them and
put together their side of the story.

When I asked Greg and Merilyn about it, they had no recollection of having seen the documentary in 1975 nor since. Nobody to
their knowledge had any video of it.

Greg had clearly tried to get things done in the 90s. When he
was on night shift in police radio operations in Newcastle in 1993, he
wrote to investigating police. I read a memo he sent to a Homicide
Squad detective, asking if cadaver dogs, which were then being used
to search for bodies near Bowral in the backpacker murders case,
could also be sent to Bayview 'in the matter of my sister Lynette
DAWSON'.

For the rest of the afternoon, Greg and Merilyn spoke candidly
about their trust in Chris and their belief for years in his story that
Lyn had not just left him without warning but that she had been in
contact with him on several occasions to say she was fine.

They accepted Chris's story despite knowing that none of it
aligned with their knowledge of Lyn as a mother who could not bear
to be separated from her daughters; as a daughter whose relationship
with her own mother was exceptionally close; and as an employee
who was always reliable and thoughtful.

The fact that *nobody* had heard from Lyn except, according to
Chris, him, did not raise suspicion of foul play in the Simms family
except with Len, who didn't take it further.

Chapter 10

Phil and Lynda

The eldest of the four children of Helena and Len, it seemed that for much of Phil Simms's life, he had been the most distant of the siblings. When we went to interview the civil engineer at Caves Beach, Rebecca's eyes widened as she took in original artwork.

Unlike his younger brother, Phil did not volunteer his nervousness. He had less to say. Over the years, he and his wife, Lynda, had been less involved than Greg and Merilyn and Pat in the different stages of Lyn's disappearance.

Phil described himself as 'not much of a talker, I'm a listener, I always listen'.

He related some of the things he had heard about his sister's husband, Chris, and his brother, Paul, before they were married.

'I heard of some funny tricks they used to do. He used to go and swap with his brother, taking girls out. That's one thing I do remember when he was taking Lyn out. But I mean, once again, that was her business if he carried on like that.

'I had heard they were quite cock-a-hoop about the fact that they could take a girl out and then the other one could take her out and they wouldn't know the difference. Now there must have been some differences. Hopefully it would not occur once they got engaged and married. It probably led onto other things, though. The goings-on at the high school and stuff like that.'

Phil recalled that Paul Dawson had 'a lot of advantages' over Chris. They were close yet always competing. On the football field, in the classroom, at college and in their personal financial positions, there was a contest between the brothers but Paul always had an edge.

'Paul had a good run through. And Chris was lagging.'

Phil told me his mother 'thought the sun shone out of Chris'.

'He was good-looking. She was happy that Lyn had found someone she was in love with . . . Even to the day that Lyn disappeared. And then things started to turn sour, I think. And the fact that he didn't report her for all those many weeks as missing.'

When Lynda was 17 and started seeing Phil, six years older, Helena would fuss and dote over Chris. 'He was going to be a teacher and she thought he had good prospects. But myself, I didn't like Chris at all. And I told Phil. It was just me and I couldn't say anything to anyone because I was 17. Who would listen to a 17-year-old? I just didn't like him. He had a tremendous ego. And he used to tease Greg, shockingly. Greg was 13, 14, and I used to get quite upset about this continued teasing. It was quite intense. And I found it quite unkind at times. It just got over the top.'

I asked Lynda to describe the character of Lyn, who was the same age.

'Lyn was quite outspoken but she was a very kind person. I can remember when our first son was being born, she'd spent hours knitting this lovely outfit for him. And she did that kind of thing for people. She was very clever with her hands and she was very attractive. She was a really nice girl.'

Lynda believed Lyn was troubled by the competitiveness between Chris and Paul. Lyn knew how it affected the less successful of the siblings. It affected Lyn, too, when she wanted to buy things for the house because Chris usually objected.

'Lyn had said to me, "Paul always comes out on top." She felt for Chris.

'I remember one day, Lyn was over with Phil's mum and she'd been out and she'd bought herself a mixer. And Chris was quite annoyed about this because she'd spent money.

'Phil's mum once said to me that she'd been talking to Lyn, who was quite unhappy. She more or less said that [her daughter] had to try harder for Chris. Her mum was a strong believer in the idea that the husband was always right. Until everything went wrong, of course.'

Lynda said Mrs Simms believed her daughter needed to be 'more compliant'.

'She did have this thing where she really thought the sunshine shone out of Chris. And of course, when that came back later for her, it was horrible, because she had thought that way . . .

'It was unthinkable that Lyn would leave her children. Lyn would have never left her children. Never, ever. She adored these kids. And we both said that at the time.

'You wouldn't go away with nothing. If you're disappearing, you'd have to have something. You'd have to pack some things . . .'

Turning to Phil, she added, 'Your dad in the beginning thought something more sinister had happened to Lyn. And your mum believed that she might come back.'

Lynda said that she was 'suspicious from the start' but it seems that she did not share this with Greg or Pat at the time.

'I kept saying she would have come back. But by the same token, we were told, we had this story, where we thought Lyn had rung.'

With the benefit of hindsight, it seemed surprising to me that intelligent adults worried about the sudden disappearance of a loving young mother would accept her husband's uncorroborated claim that she had rung more than once to say she was 'fine'. Helena and Len, Pat and her husband, Ron, Phil and Lynda and Greg and Merilyn were those closest to Lyn and they were aware of tensions in Lyn's marriage. Yet they didn't question Chris's repeated assertions that Lyn was calling only him from the Central Coast.

This unavoidable reality, according to Lynda, had been more difficult for Greg 'than probably anyone else because he was in the police force. And he probably feels they failed him too.'

'And I still feel she's in the backyard. She's on the block,' Phil said. 'Because the guy next door was building and he put over three metres of fill in the backyard at Chris's behest. It was good for him to get rid of his excavations but I think she's under there somewhere. That's the only thing I'm pretty positive about.

'If ever I win Lotto, I'll go and talk to the bloke and make a deal and buy the house and we'll demolish the backyard.'

'Because Chris used to go back every year,' Lynda added.

'He wanted to come back and see what the man had done to his house, any addition and stuff like that. But every year, I think three times he got through the bloke's defences, and straight out the backyard to see what had been done.

'And that was his excuse each time – that he'd built the house and wanted to see what had been done to the house. But he never looked in the house. And that's another reason I believe she's still there in the backyard.'

The last thing Phil Simms told me on that day in November 2017 was delivered with a sigh. His sister's disappearance had been a constant sadness for half his life. It had stolen the joy from the lives of his parents, and they had died without knowing what had happened to their daughter.

'It's dragging on,' Phil said. 'And I hope to see a resolution before I pass over.'

Three and a half years later, Phil was dead. Like his parents, he wouldn't live long enough to see any resolution.

Lynda treasured the audio file of the interview we conducted that day in 2017. Hearing Phil's voice in it was a comfort for the widow after a partnership of more than 50 years.

Chapter 11

The Murder Book

Acclaimed American crime author Michael Connelly's most famous character is a dogged old-school Los Angeles Police Department detective called Harry Bosch, who finds new leads in cold cases by exhaustively analysing all the existing documents in what's known as 'the murder book'.

Witness statements, detectives' notes about suspected serial killers, criminal histories of persons of interest, informants' tip-offs and myriad other bits and bobs are Bosch's bread and butter. The files that Bosch stays up all night reading are sometimes decades old.

But they are still tangible and they were generated when memories were relatively fresh. Going through 'the murder book' with a fine-tooth comb, taking notes and underlining parts which could be a connection to a new thread, a new angle, is my modus operandi in journalism too.

Connelly's novels ring true. The former *Los Angeles Times* police reporter's vivid descriptions of Harry Bosch discovering an obscure lead which cracks a cold case are thrilling and, at least to me, credible. I always want to read the case files before talking to or interviewing those integral to the case. Absorbing the written details first means I'm forearmed; I'll understand at least one version of the chronology and the evidence; I can challenge or question an interviewee when the version they provide differs from what they or someone else said about it 20 or 30 years earlier. The documents are a crucial mother lode in any major investigation I take on. The devil is usually in these written details. It is there in black and white. It is usually unemotional. It will not be distracting or potentially misleading like some interviewees.

I had been blessed early in Lyn Dawson's case thanks to Greg Simms having given me volumes 1 and 2 of a file called 'Brief of Evidence Concerning the Suspected Homicide of Lynette DAWSON, between 9 January and 10 January 1982'. Before attempting interviews with Lyn's siblings in late 2017, I had the benefit of having read the transcripts of their recorded conversations in 1998 with the Dee Why detective Damian Loone, as well as formal police statements which ensued.

I have seen defence lawyers demolish witnesses whose memories have, as the lawyers observe sarcastically, 'somehow miraculously improved' since their first written statement months or years earlier. We know that in the overwhelming majority of cases, memories do not 'improve'; if anything, they fade. The exception to the rule might be the return of memory as a result of recovery from a head injury.

As I compared what I was hearing from the Simms siblings in our interviews in 2017 with what they told the police in 1998, the consistency in their recollection of key events was obvious. They were not embroidering anything all these years later. Chris Dawson's lawyers might argue the Simms family were embroidering from the start, but I didn't ever believe this. I had a powerful belief in their honesty.

I saw something in the second volume of the 2001 police brief of evidence which offered hope: a typed transcript of a recorded interview of Barbara Cruise by Damian Loone. They were talking just after 5 pm on Wednesday 12 August 1998 at the Gosford police station, about an hour's drive from the Northern Beaches.

Sixteen years prior to that interview with police, Barbara was a manager at the Warriewood Children's Centre where Lyn worked as a registered nurse, helping to look after the little ones. Some of the last people to see Lyn were the women working at the childcare centre – Sue Strath and Annette Leary. They were all friends and Lyn had shared her concerns about the stresses in her marriage. These women knew about Jenny Carlson moving into Lyn's home.

In 1998, Barbara Cruise told Damian Loone, 'She idolised her two children but often spoke of some difficulties with her marriage. And she would often, as I say, she would go out of her way to try and make herself look nice, lose weight, buy clothes so that Chris would notice her and that she'd be attractive to him.'

Privately, Lyn's friendly and supportive co-workers feared that Lyn's marriage was in dire straits.

On the afternoon of Friday 8 January 1982, Lyn walked back into work with Chris after a marriage counselling session with him.

It was the last time the women saw or heard from Lyn.

'At that time, I think I'd become aware that Chris had been caught having some type of affair with a student from his school where he was teaching.'

In her police interview in 1998, Barbara recounted having been telephoned by Chris Dawson on the morning of Monday 11 January with news that Lyn had failed to meet him, her two girls and her mother at a public swimming pool on Saturday.

'Then he got a phone call, and I think it might have been the next day, from her saying that she needed a break. And that she just, you know, needed time to sort things out.

'He would ring another time and say, "Oh. I've had a further call and I don't know when she's coming back." And I was asking such things as, "What do I do with her pay? What do I do with all sorts of things?"

'But it always seemed unusual to us and we always felt a little bit uneasy about it.'

These details were unsurprising; the chronology more or less accorded with the versions from others. However, the next few sentences heralded something new: 'Sometime later, and I can't remember the time, it was probably a year even, or more, there were a couple of us wrote to the Ombudsman. I think Sue actually might have signed it, I can't remember how that came about, and suggested that perhaps she didn't disappear voluntarily, and that there might be some investigation required.'

This was promising. My understanding at the time was that it was not until Jenny Carlson had left Chris in 1990 to return to the Northern Beaches and make disclosures to police – and to Lyn's family – about certain things that had happened and her own suspicions that anyone in authority was alerted to potential foul play.

But Barbara Cruise was clearly saying that Lyn's co-workers had in fact alerted the NSW Ombudsman that something was amiss as early as 1983. If she was right, I surmised, there might be a file somewhere in the Ombudsman's archives.

But I was struggling to understand why the women who cared about Lyn – and who doubted that she had left her children, job, her beautiful home and her friends and mother and siblings voluntarily – would write to the Ombudsman with their suspicions of foul play but not police. I suspected they did not trust police.

Barbara added that she thought Sue Strath and Annette Leary might have been interviewed as a result of having written to the Ombudsman. But she seemed vague on this point, and Damian Loone didn't ask her anything about the Ombudsman. They moved on to a general talk about whether Lyn enjoyed her job.

'Yes, she did. And she was very good at it. She was a very caring person,' Barbara told the detective.

Damian Loone inquired, 'And you say that she'd discussed difficulties with her marriage. When you say that, what did she say to you?'

'Because she was telling me about this girl who came and looked after the kids, or whatever she might do. And I said to Lyn, "I don't think that's right, that he's in that house with that young girl alone." I don't remember her ever feeling uneasy, that way. But I remember thinking it sounds a little strange to me. She certainly had lost her self-esteem.

'I always felt that he wasn't that interested and she was holding on by a thread.'

Asked to characterise her perception of how Lyn was describing her marriage at that time, Barbara Cruise added, 'The magic had gone out of it. She obviously was uneasy about how it was going and felt that it was on shaky ground. Because I remember talking to her about you know, "Why don't you talk to your mum about it? Why don't you go to a counsellor?"

'And actually they did go to a counsellor because that was the last time I saw them, I think, or was that Annette? That might have been Sue and Annette who saw her. Because they came, hand in hand. Been to a counsellor and, you know, seemed to be quite bright and bubbly about it.'

Barbara recalled that nobody collected Lyn's wage packet. The other point she raised in her 1998 police interview was the mailing to the childcare centre of Lyn's Bankcard statement.

Barbara said she had opened one of the Bankcard envelopes after Lyn disappeared and looked at the statement. 'I think if I'd seen that there was a purchase somewhere, I would have remembered that. But I don't remember seeing a purchase anywhere that would alert me to where she might have been or anything. And I don't know whether it's too late to get those records. I suppose it is.

'She wasn't a runner. In other words, I think she usually, you know, faced adversity and whatever might come, unpleasantness whatever it might be. She did adore those two children. We used to know Paul and Paul's wife, Marilyn, as well, and she used to have her children in the centre. We knew them all reasonably well.'

Barbara responded to the detective's question about anything Paul and Marilyn had said about Lyn's disappearance with a comment that Chris's twin brother and his wife perceived that 'Chris was the goodie', whereas Lyn had walked out.

'Chris was the fair-haired boy. Everything Chris did had to be right. So, therefore, if there was something wrong with the marriage, it was her fault. That was how Marilyn saw it as well. I think they just thought she didn't look after herself. Marilyn's quite an attractive lady, quite slim. And Lyn had put on a bit of weight.'

Barbara strongly doubted Lyn would have gone off with a religious cult, which she recalled was a rumour at the time. 'She was a practical person. She's a registered nurse. She's not airy-fairy. Which was what I liked about her. She was a professional. She was a realist. That doesn't fit with a religious sect.'

As the manager, Barbara needed to fill the role of registered nurse at the childcare centre. She spoke to Chris about it a few times and he told her 'she still doesn't know when she's coming back'.

Later in the interview, Barbara disclosed to the detective, 'I always said, buried in the backyard. Our catchcry has always been that she's buried on that one acre, somewhere in the backyard.

'My feeling was that the only police involvement had been with people who knew Chris and were friends with Chris. And how come Annette and Sue, the last people to see her, had never been questioned? Because we've got these doubts. We've got no evidence to base it on. We just feel that he's got everything and that it's his word that she disappeared voluntarily.'

The Ombudsman angle came up again on page 22 of the record of Barbara's police interview. She told the detective that as a result of the growing concern of herself and Lyn's coworkers, Barbara went through the telephone book and called Lyn's mother to carefully explain, 'We have this feeling that maybe she didn't go.'

'She said, "I would never have thought that initially, in any way, shape or form." But she said, "I would have to agree with you now."'

Barbara asked Helena for her blessing to write to the Ombudsman. 'She said, "No, it wouldn't disturb me at all. And I'd be happy if you did it."

'So that was when we did that bit – the Ombudsman. And that's how we started.

'Lyn was not an irresponsible person. And she was an important part of my centre because she knew I had to have a registered nurse. I would have thought, if she really did do that, she would ring me and say, "Barbara, I'm really sorry to let you down." And I would understand. She had permanent shifts. As I say, when she doesn't turn up at nine o'clock, I'm in trouble because under state licensing, you know, laws, I had to have a nurse on the premises.'

Barbara was asked to describe Chris Dawson's phone demeanour during the brief conversations when he was telling his wife's boss that Lyn was still away from the home and had called him to tell him she needed more time.

'I wouldn't say he was horribly upset. He never ever sounded to me like I would like my husband to feel if I had taken off.'

She added that in Chris's calls to her, he had never asked her on a personal note, 'Why has Lyn left me?' He had never asked whether Lyn had disclosed anything about her whereabouts to her or her coworker friends at the childcare centre.

At 5.40 pm on that day in August 1998, the interview between Barbara Cruise and Damian Loone formally concluded. He asked her to exercise discretion at this early stage of his investigation; to 'keep this to yourself'.

The 29 pages of transcript threw a lot of light on some dark recesses of this case for me. The names of several more people, friends of Lyn, whom Barbara had named were new to me, and the mentions of the Ombudsman were intriguing. In my experience with government departments and agencies such as the Ombudsman, files were held for years. It was possible the Lyn Dawson file still existed.

Michael Barnes had been recently promoted to the role of NSW Ombudsman. I would be seeing him again in a couple of weeks but first I needed to meet Barbara at her home south of Newcastle and record her voice for the podcast, a medium which was as much a novelty to her as it was to me and my first two interviewees, Greg and Merilyn.

I entered a brick and tile villa with Rebecca Hazel and Eric George on a hot afternoon. We were offered cool drinks by Barbara's husband and set up our equipment. Eric frowned – the noise from the split-cycle air-conditioning system would be picked up by his sensitive microphone – but the sweaty alternative was unthinkable.

Three minutes into the interview, Barbara raised the physical mismatch between Lyn and Chris. It was crudely simplistic – loving wife and devoted mother puts on weight; good-looking muscle-bound husband prefers younger, fitter substitute.

'I think what happened with them, he's a very handsome man. Both the Dawson boys were very handsome boys. They were models. And she was a very attractive girl when they married. So when, this is something like 12 years later, she'd got a little bit bigger. She still had a gorgeous smile and was still, I would say, a lovely girl but she wasn't model material. And I think maybe Chris was about the looks by that stage. It should have been a whole lot more. She'd become a mum and not the model wife that maybe he still wanted.'

Barbara recalled that one day Lyn came into the childcare centre with a new garment. It was lingerie.

'And I said, "Oh, that's pretty racy."'

'And she said, "Oh, well, I'll put it on and I'll dance for Chris, you know, to try and bring the magic into the romance again."'

'But what alarmed me was when he brought that young girl into the home. First off, she was babysitting, the next thing, she's living there supposedly because she had problems at home. So Lyn sold it to me as if he was being a very nice person and looking after his student and caring for her because she had problems at home. My alarm bells went up immediately. I said, I guess I'm a bit older and I said, "I'm not sure if I was having any marital difficulties that I would have a 16-year-old girl living in my home", and that's how I put it to her.'

Barbara cast her mind back almost 36 years to January 1982. She freely acknowledged that she could not recall with any confidence whether she saw Lyn holding hands with Chris in the childcare centre after their marriage counselling on the Friday but she did recall that Sue Strath and Annette Leary had strong memories of the event.

'After a few weeks, we smelled a rat. Just didn't seem right.'

I wanted to circle back to the point Barbara had made in her 1998 police interview about her staff, perhaps Sue, having written to the Ombudsman within a year or two of 1982.

They were all acutely aware that the student whom they had all known as the family babysitter had moved into the house very soon after Lyn had vanished. Other parents bringing children in shared regular updates about goings-on at Gilwinga Drive, with Jenny having effectively replaced Lyn.

'And of course, we found out that he got a divorce very quickly, within a year, and then a property settlement just after, and then he married her.

'One of my staff members said to me, "I would like to do something about this. I don't believe the police have investigated this as anything other than what Chris said, that she left of her own free will." And at that stage, none of us believed that was the case.

'I kept saying, "but we're only her work colleagues". You know, we'd talk about it ourselves. I'd say, "Why is it up to us to do something – there has to be a family out there." There wasn't any big thing in the paper to say that a woman had disappeared mysteriously. There wasn't anything. There was just us, wondering where she was.

'So what I said was, "Well, before we do anything, we need to contact her family because we are only her work colleagues, her friends."

'I got Lyn's personnel file and I found her maiden name. Then I rang everybody, every Simms in Sydney, and I said, "Are you Lynette Dawson's mum?" And finally I hit upon her mum. And then I just explained to her that we felt that she may not have left of her own free will and that we would like to write to the Ombudsman but we would not do that if we didn't have her blessing.

'And she said, "Initially, I would never have thought that – anything like that . . . now, I do." And she said, "We would be delighted if you would do that."

'Then I found out that Lyn had never contacted her again. So that was the only time we contacted the family or had anything to do with them until the inquests.

'Nobody else seemed to be doing anything. And we felt we owed it to her to at least ask the question of the Ombudsman. We just didn't think there was anybody in her corner. Don't ask me why but we felt it was our responsibility to do something about it.'

I asked, 'And you made a complaint to the Ombudsman?'

Barbara replied, 'We didn't make any complaint about the police. We just asked the question "Could it be investigated from a different angle?" That was the way we couched it.

'We just wrote to the Ombudsman and said that we didn't believe there was any corruption or anything by the police. We weren't alluding to anything like that. We just felt that because Chris and Paul were popular figures, they were first-grade rugby league players and they were models. They'd been on TV ads and they would have been friends with the local police. We felt that the police only ever investigated it as if she left of her own free will. In other words, they believed what Chris said. He's the only person who ever got a phone call, according to him, nobody else did. Not another soul. So it was his word. And it was never, ever investigated as if, well, hang on a minute, maybe she didn't.'

'And did the letter to the Ombudsman prompt a response?'

'I can't honestly answer that one. I can't remember getting a response at all . . . We were really worried when we first wrote. I was really frightened. I thought, "He's going to come and have a go at us or, if he's a murderer, something worse." But we decided that we had the courage of our convictions and went ahead anyway. But for years, I can tell you, I looked over my shoulder. It was very scary.'

Barbara recalled that the first time she was interviewed by police was in 1991. I found it staggering that it took nine years for police, as Barbara put it, to 'come anywhere near any of us who worked with her'.

She added, 'When you get interviewed nine years later and you've done a lot of thinking about it and conjecture and all the rest of it, you start to get hazy.'

This timing of 1991 was consistent with the first police investigation, triggered by Jenny's 1990 return from the Gold Coast and the airing of her suspicions.

Detectives Stuart Wilkins and Paul Mayger had also interviewed Lyn's siblings and others. But every record of these interviews had disappeared. Greg and Phil Simms had speculated in their conversations with me that police friends of the Dawsons had conveniently made the investigative material disappear.

Fortuitously, however, the record of one remarkable interview still existed: Chris Dawson was questioned at a police station in Queensland, where the detectives had travelled in 1991 to seek his responses to Jenny's serious assertions of a probable murder. I knew this because the transcript of this videotaped conversation was part of the brief of evidence Damian Loone had put together after he picked up the investigation in 1998.

My interest in the Ombudsman's files from some time in the early 1980s grew. A formal investigation by investigators from that statutory agency would have generated documents and possibly records of interviews from six or seven or eight years before the first homicide investigation. If such records had fallen through the cracks, they might now be retrievable all these years later.

Barbara agreed that she and the other women in the childcare centre had formed a less than favourable view of Chris based on the information Lyn had imparted, though she was not knowingly painting him in a poor light.

'Maybe she could speak a little bit more and get a more objective opinion rather than with her family who thought he was just wonderful. I do remember a time when I said to Lyn, "Why don't you talk to your mum about this?" And she said, "Oh, no, they think Chris is just wonderful."

Finally, Barbara expressed pessimism about the case ever going to trial.

'The Director of Public Prosecutions hasn't moved. It is flimsy evidence. It is circumstantial. We'll never find a body. But I like to think that he hasn't lived a comfortable life now. He didn't get off scot-free as far as I'm concerned.

'And in the Coroners Court, you're very lucky because the coroner said, "What do you think happened?" You don't get that in a court of law. A court of law has got to be facts. But you're able, in a Coroners Court, to say, "Well, I think he killed her."'

'So you are inclined to not give him the presumption of innocence?' I asked.

'No. Not at all.'

'And is that unusual for you?'

'It is. Very. There's nothing that ever happened or was said that would make me now ever think that he was innocent. He had the means, opportunity, motive. They're all you need.'

Chapter 12

Bib and Bub

On the drive back to Sydney after the first round of recorded interviews for a podcast yet to be named, and still six months from the release of its first episode, I knew that Rebecca Hazel was already a good friend.

We had met just three weeks earlier but we trusted each other and we shared a common purpose. Rebecca was confident Chris had killed Lyn but deeply sceptical about him ever going to trial.

Rebecca pointed out the turn-off to Lake Munmorah and a vast swathe of national park and wilderness. It was where Paul and Marilyn Dawson had said they were staying with their daughters in an aunt's caravan in the January 1982 holiday period.

'It's a scrubby, shitty place, really,' Rebecca said.

I told her that our working together felt like karma. A kind of fate. Good for us. But bad for Dawson.

Rebecca agreed. I reminded her of how it had started with a telephone call in late October as she waited at Sydney Airport.

It was her turn to surprise me.

As Rebecca guided her BMW sedan on the south-bound highway from Gosford, she told me that when our phone conversation had ended, she had called the detective, Damian Loone.

'I told him if he hears from you, not to talk to you,' Rebecca admitted sheepishly.

We laughed.

Damian and Rebecca had come to know each other well over the previous six years, and hours of interviews for her unpublished book, developing what Rebecca called 'a special friendship; I think we cared about each other – he had bad flu once, also had a stent put in, he thought I'd lost a lot of weight once. It's funny how I unexpectedly found myself in those places'.

For the two hours it took to drive back to Sydney that afternoon, we went over some of the disclosures in the first round of interviews. We had warmed to Greg, Merilyn, Phil and Lynda. They were good, honest, sincere people. Was this why they had been seemingly oblivious in the face of probable evil? Was such wickedness so far removed from their decent, trusting and law-abiding lives that it meant they simply didn't think to look for wrongdoing in the early years?

How differently things might have turned out if someone in the Simms family had gone to see Lyn's friends at her workplace to ask them if they'd had any news or knew anything about the final days before Lyn disappeared.

It was well known that Lyn had worked on the last day anyone saw her. Helena spent many hours on buses and trains to the Central Coast, which was where Chris said Lyn had told him she'd gone but it seemed she never went to Lyn's workplace, where her friends and workmates spoke among themselves about her having been murdered by her husband.

Rebecca and I spoke a lot about Chris's sordid conduct and the scale of his betrayal of his wife and children. Unfaithfulness in a marriage is hardly novel but the brazenness and disrespect shown by a husband moving a teenager into the family home and having sex with her in a spare bedroom when his wife had gone to sleep after being given alcohol by Chris was hard for me to get my head around. My daughter was at this time about the same age Jenny was when her physical education teacher took her to his parents' empty house at Maroubra and had sex with her for the first time. He was twice her age.

It was, I suggested to Rebecca, pedophilia. She agreed. Rebecca was loyally in Jenny's corner at all times. I believed that Jenny was, of course, a victim but not blameless. At times, I was suspicious of her story that she had not suspected Chris of foul play when Lyn disappeared nor for years afterwards.

'How could she not have suspected him of foul play right from the start?' I asked Rebecca. 'Her own evidence was that she went with him in her school uniform one afternoon to some dodgy place where he said he'd asked about getting a hitman to kill Lyn.'

Rebecca repeatedly stressed Jenny's vulnerability as a teenager and the conditioning she had received from Chris. Rebecca made good points. She was confident that Jenny had been honest about everything. Although I valued Rebecca's judgment, I tried to keep an open mind.

In personality, background and indeed some of our beliefs and values, we were like chalk and cheese. Rebecca would prefer to read gentler editorials in the *Sydney Morning Herald* over the elbows-out pronouncements in the newspaper which backed me, *The Australian*. She had gone to university and become a lawyer and loved going to cultural events and browsing art galleries, whereas I'd left high school to go straight to the newsroom and would be perfectly happy with a meat pie and a beer at the racetrack. I told her about my omen bet on the Melbourne Cup in early November. The imported galloper was called Rekindling, I explained, adding, 'I became sure because of the name – we're "rekindling" an important story.' The horse duly won and my confidence about good karma in our investigation swelled with the winnings in my betting app.

I probably encouraged her perception of me as the politically incorrect Queenslander because she was the opposite and it provoked friendly banter about our respective differences. Her concerns about animal welfare meant she would not share my enthusiasm for horseracing. As we became closer friends and discovered more of our many differences, we would laugh them off and proclaim another reason for the improbability of our effective partnership.

This measured, thoughtful woman told me she was 'mildly neurotic'. I wasn't inclined to disagree and we laughed about this too. She has shared private things about her life that helped me understand at least some of her motivation in writing about Jenny, Lyn and

Chris. We spoke often of our children, and our rock-solid partners; in her corner, Harry and in mine, Ruth.

When we disagreed, we talked it through and it always landed us in a good place. Mutual respect and friendship served us well.

When I returned to Brisbane, we were in touch by email and text several times a day, talking about the evidence and some of the people I would need to interview. Women like Lyn's friend at the childcare centre, Annette Leary. I calculated that she would be aged 81.

'I'm coming around to your view that it will take a major break-through to make a difference in terms of a DPP decision – too many witnesses are getting old or dying,' I texted Rebecca.

Rebecca replied, 'V sad. Nonetheless, the police should be exposed for letting CD get away with murder. Do you know the legal term, *res ipsa loquitur*? The thing speaks for itself. And the facts bloody well do.'

By late November, we agreed that many of our phone conversations from that time on would be recorded at my end. My good friend, colleague and brother-in-law David Murray, a crime writer at *The Australian*, who wrote a highly acclaimed book about the 2012 murder of our friend Allison Baden-Clay, had told me there was a wealth of powerful material for a podcast being lost because my conversations with Rebecca were going unrecorded.

'I'm going to get a telephone jack and start recording. You're on notice, Hazel! We talk a big game – hope we're not gibbering and dissembling like lunatics when the tape's rolling,' I texted her.

'Bring it on,' she replied.

Although I was not privy to their conversations, Rebecca told me Jenny Carlson was on board with the podcast plan if it meant Rebecca's book about Jenny's life would get published. I looked forward to a time in late December or early January 2018 when the three of us would record several hours of interviews. To prepare, I wanted to be in total command of all the facts, allegations and timeline and before this could happen, I needed more documents, more material. I celebrated the breakthroughs with cheerful calls to Rebecca and she commiserated with me when obstacles blocked our way.

A to-do list that I kept in the Notes app on my iPhone and in my notebook grew by several entries a day. There were so many people to try to talk to but first they needed to be tracked down. Early in my career, the White Pages were invaluable but many people had abandoned the landline telephone, and mobile phones were harder to find. I relied heavily on property searches and my entries on *The Australian*'s account with a real estate database quickly mounted.

Ruth found a book by Arthur 'Neddy' Smith, a notorious underworld figure who was connected to the Newtown Jets rugby league club through his footballing brother-in-law Paul Hayward, a drug smuggler and addict who had played alongside the Dawson brothers.

Smith sought to cash in on his career of strangling, stabbing and shooting unsuspecting victims with his 1995 book, *Catch And Kill Your Own – behind the killings the police don't want to solve*. The back cover promised, 'in these disturbing accounts, one of Australia's most feared and notorious criminals, Arthur "Neddy" Smith, tells the true stories behind 37 underworld killings, all still officially listed as "unsolved."' It would make for grim reading over Christmas.

I emailed Rebecca, who was fretting about the amount of time it was taking to get a contract for the publication of her book, a photo-graph of the cover of the newly arrived book by Smith.

I told her, 'Perhaps the contract killer used his special form of leverage to speed up his publisher. I'm going to get audio of Neddy Smith. Why not? Everyone else is getting a run in this podcast.'

I drafted an email for Greg Simms to send to Neil Munro, the then director of *Chequerboard* from all those years ago. He told Greg that few productions were preserved for posterity by the ABC from the pre-digital period of 16 mm film. If there were any copies, Neil help-fully added, they would be in the ABC's archives department.

'It doesn't look promising,' Greg told me.

We collaborated in another note, this one seeking help from someone in the archives department of the public broadcaster to search for the episode of *Chequerboard* featuring Chris and Paul Dawson as exceptional twins, and Lyn and Marilyn as their faithful wives.

The email Greg sent in his name to the ABC stated:

> My sister Lyn Dawson, a married Sydney mother of two young daughters, went missing in 1982, about seven years after she appeared in an episode of *Chequerboard* about twins.
>
> The episode was called 'Heckle and Jeckle, Bib and Bub'. According to this reference link, the episode was Episode 3 in Series 11, and aired on 15 October 1975.
>
> Unfortunately, Lyn's siblings do not have any video of Lyn, only photographs, cards and letters. We would be grateful for an opportunity to purchase a copy of this episode.

The Coroners Court of New South Wales received my written request for access to the transcripts and exhibits for the 2001 inquest, which was over in half a day, and the 2003 inquest, which went for five days of public hearings. I disclosed the podcast investigation, some general facts about the case and the cooperation I was receiving from Lyn's family.

Acting State Coroner Teresa O'Sullivan refused my request to view all the exhibits from both inquests. I was advised that for $330, I could have the 25-page transcript from the 2001 inquest; however, the transcript for the 2003 inquest would not be made available for copying or inspection.

Journalists are routinely stymied when it comes to examining public records. We should not have to bow and scrape to read or purchase copies of these documents. As the official records of public proceedings, they should be made available for inspection by anyone with an interest in a case, including journalists.

I questioned, in writing, the decision to deny access to the most crucial public documents held by the Coroners Court in an emailed reply:

'I was hoping to merely read or view the exhibits during a visit to the court precinct. If there is any forensic material – such as clothing in sealed bags, for example – I would not attempt to handle it in any way. However, exhibited documents which were part of the public record in the inquests are of significant interest to me to ensure I have a complete understanding of the evidence.'

The reply of Coroners Court's acting registrar, Kazeline Dawson, held a clue that the decision was influenced by New South Wales Police: 'In an unsolved homicide and missing persons matters, the position of investigating police are also considered by the state coroner when making direction. The purpose of this is, amongst other things, to maintain integrity of investigations, and protect the administration of justice and police methodology.'

Greg Simms and Pat Jenkins had briefly mentioned to me in late 2017 that a detective from the Homicide Squad, Detective Senior Constable Daniel Poole, was reviewing the case. The brief of evidence was no longer the part-time obsession of Damian Loone, who had handed everything over in 2015. Neither Greg nor Pat expected it would amount to much because they had lost all confidence in the Office of the DPP.

I had hoped the police would welcome a podcast investigation into an unsolved case involving a suspected murder 36 years ago; the email from the Coroners Court suggested otherwise.

Greg told me that when he raised my interest and the podcast proposal with Dan Poole, the detective said that while he could not stop the family from working with me, he advised them not to, adding that he could not talk to me.

Mindful of the possible concern in the Homicide Squad about loose lips, I decided that I would not try to contact Damian Loone; it might compromise his job.

One Monday around this time, curiosity got the better of me and I drove to the Sunshine Coast and a beachside community near Coolum, where Chris Dawson lived with his third wife, Susan.

I know this area well. From the top of Mount Coolum, which Ruth and I had climbed with our children when they were smaller, you take in a stunning vista: the Coral Sea to the east, a patchwork of sugar cane fields, newly developed housing estates and the former Hyatt Coolum resort, a one-time Mecca for cashed-up holidaying families and golfers until an eccentric billionaire called Clive Palmer bought it and put in dozens of mechanised, life-sized dinosaurs he'd shipped in from China. Clive had named one of the dinosaurs – a mean-looking sharp-toothed velociraptor – after me during investigations I was doing for *The Australian* into his conduct as a businessman. I laughed each time I told the amusing story to friends when we played golf there.

As I drove slowly past Chris Dawson's house, I called Rebecca in Sydney.

'Oh my goodness,' I said.

'What is it? Can you see him?' she asked.

'No but I can see his car in the driveway, it has a personalised licence plate – the letters T W I N,' I replied.

Early in the morning of the previous week, I had taken our puppy, Molly, south to the Gold Coast enclave of Main Beach, where I had lived as a teenager before residential high-rises replaced the beachside postwar weatherboard homes. Greg Simms had told me that Paul Dawson had retired to live with Marilyn in a luxury apartment block there. I knew it well. It's a stone's throw from where I'd pedal my bike as a 13-year-old to pick up my friend Geoff Redman for our ride to high school. Every house on Geoff's street is long gone.

I sat in the car outside the building, hoping to see Paul or Marilyn walking back from the beach or one of the cafes on Tedder Avenue but I saw nobody who looked like them.

Using Facebook, I looked at the happy snaps posted by the Dawson brothers and their wives during holidays in England and Europe. In one shot, the four Dawson brothers – Peter, Gary, Paul and Chris – had their arms around each other in a show of family unity. Chris beamed, carefree in a white t-shirt as he stood next to a smiling Paul, who had wrapped his arm affectionately around Chris on one side and their solicitor brother, Peter, grinning on the other.

Gary had his arms crossed and stood unsmiling. In a nod to their childhood growing up in a modest house in Maroubra, then a relatively poor suburb known as 'Bra', just a couple of kilometres from the notorious prison known as Long Bay, the picture was captioned, 'All the Bra boys together again!'

I could see that Lyn's second daughter, Amy, had updated the cover photograph for her Facebook page in a tribute to her mother, who was sitting on a beach and smiling intently while holding a baby girl in a nappy.

'Thirty-six years old and I miss her more than ever,' she wrote.

A friend replied, 'She would be so proud of you and your gorgeous girl.'

Shanelle Dawson, Amy's older sister, added, 'Yes, she is. From wherever she is.'

Chapter 13

Schoolgirls

The Warrego Highway is gun-barrel straight for long stretches across flat and featureless plains west of the Great Dividing Range and the city of Toowoomba. In Bidyara, the Aboriginal language of the region, 'warrego' means 'bad'. It can also mean 'river of sand'. When the Warrego River runs dry, both meanings make sense.

On the last Tuesday in November 2017, I was heading for the town of Miles, four hours from my home in Brisbane. A woman called Kate Erwin had been in touch with the Simms family via its Facebook page dedicated to Lyn's disappearance.

On my second visit to Greg and Merilyn's house earlier in November they had shown Kate's correspondence to me.

'Hi, my name is Kate Erwin and I was at St Ursula's College in 1998–2002 when Chris Dawson was my math teacher and PE teacher. When I first went to boarding school, I was 13 years old and was in Mr Dawson's math class. My whole class was wooed by Dawson and gushed and vied for his attention. Frankly, he made me sick to my stomach. I was moved from his class as I found he was often trying to seek my approval. I don't know why but it was a recurrent theme through my entire time at the school,' Kate wrote.

There were further, fascinating disclosures. Chris had struck me as a closed book when it came to Lyn's disappearance, saying as little as possible. His own daughters were raised in a home in which Lyn's name was rarely uttered. I needed to talk to this woman about her experiences as a 13-year-old when, she believed, Chris was attempting to groom her.

'Thankfully for me, I was raised by a dad of steel who taught me my worth and always backed me. I am a mother of four beautiful young children. No one can replace a mother's love. Chris Dawson stole Lynette's love from her children. He knows no limits,' Kate wrote.

Kate wanted to help Lyn's family, perhaps by connecting with Chris Dawson again and encouraging him to 'say or do or implicate himself in a detail that perhaps police may or may not know'. She was wary of him but she knew how much he had wanted her approval, and probably much more, when she was a teenager.

'She wants something done. She wanted to get out and try and trap him,' Greg Simms told me.

The Facebook page was being carefully managed by Pat's daughter, Pauline, and Allyson Jennings, Lyn's second cousin. There were photographs of Lyn and a summary of the circumstances surrounding her disappearance. Many people supported it with public posts. Unseen by the general public were notes and messages written by people who believed they knew something about Lyn's probable murder. When what appeared to be genuinely promising leads were received, they would be shared with Pat and Greg and, sometimes, with police.

One of the family's unsung heroes in the police investigation to this point was Detective Senior Constable David Lillyman, who did his best work behind the scenes from The Rocks police station and was always available to follow up a lead sent to the Facebook page. Detective Senior Constable Sarah Thomsen was another quiet achiever over many years.

Allyson Jennings talked to Kate and was buoyed by the prospects. But after consulting David Lillyman, who told her that 'in no way should she put herself in danger or in a position where she does not feel comfortable or safe', the family decided that Kate must not become involved in any undercover work against Chris.

Several months after her contact with Lyn's family, I called her in Miles, where she and her husband owned and ran the Outback Motel.

After explaining to Kate the podcast investigation I had started, she agreed to meet me for a recorded interview. A few days before the drive to Miles, I bought a handheld recording device, a Zoom H2n, for a couple of hundred dollars and placed it on the back seat with its unread instructions.

At the time of the road trip, the Australian gardening and television celebrity Don Burke was under siege by allegations of gross sexual harassment. The *Sydney Morning Herald*'s investigative journalist Kate McClymont had talked to numerous women who had worked with Burke about his conduct and his alleged efforts to harass them into giving him sexual favours. The Burke stories were running hard and they were unmissable reading and viewing.

The women who came forward appeared highly credible. The journalistic investigation underpinning the stories came soon after, and partly in response to, revelations about then Hollywood film producer Harvey Weinstein. More than 80 women had come forward with allegations that Weinstein was a serious sexual harasser and, in some cases, a rapist. As the public unmasking and shaming of a once-untouchable giant in the entertainment industry gathered momentum, the #MeToo social media campaign snowballed around the world with the identification of predatory powerful men who had escaped scrutiny up until that point. It became known as the Weinstein effect.

As I gunned my car along the Warrego Highway to see Kate Erwin, ABC radio news programs aired grabs of Don Burke denying some of the allegations being levelled against him. Burke was apologetic and acknowledged many mistakes but he refused to admit to everything.

Burke used an interview with *A Current Affair*'s seasoned host Tracy Grimshaw to challenge the memories, and therefore the reliability, of several of the women who were his accusers.

'I can't remember exact things I did 20 years ago, or whatever,' Burke told Tracy Grimshaw. 'I challenge anybody to get something exactly right, something like that, quoting back all that time. And whose memory is that good? I haven't got that good a memory.'

He made a powerful point. And memories were at the heart of the Dawson case.

In Lyn's case, police had taken statements from key people who were interviewed by homicide detectives in 1990 and 1991, eight to nine years after Lyn vanished.

But, like Lyn herself, the statements of almost every single one of those people on the interview list in that initial investigation had, inexplicably, disappeared. Only the interview with Chris Dawson was still available. Hundreds of hours of investigative work by detectives and the hard evidence gathered from witnesses who made written statements about a suspected murder had been lost, through negligence or corruption.

Witnesses were interviewed again between 1998 and 2001 when the detective Damian Loone started to investigate anew. Family members, Lyn's friends and others were questioned for the first time by Damian some 16 years after Lyn disappeared. Would their memories be reliable? I had raised it with Rebecca Hazel, who agreed it was a significant problem. Recollections fade. People die. Delay usually helps the guilty.

I wondered if Chris Dawson and his brother Paul were thinking about Don Burke. Were they worried that women who had been silent for the previous 36 years would come forward in this new era where their voices could be heard? Or were they so convinced of their own infallibility that the thought never entered their heads?

Kate Erwin met me in a women's fashion store. We walked to the public library and found a spare desk down the back. I'd bought a removable memory card for the new digital recorder, still in its wrapping, and Kate looked on as I fumbled to make the device work for the first time. Each time I pressed record and began the interview with questions, it would work for a few minutes and then abruptly stop, usually while Kate was giving what sounded like a great answer.

Kate must have been perplexed at her interviewer's amateurishness but she didn't show it. I was red-faced. I had claimed to be an investigative journalist making a serious bid to solve a longtime suspected murder, yet I couldn't make the recorder stay on. Kate took the initiative and immediately understood that the memory card needed 'formatting'. Who knew? Not me.

In a heartbeat, she had it working. 'I'm a millennial,' she laughed.

When we started again, she told me that at 13 at St Ursula's, she was repulsed by Chris Dawson, yet she could see that a number of the other girls in her classes were 'putty in his hands'.

'He was literally grooming the entire class,' Kate said. 'He wanted to be our friend, not our teacher, and he made that clear.'

She described class excursions to sections of secluded beach and coastline with Dawson for exercises, running and swimming. He was the only adult.

Kate continued, 'It seemed to me like every opportunity he had to get us off the premises of the school grounds, he would seek it out. Girls who are 13 years old in string bikinis, these are my friends, these are my peers, climbing on his shoulders with their legs wrapped around his head, wrestling with each other in the surf.'

One day, in the dunes near the beach, Kate and the other girls were put through their paces by the physical education teacher. Dressed in skirts, they were on their backs and elevating their legs, then keeping them raised for as long as possible. It made their abdomens taut but Kate suspected an ulterior motive. Chris remarked that other men would be deeply envious of him at moments like those, standing above a couple of dozen pubescent girls with their legs in the air.

On another occasion, images from the 1970s of Chris and Paul Dawson wearing denim jeans as models and pin-up Newtown Jets footballers found their way into the classroom. Kate saw the teacher revel in the attention. The girls were cheering. He called himself 'the hotter twin'.

Kate told me, 'What 50-year-old man tries to seek the approval of 13-year-old girls? It made my skin crawl.'

She told me about a stage act that the skimpily dressed teenage students and some of their teachers had performed for the parents one evening. The hit song 'Love Shack' by the American new wave band The B-52s played as girls danced and writhed around.

'And then Chris Dawson came out dancing and he was the only male on the stage,' Kate told me. 'And all the girls and the teachers were dancing up on him like he was this sex magnet type of thing.'

Kate's father was appalled. 'And he's like, "Why is this happening at a Catholic school? Why are the teachers wearing miniskirts? Why are they all over this man? Why are the students all over this man? Like, how is this fun or funny or entertaining?"'

'He was furious, he was wild. He got up and he was like, "Boo, hiss."'

Kate's cousins who were in the audience were mortified but her father was unrepentant and would openly refer to Chris as 'the sleazebag'.

One day during a lesson in class, Kate went unknowingly to a very sensitive subject. 'We were talking about domestic violence and it just didn't make sense to me. Like, why is there domestic violence? How does this happen? What causes men to do this to their wives? And I remember specifically saying to him . . . "Why do they do this? What is it?"'

Kate's questions were prescient and instructive, and they triggered a volcanic response in Chris.

'. . . he just snapped. He smashed his fists on the table and I remember his neck being strained because he yelled so loud back. He was infuriated and he said, "I don't know, why would I know? Why would I know?"'

Kate called it a watershed moment. In a sudden rage, the school's favourite teacher had shown another side to his personality.

'And then the bell rang, we all moved on and just looked at each other, like, "Wow, that struck a nerve."'

Knowing the evidence of the bruising on Lyn's arms and legs, I was in little doubt that Chris had beaten her behind closed doors and threatened her with worse if she were to ever disclose it. When

Kate had repeatedly asked her teacher in a St Ursula's classroom why men assaulted their partners, had she unknowingly taken Chris back to those grim days at Bayview in the early 1980s?

I asked her about the efforts Chris made to win her approval. Driving the school boarder to and from tennis events on weekends and creating what appeared to Kate to be confected opportunities to spend time with her outside class.

'He was trying to groom me. I felt scared the entire time and extremely exposed and vulnerable. I've always had a healthy fear of him.'

When the first lurid reports broke during the first inquest in Sydney in late February 2001, about Lyn having disappeared and Chris allegedly being responsible for her murder as well as the grooming of Jenny, the St Ursula's community was aghast.

Kate was unsurprised. It all made sense to her. She kept talking to Chris as more reports appeared, including my own lengthy feature in *The Courier-Mail* in early March 2001, 'Looking for Lyn' and the pressure grew on the school to act.

Kate pressed him at this time about the disappearance of Lyn and his relationship with Jenny. 'He said that it was legal because she was over 16.'

When Greg called me the next day, he sounded optimistic. He had been following the scandal engulfing Don Burke too.

'Now's the time for people to get out and say, you know, let's band together and get these bastards,' he said. 'It's all out there at the moment in relation to Don Burke and all these people.'

Greg had some information about another potential witness: Shelley Oates-Wilding, a former Olympic kayaker who had been a student at Forest High School, where Paul Dawson was a teacher at the same time Chris was at Cromer High.

The first time I had come across Shelley's name was in 2001, when Damian Loone let me read the witness statements which had gone before the coroner for the first inquest.

Shelley was friends with another former Forest High student who disclosed to police in 1998 that she had been in a sexual relationship with Paul Dawson when she was at the school. At 33, this woman – Alice (not her real name) – had provided a ten-page statement which was, for me, the most distressing document in the police brief of evidence.

By late 2017, I had a hardcopy of the police brief and was reading each page of every document closely.

The sixth paragraph of Alice's statement, which mentioned Shelley states: 'Towards the end of 1980 I was involved in a fun run with other students from school. I was with another school friend, Shelley OATES.'

I had raised Shelley's name with Greg Simms to check if he had heard of her. She was on my list as it was possible she had fallen between the cracks and never been interviewed by police.

Talking to Alice was a higher priority but her statement was so personal and revealing that any approach would need to be handled with a lot of care. It was unclear to me whether Alice knew that her high school secrets, as revealed in her statement, had been made available.

Greg recalled that Shelley's name was raised with him by a Sydney journalist who knew her and had hinted at another relationship. Greg told me that, 'Shelley knew all about what was going on.'

I went back to Alice's statement, in which she described how Paul Dawson had approached her and Shelley during the fun run, saying the two girls could cut the run short to go to a nearby beach with him for a swim.

'I vaguely remember getting a lift from Christopher DAWSON and Jenny CARLSON back to school after the swim, because I wondered what was that girl, Jenny, doing with Chris. I didn't know then but I found out later on that they were seeing each other,' Alice wrote.

The events described by Alice and the careful chronology, if all of it were true, made it painfully obvious that Chris's obsession with Jenny at Cromer High had started about the same time as Paul at Forest High was grooming Alice.

'In 1979, I was in Year 9. I was 14 years of age and Paul Dawson was my teacher in health studies,' Alice says in her statement. 'Paul was friendly to me and one day asked me if I would babysit for him and his wife and their three children. This mainly consisted of weekends when Paul and his wife Marilyn would go out. Sometimes it was a Friday night and I would stay in the spare room and then next morning Paul would give me a lift home.'

By late 1980, Alice was 15 and a half when, she says in her statement, she was becoming 'closer friends' with Paul, who asked her on beach visits without Shelley. At the beach, Alice says, 'he kissed me on the lips'.

'I remember Paul saying words like "I love you" when he kissed me. Each time we went to the beach, Paul would kiss me. It got heavier and heavier each time. I remember the first occasion we had sexual intercourse it was black Friday in 1981 as I told my parents, as an excuse, that I was going to the movies. Paul drove me to the old gasworks at Little Manly where he parked his car, which was a light green Toyota Corona station wagon. Paul seduced me and we had sex in the car.' Alice was two months shy of her 16th birthday.

The competitive twins had been simultaneously grooming schoolgirls who were half their age. But, for once, Chris had trumped his brother: he had bedded his schoolgirl five months earlier.

Alice's statement discloses regular sex with her teacher in motels, her house, his car, his parents' place, his sister's house, and even in bushland around Belrose. But her exploitation went further, because Alice alleged that Paul wanted her to step up from what she called their 'normal sex'; he told her he wanted threesomes, anal sex, blow jobs while he drove.

'When Paul talked to me about his desires, he would often say, "I love you,"' Alice says in her statement. 'Paul was handsome and very popular with students at school. This was the first time that I liked someone and they in return liked me. I did these things because he asked me to do them and I did what I was told to do as I wanted to make Paul happy.'

More unusual sex started in July 1982, when Alice was 17. She remembered going to his house when neither Marilyn nor the children were around. Paul had told Alice he was expecting a man to come over to provide a quote to remove some stains in a carpet. He told her that she was to 'dress in a sexy outfit', dance to some music then perform oral sex on the man.

'Paul had left the house and gone up to Chris's place which was just up the road in Gilwinga Drive, Bayview. About 6 pm the carpet cleaner arrived. I took this person into the bedroom and commenced to play the stereo and dance. This guy was just standing there in shock. I then commenced to strip as Paul had wanted me to, and later I performed oral sex on this person. I did this as this was what Paul wanted me to do and I complied with his request as I was in love with him.

'About 20 minutes later, when the cleaner had left, Paul and Chris arrived. I was in the bedroom and Paul led his brother Chris into the bedroom blindfolded. Paul sat his brother on the bed and I commenced to give Chris DAWSON oral sex. Paul watched this for a while and when I had finished, Paul took the blindfold off Chris and the three of us had sex. I was supposed to be Chris's birthday present. I had complete trust in Paul and I did what he told me to do.'

Unlike the other statements in the bundle, the ten typed pages which recounted Alice's experiences included multiple notations of 'interview suspended' and 'interview recommenced'.

I tried to picture the scene: a married woman from the Northern Beaches breaking down and needing a lot of time and patience from the police officer typing out the details in a Dee Why police station over several days in September 1998.

Because of the timing, it seemed likely that she had gone to the station to support Jenny. Alice's statement was dated 17 September but she was coming and going from the station over a few subsequent days until it was completed. Jenny was there at the same time because hers was dated 18 September.

Alice next described one of the saddest scenes in this tragic saga. At the end of the touch football season in 1982, she met Paul Dawson in the gymnasium of her high school one weeknight. He had been praising her role in the threesome with Chris, and 'kept telling me that I was really good at it' and that next time a few more men should be involved.

'When I arrived, I saw at least ten guys there in the gym. These were Paul and Chris's mates. Paul had told me previously that I was to do a strip show for these guys. I stripped naked for these guys and then I was told by Paul to go to the rear of the gym where two floor mats were. I went over there and gave oral sex to some of the team members and penile/vaginal sex with the others. Paul had told me that some of these guys were Cromer High School teachers and the others were Paul and Chris's friends. I participated in this as I was told to do so by Paul.'

Paul would alternate between having Alice to himself and pimping her to other teachers, two of whom she named. By this stage, her statement says, 'everything in my personal life was horrible'.

On at least two occasions in 1983, when Alice was no longer at school, she met Paul, Chris and other teachers for sex. Lyn had been missing for 18 months in July 1983 when Jenny approached Alice and told her she wanted to give Chris a birthday present – herself and Alice in bed together with him.

Alice's statement affected me more than any of the others. The predatory, grubby antics of the Dawson brothers were depicted by Alice in a document which rang entirely true.

Alice was in no doubt about the unusual bond between Chris and Paul, describing 'an incredibly close relationship'.

'I say this because it was Paul's fantasy for Paul and Chris to be inside me at the same time, vaginally. This did occur on an occasion,' she says.

Alice heard Paul talk about the marital problems Chris was having in 1981 and she was led to believe that he wanted Jenny but didn't want to lose the house at Bayview.

In early 1982, Alice returned to Forest High for her final year. When she saw Paul, he had staked out the moral high ground. Alice recalled him telling her, 'Lyn's left Chris. Up and left him with the kids. How could a mother leave her two children?'

Chapter 14

Sex, Lies and Videotape

The most intriguing document in the police brief of evidence that Greg Simms had sent to me was the transcript of the formal interview of Chris Dawson by two New South Wales Homicide detectives at a Queensland police station on 15 January 1991.

On the same day in 1984, Chris and Jenny were married at the house in Bayview. The same house that, had alarms sounded when Lyn disappeared two years earlier, would have been crawling with police forensics officers and possibly been declared a crime scene.

A visit to the Gold Coast by detectives seeking to interview Chris on the seventh anniversary of his second wedding was a watershed event. Jenny, having left Chris in 1990, was rebuilding her life, connecting with old friends from Cromer High and telling police that she suspected Lyn was murdered by Chris so that he could have it all.

With their messy divorce playing out in the Family Court, the timing of the police visit to question Chris could not have been a coincidence. The psychological buttons being subtly pushed by detectives quizzing Chris about his missing first wife, in an investigation enlivened because of extremely serious allegations by his estranged second wife, were inescapable.

While so much from the 1990–91 police investigation went missing, and is assumed permanently lost, the original transcript and the videotape of Chris's interview by Detective Sergeant Paul

Mayger and Detective Senior Constable Stuart Wilkins had somehow survived.

It is likely that if these files had also disappeared, there would never have been a murder trial. We would not have seen Dawson's criminal defence lawyer, Pauline David, fighting to have him found not guilty during a murder trial in the Supreme Court in Sydney over several months in 2022. Nor would we have seen grainy footage of her from 31 years earlier, sitting beside Chris in a police station and correcting Detective Sergeant Mayger when he wrongly stated her surname as 'Davies' on the official videotape.

'David,' she said coolly.

Chris was not compelled to talk to the police at 3.42 pm on a Tuesday in mid-January. He was not under arrest. If he had declined to do the interview, there was nothing the detectives could do. They would have been stuck with the suspicions of a woman who was seeking to divorce him, and the recollections of Lyn's siblings and mother who had accepted for years the story that Lyn had gone away, stayed away, and started a new life.

Every case is different but criminal defence lawyer friends hold that a client under investigation for a serious crime should decline a police request for a formal interview in almost every situation. The lies told to police by many suspects are baked into the official record of their formal interviews, which are usually recorded. These are the lies prosecutors will then tell jurors are the unavoidable evidence of an accused's consciousness of guilt.

Videotaping of the interview was a relatively new innovation in 1991. For decades, defence lawyers in Queensland had argued that bent detectives fabricated confessions during unrecorded interviews and that innocent people were being jailed because of the 'verballing' culture of police. Many a suspect and witness claimed to have been 'verballed' by police records of interview which bore little resemblance to what had been said. It took an excoriating public inquiry into police corruption in the late 1980s for a suite of reforms, including longtime recommendations for the taping of police interviews with suspects, to be finally implemented.

Another curiosity was that the interview occurred in Queensland under the auspices of the northern state's legislative framework. The two New South Wales detectives had crossed the border to conduct it in a police station which had its own taping and storage equipment. Is this why the recording survived when every other interview conducted in New South Wales by the same police at the same time period were lost?

In late 2017, I studied the transcript to properly understand the structure and flow of the January 1991 interview. The more experienced detective, Paul Mayger, flooded Chris with questions about the circumstances of his marriage to Lyn and his relationship with Jenny in 1981, his first missing person report to police five and a half weeks after Lyn disappeared, his assurances to her family and friends and to Jenny that Lyn had called him to say she was fine and that she just needed more time to think things through.

He was asked about his bank accounts, apparent discrepancies in what he had told people over the years about his purported contact with Lyn, his efforts to find her and, perhaps most importantly, the so-called sightings by others of Lyn, including at a fruit barn near Gosford.

In 2014, Rebecca Hazel had emailed the New South Wales Police media team to seek an interview with Paul Mayger or Stuart Wilkins about their 1990–91 investigation.

Damian Loone had already told Rebecca that when he started investigating anew in 1998, he was handed a missing persons file for Lynette Joy Dawson.

'He has said there was one piece of paper in that file and that the interview that Mayger and Wilkins conducted with Chris Dawson had not been transcribed,' Rebecca wrote to the police media team. 'I am putting all of this in my book and am giving New South Wales Police an opportunity to explain what happened to that investigation. It would be very helpful to understand the decision not to pursue the investigation and to understand how and why the matter was concluded.'

Rebecca's request was stymied; she would not be getting any help from New South Wales Police.

Rebecca's points were strong and legitimate. Why had the Homicide Squad's first investigation fizzled out? Neither Paul Mayger nor Stuart Wilkins had given evidence at either of the inquests. Deputy State Coroner Carl Milovanovich, in his closing remarks at the second inquest, spoke of police 'losing the trail and losing documented material' including Bankcard statements and insurance policies.

Magistrate Milovanovich opined, 'I have little doubt that had this missing person report been prioritised differently at the time and some preliminary inquiries made in relation to the various persons that were involved and associated with Lyn Dawson at the time, the investigation might have taken a different course.'

Paul Mayger was difficult to locate, which was unsurprising given he must have made a lot of enemies as the state's longest serving homicide cop. I left messages with relatives but I never heard from the detective. When he retired in 2007, the *Sydney Morning Herald* published an article which quoted the then acting superintendent Ian Lynch: 'In relation to Paul's depth of experience and the level of sacrifice that he's made in terms of his family life, I couldn't speak more highly of the man. He had it all: professionalism, drive and pure dedication.'

His understudy, Stuart Wilkins, the youngest detective promoted to the Homicide Squad when he went in as a 24-year-old, was easier to find. He had risen quickly through the ranks to become an assistant commissioner and might have gone all the way to the top job but for internal politics. After 37 years of service, Stuart retired from the police force at just 55 and settled at Palm Beach, on the southern end of the Gold Coast.

When I spoke to Alina Rylko, a reporter from *The Northern Star* newspaper, about a piece she had written about Stuart's impressive career, she offered to call him and ask him to contact me. Stuart rang me the same afternoon and when I explained the case and reminded him of his connection, he confirmed he was happy to be interviewed for a podcast.

The night before I drove to Stuart's house, my sister Rebecca hosted a Christmas party and invited a number of legends of rugby league, friends who had supported her and her husband, Brett Frizelle, in their running of the Gold Coast Titans in the National Rugby League competition, and their bid to own and bankroll the team.

Among the club's many fans at this time were Chris and Paul Dawson, who regularly drove to Titans games and training. Other fans and Titans staff recognised the brothers because of their flashy playing days with the Newtown Jets in the 1970s. If anyone on the sidelines remembered the sordid allegations surrounding their teaching careers and the convenient disappearance of a wife, it didn't spoil the vibe.

Rebecca knew about my investigation into Chris Dawson; whenever she called for a chat, it was all I wanted to talk about. The twins would have had no idea that they were backing my sister's family business when they supported the Gold Coast Titans.

At the party I also spoke about the podcast investigation and the Dawsons to Matthew Johns, a legendary former five-eighth for the Newcastle Knights and a great storyteller who delved into rugby league's often murky history. His face lit up. As a small boy, he had watched the Dawson twins play for the Newtown Jets, and in later years he learned of the club's fearsome reputation and its gangland connections. Matthew Johns hinted darkly that the twins played for a team which had a criminal underbelly with long tentacles. He urged me to be cautious, even all those years later.

At his home 150 metres from the waves, Stuart Wilkins, a self-confessed 'rugby league tragic' who had played at a high level in Sydney and was seeking to give back to local teams on the Gold Coast as a coach, had been reviewing the documents I'd emailed him – the transcript of the 1991 interview with Chris Dawson, and the 1998 statement of Damian Loone. These were key pieces of evidence at the inquests in 2001 and 2003.

'I've got to say, I don't have the world's greatest memory of it,' Stuart told me at the outset. 'I suppose on reflection, my concern was those two blokes were doing the wrong thing at school as well, with schoolkids, and if that was in today's environment, they would be in the can for having sex with schoolkids.'

Stuart told me that prior to the visit to the Gold Coast in January 1991, he and Paul Mayger had interviews with witnesses including Lyn's family as part of a review triggered by Jenny's 1990 return to Sydney, and her contact with police and Lyn's family.

'It was one of those cases, in a homicide investigation where you either go all guns blazing, straight in, or you wait and sit back and get as much possible information that you can, prior to interviewing any potential persons of interest or suspects. Of course, the last thing we would have done was come and spoken to Christopher Dawson,' he said.

'I do distinctly remember using some modern technology back then, or groundbreaking technology, and that was the ground impulse radar because there was a suggestion that she was deceased or she had been murdered, and the possibility that we thought was that she may very well be underneath the pool that had been built at the family home. We used that ground impulse radar to have a look to see if we could see any skeletal remains in the ground around the pool.

'Then we flew up here to the Gold Coast and spoke to one of the persons of interest, Christopher Dawson.'

When I asked his view about what had happened to Lyn, Stuart said, 'Sometimes you come to a suspected homicide and you have all the suspicions in the world and you have all the information you can possibly get. And sometimes it's just not enough.'

Chris's answers in the 1991 interview were, Stuart believed, vague.

'And whilst there's suspicion attributed to them – and there's no question in my mind that that poor woman is deceased – but to actually go through the process of attributing enough evidence and getting to a case where you would be able to prosecute, the answers in this interview and the information and evidence were probably just short.

'You'll see during the interview that he was cautioned that he need not answer any further questions. In our minds, we had potentially enough evidence to head down a criminal path.

The caution is of course that anything you say will or can be used against you in a court of law. We don't do that lightly.

'The law expects us as investigators to ensure that if we think we've got enough evidence to at least put a charge, or put someone before a court in any format, that we should caution them before we actually speak to them, and I've been in a number of homicide investigations where unfortunately that caution wasn't delivered prior to police asking questions of suspects and the actual information and the answers to those questions have been precluded from being accepted at court because of those rules of evidence.'

Early in the interview, Chris spoke of 'some guy erecting our shed or something who was tied up in a religious sect who Lyn sought some comfort from insofar as he was asking her to come along to the meetings and giving her literature and all'.

Detective Sergeant Paul Mayger asked Chris about new information received by police.

'It's been alleged by Jenny that on one occasion prior to Lyn leaving you, sometime between October and December 1981 . . . you went to a hotel and that she remained in the car whilst you went inside and you came out a short time later and you drove back to Bayview, and that some weeks later you said to her, "Remember when I went out to that pub? I went to get a hitman to kill Lyn but I decided that I couldn't do it because innocent people would be killed." What do you have to say about that allegation?'

Chris replied, 'Complete and utter fabrication.'

Mayger continued. 'Also according to Jenny, from what she could see and because of her familiarity with Lyn's possessions, having lived in your house, she maintains that none of Lyn's clothing or personal belongings were missing from the house. Is that correct?'

'Very, very few of Lyn's possessions were missing, that's correct.'

The recording machine bleeped shortly after 4.20 pm and the interview was suspended, then restarted with fresh tapes.

For the first half of the interview, before the formal caution, Paul Mayger went over some of the known narrative which had fallen from Chris's mouth over the previous nine years.

'Would you care to tell me now what transpired at that time, please?'

Chris said, 'Prior to my wife leaving me in January 82, we were having some matrimonial problems. I went on a brief time away to try to clarify how I felt. I came back from a few days up here in Queensland, Lyn and I went to marriage guidance to try to sort things out.'

He confirmed that the marriage counselling at Manly appeared to go well for them and he left with Lyn feeling optimistic.

Mayger: 'Do you recall prior to you meeting this guidance counsellor, apparently the building that you went to see him in, you travelled up to his floor in a lift? Is that correct?'

Chris: 'Yeah.'

Mayger: 'Do you recall when you and Lyn were in the lift together that you grabbed her around the neck and said, "If this doesn't work, I'll get rid of you"?'

Chris: 'No. Not at all.'

He said that he took Lyn to the Mona Vale bus stop in the morning, then returned home and had breakfast with his daughters before the three of them headed to Northbridge Baths. When Lyn's mother, Helena, arrived by bus from the family home of Clovelly after lunch, Lyn still had not arrived and, Chris said, 'I was sort of asking where my wife was'.

'She said she didn't know so we presumed she was still shopping and would meet me at work during the afternoon some time. The girl who worked in the shop called me over and said there was an STD [long distance] phone call for me, she'd taken the call. I went there, I took the phone call. It was Lyn. She said she needed time away, like I had had prior to that day and she'd ring me in a few days after she'd had time to sort things out. I had, in the following few weeks, several phone calls from Lyn, all STD calls, saying that she needed extra time, she needed more time to sort it out.

'Then after about the third phone call, she said she needed a lot more time and she didn't know if she would be returning. I had friends at Belrose Rugby League Club who worked in the police force and I asked them to try and help locate Lyn's whereabouts. A friend of mine on the Central Coast told me she'd seen Lyn in a car on the Central Coast. In fact, my friends from Belrose told me that if they located her, although they weren't supposed to tell me, they'd sort of let me know where she was so that I could speak to her if she didn't want them disclosing her whereabouts.'

He said that he was 'constantly in touch with people' to try to find Lyn, however, her telephone calls to him had ceased after a few weeks.

Paul Mayger revisited Chris's opening spiel about having gone away to clarify how he felt about the marriage. 'You say you left home the previous Christmas for a few days, where did you go when you left home?'

Chris said, 'I came up to Queensland with the girl that I was having an affair with at the time.'

The detective had information from Jenny that the day after Lyn disappeared, Chris wanted her to leave South West Rocks, where she was staying with her Cromer High friends and her sisters, and return to the house at Bayview with him. Lyn's house. For me, this has always been one of the most deeply suspicious aspects of the case: moving a teenage girlfriend into his and Lyn's bed a day after Lyn had purportedly told him she needed a few days away makes no sense, unless Chris already knew that Lyn was never coming back.

Disputing Jenny's claim that she returned at his insistence, Chris told the detective, 'She telephoned me and asked me could she, like, come back, more or less, I think she wanted to get away from South West Rocks, more or less.'

Chris told Paul Mayger that it was 'a week or so after'. Later evidence would show he drove to South West Rocks to collect Jenny as early as Sunday 10 January.

'I didn't ask Jenny to come and live with me ... She ended up coming to live with me because she wasn't wanted anywhere else.

Okay, she wasn't wanted at home because she had a dispute at home. I remember going down to Manly Warringah Women's Refuge with Jenny while they were sort of counselling her on where she could stay and go. And I naively now offered she could come and stay with me until, you know, such time . . .'

Paul Mayger questioned him about his purported contact with Lyn in the weeks after she had 'left'. He asked Chris about the logic of such a drastic step by Lyn when, just the day before, she and Chris had gone from marriage counselling to the childcare centre and were seen holding hands, and later that night, Lyn had told her mother Helena that everything was going to be fine as the counselling had worked and the marriage was back on track.

Chris said he believed the counselling had been 'fairly positive' but that Lyn began to get 'negative at night time' and had started to question whether the visit to a stranger to talk about their marriage was worthwhile.

He said Lyn told him that her Simms family background was not as happy as that of Chris in the Dawson family, and she was also upset that the counsellor had blamed Lyn for the tensions in her marriage to Chris.

Stuart Wilkins put it this way as we spoke at his kitchen table: 'We asked him direct questions about his movements, what information he's given to other people. And it's almost like setting a trap, setting up to fail, for want of a better term.'

'Do you sometimes walk away from interviews with a suspect and you just have a feeling in your guts that they're right for it or not right for it?' I asked.

'It happens a lot. There are certainly cases and I've had a couple of them myself, distinctly, where you know that wrongdoing has taken place and you know that someone has killed another person. But it's just that unfortunate process that you just fall short on the evidence. And whilst you know, unfortunately knowing something and proving something are two completely different things and they're worlds apart.

'He was a significant figure in rugby league and quite a strong figure on the Northern Beaches. People probably, I suppose, didn't want to think that he could have done something untoward to his wife. And people wanted to think that Lyn Dawson's still okay. People want to put their hands over their ears and go, "This is not happening." Unfortunately, at the start, it wasn't murky and he was perceived to be the grieving husband.

'And that's maybe why it wasn't the most in-depth investigation to start with. Powerful influences or personalities can be an influence. So if they're giving a semi-plausible story about this is what's happened – and there's a timeline – sometimes people will accept it. I think that happened in this case to some degree.'

As I scoured the 42 pages of transcript of Chris's 1991 interview for clues and leads, a curious purported sighting of Lyn by someone who had known her stood out.

Here's how Chris put it: 'I mean, this friend of mine and Lyn's said she'd seen Lyn on the Central Coast, I presumed she was on the Central Coast for at least, for a little while after that, anyway.'

Chris named the friend as Sue Butlin, wife of Ray Butlin, the manager of a Gosford Rugby League Club when the Dawson twins had played there after their first-grade careers with the Newtown Jets.

'We used to spend every Sunday together. So if Sue had seen Lyn, she'd know it was definitely her . . .'

Paul Mayger asked, 'Do you recall whether she said that it was Lyn or it looked like Lyn?'

'I'd say she was fairly positive that she'd seen Lyn.'

This was a potentially devastating blow to the proposition that Lyn had been murdered by Chris on or around 8 January 1982. I tried to investigate this claim and began looking for Ray Butlin. A relatively recent image on Facebook showed him in a chummy embrace with Chris and Paul Dawson. Ray did not return my calls. His wife Sue died seven years after Chris nominated her as a witness highly likely to have seen Lyn 'in a car' at a fruit barn. I was very sceptical about it.

I asked Stuart to recall the view he formed of Lyn from the interviews he and Paul had done.

'She seemed like a normal mother, a normal wife. She worked, she looked after her kids. She seemed healthy and happy. There was no indication whatsoever that she was suicidal.'

Then I asked, 'In your policing career, can you recall cases where mothers of young children have left the family home to get away, think things over, start a new life even, and never had any contact with their children or their siblings or their parents or their friends or anyone again – but they're still alive? Have you ever come across that?'

Stuart replied quickly. 'No. Nup. Rarely does a woman up and run away. It's very, very difficult not to be found.'

'And in your view, what are the chances that Lyn Dawson's changed her identity or has disappeared and is living happily somewhere?'

'Highly, highly, highly unlikely. Never say never – because it could possibly happen – but I don't think that's a possibility in this case.'

Stuart struggled to remember if anything in particular caused the investigation to end in 1991. He gave up. I wondered at the time whether the purported sighting of Lyn by the wife of a mate of the only suspect was a factor. It was unclear to me why the detectives had not interviewed Paul Dawson and Marilyn Dawson on the Gold Coast in 1991. Stuart could not recall.

I thought about Lyn's two daughters and how they'd grown up being told that their mother abandoned them and that she didn't want to come back. The emotional cruelty left a bitter taste.

Outside Stuart's house again, a sea breeze took the edge off the heat and humidity of the December afternoon. I knew from research before our interview that he had been integral in homicide investigations in the mid-1990s, including those which led to the conviction of the serial killer Ivan Milat. Stuart helped persuade a key witness, Paul Onions, who had escaped from Milat's moving car and narrowly avoided being shot as he sprinted down the road, to give crucial evidence which sealed Milat's fate.

My close friend Terry Martin, one of Queensland's most respected criminal defence lawyers, had gone above and beyond the call of duty in an extraordinary and almost successful representation of Milat. We stood on the footpath and Stuart told me the homicide detective's unspoken subtext when questioning a prime suspect, like Ivan Milat. Or Chris Dawson: 'We know you did it. You know that we know you did it. But we've got to prove it.'

Stuart was in no doubt about Milat's guilt. I was sure he felt similarly about Dawson.

Rebecca Hazel was curious to know how the interview went. I told her that Stuart Wilkins was fair-minded, candid and interesting. 'He described a murderer's two biggest risks. One, that they will tell someone else who will give them up.

'And two, that they will leave evidence behind that is incriminating. The second risk doesn't arise. And as for the first risk, who knows? Everyone has kept their mouths shut.'

Chapter 15

Cops and Smacka

Rebecca Hazel and I planned to catch up at Circular Quay to talk about the next round of interviews I wanted to do in Sydney. On the telephone and in text messages we talked at length about the case and our impressions of some of the evidence. We shared our suspicions about some key events and moments which were conveniently favourable to Chris Dawson.

The failure of police to question Lyn's work friends and look into potential foul play after January 1982 was very odd. The disappearance of almost all the files and interview statements collected by the Homicide Squad detectives, Paul Mayger and Stuart Wilkins, as well as the unexplained termination of their investigation after the videotaped interview with Chris in Queensland, was bizarre. There has never been a suggestion of wrongdoing by those two highly regarded cops but it was impossible to give the benefit of the doubt to others.

It was little wonder that Lyn's brothers suspected Chris had been protected by police. In the 1970s and 80s, rugby league players and cops were more likely to scratch each other's backs. The police force and first-grade rugby league teams were culturally aligned: male-dominated, testosterone-fuelled and ruggedly opposed to unwelcome scrutiny.

The worshipful adulation of successful footballers made things worse. I told Rebecca that Stuart Wilkins had described the Dawson

twins as fine players with great charisma, although he had hastened
to add that it had not influenced the questioning of Chris in 1991.

'He volunteered that their good name and celebrity undoubtedly
would have influenced uninformed police to not think of them as the
worst at the time,' I texted her.

That was probably an understatement. The present era's media
interest in footballers and their lives away from the field did not exist
in the early 1980s. If a married mother of two little girls had disappeared in Sydney in 2017, it would be front-page news and the media
attention would only snowball.

The coverage would be exponentially greater if the missing
woman turned out to be the wife of a former first-grade footballer.
In Lyn's case there was not even a single column snippet in the local
newspaper, *The Manly Daily*. When Chris finally yielded to Helena's
urgings to go to the police station to report her daughter as a missing
person in mid-February 1982, the cops did the bare minimum.

The little that was known about this initial report to police emerged
during Damian Loone's 1998 investigation, and he set it out in the statement he provided to the coroner. He quoted from an internal police
report prepared in 1985 by then Inspector Geoff Shattles in response to
a letter written by Lyn's work colleague, Sue Strath, to the New South
Wales Ombudsman about the lack of police activity. Sue's 1985 letter
was among the documents that disappeared but an official rebuttal of
it survived in the Shattles report. Another suspicious coincidence.

The Shattles report states that Chris Dawson went into the Mona
Vale police station at 9.15 am on 18 February 1982 and reported to
Sergeant Gibbons that Lyn had been missing since 15 January 1982.
Chris had described the circumstances surrounding him dropping
Lyn off at 7 am on Saturday 9 January so that she could do some
shopping, her failure to come to the Northbridge Baths as planned
and her telephone calls to him about her needing some time away.

There were some further details which must have allayed suspicion. Chris told the desk sergeant that a check of Lyn's Bankcard
statements revealed she had used it on 12 January, and that she had
called him on 15 January 'and stated she needed more time to think.

He had not heard from her since that date and he was of the opinion that she may have gone to a religious group on the north coast.'

In his report for senior officers, who were being asked questions by the Ombudsman's office about the adequacy of early investigations, Inspector Shattles stated that Sergeant Gibbons forwarded information to the Missing Persons Unit at Police Headquarters. Chris Dawson was followed up several times through February and March with telephone calls and told police that he 'could not offer any further information'.

On one occasion in April 1982, Lyn's father, Len, was contacted; later in April, Lyn's mother, Helena, got a call from police. On 29 April, Constable Snook of Mona Vale detectives spoke to Chris Dawson who disclosed 'that he and his wife had marriage problems for some 18 months past. They had attended a psychiatrist on the day prior to his wife leaving home to try and resolve the issue and were to attend again. He further stated that at the time of his wife leaving, she had $500 in her possession.'

The next significant part of the report concerned a development in August 1982, when Lyn's mother and Chris were asked to prepare for the Missing Persons Unit 'a full profile on the missing person and include all sources of information, friends, associates and relatives'. These were duly completed, according to the Shattles report, with 'nothing appearing in them to lead to any suspicion of foul play'.

On its face, this was a head-scratching assertion by the senior officer, particularly after he had already documented the disclosure by Chris of marital difficulties. A little further on, his report described the routine follow-up of Chris and Helena, some purported sightings of Lyn and, on 10 November 1983, news from Lyn's mother 'that Mr Dawson had obtained a divorce from her daughter she believed in July and was about to marry Jenny Carlson, who had been the babysitter at the home'.

It was hard to read this and not be appalled by the incuriousness of trained police. They were made aware of a disappearance which was completely out of character, marital difficulties, a hasty divorce in absentia and marriage to a teenager who had been the babysitter.

Yet all these facts failed to set off alarm bells at police headquarters, where Shattles wrote a report justifying the police actions to date and effectively blaming Lyn's family.

His report adds: 'Further to this, the brother of the missing person is a senior constable in the New South Wales Police Force and he at no time contacted police at this station in regard to any suspicions he has had regarding the disappearance of his sister.'

It is a notorious fact that police corruption in New South Wales was endemic at the time. In the police Criminal Investigation Branch in Kings Cross alone, rampant bribery, money laundering, drug trafficking, fabrication and destruction of evidence, fraud and serious assaults of witnesses were uncovered. The revelations flowing from a royal commission, led by Justice James Wood for three years from 1994, exposed what he described in his final report as 'deep-seated corruption and criminality'. A criminal milieu of dangerous offenders – some of whom were sworn officers – were protected and even effectively commissioned to commit crime with immunity.

Justice Wood also identified widespread 'process corruption' in which officers were effectively useless although not receiving bribes to turn a blind eye to crime. He attributed this malaise to 'poor investigative practices, lax supervision, insufficient emphasis in formal training and, in the field, on the unacceptability of police breaking the law to secure convictions, and long-standing acceptance within the Criminal Investigation Branch and specialist squads of the notion that the end justifies the means'.

Detective Sergeant Brian 'Smacka' Gardner was a dedicated rugby league fan and, for several years spanning the Dawson playing days, the president of the Belrose club. As a copper, he was what was known with a wink and a nudge as 'old-school'. In an era with less regard for policy and procedure, Brian had enforced the law and caught criminals on his own terms.

The father of three daughters had a lofty reputation among detectives and criminals on the Northern Beaches for his community-minded contributions. His luring of the talented twins Chris and Paul as captain-coaches of Belrose was a masterstroke.

For Chris and Paul, accepting the offer to play for Belrose meant that, despite having retired from first-grade rugby league, they could still run out together, play a hard game every week and receive accolades and cash for coaching and captaining. The standard of play they were used to at the Newtown Jets, even on a bad day, was far ahead of Belrose.

In his interview with the Homicide Squad's detectives in 1991, Chris name-dropped Gardner, claiming he was told that he could rely on Brian to let him know about Lyn in the event that she was located alive and well.

When I talked to Stuart Wilkins about this at his home in early December 2017, he recounted the reference. 'He mentioned the name Brian Gardner, who I knew quite well. He was a detective senior sergeant and a very well qualified and very well respected police officer. And [Chris] just threw his name in as either an associate or "I've asked this detective senior sergeant if he can follow up on my wife."'

Stuart told me that he and Paul Mayger spoke to those officers named by Chris. One of them was Ian Kennedy, a straight-shooting detective who had gone to school with and played football with the twins. In later years, he would help solve the sadistic sexual assault and murder of Sydney nurse and beauty queen, Anita Cobby. According to Chris, Ian Kennedy had told Chris at a school reunion of a report or a suggestion in police circles that Lyn had turned up in New Zealand. When asked by investigating police about this account, Ian described Chris's claims as nonsense; a lie.

When I contacted Ian Kennedy, who had retired, he politely declined to talk about it. He had not ruled out being called as a witness if ever the case went to trial.

I learned something about Brian Gardner by finding his death notice from September 2015 in a newsletter, 'Still Talking', published by the Laryngectomee Association of New South Wales of which Brian had been a hard-working and long-standing president until he died at 77.

The eulogy said Brian loved all sporting pursuits, especially rugby league.

'His fellow police will remember him for his strong sense of moral obligation and the importance of punishing those who committed crimes or harmed others. I think all of us will remember Brian for his warm-hearted nature, kindness, sense of humour and for all the hard work he put into those causes he was passionate about. He will be sadly missed.'

Another police officer who was connected with the Belrose Rugby League Club and named by Chris in his 1991 interview had risen to become a detective sergeant in 1998. He knew Damian Loone and agreed to make a statement for the fellow Northern Beaches detective's investigation.

The cop told Damian that in the early 1980s, he was asked by Detective Sergeant Brian Gardner to play for the first-grade team in return for a free overseas trip once a year and a bit of cash.

He described the Dawson twins: 'They never had much time for the other players and really stuck to themselves. I remember on a number of occasions they would turn up for training at our oval and they would be wearing exactly the same clothing. From the jersey right down to their socks and runners.'

After a game, every player would stay in the dressing room and have a beer. Except for the twins, who would drink only Coca-Cola. After training on Monday and Wednesday nights, the players would go to the President Hotel at Belrose but Chris and Paul stayed away.

'Chris and Paul Dawson were unusual people. They were unsociable and only mixed with themselves. They were introverted and felt vulnerable without each other.'

One Sunday in 1981 or 1982, Chris arrived with a strikingly attractive teenager. 'He had a girl walking with him that was about 17 years old, blonde hair, great figure and she was very good-looking,' the detective said in his 1998 statement. 'I thought to myself, "He's having an affair with one of his students."'

The detective did not act on his suspicions.

The Crimes Act in the section relating to what was termed 'carnal knowledge' had an additional hook to ensure that people in positions of authority – 'being a schoolmaster or other teacher' – would be guilty if they had sex with a girl under the age of 17. It was punishable by a term of imprisonment of up to eight years.

The detective recruited by Brian Gardner suspected what was going on between Chris and his student. It is probable that the club's president knew too. How many others turned a blind eye?

'I'm going to try to contact and see him on this upcoming trip,' I told Rebecca.

It would be a delicate approach. A short time after the footballing cop gave his statement to Damian Loone, it was alleged that he corruptly received cash and stolen property, solicited and received bribes, tampered with evidence with the intention of misleading a judicial tribunal, committed certain actions with the intention of perverting the course of justice, obtained unauthorised access to police data, stolen cash, and made a false statement.

He had pleaded guilty in 2002 to four corruption charges and received a five-year prison sentence.

'If I were him, I wouldn't talk to us because of the likelihood of his own corruption and jail term being raised publicly again but we can try.'

I found the former detective on Facebook and sent him a message in which I mentioned having interviewed Stuart Wilkins the day before.

'It's about the Lyn Dawson case – I've read your statement about Chris and Paul, it went to the coroner and became a public exhibit back in 2001. It's a case that troubles a lot of people. I thought you might be prepared to talk about the things you raised in your statement.'

He replied, 'With all due respect, I don't talk to current cold-case detectives or journalists. That part of my life is behind me. I sit on the other side of the fence now. Once in jail, you learn not to talk. It's about self-preservation.'

Chapter 16

Pat Jenkins

In a two-bedroom flat with sweeping views over the Sydney Harbour Bridge and the city's skyscrapers, Pat Jenkins silently read pages of notes which she had written out longhand for our recorded interview in early December 2017.

This kind and compassionate widow, whom I had met back in 2001 when she cooked me dinner after my long day reading the police brief of evidence in the station at Dee Why, was no longer in excellent health. But Pat was committed and fiercely determined to do her very best for her sister's sake.

'If I'm tired, I slur, after the stroke but I'm good today,' Pat said. 'But I think I'm not going to do a good job for Lyn.'

Pat's nervousness was audible as she started to read. I exchanged a knowing look with Nick Adams-Dzierzba, one of *The Australian*'s audio producers who had come to the flat to help me with the interview. Pat wanted to speak and answer questions naturally but she was understandably anxious. The build-up to the interview, Nick's recording equipment, and her stroke were all contributing factors.

As we gently persuaded Pat to speak from the heart rather than the sheaf of loose papers, Greg Simms, who had driven down from his home near Newcastle to help his sister, offered slices from one of Merilyn's freshly baked banana cakes. He shared an update he'd just received from an ABC TV staff member as a result of his request for a copy, if one still existed, of the *Chequerboard* documentary on twins featuring Lyn, Chris, Paul and Marilyn.

'From what he was saying, it doesn't look extremely favourable that there's any recordings at all,' Greg told me.

I asked him to request that they press ahead with the search anyway, and the newspaper would reimburse him the $165 fee.

'I would just love to see Lyn and hear her talking on the tape,' I replied.

Pat told me about the former deputy head of Cromer High Hylton Mace, who had told her some 18 months earlier that he was unhappy with Chris's conduct with Jenny and had refused the PE teacher's request for a favourable reference.

'I wonder why things weren't said about things that were going on by people in charge but I don't want that said,' Pat told me.

Her reticence about calling out the cavalier approach of the school's leadership to teachers having sex with teenage students perplexed me. 'Why don't you want that? I mean, isn't that their duty to be doing these things and looking after the students?'

Pat replied, 'Absolutely. But I think a lot of things happened then, at Forest High and obviously Cromer, and nothing was done about it, between teachers and students.'

'The students in the school are surely in the care of any teacher from that school?'

'The playground was like their playground. They had their victims.'

Greg chimed in. 'They were hunters.'

Pat agreed. 'Yeah, they were. It's a good word for them.'

As Pat became comfortable and reached back four decades, I heard for the first time that Lyn felt she was on the outer not just with her husband but with his mother too.

'The twins were very spoilt. Chris's mother, she idolised them, and she could be quite nasty with a couple of things she said to Lyn. She certainly would always take his side and was rather vindictive against Lyn. She said that Lyn had champagne tastes on a beer budget, and she said, "Oh, you're just a glorified babysitter."

'And, I mean, Lyn had gone through nursing at the children's hospital. She worked for Geoffrey Edelsten over at Coogee. She'd worked for Dr Peter Baume who was later Senator Baume. Then she was on a team that was doing research at Royal North Shore into post-operative pain. She was doing her best, trying to save money for the family and that was the opportunity she had, to work at the child-minding centre.'

After Lyn's disappearance, Pat told me, Lyn's daughter Shanelle told her grandmother Helena that she had been told Lyn was 'only their pretend mother' and that Jenny was to be called mum from then on.

'They were also told their mother had left them because she didn't love them,' Pat said. 'The older daughter told me they were never allowed to talk about Lyn as they grew up. It was never said, "I remember when we did this with Lyn". And photos of Lyn, Chris got rid of them. It was as if she never existed.'

Pat began to cry as she recalled one of her enduring memories of Lyn rushing down the driveway with her arms outstretched to greet Pat and her husband Ron's three little boys, enveloping them in a big hug.

'I'll always remember that moment, it just shows her loving nature towards children,' she said.

Pat was momentarily broken. We shifted gears and went further down the memory tunnel to her childhood, growing up beside the Pacific Ocean at Clovelly, swimming and walking the coastline, and sharing a bedroom with Lyn.

'I've got a picture on my iPad of Lyn. She was only about maybe six. We'd walk around from Clovelly around Thompson's Bay which is now Gordon's Bay, right round to South Coogee and we'd swim in the middle of winter and in the summer we'd swim at the Sydney Ladies Swimming Club. When we were very little, we'd go around to a place called the Bogey Hole, which was behind Clovelly and there was always a watchful mother sitting above near the flats, watching that everything was okay.

'Certainly when she was younger, she'd call a spade a spade. She would stand up for what she thought was right. I always thought she was the brightest of the four of us.'

Pat recalled that Lyn had met Chris at a dance when they were both prefects of high schools – Sydney Girls and Sydney Boys – 'and they seemed like a lovely couple'. The schools were neighbouring and Pat recalls notes being passed over the fence by students in a relationship or wanting to start one.

'But you know, thinking back, I mean, obviously now we realise we didn't know him at all. Because, as Lyn said, there was a dark side to him that nobody knew. I don't think he really related to us. He was quiet. He didn't seem to be outgoing.'

'But your mother adored him,' I said.

Pat sighed. 'Yes, well, they had the image, Lyn and Chris, they always looked lovely together. The children always looked beautiful. Yeah, Mum thought he was a very fine young man. He didn't drink and didn't smoke. Maybe she thought he was a very clean-living person. I don't know. But her ideas about him changed, especially when Jenny was on the scene. And even at that stage, though, Mum still held out hope that she would see Lyn. There was no way that Mum could think she'd never see her beloved daughter again. She just couldn't cope with facing that.'

A calendar of Lyn's movements over the previous week is an instructive guide to her relationship with her mother. Lyn had spent the previous Friday 1 January, Saturday and Sunday with Helena and Len at the Simms home at Clovelly. Lyn had talked to her mother on the phone on Monday 4 January and again on Friday 8 January. They were close. Which made it harder to understand why the family accepted Chris's claims that Lyn was calling him – but could not call her mother or her siblings.

'He said, "Oh, Lyn said she'll ring you", meaning Mum, "when she feels she can". That was really cruel. Lyn supposedly rings Chris, the person that she's having a conflict with, and doesn't contact Mum.'

I asked, 'Perhaps Lyn went away and was struck by a car? Or had a misadventure with someone like Ivan Milat driving up the highway? Is there a possibility in your mind that something like that has happened? That Lyn wanted to get away for a couple of days and then had a terrible accident or fell into the hands of a violent, random serial killer? And that's why we've never heard from her?'

Pat gave the theories short shrift. Lyn would not have just upped and left without so much as a call to Helena to say, 'Mum, I'm having difficulties. I've got to get my thoughts together.'

'She would have rung Mum or us in the following weeks. We loved her,' Pat said. 'But Mum could never give up hope. It was only at Dad's funeral, when she kept on looking at the back door. I said, "Mum, what are you doing? Why are you looking at the back door of the chapel?"

'And Mum said she was looking for Lyn, and she knew Lyn mustn't be alive otherwise she would have come to Dad's funeral. I mean, that's not really logical but that's the way Mum felt. Mum and Dad didn't deserve that. Well, none of us did.

'Every time there's a news report of a body being found along the Pacific Highway, usually north of Sydney, you'd wait in horror, and then you'd hear, "Oh, it's a male". Or the wrong age or something. And it wasn't Lyn. Now, I really believe she's buried somewhere near the house. Around the house or out the back. It was just bushland then but now it's roads and houses.'

Pat handed me more copies of some of her mother's handwritten letters and diary pages to read on my return to Brisbane. Helena's documents were filled with contemporaneously written details and facts about who said what and when. There were loose pages and random notes, sometimes only a couple of lines for each date. Whenever Chris rang with a snippet of information, Helena wrote it down with a date.

It was a sentimental store of potential evidence for a police brief. Pat was disappointed that it had not been part of Damian Loone's file. Damian had always intended to formally interview Helena but one thing led to another and he had not got around to it before she died. Pat told me that Damian was often hard to find when she or her mother had fresh information. He was being transferred to different police stations and Lyn's case was picked up again when he had time.

One day she came across a book called *The Kingdom of Illusions* by the journalist and author Richard Shears. The book delved into the crimes and criminal connections of Chris and Paul Dawson's Newtown Jets teammate Paul Hayward and his brother-in-law, contract killer Arthur 'Neddy' Smith. The book's revelations bolstered Pat's confidence in Jenny's evidence about having driven with Chris in late 1981 to a place to see someone about getting a hitman to kill Lyn. Pat had a nagging suspicion that Chris had gone to see Smith.

Pat resolved to write to Neddy Smith, who was in Long Bay Correctional Centre. She struggled to get the tone right. Pat didn't want to accuse him of being a hitman or of being contracted to kill Lyn. Instead, she explained how much Lyn meant to her family and she enclosed a photograph of the young mother holding one of the girls. Pat disclosed in her letter that she had relations with Parkinson's disease and that she hoped he was comfortable.

'What I hope you will find within yourself to do is to write, or if you are unable to do that because of your illness someone else could do it for you, to say you had family and social connections to Paul Hayward. That is all I need and I cannot tell you how much we would appreciate it if you could do that.'

In her three-page handwritten letter, Pat assured the contract killer that she was not suggesting he had murdered her sister.

'I am very sorry if you are offended by any inference I have made,' Pat added.

Long Bay's infamous inmate had turned informant about his crimes and his corrupting of police in Sydney in the 1980s. Pat's hope was that Smith would tell her he had been approached by Chris to murder Lyn and had declined the contract. A disclosure like this might be enough to change the DPP's mind about prosecuting Chris.

A senior prisons officer replied to Pat in writing in late 2010, stating that 'while we appreciate what you and your family are trying to achieve, a decision has been made not to allow inmate Smith to receive the letter'.

Pat gave me a handful of other letters that she and her cousin Wendy Jennings had exchanged with the Office of the DPP with each formal rejection of Damian's proposal to charge Chris with murder.

'Even Mum mentioned to me that she'd seen bruising on Lyn. In Mum's way, she would find a reason for this: "Oh, she must have something wrong with her blood."'

I asked, 'Do you remember visiting the house in 1981 and noting that some things didn't look as they should have?'

'Lyn was very houseproud. I particularly noticed she had these big hanging baskets with ferns hanging down, which looked absolutely beautiful in previous times. They were all dead. The ferns were dead. And I just had that feeling that the love wasn't in the house at that time. But I had no reason to suspect that she was being bashed. No reason at all.'

Pat suggested that Lyn tried very hard to protect her abusive husband.

Greg agreed. 'She was that much under his control. She didn't want to rock the boat.'

Pat recalled talking to Lyn soon after Chris had left just before Christmas 1981 'and she didn't know whether he was coming back or not because of the note that he left, because he'd taken all his clothes and even his pillow.

'She didn't know that he'd gone away with Jenny. And we certainly didn't know. Lyn had been waiting. He was supposed to pick her up from work and she'd done a big shop and she waited for an hour and he didn't come, so she rang his twin brother, Paul, who lived just up the street, and Paul said he didn't know where he was. So Lyn got a taxi home and when she got home, she found this note on the bed and all his clothes had gone.

'Chris said, "Don't paint too black a picture of me to the girls." And Lyn told me that she said to the girls, "Dad's had to go away suddenly on a holiday". And Lyn said that she gave the girls both a kiss and said it was from him.

'When I was speaking to her on the phone, she was very distressed. She was speaking really, really quickly and I could hear the murmur of voices in the background. That was Chris's parents who'd come to support her and I could hear them, so I'm sure they could hear what she was saying about Chris's anger. And she referred to "his black eyes flashing", they were her words. She said he was angry all the time at her and she felt for no reason he'd suddenly flare up at her. She wanted him to go and see a doctor in case there was a physical reason for it. She was really concerned because if Chris had gone and was not coming back, she was stuck there. She couldn't drive. And she said to me she didn't have much money.

'She also said that she didn't want to lose her job and she only had a short period of time off between Christmas and New Year. And the third thing she said was she wanted to stay there in case, as she called him, Chrissy came back.

'I was surprised at how candid she was being with Chris's parents sitting within hearing distance. Everything was just spilling out.'

Jenny had been a regular in the house for much of 1981; things came to a head in November.

'We knew Jenny was on the scene because she was staying with them. And when Lyn told me that Jenny was staying there, I just thought, "Oh, that's the sort of thing my sister would do. Welcome a young person who's in trouble into her home."'

Chris's brief stay in hospital for a nose operation six weeks before Christmas was a tipping point. He had told Lyn that she was not to visit him. Helena, genuinely fond of her son-in-law, went to see him. She walked in on Jenny, still in her school uniform, leaning over Chris in his hospital bed and dabbing his nose in a moment of obvious intimate affection.

Helena was shocked. When she got back to Clovelly and told her husband, Len, he replied, 'Tell Lyn to get that girl out of her house now.'

Hours later, Lyn was telling the teenager to leave. She delivered the genteel riposte: 'You've been taking liberties with my husband', as if Chris had somehow been entirely blameless; the helpless victim of a schoolgirl half his age. Jenny admitted to Lyn that she and Chris were in a relationship.

Pat described her surprise at the tumult unfolding shortly before Christmas, with Chris having abruptly walked out. It seemed that was the first time she realised her sister's marriage was in grave trouble.

Pat explained it this way: 'I believe it's this image, the happy family, beautiful children, the ideal sort of life. And everything was crumbling down. I don't think she could face that, the loss that was happening to her.'

As Lyn remained missing for weeks, then months and years without contact, her brothers and sister and mother still clung to hope. The idea of foul play would have forced them to confront the probability that Lyn was never coming back. They chose instead to wish for the impossible. Who could blame them?

On an outing, Shanelle asked her nanna why she hadn't been over to see the relatively new cubby house. It was Lyn's last present to her daughters. Helena replied that there was no spare room in the house at Bayview. Quick as a flash, Shanelle said that she could sleep in her father's bed 'because Jenny does'. It was the moment a horrified Helena realised the former babysitter was living in Lyn's home and sleeping in her bed.

But the mother of four had been so hopelessly misled in her grief and confusion that instead of suspecting foul play, she judged her daughter for having walked out on her daughters and husband.

'Mum said to me one time, "Lyn might have gone back to the house, seen Jenny was there, and so left,"' Pat said. 'Mum just could not comprehend that she'd never see Lyn again. There was always that hope.'

Helena took public transport to the Northern Beaches to stand on the sidelines while Chris and Paul played on weekends for the Belrose Eagles. It was her only way to see her granddaughters but she would usually return to Clovelly distressed because the Dawson brothers and their parents started to ignore her. Lyn was gone, replaced by a teenager. Out with the old; in with the new.

Helena was even more disposable. One day, Marilyn walked up to Helena on the sidelines of Lionel Watts Reserve in Frenchs Forest and said in a friendly greeting, 'And how are you today, Mrs Simms?' After weeks of feeling increasingly ostracised on those visits, the small act of kindness overwhelmed Helena, who burst into tears.

In her own young family at the time, Pat told me, the worry caused by Lyn's disappearance led to strains which needed to be carefully managed. For the sake of her husband, Ron, and their children, Pat had to make adjustments. Not knowing Lyn's fate, worrying she was cold and alone, consumed Pat. She made a conscious decision to put her family first. This didn't mean forgetting Lyn but it did result in her deciding that Lyn had moved on with her own life, as strange as that seemed, and Pat would need to move on with her life too.

Greg, watching his older sister explain this conditioning of her heart and mind, had said something similar when relating how he and Merilyn had to draw a line. There was a black hole into which Lyn had somehow fallen and if they were not careful, it would pull the rest of the Simms family in after her.

The early December sky, a vivid blue when we arrived, was changing. A vast quilt of angry cumulonimbus clouds had been steadily darkening over the city of Sydney and were now an angry, deep purple and looked ready to envelop the skyscrapers and the iconic bridge.

Pat appeared oblivious to the dramatic change in the weather. She was still working for Lyn, making sure she didn't forget to tell me the things she had jotted down, when the clouds finally broke with an earthshaking display of thunder, lightning and rain.

'I just wonder how different things would have been if Lyn had been alive, loving her children and bringing them up in her way,' Pat said. 'They had a wonderful mother who loved those children and looked after them beautifully. And instead she was replaced by a schoolgirl who obviously couldn't cope.'

*

We paused the recording and took a break for cake and a cup of tea as nature turned on a dramatic light and sound show.

I leafed through the loose documents Pat had brought to refresh her memory and help her to make points about her mother's despair, the tightrope the family walked to try to maintain a relationship with Lyn's two daughters to whom Chris could restrict access at any time and the DPP's repeated refusal to run a prosecution in the 16 years since 2001 when the case for murder was first presented.

'Is that recording?' I asked Nick Adams-Dzierzba, who nodded. 'Pat's just handed me an email and it's headed, "News from your dad", and it's from Chris Dawson to his daughter and it's dated August 2010.'

I read aloud this document, written by Chris to his daughter Shanelle, who had forwarded it soon after to her aunt, uncle and her half-sister, Jenny's daughter with Chris. Shanelle had omitted from the list her little sister, Amy, who regarded the murder case against her father as fake news and a conspiracy.

Hi Shanelle,

I must tell you an amazing bit of news from old acquaintances I heard this week. You will remember over the years me telling you about various sightings of your mum, such as seen across the road from Mona Vale PS by another parent a short while after she left, a woman telling your grandmother she saw your mum on the Northern Beaches. Another one on the Central Coast at a fruit stall on the side of the road by Sue Butlin. Sue is now deceased. As well as seen in the city by Elva McBay, who knew all of us very well – every week at the football for six years – at the procession of Prince Charles and Diana in 1983.

But, most exciting, after chasing these past leads up to the Central Coast and so forth, something happened this week.

In his email, Chris went on to explain that an acquaintance from his footballing days and his wife got in touch with him 12 months earlier to tell him that in a British episode of the TV series, *Antiques Roadshow,* 'there was a segment that showed a woman in the background that they both believed looked remarkably like your mum'.

When the episode was repeated on Australian television in August 2010, Chris wrote, his football mate's wife took a photograph of the mystery woman on the TV screen.

> The show was filmed in Padstow, near Cornwall in England, and the likeness to your mum is uncanny and has given us a strong sense of hope that at last her whereabouts may be known.
>
> It was a segment of footage where a woman was trying to get a valuation on a silver pig and Lyn was in the background. A New South Wales police detective told me years ago that your mum was in New Zealand and could easily have travelled beyond. Similarly, as you have found after a decade of world travel, how easy it would be to travel anywhere and remain uncontactable.
>
> After at least four sightings of her over a period of time, I have not lost belief that she may one day be found. I always prayed that her life choices, like yours, could then be acknowledged and her safety and wellbeing confirmed. Just as an aside, the woman who sent me the enclosed photo knew your Mum from football over a six-year period and also showed photos years ago and again recently to a clairvoyant at the city markets who on both occasions said she had no hesitation in saying she was still alive. My girl, perhaps you would like to forward this email to Aunty Pat and Uncle Greg, who may have police contacts they could use to follow up the sighting in the UK.
>
> You may also like to consider a visit to Padstow on your continuing travels around the world. We really can't say whether the woman in the photo is likely to be a resident of the area or a tourist. So I guess it is a long shot that you could meet, unless local police could be of assistance.
>
> Thinking of you, love as always, Dad.

I made a note to try to find out what was going on with the police investigation around the time Chris wrote it. Something had prompted this email. It was highly unusual for Chris to talk about Lyn. In his email, he does much more. Asking his daughter to share the email with Greg and Pat was bizarre; they had not talked for years.

Chris knew from statements Greg and Pat had made over the years to police and to journalists that Lyn's siblings despised him and wanted him rotting behind bars, not giving them seemingly thoughtful tips about Lyn's purported whereabouts near Cornwall.

His email coincided perfectly with the interest at the same time of *The Australian Women's Weekly* magazine, which published an article about Lyn's disappearance over several pages.

Chris's story was so obviously tactical and that made it all the more wicked. Exploiting his daughter's emotions and her longing for her mother, he sought to deflect suspicion of himself as the murderer and send Shanelle on a wild-goose chase to a place called Padstow, where a woman who didn't look much like Lyn at all had briefly popped up on TV.

By this stage, I had read hundreds of pages of evidence from the police brief of evidence as well as transcripts for the five days of public hearings of the second inquest run by Deputy State Coroner Carl Milovanovich in 2003. I had moved well beyond reasonable doubt. In my mind, Chris was indeed a coldblooded killer. And he had got away with it. So far.

If the podcast went the way I hoped, with reams of evidence put into the court of public opinion, there was still a chance for justice. Although I had wanted to remain coolly detached for the months ahead and during the production and release of the podcast, my position hardened and shifted several degrees. Pat sharing Chris's email was a large part of that shift. I read Shanelle's response – not to her father but to her Aunty Pat, Uncle Greg and her half-sister, Chris's daughter with Jenny – and tried not to show how it moved me, although my voice was clearly affected.

'Hello, my loves,' Shanelle began.

I hope you don't mind. I felt a need to share this email with you. It just goes to show me the extent to which this man will go to try and cover his own neck. Does he actually love me to try and plant a false seed of hope in my heart? Surely depriving me of a loving, nurturing person in my life is enough suffering. The utter selfishness of this man who claims to love me has me feeling utterly disgusted.

I think he must be feeling threatened. Aunty Pat, be assured that he is not leading a normal life. He is indeed suffering immensely. His spirit, his heart, and now his body. As the years of lies and deception seep out into his physical world, unable to remain suppressed and contained much longer. I know the truth will come out. It is universal law. I'm wanting to play my part in this too. Not to seek vengeance, but to honour my mother.

Love and light,

Shanelle.

This proof of Shanelle's clear-eyed view of her father was not news to her mother's side of the family. Up to this moment I had strongly doubted that she would be interviewed for the podcast. Pat, Phil, Greg and Merilyn had deliberately not mentioned to Shanelle, who was living in New Zealand, that I was investigating her mother's disappearance.

Amy had cut ties with her father's accusers on the Simms side. She told them, 'I don't want anything to do with this family anymore because you're persecuting my father.'

But I hoped Shanelle would learn about the podcast soon and consider talking to me about her mother.

'She's the last contact we have with our sister,' said Greg.

He lamented what he and Pat agreed was Chris's cowardice; his refusal to give evidence at the inquests in 2001 and in 2003; his rejection of interview requests in 1998. The only time Chris has spoken on the record in a formal police interview was 1991.

'Well, I hope he talks to me. I'd like to be able to put all of these things to him,' I told Greg and Pat.

Pat had an idea. 'Could you put your hands around his neck for me and give him a little squeeze?' she asked.

Greg had the last word. 'It comes down to one main thing. We all know that she wouldn't have left those two girls. She was told she'd never have children. They were even looking at adopting. You would love those children with every ounce of your being.'

Chapter 17

Catch a Killer

The rain was teeming and traffic had slowed to a crawl as Greg Simms went out of his way to drive Nick Adams-Dzierzba and me to a building in George Street in the Sydney CBD. I was privately glad that the short distance would take twice as long as predicted. For the first time, Greg was on his own. This gentle, easygoing man must have done it tough. Lyn's little brother was a serving cop when she disappeared. Greg knew that people wondered why he had not been suspicious until Jenny blew the whistle in 1990. I told him we were on our way to see Michael Barnes.

'He's had a really interesting career in Queensland and was instrumental in solving a terrible homicide involving a kid called Daniel Morcombe,' I explained to Greg. 'Against police wishes, he ran a coronial inquiry into that, which flushed out a lot of new evidence and was the precursor to a very successful police operation that finally captured the killer of that kid.'

Greg told me he wished New South Wales and Queensland police would cooperate in a joint operation 'to set Dawson up'. It was an obvious segue and with a little prodding, he went on to disclose that he had finally got out of the police force 'with anxiety and depression' in 2001. In February of that year, the first inquest into Lyn's suspected death revealed a circumstantial case of murder.

'I was just worn out. I never really got the chance to recover. It hit me like a rock,' he said. But, he was quick to add, he did not attribute his mental condition to stress over Lyn and his powerlessness in the police investigations.

'How important is it to catch a killer?' I asked. 'The killer of your sister?'

'That'd be like winning Lotto. It's extremely important we get a result for not only Lyn, for family and friends. We get a result to put someone away that has been hiding it for so long, and hopefully we can put her to rest. That's the main thing. If we find her.'

Greg wanted both outcomes. 'I think he's had enough freedom and he needs to actually be punished for what he's done and if we can find Lyn, in the process . . . yeah, I just keep thinking about the backyard. If Paul Dawson wasn't there, would he be cunning enough or smart enough to go and bury her in his brother's backyard?'

It seemed surreal. The windscreen wipers swishing the rain away violently, a busker under a shop awning on George Street playing a cheerful tune, Nick in the back seat with a boom mic extending almost all the way forward, and Greg Simms, a medically retired cop, raising possible burial plots for a sister whom we suspected had been dead for longer than she'd lived. Greg wanted to go back in time and stand outside the house in Gilwinga Drive 'and see things happen'. Not the crime of murder but the events leading up to it. And after it.

'Like they do on TV,' he said. It was a fantastical idea.

More realistic but still remote was a breakthrough in the ABC's search for video featuring Lyn, Marilyn and the Dawson twins in a long-lost 1975 documentary.

'We've got no recordings or anything of her. You never know. They might find something. I might be able to hear Lyn's voice again.'

Chapter 18

Michael

Some of the smartest and most interesting truth-seekers in the criminal justice system are the least heralded. As Queensland State Coroner for a decade until 2013, Michael Barnes was integral in helping crack open unsolved murder cases. In New South Wales, he struck several major blows with his coronial investigations of unlawful killings which were crying out for prosecution by an intransigent Office of the DPP. Michael is also endlessly curious and had become interested in Lyn Dawson's case since our catch-up at Icebergs a month earlier.

He agreed to be interviewed about missing persons cases generally. His observations of the circumstances of the early investigation of Lyn's case were logical. He acknowledged the very poor response by police in the 1980s.

'Equally, though, you've got to wonder about her parents just accepting it, including her brother who's a copper. I mean, they're the strange aspects of the case, aren't they?'

In a missing person investigation such as Lyn's, there is no obvious crime scene, no body and all the leads are cold. The longer it goes, the harder it is to rely on people's memories about what they saw or heard. Telephone records, credit card records and CCTV footage – all the information you would normally rely upon in a murder investigation – are all lost or destroyed. For far too long, investigative agencies did not countenance the probability that a significant number of missing person cases were in fact well-concealed homicides.

Michael offered an explanation as to why inquests are an effective mechanism for investigating suspicious cases.

'Police have thousands of files. Each detective is working on many, many matters. The trouble is, as occurred in this case and lots of others, people are quite adept at making the abnormal sound normal. The officer who receives the report knows nothing about the missing person other than what he's been told by the person reporting it. He can speak to that person. He can speak to other members of the missing person's family. But unless they raise concerns, it's difficult for the police to do anything else. It really depends upon what the officers are told by the only people who can give them information about the missing person.

'An inquest is looking at one case and it's putting all the resources into that one case and is doing it in a different way, through a different lens, than the usual police investigation. I'm not saying that lawyers are smarter than coppers or anything like that but they do look at things differently and test evidence differently. They're less likely to accept assurances or make presumptions. And that's easier to do when you've only got one case to look at. Someone else has done all the spadework and removed all the dross. So you can look at the bare bones of the investigation.'

In Lyn's case, however, the DPP had refused to run a trial after two coroners, Jan Stevenson and Carl Milovanovich, had each separately reached a conclusion that Lyn was dead and a known person could be successfully prosecuted over her murder.

I believed that the DPP had misunderstood some key evidence, resulting in a misguided belief that Lyn had been sighted after she disappeared. There were clues in the letter exchanges between Pat, her cousin Wendy Jennings and lawyers in the Office of the DPP, and their telephone conversations. Pat and Wendy, who took notes at the time, were adamant that a senior lawyer in the office made it clear to them that one of the reasons for declining a prosecution was the so-called sighting of Lyn by her mother Helena, some time after her disappearance; and, separately, at a fruit market near Gosford by Sue Butlin, who died before the first inquest. Helena had been looking for her daughter from the day she was supposed to see her at Northbridge Baths on 9 January 1982 until Helena's death, aged 85, in September 2001.

Wendy's handwritten note states: 'In August 2003 I spoke to a female solicitor in the DPP's office. She was part of the decision-making process on Lyn's case. A few issues she raised with me caused me enormous concern . . . this woman told me Lyn had been sighted by her own mother after she had disappeared.'

Pat told me she had spoken to the same solicitor who told a furious Pat the same thing about Helena having supposedly seen her daughter again. It was a nonsense.

And there was no evidence that police had talked to or taken a statement from Sue Butlin. I suspected it was a completely bogus sighting which had possibly led lawyers for the DPP up the garden path.

But there was no accountability mechanism; the DPP is not required to provide reasons for any decision. This statutory framework, Michael suggested, which allowed prosecution decisions to go unexplained 'might be a little unusual in this day and age, when almost all public officials have to give reasons for their decisions so that the community or their stakeholders can understand the basis of those decisions. But that's the system we've got'.

Michael had only been in the job as State Ombudsman for a few weeks. It was far removed from his brief stint as a journalist in Brisbane at a now-defunct tabloid newspaper, many years before I had met him.

'I was too careful. I used to think you had to get it all right. And someone said to me, "Don't get it right. Get it written. Doesn't matter if it's right as long as someone said it."'

It was an apt metaphor for truth as a relative concept.

I told Michael we were finding people who hadn't been interviewed for 20 years. I had no way of confirming that what they would tell me about Lyn, Chris and the events of 1982 was right or true but all of it would be part of the broad narrative arc of what I firmly believed was a case of coldblooded murder.

The next day, I would be going to the Northern Beaches to see Sue Strath, who worked with Lyn at the childcare centre.

'And in 1985, she'd become so frustrated and concerned that nothing had been done and that people had just got on with their lives, although Lyn's family was worried sick, that Sue put in a complaint to the Ombudsman about the police inaction on it and that led to a bit of a shake-up and attempted reinvestigation. Although we don't really know why that didn't go anywhere. I don't know whether it would be in the archives – Sue Strath's original complaint to the Ombudsman?'

Michael suggested it 'probably would be filed away'.

I needed to find it. If there had been an investigation by the Ombudsman in 1985, the possibility of documents and records of interview that had not been seen since could not be ruled out.

Rebecca raised it as we sipped tea in a cafe after leaving Michael's building.

'We don't have that full report. And that would be great if we could get our hands on that. You mentioned it to Michael today,' she said.

'I was hoping he'd say, "Oh, let me just fish that out of the bottom drawer,"' I replied.

When Sue Strath, Lyn's friend from the childcare centre, returned my call, she had lost none of the vim which saw her make a formal complaint to the Ombudsman in 1985.

'One of my aims is to get Chris Dawson before he dies,' she told me on the telephone before we met. 'The police were like, "Oh, the poor guy. His wife's left him". Like, come on. Why wasn't he ever prosecuted for having sex with underage girls? He and his brother? Why did that never happen?'

I knew there was a lack of interest from police in the lesser offence of carnal knowledge. A murder conviction was the main prize. But there were other reasons too.

'I suspect that for them, in their fifties now, this isn't something they really want to relive in terms of having to give evidence in public and put themselves out there and go through all the humiliation,' I replied.

'Yes, I understand that that can be hard,' she said. 'But with what's coming out now in the media and stuff, people are more prone to talk about what happened to them when they were 15 and 16 and being sexually abused.'

As Rebecca Hazel remained confident that I would be interviewing Jenny Carlson later in December, I had good reason to scoop up all the recollections of Sue and other people. I wanted to be able to ask Jenny about all the obvious things but I also knew that the more background interviewing I did, the better informed I would be and the more she would be prompted to disclose when asked the right questions.

Parts of Jenny's story were not sitting quite right in my view. I asked Rebecca, a staunch Jenny ally, if a teenager would want to remain with an older man who had told her he had been to see a hitman about having his wife murdered. Wouldn't a teenager be fearful that if he could have a mother of two little girls killed, he could easily have his girlfriend killed too?

And notwithstanding Chris's claims several months later that Lyn had voluntarily gone away, wouldn't Jenny be deeply suspicious that he had murdered her with his bare hands, or organised a hitman to do the deed in January 1982? Lyn had ordered Jenny out of the house at Bayview the previous November. I tried to imagine the reasoning of a girl returning nine weeks later, and not just to the spare room but to Lyn and Chris's room. To Lyn's bed. Putting all her things in Lyn's wardrobe and taking over Lyn's bathroom and kitchen. Pat, Greg and Merilyn talked about how houseproud Lyn was, constantly buying decorative things. The living areas must have had Lyn's presence stamped all over them. Wouldn't Jenny be terrified at the prospect of Lyn returning unannounced while Chris was at work?

These questions, which suggested that perhaps Jenny had suspected more than she had said, needed to be asked. They were not raised by Damian Loone in his lengthy interview with her in 1998, and they weren't asked by either the police prosecutor Matt Fordham or Chris's solicitor brother Peter Dawson when Jenny was in the witness box in the 2003 inquest.

I could understand why.

For Damian Loone and Matt Fordham, the prospect of convicting a suspected killer relied on the testimony of a woman who, as a teenager, was unaware of foul play because of the coercive control to which she was subjected. For Peter Dawson, lawyering a pathway to the exoneration of his younger brother meant casting Chris as an unknowing, abandoned husband and Jenny as a vindictive fantasist. There was no upside for Team Dawson in painting her as someone who suspected anything untoward.

Rebecca understood why such questions would be on my list, and she was sure that Jenny would meet them without equivocation.

At her house at Ocean Grove, Sue Strath had just finished her exercise for the day – kayaking at Narrabeen Lakes. She handed me a large yellow folder filled with dozens of newspaper clippings, the earliest dating back to 1998, when Damian Loone organised a *Manly Daily* story appealing for people with information about Lyn's disappearance to come forward to police.

'I've been collecting things as they appear in the papers about Lyn,' Sue said.

I had read Sue's statement to Damian, as well as her evidence when she was a witness in the 2003 inquest. I had watched the old footage of her from the ABC's *Australian Story*. Her loyalty to Lyn, even after so many years, was touching.

There was a missing piece in the puzzle, however, and it revolved around Sue's action in 1985, when she complained to the New South Wales Ombudsman about the failure of police to properly investigate Lyn's disappearance. Implicit in Sue's 1985 complaint – the submitted form of which seemed to have disappeared – was a strong suggestion of Lyn having been murdered. As this was five years before Jenny's worrying disclosures to police and to Lyn's family triggered the first investigation of a suspected murder, Sue must have been the first to officially raise the alarm.

I was still hoping to discover her original complaint file in a dusty archive somewhere. In the meantime, I could only ask questions.

Sue told me she had written to the Ombudsman in 1985 because in the three years she had waited for police to do something 'nobody came to the Children's Centre to interview any of us'.

'I just kept waiting. Even now, I think I should have gone in earlier than three years. But I kept thinking that someone else is doing something. I'm only a work friend. Surely someone else is doing something. No one was doing anything. A person goes missing and no one cares. That's really sad.

'I thought that if someone goes missing, surely there are people that care about them. I would hate to think if I went missing, no one ever complained or came looking for me. That's why I wrote to the Ombudsman. And I complained that no one followed up when she went missing.'

Sue recalled seeing Lyn on Friday 8 January 1982 at the centre 'and she was very positive. I remember her going off with Chris and she said she was going to see a counsellor . . . and she was like, "Oh, this is going to be really good". And I remember them coming back and holding hands and that was a bit of a shock.

'I thought, "Wow, that must have really been a successful session."

'She was feeling really positive when she came back. She said it was really good and, you know, "I'm hoping that everything will be worked out." That's why I was in such shock that she went missing the next day. She was looking forward. There were stories about her going away with some religious group, which is absolutely ridiculous. She wasn't even religious. She was such a loving mother and wife. She adored Chris. She would never, ever have left her children. And the older one was just about to start school. She had the school uniforms ready.

'I used to always say, "Oh, she's under the pool and no one's caring about her."'

Lyn had been confiding to her friends at the centre for months that some things were troubling her about Chris's contact with the family babysitter. Lyn had told Sue of coming home from work on a hot afternoon to find Jenny swimming nude in the pool when Chris was nearby in the house.

Sue was in no doubt back then that the teacher and his student were in a sexual relationship but Lyn appeared unwilling to accept the plain truth. 'Jenny was supposed to be the babysitter, looking after the kids. She was swimming naked in the pool and her bikini was hanging up on the line or something. And I said, "Lyn, what are you doing? Get her out of there!" I said, "She shouldn't actually be at your house, you know, don't you think something is going on?"'

'You would have been that blunt?' I asked Sue.

'Oh, yeah. Sorry, I'm very blunt. I just tell it as it is.'

A calling card from Detective Sergeant Paul Mayger of the Homicide Squad at Chatswood appeared among the newspaper clippings.

'Yeah, that's the card. It was sitting in the bottom of my kitchen drawer for years,' Sue said.

She recalled a visit by the experienced cop. She suggested he came by in 1985 to respond to her complaint to the Ombudsman but the visit must have been five or six years later, with Jenny's return to the Northern Beaches triggering the first murder investigation. After that one had fizzled out in 1991, Sue badgered her friend Helen's husband, a senior cop called Paul Hulme, constantly asking him, 'When are you going to do something about my friend, Lyn?'

'And he thought, "I'll just shut Sue up, I'll send my best detective" – because it was Missing Persons Week – "to go and have a look at this case". So he got Damian Loone. He gave him the file, got him to look at the case and Damian came back and thought, "There's a case to answer for here. I really think we need to follow this up." From then on, Damian has been following this case and every couple of years he contacts everyone and says, "Yep, we're still going, case is still happening." And I'm hoping he's going to eventually do something about it.'

Sue disclosed her disappointment. She had her folder of news-paper clippings, which bore witness to the media interest. She monitored the TV current affairs programs for their occasional ten-minute burst of reheated innuendo about the unsolved case. She was often willing to talk to the journalists whose questions would transport her back in time to a childcare centre and a trauma over what she had always been very confident was her friend Lyn's unsolved murder. All of it was wearying and, Sue lamented, 'nothing gets done'.

'The reason why I think all of us keep going, keep pushing it, even accepting an interview again, because it would be very easy to say no, is her daughters,' she told me.

An older man without a shirt walked across the front lawn.

'The guy next door – he worked with Chris Dawson,' Sue said. 'And he was a teacher. All the teachers knew they were having sex with the girls—oh no, I can't say that.'

She told me his name was David Clarke and assured me that he was not part of any wrongdoing. When I asked whether he would talk to us, Sue confidently predicted that he would.

Twenty minutes later, she walked outside and when she returned she said, 'I told him I've got someone from *The Australian*, I need you to come and talk to him. And I told him he needed to put his shirt on.'

Sue asked me whether I knew this place, the Northern Beaches, was different from the rest of Sydney. Once you crossed The Spit bridge to the insular peninsular, life was lived in something of a bubble. The grapevine worked particularly well. Its most ardent users soon knew with whom you were sleeping, how you were going in your business or job and what your children were up to.

'Everyone knows your business, especially if you grow up here,' she said.

That seemed true enough. In passing, I had mentioned my Uncle David, a fitness fanatic who lived at Collaroy and kept older locals fit with personalised training. It had been years since we caught up.

Sue was onto the connection immediately. 'David Hooper – is he your uncle?' she asked. She caught up with David regularly at a favourite coffee shop.

David Clarke, a retiree who spoke with an American accent and lived with his wife, Bev Balkind, also a former teacher, in a modest house right on the oceanfront, smiled and told me drily, 'We don't play the banjo up here but we can tune it'.

David casually told us that some weeks after Lyn had disappeared, Chris transferred to nearby Beacon Hill High, where David was teaching. At this time, many teachers and students knew his wife had vanished and a teenager from Cromer High had moved into the house.

Chris still had celebrity status. He and Paul had been in a catchy television commercial for corn chips; their roles saw them nodding a lot to the slogan '*Just say CC*'. David recalled grinning students would suddenly start nodding in unison whenever Mr Dawson was nearby. It was an act of familiarity, endearment; they liked that he was a bit special.

David had heard the stories of Chris and Paul and female students but he hastened to add that he had not seen anything, nor did he have the sort of evidence that would withstand a good lawyer's cross-examination.

'We're all aware that it happens. I've worked in six different high schools and in five of them, there were relationships between students and teachers,' he said.

Sue gently laughed when I said I was looking forward to talking to Chris.

'Do you think he could give an interview that would persuade you that he's been an innocent victim in this and he's been unfairly accused?' I asked her.

'Definitely not,' she replied.

Sue and her then husband, a footballer himself, had hosted Chris and Lyn for dinner at their house. She saw him like many others in the community did at the time: handsome, popular and charming. However, she also knew he was a 'control freak' who had conditioned Lyn to accept his brazen lies as unimpeachable truths.

'Naive would be a good word,' Sue sighed. 'No, she wasn't foolish. She just idolised him.'

Across the Northern Beaches, Sue told me, knowledge of Lyn, the exploited schoolgirls and of the failures of the criminal justice system to put Chris beyond bars was a part of the local lore. Women in their 70s who were 30-something mums in 1982 still talked about it to their adult children. Sue's daughter, Lulu, had grown up hearing the stories.

I made a note to come back to talk to David Clarke's wife, Bev, who had taught at Cromer High. Chris's grooming of Jenny appeared to not be an isolated incident, and I hoped Bev might be able to speak to the apparent culture of teachers having sex with schoolgirls in the 1980s in high schools on the Northern Beaches.

Unlike his neighbour, David knew Jenny when she was a single mother and taking her athletic daughter to play in weekend sport events with David's son. David got involved in coaching the softball team and Jenny helped him run it.

'And finally the penny dropped with me, and she just sort of smiled and said, "I wondered how long it would take you to work this one out,"' David explained. 'She was quite open about it. She's a lovely person.'

Sue walked Nick Adams-Dzierzba and me out to the footpath, where a taxi was waiting to take us to meet Lyn's other friend from the childcare centre, Anna Grantham.

'Is that you, Hedley? What are you doing here?' a shirtless man in wet boardshorts yelled. Matthew Johns, the former rugby league legend who had been giving me tips the week before, was walking back from his late-morning swim off Ocean Grove Beach.

The coincidence was too much. Sue was right; unexpected things happened on the insular peninsular.

Nick was quiet on the taxi ride, then as we set up in Anna Grantham's house, he told me something in a hushed voice. He had been listening intently as Pat, Greg and then Sue Strath recalled and described a woman whom nobody had seen for three and a half decades.

'At first, when I was hearing the family talk, you think, is that all that your life comes down to in the end? A couple of people thinking about you 35 years after you're gone? And there's a bystander effect where everybody was like, "Oh, somebody else will do something." But Sue sounded like she was the one who didn't take that view. She was, "I'm not going to wait for somebody else to act. I have to."'

Nick's insights were always perceptive. Still waters run deep. I agreed with the quiet young man's appraisal of no-nonsense Sue.

In my first conversation with Anna on the telephone, she had begun to cry. Her friend Lyn was often in her thoughts. Anna stayed in touch with Sue, Barbara and Annette from the childcare centre, and since the inquests in 2001 and 2003, she had become good friends with Pat Jenkins. This led to a friendship with Lyn's daughter, Shanelle, to whom Anna would send packages of clothes for Shanelle's little girl. When Anna and Lyn were young mothers, their daughters played together, and now those girls were young mothers too, the baby garments were being recycled.

Before I arrived, Anna had looked for a picture frame made of glass, a Christmas gift from Lyn in 1981. It had disappeared recently. Anna feared the cleaner had accidentally broken it and thrown the pieces away. Years earlier, Anna had asked a woman who said she could feel and see things from the spiritual world to hold this item, which Lyn had once held, to try to connect with Lyn. Anna was shaken by the woman's disclosures about having seen an image of a woman's body rolled up in a carpet.

Anna cherished her times with Shanelle. 'She really believes that the time is coming, it's very close, for her to find out about her mum,' Anna told me.

She recounted recollections from the early 1980s. There was the time Anna and Lyn sold some old clothes and bric-a-brac from the back of Anna's car boot at a weekend market. Chris came by, according to Anna, and he appeared aggressive and angry. Anna mentioned it at the childcare centre when they were next working together, and Lyn told her, 'He can be quite nasty', and described a time when he had grabbed her hair and pushed her face into mud around the newly built swimming pool. Anna recalled Lyn saying, 'I couldn't breathe.'

When Anna went to the house at Gilwinga Drive, Lyn showed her the master bedroom with its many mirrors and windows. Lyn sat on the bed and confided that she hated getting out of bed in the morning in front of Chris, because she believed her legs were thick and heavy.

'I said, "You look amazing all the time. You dress so beautifully and you're so lovely,"' Anna said.

But Anna remembered Lyn was looking very drained in the months before she disappeared. Lyn had talked to Anna about Jenny. 'She said to me, "She's having a lot of trouble at home and she's doing exams and Chris wants her to move in."

'Her answer was, "Well, that's what Chris wants ... she needs help. She has got nowhere to go."'

Lyn left the childcare centre early in a taxi one day because it was school holidays and she wanted to see if anything was going on at home with Chris and Jenny being there on their own. She returned, Anna said, 'looking very pensive and worried'. Not long after, Lyn told Anna, she went to Cromer High after school hours for an event. One of the female teachers approached Lyn quietly and told her that Chris and Jenny were in a relationship. Anna remembered another conversation in which Lyn spoke of being in the kitchen, cooking the evening meal, as Chris and Jenny edged closer to each other until they were touching in the lounge room. They believed Lyn couldn't see what was going on.

After Lyn disappeared, Anna told me there was suspicion in the childcare centre but there was also fear. Sue had not mentioned being scared of Chris, while Anna said that they were all scared of repercussions. Barbara had also expressed her fear. On the insular peninsular, police and footballers were bosom buddies. There were other teachers involved with schoolgirls. The wrongdoing was widespread. And Chris was a large, powerful man.

This helped explain the delay in doing anything. It also helped to explain Sue's 1985 complaint to the Ombudsman about the lack of police investigation, when the more direct pathway would have been Sue or Anna or Barbara Cruise or Annette Leary or all four of them going together to the closest police station, asking to speak to the most senior detective, and saying, 'We believe our missing friend Lyn has been murdered by her husband'. Nobody did this. Everyone assumed someone else would do something.

'How often did he ring you or come and see you to ask whether you'd heard from his wife?' I asked Anna.

'Never. He never bothered to contact anyone like that,' she said.

Of course, Chris wouldn't do it if he already knew there was no point. He wouldn't contact her friends to ask if she'd been in touch if he already knew she was dead. But if he had played the role of the distraught husband, perhaps he would have invited slightly less suspicion.

'I wish I could've done more,' pleaded Anna. 'Why didn't we? How could we just let it go like this? Years and years? I do regret not doing something at the beginning. We all do.'

Chapter 19

The Long Driveway

'What do we call the podcast series? And book?' I texted Rebecca Hazel one day in December between interviews.

Rebecca suggested 'This Empty House' for her book and 'Cromer High' for the podcast.

I responded, 'I thought of something else for your book or the podcast – "The Teacher's Pet". Your publisher would probably like it, not sure how Jen would feel.'

When Rebecca replied that she wasn't keen on it for her book, I was privately relieved; instinctively, I knew that it would be the podcast's title.

The idea must have been influenced by the 1998 interview at the Dee Why police station between Damian Loone and Jenny's younger sister, Naomi. She told the detective that when she was at Cromer High, she used to 'hear things, you know, whispers, rumours' about a relationship between her older sister in Year 11 and the popular PE teacher Mr Dawson.

'In fact, one of my friends who lived across the road said she saw them kissing when he dropped her off from school one day. I mean, he was a good-looking teacher and it was exciting. I feel ashamed of it now but that's just the way you feel when you're 13 and everyone's got a crush on him. Children at school used to sing a song to me, that Police song – "Don't Stand So Close To Me."'

The song was a smash-hit in 1980, just as rumours among students and staff about Mr Dawson and Jenny swept Cromer High. In her interview with the cop 18 years later, Naomi began to recite some of the evocative lyrics sung by Sting, a schoolteacher before he became a rockstar. The lyrics described a teacher and a beautiful schoolgirl. The teacher's pet.

On my visits to Sydney for interviews, my sister Kate and her husband, Paul, hosted me at their house, a couple of hundred metres from the 1970s Simms family home. The three of us walked around it and I showed them a park bench near Lyn's old house with a modest plaque honouring a carefree teenager who used to sunbathe there: *Lynette Joy Dawson.*

As Paul was the editor-in-chief of *The Australian* and a powerful supporter of the podcast, he would pepper me with questions about how the investigation was going. It was a risk for him too; our costs were mounting, and that was before we had commissioned legal advice on the defamation risks, which were manifold. His support was rock-solid and his interest grew as I briefed him over morning coffee about the interviews lined up for each day. In the evenings, he had many questions about what people were saying to me.

Three decades earlier, Paul and I had been flatmates on the Gold Coast. He had even talked to Chris and Paul Dawson for a human-interest story published in *The Courier-Mail* in February 1989. I had found the story while trawling the newspaper's library and electronic archive soon after the first inquest in 2001.

Paul, an identical twin himself, was a 19-year-old cadet reporter when he wrote the story, headlined, 'Seeing double means extra trouble at Coombabah High', about the school's 12 sets of identical twins. The celebrity Dawson brothers featured most prominently: 'Paul Dawson – or was that Chris – said it was great being a twin because you had a friend for life no matter what happened.'

One of the twins told my journalist friend, 'We love it – we always asked to be in the same classes at school and we have played the same sports together all our lives.'

*

'Where are we now?' I asked Rebecca as she leaned over the steering wheel of her large BMW somewhere north of Anna Grantham's home.

'We're at Mona Vale and you turn inland here towards Bayview,' she replied breezily. 'We'll climb up there and we'll go to Gilwinga Drive and we'll see the house that Chris and Lynette built. Where they lived with their little girls, where Jen moved in with both of them for a while. The same house that Jen moved back into once Lynette had disappeared.'

On the winding road up to the suburb's escarpment, mansions vie for multimillion-dollar views of the beautiful blue expanse of Pittwater, a boating playground in which my father became an avid sailor.

When I was a teenager on the Gold Coast, Dad bought a graceful sloop called *Dalliance*, and we made plans to take a year out and sail around the world. It was a nice pipedream. On one brief but memorable journey, which was part of the preparation for the planned big one, we set sail from Southport and were caught in massive seas off Coffs Harbour where the waves dwarfed *Dalliance*. Gale-force winds, driving rain and the fury of this tempest in which I felt helpless left its mark. Dad, standing with characteristic calm and stoicism at the wheel, had ensured we were attached to the rails with safety ropes in the event that we were swept overboard by a wave or lost our balance as *Dalliance* surfed at a seemingly impossible angle down the face of a wave. When he asked me to go to the bow to take some of the sail down, it occurred to me that this would surely increase the chances of me ending up over the side. I swore and defiantly shouted, 'No!' Dad got the message. The head sail could rip itself to bits. We laughed about it afterwards.

My cadetship at the *Gold Coast Bulletin* and Dad's commitments in commercial aviation took priority over the idea for an ocean crossing. *Dalliance* was sold. Twenty-five years later when Dad was turning 70, he flew to San Francisco and bought a local retired dentist's sloop, fitted it out for a long-distance journey, then set off to Australia. Crossing the Pacific Ocean alone at his age carried inherent risks. Whales, container ships and partly submerged debris could have sunk his vessel. He would snatch sleep intermittently, never more than a few hours. Massive seas, whipped up by a cyclone near Fiji, and a severe hand injury threatened disaster but Dad got lucky, making it back to Moreton Bay and playing down his extraordinary feat as unremarkable. Like a Sunday ride on one of his powerful motorcycles in the hills behind the Gold Coast.

I had thought about my father every day since his death at 77 earlier that year. Driving around the Northern Beaches with Rebecca, reflecting on the earliest parts of Dad's life and his experiences in the same places I was visiting, I felt closer to him.

'We'll also see Paul Dawson's house, Chris's twin, it's just a couple of hundred metres down the road,' Rebecca said.

Rebecca and I had been comparing notes and wondering where Lyn's remains might be. Almost everyone I had interviewed nominated the immediate surrounds of her old home at Bayview. Rebecca told me that detectives from Paul Mayger in 1990 to Damian Loone a decade later might have targeted the wrong area because Jenny 'said she kept telling them to dig in the soft soil below the girls' bedroom windows'. But Damian had never done so.

'And I took that bit of information back to Damian. And he kind of got quite angry because he told me that she had been at the digs and she'd never suggested that,' Rebecca said.

As we turned towards Gilwinga Drive, a large road sign with a sketch of one big human eye came into view. It was unlike any road sign I had seen before. It was meant to deter wrongdoers: *Neighbours alert area. We look out for each other.*

A couple of lizards ran across the bitumen in front of the long, steep driveway to Lyn and Chris's old house. Rebecca pulled over to talk about what had transpired up there in late 1981, when Lyn's life was shortening, on a seemingly unstoppable countdown of months, weeks, days and, finally, hours.

We were so deeply immersed in Lyn's story that we wanted to go inside her old house, which she had gone to so much trouble decorating. Inside Lyn's bedroom before it became Jenny's bedroom.

Around the side and across the soft soil where Julie Andrew had seen Chris berating a crying Lyn as she held their daughter.

It had been more than 12 months since Rebecca completed her manuscript. She told me outside Lyn and Chris's old house that she had resisted going back into the traumatic nitty-gritty of it all. There were times when she was writing or typing up notes from her conversations when the sadness became too much; the litany of lies and betrayals too overwhelming. She tried to undo the hurt and misery with a hypothetical what-if. If Chris had simply said to his high school sweetheart and mother of his two girls, 'I'm sorry, I can't be here anymore.' But the scenario withered in the face of passions, property, money and unfettered custody.

'I found it really, really upsetting. But I realise I need to go through this again with you,' Rebecca said.

Lyn's torment about Chris's infatuation, dressed up as concern for a teenager who had moved into the home, overlapped Jenny's relief at being there. A woman seeing all she loved slipping away while a girl simultaneously experienced sanctuary, protection and the care of a charismatic schoolteacher. As his discarded wife fell asleep or went shopping, he wanted to make love to the girl.

'She would have had some happy memories from early on, when she was babysitting for them and she suddenly had a bit of a warm embrace from a family,' Rebecca said.

We talked about some of the tumultuous events soon after. Lyn telling Jenny to pack her things and get out, resulting in the teenager walking down the road to Paul and Marilyn's house, being allowed to sleep there but getting up early and hiding in the bush so that their girls wouldn't see her and tell their cousin Shanelle or Aunty Lyn that Jenny had moved in. Chris and Paul Dawson were joined in their betrayal of Lyn.

'I've tried to imagine many times that you're living in this extremely isolated location and the three people, the three adults in your world who are helping you, who are closest to you, are conspiring against you,' Rebecca said of how Lyn would have felt.

'These people around me, this little community I have that was supposed to really love and do everything for me, are actually all betraying me, including this young woman who I've moved into my house as an act of kindness, who I'm pretty sure is having an affair with my husband. There's a part of me that, I think, I could imagine just walking out the door.'

Lyn was being gaslit. She lived in a microcosm where nothing was as it seemed.

I asked Rebecca if Jenny liked Lyn.

'I've asked her that exact question,' she said. 'And what she said to me was, she started to cry, and she said, "Lynette Dawson showed me more kindness than anyone else ever has in my entire life." So I guess that's yes, and in quite a profound way. She feels terrible. That's why she cries. When we really talk about it she would often put her head in her hands and say, "It wouldn't have happened except for me." It's a terrible burden she carries. Of course, it's not her responsibility at all.'

When I rejoined that, even as a 16-year-old, Jenny could have separated right from wrong in what she was doing behind Lyn's back, Rebecca countered.

'She had no way of knowing he might have been going to hurt her. There was no conspiracy. I think she hoped at certain points during her final year of school that he would leave her and they could be together. But I don't think she thought he was going to hurt her.

'That was one of the first things I asked Damian, did you ever think she had anything to do with Lynette's disappearance? And he said, "No, not for a minute, because she came to us and she told us what she knew." He said if she had something to do with it, you would not put yourself in that position.'

'Could you live there, knowing its history?' I asked.

Rebecca didn't hesitate. 'Yeah, I could. Because if she's there and if it happened under the circumstances it did, I could, I could take care of her. I could make it nice, you know? If that's where her resting place is. If her family thinks that's where she is, there's a place where they could come and speak to her. What about you?'

'I think it's a beautiful thing that you just said but I reckon that I'd be pretty uneasy,' I answered. 'I think I'd dig the place up.'

I wanted revelations and public concern arising from the podcast, still months away from release, to effectively force a situation where police would return to the property and do just that: a proper dig.

As we talked over the noise of the cicadas and debated what to do next, Rebecca's idea to walk up the driveway and talk to the relatively new owners felt increasingly unattractive. I tried to put myself in the owners' shoes, being told by a couple of strangers that a missing woman's body was possibly buried in the yard. It would be better to property-search the address to identify the current owners, then explain in writing what was intended and why.

'It's a great idea. Much more elegant than just knocking on the door,' Rebecca agreed.

'This is the reason why I'll listen to this podcast,' Nick Adams-Dzierzba piped up from the back seat. 'This conversation that's happening in the car, right now. Knowing that you're sitting out the front with a dilemma – the morality question – do we go in or not? And if you don't, whether you're just as complicit as everybody else these past 36 years.'

Rebecca started the car. We drove away.

Chapter 20

Lost Files

Back at my desk at *The Australian*'s office in Brisbane, I gave Michael McKenna, the bureau chief, an update. I ran through the interviews already recorded. I had many hours of audio files for the recorded conversations with Greg and Phil Simms, and Pat Jenkins; Greg's wife, Merilyn, and Phil's wife, Lynda; three of Lyn's work friends, Barbara Cruise, Sue Strath and Anna Grantham; Jenny's friend the author Rebecca Hazel; NSW Ombudsman Michael Barnes; the former homicide detective Stuart Wilkins, who had interviewed Chris Dawson in 1991; and Kate Erwin, a former student of Chris Dawson when he taught at St Ursula's College in Yeppoon.

In my experience of reporting unsolved alleged serious crimes, most people are generally reticent to point an accusing finger. The risks of being sued or of maligning someone unfairly are such that condemnation comes only after a jury or judge's formal verdict of guilt.

In Lyn's case, almost everyone I talked to was convinced Chris had killed his first wife, and unafraid to declare it openly, on the record.

The ballast crucial for an investigation such as this was mounting in paper and digital form. Transcripts of the first inquest in 2001 and the second in 2003; the police brief of evidence from 2001 which contained witness statements and typed transcripts of interviews; my original files and notebook of 2001 retrieved by Alexander from the roof space of the carport; as well as two books about organised crime

and contract killings, numerous letters including handwritten correspondence from Lyn's mother, Helena; diary notes, photographs and
newspaper and magazine clippings from Lyn's family and friends; and
letters to and from the Office of the DPP over its refusal to prosecute
Chris Dawson and my own research.

Each new interview I recorded produced new leads and more
names of people who would go on my list to find and follow up. Even
more leads and names came from close reading of the police brief.

Michael knew that a lot of ground had been covered already but
there was a long way to go before I would be ready to start writing.
I didn't let on that I was feeling intimidated by the enormity of Lyn's
story. Every time I thought about writing episodes for the podcast,
it seemed too important and vast for me to do it justice. I handled it
by turning a blind eye and adding more names to the list of people
I wanted to track down. I would worry about weaving it all together
some other time.

Sue Strath's recollections of her complaint to the Ombudsman in
1985 about the complete lack of police investigation for the first three
years of Lyn's disappearance were strong, and her manager from the
childcare centre, Barbara Cruise, had similar memories.

Between interviews, I wrote to Michael Barnes and explained
more fully that a formal complaint lodged with the Ombudsman in
1985 by a woman, Sue Strath, (whose surname then was Browett)
must have come to the attention of investigators from the Ombudsman, as well as high-ranking police at the time, as it had triggered
internal reports by Inspector Geoff Shattles.

An extract from the Shattles report had been discovered by Detective Damian Loone, who noted it in his statement for the coroner's
inquest in 2001 but the location of the rest of the file – all the documents that must have been generated in the Ombudsman's office in
response to Sue's complaint – was a mystery.

'The Ombudsman took it seriously at the time in '85 and produced
a report – but I don't have it and Sue the complainant doesn't have it
and it would be informative to have it now,' I texted Michael Barnes.
'Do you think the file would be archived as a public record with the

Ombudsman, or perhaps on microfiche or a shelf in the organisation, and would it be possible to obtain?'

After asking some of his staff about the availability of old files, Michael relayed some general feedback that Sue's complaint file from 1985 was unlikely to exist. Most of the Ombudsman's records were kept for seven years. I strongly doubted I would get anywhere with the police who, in my experience, were mostly culturally hardwired to be the antithesis of transparent.

A stickler for correct process, Michael gave me the name of the manager in his department to whom Sue Strath should write with details of her 1985 complaint file and a request that it be retrieved and copied to her, if it still existed.

I drafted an email to Sue, who approved the wording and sent it under her name.

'Sorry, Hedley, couldn't help,' she told me the next day.

A prompt reply from the Ombudsman advised her that a search had revealed no documents. Disappointingly, the manager added that a file as old as Sue's 'would have been disposed of after a certain number of years of storage at the government records repository'.

'Nothing ventured, nothing gained,' I told her.

When I telephoned him, the long-retired police inspector Geoff Shattles cast his mind back to the case he looked into and played down in his internal report in 1985.

'I just remember that she was missing and so forth. There was a bit of suspicion. We had the husband and some schoolgirl or something. I put everything in there at the time, and I think I had a detective sergeant look into it and so forth.'

He politely declined my offer to visit him with copies of his documents, which might refresh his memory. 'I can't help you anymore. Too old now, not interested in that, thanks very much.'

Another dead end.

But Sue's folder filled mostly with newspaper clippings held one gem: a business card for Roslyn McLoughlin from when she was a case worker in aged and disability services for the Mosman Municipal Council. The women had met at the second inquest in 2003.

Ros had left the council and was semi-retired in a country town called Gunning, near Canberra, and a Google search revealed that she had been named the town's Citizen of the Year in 2015 for her many good deeds, including volunteer work for the town's Lions Club.

It was Sunday when I called the Lions Club of Gunning on the off-chance somebody would be there. Ros picked up and was happy to talk to me about Lyn.

In the testimony of Ros at the inquest in 2003, and in her earlier statement to Damian Loone, she recalled a weekday – sometime between the second and third week of December 1981 – when, after they'd finished their game of doubles, Lyn expressed an urgent need for one of her tennis-playing friends to go back to the house with her.

Ros recalled that Lyn's plea occurred in the week leading up to Christmas, not a weekend. When Ros spoke to me, she believed it would have been Monday 21 December.

A proposed sale agreement with a real estate agent who had been contacted by Chris was dated Monday 21 December. It was found, signed by Chris but not by Lyn, in Lyn's dressing gown, which had been in one of the many garbage bags Chris had delivered to Helena's home in 1982.

It seemed obvious that things were coming to a head in Lyn's unhappy home in December 1981. I speculated that an increasingly angry and frustrated Chris had told Lyn that he wanted the house sold so that he could start again with the babysitter. It followed that the sale agreement was subsequently presented by Chris on 21 December and that Lyn refused to sign, resulting in Chris persuading Jenny to pack and leave with him to drive north for a new start in Queensland, a couple of days before Christmas.

Ros and Lyn were not tight friends. They had met because Marilyn Dawson and Ros were close. Once, perhaps twice, Ros had been up to Lyn and Chris's house to babysit their two daughters. Yet on this particular day, after tennis in the third week of December 1981, Lyn was pleading with Ros to return to the house with her.

When Ros explained that she had too many things to do in that busy week before Christmas, Lyn asked each of the other women there. Nobody had the time to spare.

Lyn's motive for imploring Ros was playing on my mind. 'I've wondered, was she wanting to socialise more and just pour out her heart to someone who didn't know Chris very well and therefore she could explain everything, without feeling that he would find out about it,' I asked Ros.

'I think she was scared and she wanted someone to go back to the house,' Ros replied. 'That was the last time any of us saw Lyn.'

'She really begged me to go to her place with her. The tone in her voice when she asked me, it was "please come back". I had my own issues at the time and a couple of kids and just went, "I can't, no, I can't do that." I did sense a desperation in her request and in hindsight I would have definitely gone.

'On that occasion, she didn't appear to be as happy as she could have been. She had tennis gear on. On top of her thighs, she had a really large grapefruit size bruise. Certainly, bruising on her upper arm. I remember because it was so large. And I remember thinking, "I wonder how a person would get that?" The alarm bells did sort of ring.

'I wasn't thinking of anything happening to her. Things like domestic violence weren't talked about very much. I didn't know her well enough to inquire, "How did you get those bruises?" But it was unusual.'

When Ros and the other women next caught up for tennis after their children had gone back to school in January, they talked about Lyn having disappeared on 9 January, her pleas to Ros and other friends at their tennis catch-up just prior to Christmas and the large, purple bruises on her legs and arm.

'We did suspect that maybe Chris, her husband, had done something to her. We talked about that,' Ros said. 'She would not have gone off and not taken her children with her. Her whole focus was her two girls.'

In May 1999, Ros made a two-page statement to police. She had seen a story in the *Manly Daily* newspaper featuring the detective Damian Loone talking about his investigation into Lyn's fate. Ros had changed careers and become a social worker; she now understood domestic violence and its prevalence, and how people remain silent. None of the women with whom Ros played tennis before and after Lyn's disappearance had been to the police about their suspicions in the previous 17 years. They all presumed that Lyn would reappear – or her body would be found.

Amid public interest in the inquests in 2001 and 2003, numerous photographs of Lyn taken when she was younger were released and published across the media. The images of a beautiful looking young woman were very different to how Ros remembered Lyn in December 1981. She appeared worried; tired and drawn. Ros said Lyn had 'lost her sparkle'.

I asked Ros, 'Do you think it would have been possible in early 1982 for one of Lyn's friends to go around to the other friends and say, "Look, this doesn't make sense that Lyn would leave. We did notice this bruising and she was begging for us to go back just before she disappeared. Do you think we should go to the police and just air our concerns?" Or do you think that would have been a very unusual thing to do at the time?'

Ros replied, 'We certainly discussed everything that you just mentioned; the bruising, the fact she was really wanting us to come back to her place, that her disappearance was really out of character. And if she was just going to go away, she would have taken the kids. And we probably talked about it a few times. But going to the police . . . I have no idea why no one went to the police.'

Chapter 21

Julie Andrew

In late 2017, I spoke to Dennis Watt about my investigation.

Dennis was the new chief at the Gold Coast Titans and had witnessed the public interest in the Dawson brothers. As *The Courier-Mail* newsroom's chief of staff 25 years earlier, Dennis had been my boss and I respected him enormously.

The Dawson brothers still had no inkling of the podcast I was planning, and I wanted to keep it that way for as long as possible to minimise the risk of people I intended to talk to being warned off. My sister Rebecca expected that the Titans would lose a couple of fans when Chris and Paul Dawson learned the club's part-owner was related to the reporter who first wrote about them in 2001 and had returned for a new investigation and a podcast in 2018.

In the meantime, as I suggested to Dennis, it would be helpful if a photographer with a long lens could be alerted to take some pictures of the brothers when they were next at Titans training. I wanted Dennis to let me know when he next saw them there.

To his professional credit, Dennis never did. Instead, he and Matthew Johns told me to talk to Paul Broughton, who had coached the Dawsons at the Newtown Jets.

When I called him, Broughton was struck by the coincidence; he ad talked to one of the twins in a shopping centre just the other day. as the first time in many years.

'He asked how I was, he hadn't seen me for a long while. And he said, "I had to ask one question that's intrigued me for 40 years,"' Broughton said. 'And he said, "Why did you drop me after game one?"'

The question must have been asked by Chris Dawson, always in the shadow of his better performing brother.

The veteran former coach remembered exactly why he had dropped the fit and talented player. 'I had a misguided, perhaps misguided, belief that their first concern would be for their brother, for either brother for himself, rather than for the team as a whole,' he replied. 'They both felt they should be in the team together. I know they are very strong for each other, their loyalty to each other was exemplary. They just never played really well together.'

The odd closeness of Chris and Paul Dawson was constantly remarked upon in statements from the police brief of evidence, and in my interviews with Lyn's family and friends.

Ahead of a planned interview with Julie Andrew in her home in Balmain, I browsed the busy shops nearby. She recommended her local pub, The Riverview, for pizza and Guinness. Thirteen years earlier, Ruth and I had stayed with Kate and Paul in their apartment in the converted old Colgate-Palmolive factory, which once manufactured soap and toothpaste near Balmain peninsular. The trendy inner west enclave of terraces on small blocks and bustling cafes is 35 kilometres from Julie's old home near the bush of Bayview on the insular peninsular. The vibe could not be more different.

Around a kitchen table in a cosy terrace in Balmain, I listened and watched as Julie Andrew described the brothers' narcissistic connection.

'It was a twin relationship that seemed to be even more connected. Everything they did in their lives was mirrored, right down to all their part-time jobs and the way they did everything. The way they looked, the way they interacted. They always lived just a few houses apart. They sort of drove the same cars. They were too entwined. It was almost like they'd never been able to function separately. They functioned as one person, connected.

'They were really quite strange. I've not come across anyone in my life that presented to me the way they did. It was like two people who were actually one person. And they both were very secretive. I was on the outside looking in and that was how I perceived it. They didn't take a shit without the other knowing about it.'

The police statement provided by Lyn's friend and neighbour in 1999 was moving. In the flesh, the diminutive widow was extraordinarily powerful. It was as if she was still there on the hill at Bayview, hovering over Lyn, Chris, Jenny, Paul and Marilyn.

Julie exuded strength, deep insight and unflinching honesty. For 16 years, she had not acted on her certainty that Lyn was killed by Chris in January 1982, and I believed that she suffered with guilt, despite her insistence that regret was a waste of time. In her own first marriage, Julie had been hurt and when she reflected on the early 1980s and her relative powerlessness, she spoke for millions of women who were treated like second-class citizens.

She placed an old colour photograph on the table, showing the backyards of the acreage properties and the direct line of sight she had through the bush. Julie said that she had 'always' believed that Lyn was buried nearby, in the bush, and that her body was possibly moved later. Like Lyn's siblings and colleagues from the childcare centre, there was no uncertainty; no attempt to qualify or prevaricate. She was adamant: Chris murdered Lyn and got away with it.

I raised with Julie that she had not hesitated to use the word 'murderer', notwithstanding the presumption of innocence that any accused person would enjoy in our legal system as a fundamental human right.

'And that's a word I don't take lightly. I've never used it for another human being in my life,' she said.

She conceded there would be some prejudice, some faulty recollections 'but all in all, we're solid, intelligent people who could think clearly and logically and laterally and knew the guy and knew what he wanted'.

'He wanted Jenny. To get Jenny, he had to get rid of Lyn. And then Lyn's gone. Where's she gone? Just wandered off? Wandered off with some God botherers, never to be seen again? She didn't take anything. Didn't have any money. He said she took $500. She didn't have two dollars to rub together. She worked part-time and he gave her this little, tiny bit of money. Again, control! She had nothing. She didn't take anything. She didn't take a pair of underpants. She didn't take any of the beautiful fiddles that she loved. And she didn't take her two children and she would not have let go of those little hands.'

Julie remembered Lyn's little voice and her wariness around Chris.

'She was careful. Careful not to ruffle any feathers. She was very softly spoken. So there's this really calm, quiet, serene woman. And then around him, she just had this edge of caution. She wasn't frightened of him, although I do think that he physically abused her at times. Towards the end, he could be rough. I know that every now and then she'd have grab marks on her. I saw marks but I never asked her how she got them. I should have said, "How did you get that?" And the woman I am today, I would ask that.'

Her recall of the baskets of costume jewellery Lyn's daughter Shanelle would wear, of the obvious sexual attraction between Chris and the teenage Jenny, and Julie's blunt statement to her friend that Chris was 'fucking the babysitter' all painted a cinematic picture. She took us back in time, to Bayview when the cicadas sang nature's summer soundtrack while Julie implored Lyn to stand her ground and refuse to permit Jenny to come and live in her house. Back to when Lyn would have a quiet cry and share her self-loathing, because her varicose veins were showing and her bottom had widened, and the sadness she felt each day coinciding with the washing in the laundry piling up and the dishes in the kitchen sink staying there, dirty, too long. Lyn was not coping. And all the while, Julie recalled, Chris 'strutted around like a peacock', Lyn knew 'Chris doesn't like the way I look'.

Back to a time when Julie noticed that Lyn was not around the house anymore. She wasn't asking Julie for lifts to Mona Vale. She wasn't walking home with the shopping or hanging the clothes out on the line. Lyn was invisible and silent.

But Jenny had moved back in.

After an absence of just eight weeks, Jenny was back swimming in the pool, topless. Lyn's two little girls were laughing and playing around her. Chris was ebullient. The relationship was, Julie recalled, 'now out in the open'.

Julie tried to telephone several times in this period. Nobody picked up. When she spoke to a friend on the other side of the road, the married woman told Julie of having recently walked up the driveway and seen Chris and Jenny in bed together. Lyn's bed.

Julie was dumbstruck that no one had ever bothered to come and talk to her. Nobody from the police and nobody from Lyn's family. She shared her theory about the failure of police to look into it. Chris had friendships with senior police, she told me, adding that it could have been as simple as him saying to one of those officers, 'You know what women are like. She's just taken off.'

I had to ask the obvious question: why did Julie not go to the police herself and share her suspicions in the beginning?

'Women are very different now. And the knowledge that I've gained as a mature woman, an older woman, I'm a different person to the one I was back then. Back then, you believed your police and judiciary. If your doctor told you something, you did what you were told. They know, they can be trusted. So if police aren't going to do anything, then they must know something more than I know. But I never expected to see her again. I just knew she'd been killed.'

Near the end of the interview, Julie asked me about my confidence that the podcast would make a difference. Then she spoke.

'What I've got to offer, really, is minuscule. But you're putting pieces together of a puzzle. And a piece that I might be able to add might help you to move forward and add another piece.

'I can be instrumental in adding the smallest piece to help you to move forward in some way so that something comes out of this, so that she finally gets the justice she deserves, the recognition that she deserves, and that's why I'm speaking to you. I loved her. She was a really important part of my life.

'I've never discussed it as in-depth with anyone, other than my brother, than I have with you today. I hope with all my heart that you're very successful in your endeavour and we get some closure for Lyn.

'You don't accuse somebody of murdering somebody else – it's not something you can say lightly. It's heartfelt. And it's not anger or aggression. It's sorrow. I'm sorrowful. I've lost a dear friend and I've carried it for years. And I miss her every day. I just want justice. I just want justice for her and her family. And I would love for her little girls to know she didn't leave them. She never walked away from them. She was taken away from them by the person who was supposed to protect her.'

Julie was mesmerising. Her words and the conviction with which she delivered them carried the weight of decades of rumination, sorrow, love and determination.

On the way to our next interview, Rebecca told me she was blown away by some of the disclosures. In about 45 minutes, we would be meeting Carl Milovanovich, who ran the 2003 inquest which heard from numerous witnesses across five days. But Julie was not one of those witnesses. We wondered whether it would have made any difference to the decision-making of lawyers in the Office of the DPP, who received the transcript from the inquest, if Julie had been cross-examined.

Julie had reflected on giving Lyn strong advice to push back against Chris, to stand against what he was insisting should happen with Jenny coming into their house. Julie had worried for years that it might have pushed things over the edge.

'I don't think she's a hater, yet she was declaring him a killer without equivocation,' I said to Rebecca.

'She did that because Lyn was such a good friend,' she replied. 'Lyn was someone she loved. Someone she felt was taken away from her and from her family and from her daughters.'

I wrestled with a conundrum. The idea that an intelligent and caring woman would wait for months and years for police to knock on her door but not pick up the telephone to the local police station and say, 'I think my neighbour has been murdered. She's missing and I believe her body is on the block.'

Julie told us that her husband at the time had even said to her, 'Leave it alone, Jules.'

'The people that we're speaking to are all good people,' Rebecca said. 'I don't think they're lazy people. I don't think they didn't care about her enough. They didn't have confidence. They didn't know how to interact with police. Did they have the right? Would they get into trouble? Maybe they were scared.'

Rebecca suspected that for some of the witnesses, including Julie, their insistence now that they were almost certain of foul play right from the beginning couldn't be right.

'I think people mix up all those years and times and feelings and places,' she said. 'This is going to be the problem with any prosecution.'

Chapter 22

Carl Milovanovich

'Do you think Jenny is looking forward to telling her side of things?' I asked Rebecca as she pulled onto Victoria Road in Sydney's inner west. We were running late. Again.

'No, I don't think so,' Rebecca answered. 'I mean, she wants it out there. But the actual telling, no, I think that's quite traumatic for her.'

Speeding to the home of Carl Milovanovich, I wondered about Jenny's state of mind. The woman in her mid-50s whose identity had been framed around her life as a teenager, a babysitter, a high school student; a teacher's pet.

I wanted to ask Jenny questions that would go to the heart of what she knew or suspected and when. Jenny went from being oblivious to the probable murder of her predecessor to being strongly suspicious but that could not have happened overnight. It seemed more likely it was something that seeped gradually into her consciousness over a number of years. Chris was her protector and the father of her child; she must have believed in his innocence for a number of years. That made more sense, especially in light of Rebecca's suggestion that, contrary to their 2017 perceptions of having strongly believed in 1982 that Lyn was murdered, Lyn's friends did not at first suspect the worst of Chris.

The day before meeting Carl Milovanovich, he was in the news for a starkly different case. After a complex and long-running

Australian Federal Police investigation, a Sydney man was embroiled in allegations he had tried to sell ballistic missile components and highly classified information about weapons of mass destruction to the rogue state of North Korea. The accused appeared before Magistrate Carl Milovanovich who, having retired as the deputy state coroner, was back as an acting magistrate to help clear a backlog of court cases.

Before we arrived, he had done some research on 'no body' cases of suspected murder.

'It's very, very hard, isn't it, to get a conviction without a body,' he said as we set up equipment for the interview.

This was another significant breakthrough – a former coroner talking on the record about a case which had troubled him greatly; a case he believed should have been prosecuted by the Office of the DPP. It is unusual for former judicial figures to grant interviews. My request to interview the retired magistrate Jan Stevenson, who ran the 2001 inquest, had been declined. I believe that Carl took the view that, while unorthodox, the public interest would be served by him sharing his views in a podcast series.

As Nick Adams-Dzierzba began recording, Carl explained why circumstantial evidence in a case such as Lyn's was particularly challenging. If the accused can point to a reasonable hypothesis consistent with innocence, it's very hard to secure a conviction.

'And no doubt the DPP would have been thinking one hypothesis is that she's just gone away and started a new life,' he said. 'When you haven't got a body, that's a hypothesis that can be raised. I don't think it's a reasonable one. Not when you've got two children and you've got a family, a community, a job and all those things. The circumstances, all the circumstances when you put them together, are so remarkable that I just could not accept that Lyn Dawson would just disappear off the face of the earth without there being some human intervention. It just defies all logic that a mother would leave a four-year-old, a two-year-old, a family, a job and friends and just disappear.'

Carl described the purported phone calls from Lyn to Chris, and the alleged sightings of Lyn on the Central Coast and elsewhere, as 'lies' told to muddy the water. He criticised the initial police investigation for having treated Lyn as merely another missing person.

'They never looked at the issues of domestic violence. They never looked at the reality, or the possibility, that this was a homicide,' he said.

Back in 2002, before the public hearings for the February 2003 inquest, Carl met regularly with Damian Loone to go through the brief of evidence and look at other avenues for investigation. It's always a truth-seeking exercise where the magistrate effectively takes a hands-on approach to try to ensure nothing gets overlooked, grants further warrants to search premises and determines the witnesses who should appear. When he did this in Lyn's case, Carl told us, his initial reaction was, 'Why haven't the police charged this fellow with murder?'

The transcripts of the inquest proceedings in 2003 made for fascinating reading as I prepared to interview Carl, who had butted heads with Peter Dawson, the solicitor appearing on behalf of his brothers Chris and Paul, and Paul's wife, Marilyn.

Peter Dawson mostly practised family law but had appeared previously in the Coroners Court, acting for his brothers and Marilyn at the 2001 inquest. The solicitor had told the court at that time that the focus of Detective Damian Loone on Chris as a probable murderer was completely misguided.

'If anybody stood to benefit from the death of Lynette Dawson, it was Jenny Carlson,' Peter Dawson said. 'And if this suggestion about a hitman was to have any weight, surely in an isolated area in Queensland, when he's living with Jenny Carlson, why wouldn't he do the same thing? It's just rubbish, Your Worship, and there is just no evidence to support this allegation at all.'

Peter Dawson had also rubbished the police brief of evidence. It was, he submitted, a tissue of lies and exaggeration. 'No prosecutor could even look at it. Now I don't put that on a light basis. I've been a Crown prosecutor for a certain period of time. No one would look at it, Your Worship. The investigation of this particular disappearance has been atrocious. It's not for Chris Dawson to pay the penalty for that. There's no evidence there at all that he did any harm to Lynette Joy Dawson.'

In 2001, State Coroner Jan Stevenson's decision to terminate the inquest and refer the matter to the Office of the DPP occurred after she had studied the police brief of evidence in her chambers. There was less than half a day of evidence heard in court and only one witness, Damian Loone. The transcript is a mere 25 pages.

The 2003 inquest was different; Carl wanted numerous witnesses to testify over five days of public hearings. The transcript runs to more than 300 pages.

On the first day of the inquest, Peter's heated cross-examination of Detective Damian Loone prompted an interruption by the deputy state coroner. 'I don't think emotion should really take over your role as a solicitor and I tend to detect that you are emotional in this matter and that may be clouding your judgment in relation to the manner in which you're conducting yourself in court and the way in which you're asking questions,' Carl told him.

Peter insisted that his role would not be adversely affected by emotion.

Carl told me that later, in his cross-examination of the detective, Peter's questions were repetitive and irrelevant. Carl had heard enough, advising Peter, 'You are regrettably not assisting me any further. Unless there are further questions of relevance, please sit down.'

Peter Dawson asked, 'Would Your Worship note my objection to what I regard as Your Worship gagging my line of cross-examination?'

'You can't object, Mr Dawson,' Carl explained. 'This is my inquiry. I indicated to you earlier, this is not a criminal court. I know this case backwards.'

Peter Dawson cited figures about missing persons generally, telling the detective that of the 8000 people reported as being missing in New South Wales each year, all except 0.4 per cent, or about 32 people, were located. He was trying to say that Lyn had left voluntarily and elected to stay away and that she was in the tiny percentage of missing people who were never found.

Their fate was of particular interest to Carl, who had made strong recommendations to reform the lackadaisical approach of police when it came to investigating missing persons reports.

'We know all these statistics, Mr Dawson,' the deputy state coroner said. 'We also know that of the 32 that are not located, they are usually victims of homicide.'

In the comfort of his lounge room, I asked Carl about the tensions during the inquest at Westmead in February 2003, where he was a stickler for formality and procedure.

'I wasn't impressed with the fact that he was appearing for his brother,' Carl said. 'I thought that as a lawyer, ethically, he might have considered that it might have been inappropriate for him to appear. It was obvious he had no experience in the coronial jurisdiction. I don't think he understood the purpose of cross-examination, nor did he understand at the end of the inquest what my role was. It muddied the water a little bit but that's about all. I don't think it affected my decision in any way to refer the matter to the DPP. That was based purely and clinically on the evidence.'

Carl's candour and his obvious confidence in the strength of the evidence he assessed in 2003 gave me hope that justice just might, finally, prevail. Carl had reached a certain view about Chris Dawson. If he were on a jury in a murder trial, Carl would almost certainly have voted to convict.

These two legally trained professionals, Carl and Peter, who were far apart in their approach and in their assessment of the facts were a similar age. Before he became a legal studies student, Carl had intended to be a schoolteacher. He was unemotional but there was no disguising his disdain for Chris Dawson.

'He knew she wasn't coming back. That's so evident. That's circumstantially so strong. I thought that out of all the cases that I had referred to the DPP . . . this was one where I thought they would (prosecute).'

When Jenny gave evidence in 2003, she was cross-examined by Peter Dawson, who didn't extract anything of note from his former sister-in-law. Plainly, as their testy exchanges revealed, there was no love lost between the two.

'I was impressed with her and I thought she was a witness of truth,' Carl said. 'You always had to balance the fact that she was very young at the time when the relationship started, about 16. She had been with Chris Dawson for ten years and obviously the marriage had broken down. There would have been some acrimony there, and you have to look very carefully to try and sift through whether there is any animosity in that evidence towards Chris.'

Carl highlighted the unseemly haste with which Chris went to South West Rocks to collect Jenny and bring her back to Bayview, just 24 to 48 hours after Lyn had disappeared. This timing, in the former deputy state coroner's view, was a powerful feature of any future prosecution case. It 'defies logic' that a husband would install his teenage girlfriend in the house if he truly believed his wife might return after taking some time on her own to think things over.

But if a husband knew his wife would never be coming back?

'That is, I think, Chris Dawson's Achilles heel. If you put all this evidence before a jury of normal people, they would come back with a guilty verdict.

'You've got to try and go back to the DPP and say, "Have another look at this." Maybe the family can push that. They could say, "Well, look, the scenario about her possibly going up and joining a commune or something or some religious group – after all these years, if she was alive, she would have contacted the family." She's got daughters who are probably married now and got kids. And her mother's passed away and just missed out on all those anniversaries and all those milestones. It's just not normal human behaviour for a woman with her intelligence, her community ties, the fact that she was employed. She had two kids. A lovely home. It just doesn't add up.

'One might speculate that if the circumstantial evidence is so strong as to suggest that Chris Dawson murdered Lyn and disposed of her body, he may have needed some help.'

The one part of Jenny's evidence which he regarded as weak, albeit potentially factual, was the drive with Chris across the Sydney Harbour Bridge to see a hitman about getting rid of Lyn. Jenny's uncorroborated testimony about this purported event would come under fierce attack in any criminal trial.

'Is she venting a little bit of spleen in relation to a marriage that broke down and so forth?' Carl asked. 'I could see a lawyer tearing her apart in relation to that piece of evidence.'

At the end of a long day, Carl's energy was contagious. I had a spring in my step and Rebecca looked invigorated as we pulled out of the driveway, with Carl and his wife warmly waving goodbye.

The former deputy state coroner clearly saw the merit in giving this unsolved case a big push. Fifteen years after he had completed his own scrutiny, he still wanted the DPP to reverse its decision. Carl was prepared to express his disappointment in a system of which he was still a part. It was a brave call. In my experience, judges and magistrates kept their lips sealed unless they were making pronouncements from the protection of the bench. But in Lyn's case, good people like Carl were deeply invested to try to ensure that Chris Dawson would one day be made accountable.

Rebecca and I agreed that Chris Dawson was not a criminal mastermind. Police incompetence, the trust of Lyn's family and the passage of time had conspired to help him get away with murder. He just got lucky that it all fell in his favour while the trail went cold.

We debated Carl's suggestion that we pay for a senior lawyer to review all the evidence and provide a written opinion about the prospects of a successful prosecution. It would cost upwards of $10,000 in legal fees and Rebecca visibly winced at my suggestion that we put a big bet on a racehorse to try to win the kind of money a lawyer would want.

'What do you think the chances are that we can somehow bring closure and solve it?' I asked.

'So much is stacked against us after 36 years,' Rebecca replied.

'But, sometimes, it happens.' I was feeling more confident after the interviews with Julie Andrew and Carl Milovanovich.

Rebecca looked anxious while driving unfamiliar back roads in western Sydney at night. There was no street lighting, and her BMW's front lamps scarcely illuminated the way ahead.

'It's only going to be this dark for a very short distance,' she said hopefully.

Our deep-thinking friend and audio producer Nick Adams-Dzierzba, still dutifully holding the microphone in the back, responded, 'Are you talking about driving or the investigation?'

We looked at each other, confused.

'Sorry. It's an analogy about how dark it is and not seeing where you're going.'

He made a fair point.

Chapter 23

Ocean Grove

Seaplanes tracking the coastline to the northern playgrounds of Palm Beach and Pittwater flew in cloudless skies directly over Bev Balkind's house as the retired teacher welcomed us inside. Her father found the bungalow when he knew he was dying. He wanted to live his last days next to the Pacific Ocean, waves lapping the curving coastline to Long Reef Point.

After her mother's death, Bev, by then a young schoolteacher, moved in. She and her husband, David Clarke, made it their home and raised two children there, long before property speculators and wealthy elites helped drive prices for oceanfront property into the stratosphere.

As Bev offered homemade cookies flavoured with ginger and cinnamon and sprinkled with pecans, she picked up the narrative from where David had left off a couple of weeks earlier.

Lyn had been gone for several months when Bev, a physical education teacher, successfully applied to transfer to Cromer High in the first half of 1982. She filled a position newly vacated by Chris Dawson, who was moved to Beacon Hill High.

Jenny Carlson, who had completed her final year of school the year before, had been living with Chris as his de facto since about 10 January. Teachers and students were talking. It needed to be managed. Education officials managed it by moving Mr Dawson from Cromer High to Beacon Hill. Problem solved.

Bev became acutely aware that the sexual contact between Chris and Jenny had begun when the girl was still at school.

'I had a class of special needs children and when we were inside the gym doing gymnastics, they'd say, "You don't have to stay with us, miss. Mr Dawson used to go and spend the time in the storeroom with Jenny,"' Bev recalled.

'He would go to the storeroom with Jenny and leave them alone in the gym to do whatever they wanted. These kids were just very open and honest because of their disabilities. They didn't understand there was anything wrong with what they said to me. They didn't see that they were telling tales or saying anything they shouldn't.'

I didn't ask Bev what went on in the storeroom but she left me in no doubt that the teacher and the student were having sex while his class of special needs students went unsupervised.

The reaction of a number of the other male teachers, several of whom were emulating Chris in their exploitation of female students, troubled her greatly. Instead of being appalled at the conduct which necessitated his transfer, the reaction, she recalled, was, 'Poor Chris, he got caught'.

'I was new to the school and when you're a newbie anywhere, you don't make waves or carry on,' Bev said. 'I was offended by it but I didn't want to make enemies right away. And I convinced myself that if I didn't see something happen with my own eyes, then I certainly couldn't report it. That washed my hands of any responsibility.

'You didn't know who you could trust in the hierarchy of the school. You didn't know if you could go to the principal or your head teacher and say something and it would be believed or if you'd be the one who'd be moved on next.'

Bev could not recall having ever met Chris Dawson. However, she had regarded him as a 'lowlife and reprehensible' since she started to teach at Cromer High in 1982. Most of the women on staff, she believed, felt similarly about his abuse of power. But not the men.

Some years after Lyn's disappearance, Bev's views of Chris hardened as she came to know her new neighbour, Sue Strath, and heard Sue's stories of Lyn's love for her girls and how unlikely it would be for Lyn to up and leave. Like Sue, Bev had been cutting out and keeping articles from the newspapers over the years.

'And each time something comes up about Chris I'm thinking, "They must get him this time. They have to." And yet they never do. He's still walking free. I believe he's as guilty as sin.'

When we talked about physical education teachers in high schools and whether they were overrepresented when it came to sexual misconduct with students, Bev was adamant, citing her own experiences over decades of teaching; a certain number of male PE teachers never grew up and behaved like adolescents in adult bodies. Yes, she was making a sweeping generalisation, and no, of course it didn't apply to the majority. Still, it did have a ring of truth to it.

'And that was what they were like when we were at college with them. They were alley cats, all of them. Well, most of them. There were a few good ones there,' Bev said.

A few days before I met Bev, Australia's longest-running public inquiry, the national Royal Commission into Institutional Responses to Child Sexual Abuse, had delivered its final report, exposing pedophile priests in the Catholic Church, Anglican Church and others, pedophile schoolteachers in church-run schools, and dozens of cases of the failure of authorities to respond ethically, morally and lawfully to the molestation of children. In this overdue inquiry, public hearings around the country heard from many survivors of sexual abuse. Some of the most senior figures in Australia's churches were investigated and cross-examined about wilful failures to report abuse and actively covering up abuse. Criminal prosecutions of the allegedly guilty were inevitable after so much damning evidence and investigative effort. There were hundreds of recommendations to help keep children safe from predatory adults.

Tens of millions of dollars from the public purse were spent over five years on a retired judge, lawyers and other professionals to get to the bottom of it all. Oddly, public schools were all but ignored in the investigative sweep. Nobody had lifted a finger to examine the culture and conduct of the teachers at the schools on Sydney's Northern Beaches. Nobody from the public inquiry's vast staff looked at how the grooming of one student by a popular teacher had led to the probable murder of a loving wife and mother of two girls.

I told Bev and David about the harrowing police statement of the former student, Alice, who described what she said had occurred between herself and Paul Dawson, his brother Chris and other teachers, including in the school's gym. They appeared shocked. Revolted. It was the same reaction I experienced every time I read the compelling document. I had used Google and Facebook to find these men. I had found so many photographs and posts about them as grandfathers in peaceful, respectful retirement. Would it be unfair to hold them accountable now, so many years later?

Bev, who freely admitted that she had been 'a chicken' when it came to calling the abuse out when it was happening around her in the early 1980s, replied, 'As the royal commission has shown us, people who commit these horrendous crimes have to be taken and made to account for themselves. Otherwise, you'd say war criminals, just because they're old, shouldn't be prosecuted. It's the same thing. If you're a criminal, you're a criminal. Sorry to be moralistic but that's how I see it.'

Later, David reflected on whether he looked back and saw himself as part of the 'boys club', having turned a blind eye to what he had heard, and suspected, was occurring between fellow male teachers and female students.

'You hear things,' David said. 'Are they true? Do you really know when you hear things? None of the people I've worked with ever said, "Guess what I'm doing?" You don't make waves. I mean, you've got to work with these people. You don't know where the bodies are buried. You don't muddy the water. Don't pick a fight. Don't accuse someone of molesting a Year 11 student. That's not going to go down well.'

*

We drove from the beachfront to the nearby home of the retired Detective Inspector Paul Hulme, whose wife, Helen, had been friends with Sue Strath since their teens. Through the 1980s and 1990s, Sue kept lobbying Helen and Paul about the need for police to properly investigate Lyn's suspicious disappearance.

By 1998, a promotion for Paul Hulme gave him the seniority to get something underway. As the new crime manager at Dee Why police station, he asked one of his most promising detectives, Damian Loone, to look into Lyn's disappearance.

'I'd love to see somebody get what he deserves,' Paul told me as we entered his home.

Nick Adams-Dzierzba, mindful of interfering audio noise, politely asked that the radio be turned off. It was mid-song – Carole King's 'You've Got A Friend'.

Helen began to talk about the dedication of Sue Strath. 'She is a determined person and Lyn was a very good friend of hers,' Helen said. 'She was extremely troubled that nothing really eventuated. So that's when she spoke to me . . . She thought, "Well, now's the opportunity . . . can you get Paul to do something? She's too important to just be forgotten."'

Paul nodded. When he tried unsuccessfully to find any evidence of proper investigation in the 1980s, he was, he recalled, 'pretty well disgusted'.

'To me, it was a stand-out that there were no other suspects. It could only be him. I just couldn't believe that you wouldn't attack it from that angle. Somebody should have been handed that to take over and do it. I just think it was obvious that you're looking at the husband.'

Paul believed that the credibility and popularity of Chris Dawson affected the police response in the early days. The former Newtown Jets first-grade footballer could call in favours.

'You weigh up all the options. Is it possible she would just walk away and leave? No. She was a good mum, I believe. Plus, there's the fact of his character. He was abusing his position at schools with girls. I'm not saying that makes him a murderer but it certainly shows that he had reason to get rid of her. Especially with the babysitter moving in and him marrying her. I mean, I think anybody picks up the book and says, "Oh, you've got to be kidding. If it was not him, who is it?" I've been involved in a lot of missing persons cases. And a lot of them have been murdered.'

Paul Hulme wanted Damian Loone on the job because he knew the detective was like a dog with a bone. Damian and Sue Strath shared that quality, which meant Lyn's case was never completely extinguished, despite the official incompetence and inaction which followed her disappearance.

Without identifying Chris, I asked Paul, 'What does it take to catch a killer in this case?'

'A confession would be handy, from Chris,' he replied. 'He's approaching old age. Maybe if he gets sick, or something, and he wants to clear his chest.'

Several hours later, over beers in my room at the former Manly Pacific International Hotel, Rebecca told Nick and me about the businessman who had previously owned the oceanfront building, Andrew Kalajzich. Having become wealthy and widely respected in the community after starting out in the family fish and chip shop, he opened the hotel in 1983. Three years later, his wife, Megan, was murdered in her bed. A gunman entered their house on 27 January 1986 and fired two bullets into her head as Andrew lay beside her.

The ensuing homicide investigation uncovered Andrew's plot to have the mother of two killed and he was charged over her murder. The former leader of the Manly Chamber of Commerce protested his innocence but few people believed him; the evidence of him having paid the killer $20,000 and helping with the staging were irrefutable, and he was convicted and sentenced to 25 years. He was released in 2012, still protesting his innocence.

I shook my head and shared happier news: Lyn's brother Greg Simms had telephoned.

'The ABC has contacted him about that program, *Chequerboard*, on the twins. They've got it. And he said, "I've got goosebumps. Lyn is going to be in there, talking, and we will be able to watch her and listen to her." They don't have any tape or audio of their sister. And now he's going to get this as an MP4 video file. He's so rapt and emotional. He said three times, "I've just got chills from this."'

Up to this point, we knew Lyn only from photographs and what others said about her. Soon, though, we would be able to watch her and listen to her on a screen. And watch and listen to her husband and her brother-in-law.

Twenty minutes after Greg shared the happy news, the Coroners Court's acting registrar, Kazeline Dawson, called me. My request for duplicates of the audio recordings of the coronial proceedings in 2001 and 2003 had hit a major roadblock: the audio had been destroyed.

It is hard to understand why anyone in the Coroners Court, a well-resourced and integral part of the administration of justice, would want to destroy audio-cassette tapes of witnesses and lawyers in five days of legal proceedings revolving around a suspected murder.

The ABC had kept video of the *Chequerboard* program in its archives since the 1970s; for 17 years, I had kept my files about Lyn in my desk and in the roof space of my carport. And yet someone working for the government had decided these audio records, involving the most serious allegations that can be levelled, were dispensable.

Two steps forward, one step back.

Chapter 24

Bruises

'I'm downstairs with coffees,' Rebecca texted a little after 8 am on 20 December. We were on the home straight now. Just two more interviews before I could return to Brisbane and take some time off with my family.

Annette Leary had sounded very fragile when I spoke to her on the phone. She had been in hospital and I feared the worst. As her grandchildren splashed in the pool, we sat around her dining table and Annette talked over the noise from the cicadas about her recollections of Lyn's last days. The mating ritual of these ruthless insects was deafening and we needed the windows closed to ensure the recording would be audible. Without air conditioning, the room had become a sauna due to heatwave conditions.

After 45 minutes, I was drenched in my own perspiration and Annette looked ill but at least the interview was just about done. I glanced at Nick Adams-Dzierzba, holding the microphone, to signal we could wrap things up. Annette had answered all our questions. She recalled that Lyn had told her that on her way to marriage counselling with Chris, he had put his hands around her neck and warned, 'If this doesn't work, I'm getting rid of you'. It was something, Annette added, she'd never forget.

It was an amazing quote, a great grab for a podcast. But Nick looked deeply worried. After another minute of frantic button-

228

pushing, he looked crestfallen. Inexplicably, the recording equipment had failed. There was no audio, and we were running late to talk to Lorraine Watson, a former dressmaker who lived in a nearby aged care centre. We would have to return to Annette's house later that day, when the heatwave had made everything hotter.

On the way, Rebecca and I talked about a scenario in which Lyn had been near-strangled in the lift on the way to marriage counselling on 8 January 1982. It was not hard to picture Chris putting his powerful hands around Lyn's throat and squeezing, just as Jenny had alleged he had done with her. But it was difficult to imagine Lyn telling her friends at the childcare centre afterwards that everything had gone well, and repeating this to her mother on the telephone that night. How Lyn could have possibly believed her marriage might come good again after such an event, if it had happened as described, was unfathomable.

At the aged care centre a short drive from Annette's house, the residents were singing Christmas carols and decorations filled the lobby. Lorraine was a popular resident. The staff clearly doted on this forthright woman, who had come forward to talk to Detective Damian Loone in 2003 after the screening of the ABC's *Australian Story* program. When she watched the program, Lorraine recognised Lyn as a woman who had come into her dress shop in the Strand Arcade on several occasions to have a dress made for a special event. Lyn's visits were memorable because Lorraine saw what she described as 'massive bruises' on Lyn's body when she took off her clothes for a fitting. Lorraine and her husband, Ron, got to know Lyn a little more while giving her a lift home from the city.

'My daughter's not really happy about me doing this,' Lorraine told us as we started the interview. 'She said to me, "Mum, don't get involved, you know, it's a murder."'

Lorraine wondered whether we thought Chris Dawson would come after her if the case went to court. 'I don't think so though, do you?' Lorraine asked.

I explained that we had already interviewed a number of Lyn's friends who had made strong comments about Chris. Nobody was holding back. Lorraine ploughed ahead, recalling her contacts with Lyn.

'I can remember distinctly what she told us, because we became quite friendly with her. When we took her into the dressing room, we noticed on her arm, on both her arms, like finger marks. And I thought, "Oh, that's strange." But I said nothing because we had just met her.

'Then when we gave her the first fitting and she had to take her clothes off, I noticed on her thigh an absolutely massive bruise. A bluey-purple bruise. It looked as if someone had kicked her. And I said to her, "What in the hell have you been doing to yourself?"

'She said, "Oh, it's a long story."

'So after a while, we got talking to her about her children and everything, and she said, "I'm not in a very happy marriage. I'm married to a very violent man."

'And I said, "Did he do all those bruises on you?" And she said, "Yes but he's done other things to me as well."

'She told me that he used to belt her around. We said, "Why don't you leave him? You know you can't stay with somebody that's like that."

'She said, "Oh, where would I go? I've got a house, I've got two beautiful children. What would I do?"'

Lorraine didn't see Lyn again. I asked her about her confidence that the woman in the photographs on *Australian Story* was the same one who came to Lorraine's fashion salon.

'I'm absolutely positive,' she said. 'And as soon as the show finished, I rang Damian Loone, who took my call straight away, and I said to him, "I know that girl." And I told him over the phone what I'd seen, and he came round to see me the next day.'

Lorraine had made her mind up about Chris Dawson. 'Damian Loone said, "He's definitely guilty." And he said, "Well, we'll get him in the end."'

We chatted for a while and Lorraine answered all our questions. I asked whether she was still worried or did she feel better having spoken on the record about it.

'I think I'm doing the right thing, if what I've told you can help with the case,' she said.

Back at Annette Leary's house for the second time that day, her husband, Brian, exhibited his pride and joy, a beautifully restored fire chief's car from the 1920s. He showed us one of its original novelties – a little contraption to remove horse-shoe nails which, back in the day, would become embedded in the tyres.

The cicadas were still out of control. We worried about subjecting Annette to a second interview in her overheated dining room but she was insistent about doing what she could for Lyn.

'There was only the two of them in the lift and they got in together and he pushed her up against the wall and holding her by the throat, he shook her and said, "I'm only doing this once and if it doesn't work, I'm getting rid of you."'

'And just to be clear, you were not a witness to that event?' I asked.

'Not a witness. No. We only heard what she said had happened. She seemed a bit shocked but laughing it off. Because she loved him and she pretended that, you know, he was only being silly and he wouldn't really hurt her. She couldn't believe that he would. We found it very strange, very hard to understand. She had bruises on her neck. And that's why we were shocked. We asked her what had happened and that's what she said. When she came back after that counselling session, she told us that she thought it was going to work and she could save her marriage.'

The conundrum that Rebecca had identified was front and centre: it was difficult to reconcile the two post-counselling statements. On the one hand, Lyn telling her friends at work about her throat being squeezed by her husband as he's talking about 'getting rid' of her; on the other hand, Lyn telling the same friends that her marriage is going to survive.

'I really think she was fooling herself,' Annette added. 'She couldn't bear to think that it would really break down. So she again was pretending that what he did was just playing around and he wouldn't really hurt her.'

Annette regretted that she had not been outspoken much sooner about her suspicions. She didn't mention them to Lyn's mother, Helena, when she called asking if the women had heard from Lyn.

'I think we all dropped the ball when it really came down to it,' she said.

'We all should have put our thoughts together about what had happened and gone to a police station and said, "This has been happening, now this girl has disappeared. She hasn't come back to work or home and we're worried about her." It would have been the thing to do. Back then in the eighties, we weren't as confident in ourselves to go to the police and say, "You should be doing this." We felt we just had to wait for them to do what they had to do but it just went on and on and on.

'I can still see those two little girls when she'd bring them to the centre, waiting for her mum to pick them up. Or Chris. And she couldn't be more proud of any little thing they did. Just loved them to bits.'

We left Annette, exhausted, overheated and dehydrated. I had time for beers in Manly with my friend Chris Mitchell, *The Australian*'s longtime editor-in-chief before the baton was passed to Paul Whittaker. When I was given the green light in 2001 to go to Sydney and bring back a big story about a missing mum, Chris was running *The Courier-Mail*. The culture he instilled in us was great for journalism. Chris left a massive hole at the newspaper when he left to return to Sydney.

Then I'd take the Manly ferry back to Circular Quay, a train to the airport and the 6.05 pm flight back to Brisbane.

'We've had a very fortunate three days, talking to as many people as we have. We just have to now put it away for Christmas,' I said to Rebecca.

She looked lost in thought. 'I had a really, really spooky feeling in there at the end,' Rebecca said. 'In everything we've been hearing and learning in this really condensed period of time that we're going to see people, Lynette knew where it was going. Lynette knew it was over.

'And I just had this horrible image that when he went to kill her, she let him do it.'

Part 3

Juggernaut

Chapter 25

Chequerboard

January 2018

A twenty-minute drive from Chris Dawson's house near the beach, I walked popular trails across Noosa National Park and looked for a killer.

Chris was in my head. Lyn's death was on my mind every waking hour. I had been told by several people how tight-fisted he was with money. He would not have wanted to expose himself to repercussions, including extortion from a contract killer. For these reasons, I believed that Chris had done the terrible deed himself. There was no hitman. I pictured him smothering Lyn with a pillow or strangling the life out of her, having made her drowsy with a sedative in her 'lovely drink'.

I scanned the crowds at nearby Peregian Beach and Sunshine Beach. Early one morning, I was sure I saw him striding purposefully towards me on the coastal path winding back from the oceanfront cliffs known as Hell's Gates. For a moment such as this, I had silently rehearsed a spiel: *Chris, you know I've been interested in Lyn's disappearance for a long time, and I'm going to tell the story again but in a lot more detail than before. It is an opportunity for you to finally tell your side and I'm offering an unedited interview.*

The elderly man smiled and cheerfully remarked on the beautifully sunny, windless day; he was not Chris.

My pursuit had become an obsession. It started to chafe with Ruth during a family holiday when I was supposed to be giving time and attention back to my wife and our remarkable teenagers, Alexander and Sarah.

I was confident Chris by now knew something about the investigations and interviews I had been doing for the podcast since November. Jenny had been aware of the podcast plans for a couple of months. It would have been surprising if she had not told her then 33-year-old daughter and as the young woman maintained a relationship with her father, it followed that she could have mentioned it to him.

I had also begun to worry about how much there was to do before the proposed release of the podcast series in a few months. There were still many more people to find and interview, and while Rebecca was trying to organise a date for our meeting, Jenny had not confirmed. When all the interviews with Jenny and others were completed, I would need to write the equivalent of a book, with a 10,000-word script for each of at least eight episodes, run all of the copy past the newspaper's defamation lawyer, John-Paul Cashen, and finally, I would need a crash course from skilled audio practitioners in 'microphone technique' so that I could narrate the story in a studio for a podcast which I knew I wanted to call *The Teacher's Pet*.

For ideas and inspiration I listened to the true crime podcast *Dirty John* and revisited the earlier smash-hit, *Serial*. The more I listened to these stories, the more certain I became that Lyn's story was about much more than the murder of a dedicated mother and wife. Somehow, I needed to convey an injustice on an epic scale. The bureaucratic incompetence and the longing of loved ones and the unforgivable betrayal over almost 40 years had to be clear.

Ruth, who had helped me write a draft of Lyn's story before it became my 2001 feature-length article 'Looking for Lyn' for a Saturday edition of *The Courier-Mail*, was a patient sounding-board as I dived down rabbit holes with the many mind-bending facets of the case.

A new and vivid technicolour version of Chris and of Lyn came
into sharp focus with the ABC's discovery of the *Chequerboard*
episode from 1975. Greg emailed the video link to me. The first time
I watched it just before Christmas Day, I sat affected by the obvious
charisma of Chris and Paul Dawson. The twins' fascinating interviews with the journalist, Robin Hughes, and her skilful weaving of
the storyline to include Lyn made a powerful impression.

For Lyn's siblings, Phil, Greg and Pat, it was an emotional experience. They had accepted that Lyn was dead and never coming back
but here, they could see her moving and smiling and talking in her
softly soothing voice.

Lyn was speaking with adoration about the love of her life, Chris,
years before he would cheat and scheme against her. Or was he
already cheating and scheming?

I felt certain every time I watched it that it would be a special driver
for the podcast series. Listeners who went to our website would not
only hear the goodness in Lyn, they would also see it. They would see
and hear the twins Chris and Paul admiring their reflections while
pumping iron and talking about their strange closeness; viewers and
listeners would be transported back to a high school football field
in Sydney in the mid-1970s, and the house in which Chris and Lyn
lived before they moved to Bayview; the audience would witness a
dining table for a celebratory lunch to mark the twins' birthdays, and
a kitchen where Lyn took care of the meal and the dishes.

I found myself smiling at the twins' good humour and easygoing
banter. When I didn't imagine him squeezing the life out of Lyn, it
was hard not to warm to Chris Dawson, to both the twins; to like
them as they traded friendly insults about Paul being the firstborn
and the leader of the duo.

'I joke Chris was too stupid to find his way out by himself,' Paul
says.

Chris immediately adds, 'I always say the stock reply that because
he was so stupid, I had to push him out first.'

On a more serious note, Paul says, 'It's a very hard relationship to
explain to anyone that's not a twin. And, you know, people straight

away think, "Oh it's not a homosexual relationship, it's not like a husband–wife relationship." It's not a . . . normal brother–brother relationship, it's something apart from all those.'

They spoke in the documentary of a secret language they shared as children that nobody else could understand.

Paul explains. 'Well, we had our own language, and we had to go to sort of speech therapy, at five to seven years of age to learn to speak properly.'

By their own admissions, their closeness is bizarre. It was unlike anything I had witnessed in some of my own friends who are twins.

I emailed Rebecca Hazel, and Greg and Merilyn.

> This program with Chris and Paul and Lyn and Marilyn is mind-blowing.
>
> I had wondered until tonight whether the frequent references by people we have been interviewing to the 'charisma' of the Dawson brothers were being overstated or cliched. In fact, it's true, they come across in this program, I think, as likeable, articulate and charismatic.
>
> If we were not aware of the stacks of evidence and their admissions about their conduct, I reckon we would want to know them. There's a quiet, reserved confidence that falls short of smugness.

Lyn's elegance and gentleness shone through. She came across as beautiful, sparkling, radiant, well-spoken and hopelessly in love with her husband.

Lyn says of her husband and his connection with Paul, 'And I hadn't properly thought about sharing him until somebody a couple of years ago said, "What is it like sharing a husband?"

'To me, it just seemed so silly because I hadn't really thought of it and you just join in. You encourage their closeness – not that it needs encouragement.'

There was something about the tone of Lyn's brief rejoinder – those five words 'not that it needs encouragement' – which spoke volumes. Lyn seemed to be suggesting her husband and Paul were exceedingly close. Too close.

'Her eyes really are alight,' I wrote to Greg and Merilyn. 'This program is about 45 years old and it was before Princess Diana's time but there is a look of Diana about Lyn. Ruth pointed it out. Marilyn looks devoted too. What she has to say is less interesting. Lyn's classiness shines through and overpowers Marilyn, I believe.'

Marilyn says in *Chequerboard*, 'They are very dependent on one another, I'm the first to admit that. And they consult one another all the time but I think that is a fantastic bond between them, that's part of their twin-ship – that they love one another and they want to be kind to one another and that comes out all the time.'

Pat and I spoke on the telephone. She had been teary about seeing her sister talking for the first time in 36 years.

'It's a treasure, it's a gift,' Pat said. 'Back then, there were very few videos and we didn't have a video recorder. So there's no live videos of Lyn or of anyone in the family. I probably value it too much.'

'When Lyn comes into it, she's lovely, she's very classy, and everything you've told me about her just made sense, it fell into place,' I replied.

But Pat sounded sad. It had taken her until 2 am to get to sleep; she'd been lying awake, thinking about Chris and Lyn in happier times. Thinking about the betrayal of her family. About the sadness of her mother. On Facebook, Pat had seen recent images of a beaming Chris holding his grandchildren, and these troubled her greatly.

'I just think he's the face of evil, sitting there grinning, holding these two little babies,' she told me.

Pat had also come across a photograph of Paul and Chris together at a recent family wedding.

'Oh, that was such a shock. It was just awful to see it. I try not to look at him. That's something I think I didn't express very well, why I said I hate him. It was because of what he'd done to so many people through his own selfishness and what he wanted but especially what he did to my mum, because I saw how my mum suffered and that I could never forgive. Never, ever. I don't dwell on him. He's taking too much from me, again, if I dwell on him all the time. I try not to let him enter into my life at all.

'But if I see a picture of him, I just see evil. I really see evil.'

I had asked Pat to collate her mother's diary entries and letters for me. Going through all of the correspondence and re-reading the spidery scribbles and handwriting of Helena had been distressing. It had also been irksome for Pat because it reminded her that Damian Loone had not taken a formal signed statement from Helena Simms. She was an important witness, having talked to a groggy-sounding Lyn on the evening of Friday 8 January, when Lyn had told her that everything went well at marriage counselling and Chris had just made her 'a lovely drink'.

Pat knew that I believed she was, in her words, 'a bit hard on Damian' for his failure to interview Helena, and for not having appreciated the evidentiary value of all of Helena's diary jottings and letters to her children about the claims from Chris about Lyn's purported contacts with him. These documents were an invaluable chronology.

'I really appreciate what he did and how he got things started but he did sit on Lyn's case for many, many years without actually doing anything,' Pat told me.

'He was always going to get Mum's diaries from me and he never did. He was always going to interview mum and he left it too long.

'And she was trying to be helpful and everything she knew she was putting down on this written statement. She handed it to the police but she hadn't been questioned about it and if she was questioned she would have been able to say, "This is what Chris told me". But Mum was putting it down as if it was fact.

'They never got around to questioning her and in the end it was too late, she was too unwell and couldn't do it. He wouldn't contact us and I'd chase him all around the police force. But then when he actually did give us his mobile phone number,

it was much better. It should have gone to the Unsolved Homicide
Squad probably a decade before.'

Pat spoke of going to Dee Why police station and sitting there for
hours in the hope that she would see Damian on his return from
whatever investigation he was out on.

My perspective on Damian's efforts came from the bundle of
documents and witness statements which formed the police brief
of evidence for the 2001 inquest. The outcomes of both inquests
were a testament to his effectiveness with the police prosecutor Matt
Fordham, though so little appeared to have been done by police
before Damian started investigating that his efforts looked particularly impressive.

Pat was undeniably grateful that Damian 'got the ball rolling', as
she put it. She noted that the affable general duties detective appeared
to enjoy the publicity which came with his handling of the case.

Damian's nickname among other cops was 'Hollywood' because
of their perception of his enthusiasm for the camera. I took the view
that he orchestrated publicity for Lyn's case when it was tactical to do
so. Sometimes he did it when he had been authorised to have covert
intercepts on Chris and Paul Dawson's telephones and he wanted to
hear what they would say about stories in *The Daily Telegraph* of a
new dig, or the re-testing of what was believed to be Lyn's cardigan,
found in layers of dirt around the swimming pool, for DNA. The
phone taps were useless – Chris and Paul said nothing incriminating – but other people who knew Lyn or Chris or Paul did come
forward with snippets of information thanks to the media interest.

Pat recalled an occasion at her house when Damian arrived with
an official police camera operator to film a meeting around the dining
table with a self-described clairvoyant, Debbie Malone. Greg sent me
a copy of the video of the bizarre event from October 2003. I had
watched it with growing astonishment. I saw the pleading, desperate
hope in Lyn's siblings as Debbie put her hands around her own neck
to reproduce what she claimed Lyn, in the 'afterlife', was channel-
ling about the circumstances surrounding her murder – purportedly

with a plastic bag over her head while she was sleeping. Debbie says in the police video that Lyn is right there with them, looking down at the dining table and willing Damian to solve the case because 'it's taken so long'.

Debbie says of the property at Bayview, 'I think the body's still there. She's lying really flat.'

As a sceptic, I found the lengthy video excruciating. Although I begrudgingly agreed with Debbie Malone's speculation about the whereabouts of Lyn's body, she offered nothing which she could not have gleaned from reading the media's coverage of the inquests or watching the ABC's *Australian Story* program about the case. Nevertheless, she projected certainty that she was actually communicating with the spirit of a long-dead Lyn. I shrank at the reactions of Greg and Pat. I could see from the video that while they appeared dazed by the theatrics, they were persuaded of Lyn's presence in the room. On a couple of occasions, it looked like Damian was convinced too.

Years later, when Pat raised it with me, her concern was not with the strangeness of a clairvoyant being invited by a detective to become part of a murder investigation – Pat was fine with that part – but that she had not been forewarned about a photographer and journalist from *The Daily Telegraph* being invited by Damian to come to Pat's house to observe it all for a story.

'And he didn't even say, "Oh, do you mind if we have *The Telegraph* here,"' Pat told me. 'He did like the publicity but maybe that was the way it got things started at the beginning.'

Damian did not limit it to *The Daily Telegraph*. In the folder of clippings that Sue Strath had given me at her house at Ocean Grove in December, I remembered a front-page story by Jacinta Koch in *The Manly Daily*. The headline was 'Body in bush tip', and below it there was a prominent photograph of a sombre-looking Pat sitting at a table with Debbie. Damian and Greg were standing nearby.

I knew Jacinta, a friend whom I had met a few years earlier when she worked at *The Courier-Mail*. The story began: 'Police plan to search an area of peninsula bushland for the body of a woman who disappeared mysteriously 21 years ago. The development follows a tip from a psychic who "made contact" with the dead woman in Seaforth this week.'

Jacinta's story quoted Damian saying that he was, at first, sceptical but that he went ahead with the session as he 'had to keep an open mind'.

'I haven't ever worked with something like this before, no. It's worked in the [United] States.'

In her mild-mannered way, Pat had started talking to Lyn's daughter Shanelle about my investigation. A single mum, Shanelle had recently moved back from New Zealand and was renting a house at Hervey Bay, a couple of hours' drive north of Noosa Heads, where I was spending time with my family in January.

'I told her all about it and her initial reaction, she said, was fearful, and then she said that she's excited about it,' Pat told me. 'She really wants answers and she wants justice.'

Pat agreed to let Shanelle know that at a private meeting, I would explain my approach to her mother's probable murder and what I intended to do with the podcast investigation. Implicit in this was the fact that Shanelle would need to go behind her father's back to meet me.

There were big risks for her. She strongly suspected that Chris had murdered her mother. Somehow, Shanelle had still maintained a relationship with him. Shanelle got along with her second step-mother, Susan, who was a science teacher at Coombabah State High on the Gold Coast when Chris and Paul were teaching there. But Shanelle's bigger worry was her younger sister, Amy, who believed her father was being unfairly targeted and had done nothing wrong.

Shanelle sounded intrigued when we finally spoke on the phone in January. She showed a cautious willingness to be involved somehow. She wanted to know more about my investigation and she deserved a thorough backgrounding even though I had not yet approached Chris Dawson for his side of the story.

Shanelle agreed to meet me at her house in Hervey Bay, a popular destination for tourists to take whale-watching tours. When I turned up with a box of mangoes, bought from a stall beside the Bruce

Highway, her warmth toward me, a stranger in her newly rented cottage, was immediately obvious. Shanelle was still settling into the community and she apologised for not having a knife sharp enough to cut the tropical fruit.

We spoke for hours. Shanelle wanted to know my views and I made it clear that the evidence I had collected and the interviews I had done to date meant I strongly believed her father had killed her mother. I couldn't sugarcoat or pretend but I assured her I wanted the podcast to reflect her father's side of the story and be as fair to him as possible. I told her I believed he should be put on trial for murder, and that anything was possible.

Shanelle saw where the podcast was going. She saw that it would be lining her father up as a probable murderer in an investigation which, when aired, would trigger enormous public interest in her family. She told me that her father remembered and hated me because of my reporting in 2001 for *The Courier-Mail*. Chris was convinced that those reports had been the catalyst for actions by the state's education authorities and the heads of the Catholic girls' school he was employed by at the time. The details in the stories and local publicity had forced him to quit, leaving behind the playground and the adolescent girls in their uniforms forever.

He was almost certainly right about the impact of my reporting in 2001. Exposing his conduct at Cromer High meant that bureaucrats had to respond to at least some of the facts from the early 1980s, terminating his Queensland teaching career. It was the right outcome and possibly saved numerous girls from grooming or worse, but his anger over my role meant he was extremely unlikely to agree to be interviewed for the podcast.

Chris was unaware that Shanelle had talked to the detective Damian Loone and had been videotaped while under hypnosis in 2013 during his investigation. It was a desperate effort to see if she had any memories as a toddler of the night her mother was believed to have been murdered. Shanelle told me that the professional hypnotherapist organised by Damian had elicited recollections from her as a small child in January 1982, including being woken up and put in a car at night. In these recovered memories, she said she was in the car and could see her father outside, digging up ground. But nobody would be able to prove that Shanelle's memories were genuine. All of it would be inadmissible in the event of a trial.

Shanelle had another conundrum. When we met in her home as her daughter played around us, Shanelle made no secret of her view that her father had killed her mother. She knew he was a narcissist and a liar. She was intimidated by him. He frightened her. But she loved him too. He could be funny and caring. She knew he loved her and wanted their bond to continue. She also knew he was masterful at manipulation.

Shanelle wanted to honour her mother by participating in the podcast investigation without immediately burning her relationship with her father. She loved her sister. We had a lot to think about before either of us could take the idea forward for an on-the-record interview. I was prepared to do whatever it took to accommodate Shanelle. She had lost so much and wanted justice.

Her voice, gentle and lovely, reminded me of her mother's voice. Her seemingly limitless patience with her daughter during some toddler naughtiness reminded me of things Lyn's friend and neighbour Julie Andrew had told me about Lyn's patience with Shanelle when she was a toddler.

After our meeting in Hervey Bay, I felt a stronger sense of righteous purpose. Shanelle, I believed, knew that I was sincere and that my connection to the story since 2001 was meaningful. She had told me about her attempts to reach her mother via so-called psychic mediums. She wanted knowledge. Answers. These, she hoped, would finally bring her some peace.

Leaving the cottage, I headed to a house a five-minute drive away.

Pam Eckford, who had worked in the women's refuge on the Northern Beaches and helped hundreds of fleeing, and sometimes bruised, housewives, greeted me warmly, and then revealed that we were distantly related. She was a longtime friend of Jenny's mother, Ann, and had known Jenny as a child and again, years later, as a scared young mother who wanted to talk to Lyn's mother or anyone in the Simms family about her suspicions over Chris.

Pam was an important witness; she had heard Jenny's story immediately after she fled from Chris. At Jenny's instigation, Pam became a bridge to the Simms family.

'I was working as a welfare worker officer at the Women's Resource Centre in Dee Why when Jenny came in as a young woman in a case of domestic violence and fleeing her husband. I became her caseworker,' Pam told me.

At this time, in early 1990, Jenny and Chris were formally ending their marriage. There would be a struggle over assets, property and, of course, their daughter. With her years of experience in helping women extricate themselves from abusive relationships, Pam had dealt with many discarded or runaway wives marred by violence, hurt and tragedy. Jenny's story was something else altogether.

Pam was aware that Chris and Jenny became infatuated with each other when she was 16. 'It was almost like she was in a trance. Her life and what she was experiencing with this schoolteacher, it was incredible.'

The suggestions of foul play being raised by Jenny in 1990 were unavoidable. She wanted Lyn's mother to know she was suspicious but she didn't know how to go about it. She wanted Pam to help her to manage this delicate part.

Helena had first met Jenny when she was a quiet high school student and babysitter helping Lyn in the house at Bayview. After Lyn vanished and Jenny took up her new role as Lyn's replacement in the house, in Lyn's bed and in caring for Lyn's daughters, Helena despaired but she swallowed her pride to maintain a connection to the little girls.

By August 1984, Chris had obtained a divorce and property settlement from Lyn and was married to Jenny, pregnant with a baby girl. In one of the many letters passed to me by Pat, Helena had written about having gone to a school with a birthday gift for Lyn's eldest daughter.

She wrote: 'I could see Jenny watching me from a distance. She was standing outside the gate and there were many other mothers around, and as the children came out she grabbed them by the hand and hurried them toward the car away from me. I called out, "Shanelle, Nan has a little parcel for you."

'Jenny turned and in front of everyone said, "We don't want anything from you after the nasty letter you sent."'

Jenny's rebuke cited a letter sent by Lyn's father, Len, to Chris to call in a loan that he had extended to his daughter and Chris when they were newlyweds saving for a house.

'I said, "I didn't send it."'

'She said, "Your husband did and Chris said if you come to the school, you are not to see the children."'

'I'm afraid I looked at her and said, "You little slut!"'

'I was so incensed. I came home seething. She damn well got everything we ever gave Lyn.'

Six years later, it must have taken a lot of courage and conviction from Jenny to want to see Helena.

On Jenny's behalf, Pam telephoned Helena. Pam recalled that the older woman was 'hesitant at first but then she warmed after a while talking about Lyn and how she can't believe what had happened'.

Pam told me that Lyn's mother had described the last time she spoke to her daughter on the evening of 8 January 1982. 'She said that Lyn had rung and said, "Everything's going to be all right, Mum. We're going to work it out." The mum said she sounded a little bit funny and that Lyn said, "Oh, Chris has made me a lovely drink."

'That was the night before she disappeared. And to me, when the mother said that, I found that there was obviously something very suspicious in the whole case.'

Pam shared the information with Jenny. Although Jenny feared that Chris had killed Lyn, until 1990, she had no inkling of what Lyn had told her mother on her fateful last night.

Lyn was not a drinker. Jenny remembered that when Chris wanted to have sex with her in the house at Bayview in 1981, he would mix his wife a drink and she would fall asleep. But on the night of 8 January 1982, Jenny was not there. The usual motive for Chris to mix a drink for Lyn did not exist. It raised a far more sinister motive for the 'lovely drink'.

Pam told me, 'Mrs Simms didn't think Chris had done anything wrong.'

Helena did not want to talk to Jenny. She told Pam she just couldn't. The hurt was deep. Instead, the older woman telephoned her son Greg and his wife, Merilyn, to explain the surprise contact.

Initially, the Simms family consensus was that they would let sleeping dogs lie; they did not want to meet or talk to Jenny. Merilyn, however, gently turned things around. Merilyn believed Jenny might have important information to disclose. They agreed to talk to Jenny at Pam's mother's home near Gosford. The meeting went well. There was no hostility. Everyone left on good terms. Jenny felt like a weight had been lifted from her shoulders. She held no direct evidence but at least she had shared her suspicions with Greg and Merilyn.

Jenny had told them about the remark Chris made to her that he had gone to see 'a hitman' about getting rid of Lyn. She also revealed that on the occasion when Chris had left Lyn, a couple of days before Christmas in 1981, he had driven north to start a new life with Jenny. At her instigation, they turned the car around and drove all the way back from Queensland. And Jenny explained his haste to install her in the family home so soon after Lyn vanished, a fortnight after Chris's pre-Christmas abandonment of his wife and girls. She talked about his controlling and abusive behaviour. She confided that she was scared of him. Sharing her suspicions about him having murdered Lyn – and what she feared he was capable of doing to his second wife – afforded Jenny protection too. Pam recalled that after the meeting, Jenny 'felt very happy'; she knew she had done the right thing.

Pam believed that everything Jenny had told her and the Simms family was true. Pam's only caveat was that she believed Jenny held much back. I thought about Jenny's two police statements of 1998. In the second one dated 6 November, about six weeks after the first one, Jenny acknowledged that 'there were a number of other incidents which I did not volunteer as I did not recognise their significance'.

One, she said, revolved around her concern in 1982 after moving in with Chris at Bayview that Paul Dawson was being less friendly towards her. Jenny told Chris that things had 'cooled' between Paul and her. As a result, it was suggested that 'if I had sex with Paul then this might improve my relationship with him'. Jenny told police that one day while Marilyn was collecting the children, Chris raised the idea with his brother and 'Paul was agreeable'.

On a night when the twins were meant to be taking the Belrose Eagles team for training, they stayed home and had sex with Jenny, who said she agreed 'in order to please both Chris and Paul and keep the relationship on an even keel'. A few days later, Paul visited again. But this time, Chris went out, leaving Lyn's teenage replacement in the bedroom with his brother. Afterwards, Jenny explained, Chris became jealous. She said that it changed their relationship. It did not happen again despite Paul's overtures.

Pam Eckford told me that as the relationship went on, Jenny began to feel like chattel, a possession that Chris wanted to keep under lock and key. She was restricted in where she could go and who she could see. When Chris was not around to monitor her, Paul and Marilyn were there. She knew they reported back to Chris.

I circled back to 1981, when Jenny was still a student at Cromer High.

Pam could not fathom what she called 'the logic' of Chris bringing a student into his home to have sex with her while Lyn was still there. There was no logic. There were no boundaries. Unlike most men, who would do whatever they could to keep a wife and a girlfriend far apart, Chris had put them under the same roof. The risk of being caught escalated.

'Of course,' Pam agreed. 'That's the way that this man obviously lives. On the knife's edge. He thinks he's infallible. He thinks he's okay and that he can get away with things. He thinks he's so smart and he could do whatever he wanted to do.'

As I sat sipping water at Pam's kitchen table, she produced a cassette tape. It was the audio recording of her 1998 interview with Damian Loone. Pam had found it in a drawer in her bedside table shortly before I arrived.

'I nearly died when I saw the name Damian Loone on it. It's still got so much dust in it and it didn't seem to be playing very well. You can have it. I thought I sounded very nervous in it.'

Back in Brisbane, Damian's familiar voice boomed through the speakers of the old audio player I had bought to listen to obsolete cassette tapes. He started the interview at 11 am on 26 August 1998.

Pam sounded much younger on the recording. She described Jenny as a 'very, very, very frightened young woman', adding that until she left Chris, he was 'enclosing her like a vacuum'.

'She couldn't move. She couldn't do anything. She couldn't have any friends. She couldn't dress appropriately. He had complete control of it all and she had to get away.'

Pam's newly discovered recording of what she said in 1998 was broadly consistent with what she told me in January 2018.

Near the end of the interview, Damian asked Pam, 'Is there anything further you wish to tell me?'

Pam replied, 'I know that at the time I thought everything was just so suspicious. Something should have come to light then. And it hasn't. Hopefully something will come to light now.'

Although clairvoyants left me cold, the concept of karma rang true. What goes around, comes around. Pam's chance discovery of evidence from two decades earlier was another positive omen, another strand in a rope which I hoped would be used by prosecutors to bind Chris to a charge of murder when the public started hearing this travesty in the podcast – which I had not yet started writing.

I realised how integral Pam had been in this case. Her helping Jenny in 1990, when the frightened and newly separated young mum had returned to the Northern Beaches to start raising the alarm about Lyn, was crucial.

Another heroine at the resource centre, Barbara Kilpatrick, died before my investigation, but she told the 2003 inquest that she alerted Jenny's mother Ann to the relationship with Chris in 1981. Ann was 'really concerned' but not enough to act. She had major problems with her violent alcoholic husband, Ron.

In 1982, Jenny was upset at having to look after Lyn's two girls. She spoke back then to her mother's longtime friend, Barbara. Jenny wanted Lyn 'to come back and get them and she wanted to live happily ever after with Chris'. Barbara recalled telling Chris, 'Why does Jenny have to be there? She should be allowed to live on her own for a little while or maybe go and live with some friends'.

But nothing happened. 'She wouldn't have gone against his wishes,' Barbara said.

In 1990, Barbara helped Jenny start again as a single mum. Jenny confided that Chris 'always wanted her to be young, he didn't want her to grow up . . . and if she didn't do what he wanted, he would be very angry with her. He wanted her to dress like the girls. She said she was very frightened of him.'

I had been waiting for Rebecca Hazel to give me the green light to come to Sydney and sit down with Jenny over a few days for the interviews we had planned. Rebecca and I believed these were a foregone conclusion, and important for the podcast. But Jenny had suddenly gone quiet.

Something had caused Jenny to change her mind about telling her story for the podcast. When she severed all contact with Rebecca over January, my newest good friend was devastated. In Jenny, whose capacity to trust people's good intentions must have been hit hard when she was a teenager, Rebecca had also lost a good friend, and her book was possibly doomed. She was dealt a painful blow.

We speculated that Jenny's sudden and unexpected withdrawal was possibly designed to cause the podcast's abandonment. Not interviewing Jenny was a setback but I was in too deep to spike *The Teacher's Pet*. I reasoned that I had received Jenny's evidence in paper form: the transcript pages of her testimony in the 2003 inquest and her written statement to police, which had been based on a lengthy record of interview in 1998 with Damian Loone. That hour-long interview was recorded on an old-fashioned cassette tape. A transcript, in the police brief given to me by Greg Simms, ran to 37 pages and listed 206 answers. The spooled tape contained all of Jenny's disclosures in her own words. Her own voice.

Chapter 26

Shanelle

The dangerous young man in the courtroom high above Brisbane glared at the onlookers and smirked at his family and friends. Ruth and I shuddered at the evidence. He had subjected his former girl-friend, the mother of his child, to a terrifying ordeal. He had bashed her, led her blindfolded through bushland and, when she must have believed that he was about to finish her off, he bound her to a tree. Having swung at her with a machete and a hammer, he sliced her skin and poured bleach on the open wounds. He doused her with fuel when she was holding their baby and threatened to light her up. In late January 2018, one of our closest friends, District Court Judge Terry Martin SC, had the task of determining the severity of the sadist's prison sentence.

Ruth and I had come to court to watch Terry's last case as a judge. Terry, always scrupulously fair and sensible, had taught me a great deal about the criminal justice system and the duties of lawyers. He was always reliable, straight-shooting and, before his appointment to the bench, a powerful advocate for some of the most despised defendants during his tenure as a criminal defence lawyer. Terry's defence of the serial killer Ivan Milat should be an informal case study for lawyers who ever question their obligations to an accused person. Terry never indicated doubt. The accused must be presumed innocent – the rule of law depends on it. And when they told him they were 'not guilty', Terry would do everything in his power to see them acquitted, no matter how grave the case. He must have privately struggled with such a heavy duty.

His integrity and wisdom influenced me over many years to be more measured in my journalism and not rush to judgment about alleged criminality. But it was hard. My natural instincts were front-footed and my style was usually prosecutorial. I often fell short of a fair-minded defence lawyer's expectations. But I struggled, too, with a justice system that I had seen let down so many victims, and free monsters who had ruined lives.

Terry was intrigued at an early stage by my podcast investigation. He offered to read some of the documents when he had formally stopped working as a judge. Whereas some lawyers strived to be in the limelight, Terry eschewed publicity when he was a barrister and kept a low profile for his decade as a judge. I knew that if Terry were to help in my investigation of the case surrounding Lyn's disappearance, it would be on background and without attribution.

After Terry calmly delivered sentence upon the guilty grub who had struck terror in a young woman on the rural outskirts of Brisbane, we went to lunch. I shared the encouraging news that Shanelle Dawson had agreed to let me interview her. The newspaper was sending our thoughtful sound recordist Nick Adams-Dzierzba to Hervey Bay on the same flight from Sydney as Shanelle's aunty, Pat Jenkins, on 25 January.

I was on a deadline for personal reasons. Twelve months earlier on Australia Day, 26 January, Dad and I had gone to a steak restaurant and enjoyed our best time over lunch together. We had talked and laughed for hours about family, friends, journalism, politics, aviation and his own childhood. He spoke more candidly than ever about the loss of his mother. At the end of the lunch, as we were walking to our respective cars, Dad needed to stop and sit down; he felt an acute abdominal pain. We had no idea it was an aneurism. He died seven weeks later.

A year to the day after our lunch, I wanted to take my son, Alexander, to the same place to eat steak, acknowledge Australia Day, honour my dad, a quiet patriot, and reflect on the last great time and conversations we had together.

Shanelle told me that she had not told her dad about her decision to talk to me on the record. It was a wise decision.

'I don't want to come across as an airy-fairy, new age dippy kind of person,' she said as Nick leaned in close with the mic.

'But you are living an alternative lifestyle, aren't you?' I asked.

'Yes, I guess you could call it that.'

Having left home at 17 to study primary school teaching, then gone travelling overseas before graduating, Shanelle had lived in hippie communes, such as Wind Spirit in Arizona, and eschewed materialism. As poor as a church mouse, she lived hand-to-mouth in Hervey Bay with her four-year-old daughter, whom she nicknamed Lala. Her values were imbued with compassion and she craved a gentler lifestyle which respected Mother Earth and the environment ahead of career and the accumulation of assets.

'Society's just a bit too harsh,' she told me. Over the next several hours, I would learn how harsh, how unjust, life had been for Shanelle as she spoke of Jenny's treatment of her and her younger sister.

'I remember really liking her in the beginning and being excited to see her, and then she became a mother and she was not very kind,' Shanelle said.

'There was always this foreboding. And my sister and I sort of walked on eggshells and we were always getting in trouble. We did what we were told. We were scared.

'It just wasn't a normal childhood.'

Shanelle could not recall any affection after her mother disappeared. The tension in the house at Bayview, and then on the Gold Coast, was palpable. Jenny acknowledged in her 1998 statement that she had treated Lyn's children differently to how she treated her own daughter.

'I remember being jealous, actually, of my cousins for being allowed to hold [Jenny's daughter] for a photo and thinking, "What? We're not allowed to touch her and hold her, this little person who's come into our lives,"' she said.

The Gold Coast's newly opened theme park of Dreamworld became all too familiar; Shanelle and her sister would be dropped off for the entire day. Dreamworld was where Jenny also found solace over several unhappy years leading up to her decision to leave Chris. Sometimes she would linger there with her friend Toni Melrose, who had a job role-playing a gum-nut fairy called Coo-ee.

'We used to go and chat to some of the staff,' Shanelle said, 'because one lady in particular used to sometimes give us little candy canes. We worked out sachets of sugar were free, so we'd put that into water, which was also free. Jenny was a lot kinder to us when Dad was around. So my perception or my memory of what it was like is that, when Dad was around, it was more relaxed and fun.'

I asked Shanelle what she understood now, as an adult, in terms of why Jenny may have treated her this way.

'I guess I've come into some compassion for her ... that she must have been repeating patterns that she had learned, or that for whatever reason she was feeling disempowered. So she was trying to take her power back. Subconsciously. She perhaps had been treated very harshly,' she said.

Long after Jenny left the house, Chris and Lyn's girls still hoped for an apology from their stepmother. Shanelle had just vague and fleeting memories of her own mother.

'I believe she was a very nurturing and beautiful mother from what everyone else tells me. And unfortunately, I don't remember her. I have really small flashes of memory which are fairly insignificant. I kind of remember looking out the front door and I would guess that I was looking for my mother and waiting for her to return. I'm sure as a little girl I yearned for this loving figure that nurtured me since birth. It's definitely been in my consciousness throughout my life and I had hoped and believed that she was alive for a long time.'

I thought of my father. My grandmother. They were always there, mirage-like, on the edge of this story, helping me understand.

'Although I have abandonment issues, I don't believe she's actually alive anymore,' Shanelle added.

There was no consensus among the purported psychics and clairvoyants who would take Shanelle's money – some saw Lyn dead and some saw her alive. Shanelle clung to hope for years but not anymore. She wanted her father to face trial for murder while making it clear to me that she would not be saying anything like that in our interview. She remembered that if a visitor to the childhood home mentioned her missing mother, there was 'really uncomfortable silence'. It was 'a taboo subject'. Nobody talked about it.

In the days before the interview, Shanelle had repeatedly watched her mother in the newly recovered *Chequerboard* video from 1975. It was the only footage she had ever seen of Lyn. There were no photographs of her mother in the house when Shanelle was growing up.

'I guess I do have a memory of the essence of her. I don't recall any actual physical memories of her,' she told me.

Nick Adams-Dzierzba, who had been listening intently while recording every word, played a little piece of my interview the previous month with Lyn's friend from the childcare centre, Annette Leary, who said, 'I can still see those two little girls when she would bring them to the centre. She couldn't be more proud of every little thing they did. Just loved them to bits.'

Shanelle brightened. 'Oh, I already knew that. But it's nice to hear it from someone who witnessed it.'

'So many people that we talked to echoed what Annette just said,' I replied. I leaned back in her chair and heard a sickening crack; I had just broken one of her few pieces of furniture. Shanelle laughed long and hard.

In her police interview in 1998, Jenny had volunteered how difficult it was to be a mother to Lyn's girls because Chris was sensitive to them being disciplined by her.

'It sounds to me like she's had to tell herself that to feel better. I don't think she had any problems disciplining us. When Jenny was there it was "don't breathe, don't move, don't make a sound". And then you still got in trouble anyway.'

Her father was heartbroken when Jenny walked out and he sought his girls' blessing to try to patch things up with her. But there was no going back for his second wife.

He became engaged to another woman, who would walk around the house partly naked, prompting a pubescent Shanelle to call her a vulgar name. There was an altercation, an attempted face slap and the plate in Shanelle's hand accidentally cut the woman's chin, which opened and bled. After this event, the relationship was doomed.

It was time to get something important on the record. Listeners would want to know.

I asked Shanelle, 'Before we started these interviews, you said that under no circumstances would you answer questions about the allegations levelled against your father, the police brief that paints him as a murderer and your mum having been the victim of foul play. I have to ask you, again, is that still your position? Is there any part of that you want to address in this interview?'

Shanelle shook her head. She would not go there.

We looked at some family photographs of a young Jenny, just a teenager herself, beaming while seated with two little girls who looked the right age to be her sisters, not her stepchildren.

'She must have, on some level, realised the way she was treating us wasn't okay.'

Shanelle showed me a letter she had written but not sent to Jenny the year before, 2017, on the 35th anniversary of her mother's disappearance, parts of which are reproduced below:

To Jenny,

I see this letter as a necessary step towards full forgiveness. And so I write to try to bring healing to myself to neutralise the toxic poison that I feel inside, to let you know the ways that actions and choices have affected me. I want you to know that after all of these years, I'm still affected, as is my mothering and general character, which is at times harsher than necessary because of the patterns of behaviour and programs passed on by you.

These are my memories as I remember them. Perhaps there were happy ones too, but if they were, they have slipped away

amidst the harshness and trauma. We were good and kind children
and didn't deserve how we were treated by you.

We never ever dared to talk back to you, defy you in any way.
I know you didn't have a good upbringing and there were other
reasons behind your treatment [of us]. You were very young when
you started an affair with my father and then suddenly had full-time
care of us.

Shanelle remembers her upbringing as harsh and dysfunctional. Even
Jenny's father and sister said in their interviews with Damian Loone
that Lyn's girls were not lovingly treated. But Jenny must have also
been in a world of pain, isolated from family and friends and coer-
cively controlled by a sociopath. I wondered whether Jenny resented
the two little girls who were daily reminders of Lyn, the woman who
had tried to help her as a schoolgirl. It is difficult to imagine how
normal family life could ever have been possible while Jenny lived
with Chris under such circumstances.

Towards the end of the interview, Shanelle told me what she
wanted from the podcast investigation.

'Answers would be wonderful. It would definitely help the healing
process. I just really don't believe for a second our mother, especially
given as loving as she was, would have left us willingly.'

Shanelle wanted more than answers. She wanted to signal to
her father that she supported the journalist he loathed in a murder
investigation via a podcast. In a couple of months, Shanelle would be
travelling to Fiji with her father and his third wife, Susan. They had
planned a trip for themselves and their children to help celebrate a
significant wedding anniversary.

'Your father's yet to be approached by me for an interview. How
do you think he'll feel about you talking?' I asked Shanelle.

'I hope that he sees that I was honouring my mum and that's been
a real need in me throughout my whole life.'

We wrapped things up and went to dinner after a walk down the
long pier stretching several hundred metres into the bay, between
the mainland and K'gari, or Fraser Island.

Five days later, Shanelle disclosed the fact of the interview to her father, and then she texted me.

'It is safe to say my father won't be talking to you in this lifetime.'

It was about 'his anger at your first article and now he's obviously feeling threatened and going on and on with more lies and excuses and anger,' she explained.

'He started to guilt me and claims it's the first he's heard about his brother having affairs with schoolgirls, to which I responded, "Bullshit."'

There was a fortnight's silence between them. Chris got a new phone.

'He claims he doesn't know how the last screen cracked,' Shanelle told me. 'I suspect it was after I hung up on him. We're back to ignoring the herd of elephants in the room.'

When I spoke to Pat Jenkins after her return to Sydney, she had heard more from her niece.

'Did you hear the reaction of Chris?' Pat asked.

'He spoke quite viciously about you. He's very nervous about it all.'

Chapter 27

Are You There, Chris?

We were getting close.

Over the previous five months, I had made six trips to Sydney and Newcastle and retrieved and read thousands of documents from the police brief of evidence, the two inquests and the archives of newspapers and high schools.

I had recorded dozens of face-to-face and telephone interviews with numerous people. From family, friends and work colleagues of Lyn to former cops, independent witnesses and the former deputy state coroner. I had questioned good friends, my former fellow students Vitto Ulliana and Les Green, and our popular PE teacher Glen Hoppner from Keebra Park High on the Gold Coast, all of whom remembered Chris from his time teaching there.

But instead of listening to the audio files from these conversations and marking up the transcripts for use in the podcast, I kept chasing. It was classic avoidance. Investigating, identifying angles and leads to follow up, tracking people down and interviewing them: this was my comfort zone. I felt confident doing these tasks but it meant I had still done no writing for the podcast.

I had audio files taking up dozens of gigabytes on my MacBook Air, more interviews coming and, as the deadline for a release of the podcast loomed, growing anxiety from not pausing, surveying the many folders of files and asking, 'What have I got and how am I going to use it?'

Having agonised for weeks about how to even start the first episode, I went to meet a good friend with a plea for help.

Karryn Wheelans, a former top investigative journalist for television current affairs, quickly grasped the problem, and the remedy. She told me I needed to stop. Stop investigating and finding more people to interview. Stop reading the evidence. Start listening to the audio. And start writing.

Karryn also told me to take better care of myself. We'd met for an impromptu lunch at the Hundred Acre Bar at St Lucia Golf Links and she could see I was running on empty, draining the bottle of wine like it was lolly water. Karryn told me much later that I looked and sounded seriously, unhealthily stressed.

With her advice ringing in my ears, I answered the fundamental and most obvious question about where to begin a story this vast: it had to start where it ended. Where, I believed, Lyn had been murdered. It needed to start at Bayview. I wanted to describe this place, with its escarpment and magnificent water views of Pittwater and the Northern Beaches. I wanted listeners to hear the evocative sounds and imagine they were at the house in Gilwinga Drive, with its surrounding bushland and those noisy cicadas which had infiltrated my recordings from the area. What caused them to make such a racket? I found out with a Google search. It was a mating call by the male cicada. It gave me an idea and I smashed out a few paras, the opening for the first episode which would be called Bayview:

'There is a hilltop of rugged beauty above Sydney's sunny Northern Beaches. A place of dense bush and rocky outcrops, and long driveways snaking across acreage properties to comfortable family homes.

'It is noisy here at Bayview in summer. Male cicadas crawl out of the soil, then violently deform their bodies to pull off a complex vibration – and an ear-splitting buzzing. Nature's summer soundtrack can be deafening. Maddening. The secretive cicadas are desperate to find a female for a frenzy of mating.

'It will ultimately be fatal.'

I knew I needed a compelling voice to follow my opening narration. It would be best to introduce a new witness, someone who knew Lyn well. Someone who knew Chris. Someone who was close to Bayview. Someone whose spoken words would cut through and hook the listener. If Lyn's case was going to be solved, the podcast needed to be widely shared and trigger a public backlash which might force the authorities to do their jobs properly. There had been many memorable interviewees in my investigation to date but one stood out.

Julie Andrew's evocative descriptions of her good friend and neighbour, Lyn – and of Chris, and of the time and the place and the strange twin relationship with Paul – were spellbinding for me when I sat around Julie's kitchen table a week before Christmas 2017.

These words from this remarkable woman followed my opening:

'The best way to dispose of a body when you live in the bush is to put it in the bush. And that's what I think he did on the Friday night.

'I don't think I believed she was murdered straight away. I think I thought, "He's got rid of her somewhere. What's he done with her? Where's he put her?" And then when Jenny turned straight up, like a few days later, she's there, I thought, "You've got rid of her, you've got rid of her, you've done that. But no, you wouldn't have done that."

'Would he? And then I became absolutely sure.'

I then came in. 'My name is Hedley Thomas and for the past six months, I've been investigating the sudden disappearance and probable murder of Lyn Dawson. This is *The Teacher's Pet*, a podcast series about a star footballer, his schoolgirl lover and a wife who vanishes.'

The episode included recollections from Lyn's sister, Pat, and her two brothers, Greg and Phil, and brief profiles of Lyn, Chris and Paul. Listeners would hear an executive summary of the case and an insight into Chris's accuser, Jenny, who had raised allegations of foul play after fleeing him and ending their marriage in 1990, eight years after Lyn's disappearance.

Boldly, I disclosed that my investigation had discovered new evidence and clues 'that were missed by New South Wales Police when they finally started suspecting a murder and began asking hard questions, years after Lyn vanished'. I added that, 'Key witnesses who did not go to police at the first opportunity have divulged important facts'.

'If these lead to the recovery of Lyn's body from the ground at Bayview, where I think she lies, it is likely that murder charges would be levelled against the suspect police have circled for a quarter of a century,' I said.

It was a risky gambit but everything about this story screamed risk. The most important stories always did.

In a stroke of luck that changed everything, I had met a genius musician and audio engineer, Slade Gibson. Our mutual friend, the remarkable journalist for *The Australian*'s *Weekend Magazine* and author of *Boy Swallows Universe*, Trent Dalton, knew we would hit it off.

Slade, who had been a guitarist for the pop band Savage Garden, lived quietly at the end of a little cul-de-sac a 20-minute drive from my home. When we started talking, it was to record my voice in his home studio for a brief audio trailer for the podcast series. He was immediately curious but not pushy. Slade had a gentle and tactful approach which calmed my nerves behind the microphone.

In the beginning, I thought the audio engineer would contribute only technical prowess but Slade's instincts about story angles, tone and fairness were second to none. As he listened to the voices and heard my feedback, the married father of two little boys volunteered observations which were poignant and true. Although he had met none of the people, he had worked out things about Lyn, Chris, Jenny, their families and friends which had eluded me.

The more we talked about podcasting and the story of *The Teacher's Pet*, the more I realised that Slade should produce the series and compose the music. Working ridiculously long hours for relatively modest remuneration, he wrangled the audio files I had recorded, with their dodgy levels, smoothed my voice in the narrations, and sensibly counselled me about numerous story points which, if I had not listened, could have had disastrous consequences.

We never had a cross word. Slade had never worked in journalism before. Until we got together, he had never produced a podcast – we were both rookies – but he understood storytelling, life, tragedy, justice and nuance.

I lobbied Paul Whittaker to come up with money which wasn't budgeted to fund Slade to write the music and produce the audio for the eight episodes I expected we would need to tell the whole story. Paul knew I was in deep. He was sensible with the company's money but he was also hooked on the story. He grumbled about the time, and now the extra cost, it was taking. The alternative was an in-house production by existing staffers of *The Australian*. I knew that wouldn't work as smoothly. Audio was a sophisticated science. We had much to learn. And we needed to be in the same city. Slade underquoted with his fee proposal because he was intrigued by the story. The chemistry between us was always positive. He had a hunch that we were going to create something very important, something which might change lives for the better and right a longtime injustice. We both felt it.

We worked closely with Kel Southan, one of *The Australian*'s digital managers, who had been gripped by a draft of the first episode Slade Gibson and I had previewed to our colleagues in Sydney. Their feedback was strongly encouraging. Another test audience occurred at our house in Brisbane, where Ruth hosted her book club friends for dinner, wine and an early listen. The unvarnished honesty from these intelligent women was greatly appreciated. As I knew the story inside out by this time, there was a risk that I would assume that everyone else knew it as well. The fresh ears of Ruth's friends, all of whom I had known for years, were vitally important, as was the expert advice from my friend David Murray and Kel. Slade and I made a number of subtle changes and tweaks to help the story's flow.

The next challenge was legal. We needed to not cost the company millions of dollars in damages payouts and also, preferably, stay out of prison.

Too many times I have seen lawyers, skilled in the vagaries of libel and defamation, take the easy way out. They examine the drafts of unpublished stories and advise editors and journalists to effectively emasculate the text, watering down the allegations to minimise the risk of being sued. This weak response is sometimes justified if the claims and their footings are questionable. Other times, it's just a cop-out which turns what should have been a courageous, hard-hitting, and well-researched story into a damp squib. Few things sap an investigative journalist's morale faster.

Paul Whittaker had been a fearless reporter. As *The Australian*'s editor-in-chief, he always fought to publish the strongest potential version of every story in which he had confidence. Paul challenged the lawyers if he suspected they were being overly risk-averse. At another newspaper, *The Teacher's Pet* could have easily been put into the 'too hard' basket, where it would have curled up and died.

The overwhelming inference from my podcast would be that Chris had got away with murder and child sex offences. My journalism would seriously damage his reputation, risking a defamation suit. It was unavoidable. We couldn't dress it up any other way because this was a key driver – a probable killer was free because the criminal justice system had failed a murder victim.

Defending a defamation action is extremely costly, and in my view the law and most judges in Australia generally favour plaintiffs. Peerless ABC investigative journalist Chris Masters, whose extraordinary efforts exposed police and political corruption at the highest levels in Queensland in the 1980s when I was starting out as a cadet reporter, talked to me many years later about defamation actions which entangled him and the ABC for their program, *The Moonlight State*. He lost a decade to the defence of defamation proceedings, which took a debilitating personal, professional and financial toll. He called it 'death by a thousand courts'.

Paul Whittaker understood the risks for his editorship, career and the newspaper's balance sheet. He didn't flinch. The question for our lawyers was whether we could successfully defend our journalism in the Supreme Court or the Federal Court at a cost of around $20,000 a day in the event of Chris launching defamation proceedings and going to trial. Such a case might cost us millions of dollars and, if we lost, more in a damages payout.

For years, I had worked closely with defamation lawyer John-Paul Cashen. He delivered reliable advice every day across the newspaper. John-Paul grasped the key issues quickly. He understood our priorities. If he was in doubt, he called me and when he identified serious risks, he tried to rework a story's angle, tweaking it or adding a line which would minimise the risks. If he and the law firm's partner Justin Quill were on it and we were prepared to make some concessions, we were usually good to go.

I would always try to give John-Paul, Justin and Paul Whittaker as much context as possible in an often-unsubtle lobbying campaign to improve the prospects of publication. The biggest question turned on if Chris would sue. I strongly doubted it. His daughter Shanelle agreed. In a defamation proceeding, he would have to get into a witness box to answer questions under oath. In the 36 years since Lyn's disappearance, Chris had worked hard to avoid a courtroom. The only time he had entered one was to lay claim to Lyn's share of their assets – the family home – when he divorced her in absentia in 1983. He had not bothered turning up at either of the two coronial inquests into Lyn's disappearance.

I could find only one sit-down media interview Chris had done about Lyn. In late May 2003, a few months after the second inquest, *The Daily Telegraph* published a staged photo of him looking reflective next to a headline: 'I did not kill my wife'. It ran on page 17 with: 'Now he breaks his silence to Kara Lawrence'.

'I've thought of suicide but I've got the most beautiful family I would ever want and I know if I did that, people would just say he's guilty,' Chris said. 'I made mistakes at the time but I don't know how that comes close to murdering somebody.'

He repeated his story that Lyn had called him in January 1982 to say she needed some time away. It was 'a shock', he told Kara, adding, 'I was upset but I wouldn't have been critical because I was partly responsible for the state our marriage was in. I've got no reason to believe she's not alive though I can't understand why she didn't contact her family'.

I grew hopeful that Chris told Kara more than this. Perhaps it was cut from her carefully balanced story for space reasons. When I spoke to Kara, her memory of the interview with Chris 15 years earlier was, understandably, hazy. If she had audio of the rare interview, it would be great for the podcast, and I promised I'd buy Kara and her friends a long lunch. She kindly offered to play a few obsolete cassette tapes which were still lying around. But Kara's efforts ended in disappointment.

I was curious about the timing and the motive for his interview with *The Daily Telegraph*. But it seemed that Chris was being tactical. The producers of the ABC's *Australian Story* program started talking to Lyn's family in early May 2003. The producers reached out to Jenny, and to Chris and his third wife, Susan, too. Chris refused to be interviewed for the TV cameras. But he knew the ABC's long-form story was coming and that it would probably be bad for him. He got in first.

I sent John-Paul, a towering figure with an easygoing nature and a gift for explaining legal strategy in layperson's language, a raft of key documents – the findings of the two coroners, who had recommended in 2001 and in 2003 that Chris should be prosecuted for murder; the draft scripts for several episodes in the series; a racy video trailer crafted by Brisbane producer, Gwyn Dixon; and some notes about Chris Dawson's past disinclination to bring a defamation action against anyone.

In an effort to be as candid as possible, I had shared the almost-finished video trailer with Shanelle too. It hit her hard.

'Probably shouldn't have watched this in the library. Bawling my eyes out now. It's very effective.'

I knew Shanelle liked to sit with the important things and reflect before making her views known. The video trailer's montage of voices and images included those of Shanelle saying she did not believe her mother would leave voluntarily, and Jenny calling Chris 'narcissistic'. It was powerful and it wounded Chris's eldest daughter.

'I naively didn't realise you were going in that hard, I thought it was a little more objective,' she wrote to me a day after she broke down in Hervey Bay's public library. 'It was so dramatic, I felt like I'd been punched in the stomach and then I bawled in the middle of the library. I'm even more stressed about Fiji and won't be able to look my father in the eye.'

Shanelle was worried about the reaction from her younger sister, loyally dedicated to their father. I feared she was teetering and would try to persuade me to not use her interviews in the podcast.

She did not want to talk on the phone for a while. We exchanged text messages instead. Layers of emotions, secrets and betrayals, wrapped up in a tragedy which began unfolding when Shanelle was a toddler, were about to be exposed to sunlight, and the 100-second trailer was just the beginning. It was a sensationalised preview and not emblematic of the long-form, slow-burning storytelling I had in mind with a podcast series which, I told her, would be about eight episodes, 45 minutes to an hour each.

'There's a chance we can resolve this once and for all – I really mean that. Trust me.'

Shanelle walked back from the brink and began to steel herself for the blowback from her father and the rest of the Dawson clan. Only half-joking, she concluded it was time to cease resisting her 'fate of orphan-ship, and cease worrying about what my family think of my choices.'

Shanelle apologised 'if I momentarily lost some faith in you'. She soldiered on and resumed her habit of sending me thoughtful notes of encouragement for an investigation she knew had become exhausting and potentially dangerous.

I told her I'd stumbled on an encouraging breakthrough which had given me hope that Lyn's remains would be recovered. Shanelle didn't press me to tell her about it but asked if I would share the information with the Detective Senior Constable Daniel Poole, who was running the Homicide Squad's reinvestigation.

The police had made it plain there would be no cooperation from their side. I had written a lengthy note to Paul Whittaker for him to share with New South Wales Police Commissioner Mick Fuller, explaining what was intended with the podcast series. I asked for interviews with Poole and his predecessor on the case, Damian Loone, and sought the audio files from past interviews with Chris and Paul Dawson and others. Optimistically, I told the police chief that the podcast and associated publicity was 'an overdue opportunity to solve this case which has troubled many people for 36 years'.

We were rebuffed.

Behind the scenes, the old police brief of evidence – which the DPP had repeatedly deemed too weak to support a prosecution of Chris Dawson for murder – was being reorganised, with new evidence and statements from people who had been interviewed by Poole. An updated brief was imminent. Pat Jenkins and Greg Simms had no idea what was in it apart from the evidence they had seen and heard in 2003, as well as subsequent bits which Damian Loone had told them about.

While Loone had shared news about his investigation when he had the time, Dan Poole was a closed book. He stayed in touch with Lyn's side but he would not disclose anything which might be taken out of context or leak and tip off the only suspect. In this vacuum, Lyn's siblings had little confidence that the most recent police work on the case and the promise of yet another referral of the brief to the DPP would count for much. As the recommendations of two coroners in 2001 and in 2003 had failed to persuade the DPP, it would take something unusual to make a difference all these years later.

I believed that a new lead about the whereabouts of Lyn's body held a lot of promise. It had come from a most unlikely but highly credible source: Magistrate Jeff Linden.

I contacted him because, as a law student and then a young solicitor, he had known Lyn, Chris, Paul and Marilyn in the 1970s and early eighties. Jeff had played rugby at Easts with Chris and Paul, and friendships blossomed around the green expanse of Woollahra Oval and the Easts clubhouse near Rose Bay. Years later, Jeff had been to the Dawson home in Gilwinga Drive for social occasions. He played tennis with the twins. He and his first wife were particularly fond of

Lyn, watching her progress from a young girlfriend besotted with Chris to newlywed and finally to affectionate, caring mother.

Although he had never made a statement to police, the brief of evidence did include some legal documents relating to Jeff. As a solicitor, he acted for Chris during the process of divorcing Lyn, a year and a half after her disappearance.

Rebecca Hazel, who had talked to Jeff and found him warm and friendly, encouraged me to try to interview him for the podcast. I expected that Jeff would probably tell me he never saw anything untoward and that Chris had been a good footballer, friend and client, and appeared to have been a dedicated husband and father.

Over the years, Jeff had seen Lyn's family making public appeals for information.

'They've been tortured by it ever since it started,' he told me during a brief break from his court duty as a magistrate in northern New South Wales. I was driving near home on Gold Creek Road and making arrangements to meet him for an interview near his home on the outskirts of Byron Bay, when his next comment caught me by surprise.

'There's one particular aspect that I'll be talking about that you may or may not already know anyway. It's about a meeting I had with a fellow who was doing some renovations to the house,' Jeff said.

I could not wait a week. I asked Jeff to describe what the new owner of the Dawson house had told him.

'I mentioned that I knew Chris Dawson, who used to own that place, and he said, "What do you know about him?" And I went on and told him the story about Lynette and my personal view is that she didn't walk out. And I saw the blood drain out of his face and I said, "Why do you ask that?"

'And he said to me, "We're doing renovations there and he turned up completely out of the blue, the other day", were his words, "and asked where we were digging."

'That just sent shivers up my spine as well. But he said to me, "If she's there, she's under six inches of concrete."

'That meeting, in my mind, was just chilling.'

The conversation occurred in 1987, five years after Lyn vanished.

Jeff was then a solicitor at Mona Vale, chatting to the new home owner about an unrelated legal matter. It was sheer coincidence.

Having helped Chris with the divorce process in 1983, resulting in a property settlement, Jeff knew that Chris had sold up in late 1984 to a young family who, in turn, sold it in 1987. The man Jeff spoke to in 1987 was the then owner, Neville Johnston.

I pictured the scenario: Chris turning up without an invitation to his old house to see it undergoing significant landscaping and reno- vation works, and asking the new owner, Neville, 'Where are you digging?' A few days after this memorable exchange, Neville chatting with his local solicitor, Jeff Linden, and learning that the original owner's ex-wife – who was besotted with her husband and daugh- ters – had been missing since 1982.

The timing of my connection with Magistrate Linden was uncanny. The day before, I had been questioning Neville's wife Sue. I was intrigued by the information Sue and Neville had given police in 1998 about Chris's visits to the house.

We talked at length about the potential for a body to have been buried up there. Sue, a retired schoolteacher who had heard the rumours about Chris, was very helpful but sceptical. In her spare time at Bayview, she was a keen gardener and she distinctly recalled the ground being so hard, she could barely penetrate it with her pick.

Sue told me that she and Neville had thought it very odd at the time that Chris kept turning up to look around. He visited on several occasions, uninvited. But Sue was unaware that Chris had asked Neville, during one such visit, 'Where are you digging?'

Jeff told me that, in 1987, when he explained to Neville that he had known Lyn as a loving and dedicated wife and mother, and certainly not someone likely to have run off, both men were shaken, under- standing the implications. Neville asked Jeff to keep the information secret from Sue.

'He said, "Whatever you do, don't tell my wife about this or she'll never want to live there,"' Jeff recalled. 'Not only did [Chris] turn up but the bloke made the point that he turned up uninvited and without making any contact with them at all, just turned up.'

Jeff's information gave me hope that we might find Lyn's body. Perhaps she really was still in the bushy acreage near the house. On drives past the house, Jenny had told Rebecca, 'She's up there.'

I drove three hours to Byron Bay and west over the hills and volcanic landmarks to the town of Lismore, parking in the shade of a river gum for an interview with Magistrate Linden. We met during his break from the demands of busy Court 1.

'Oh, she was terrific,' he said when I asked how he remembered Lyn. 'She was just a lovely girl and a great mother, a really devoted wife and a really, really, really nice girl. I liked her a lot.'

As a longtime magistrate, Jeff understood the potential ramifications of the information he was sharing with a journalist working for a national newspaper on an unsolved murder. He had permission from the chief magistrate's office to talk to me.

Jeff candidly disclosed that his former teammate's question – 'Where are you digging?' – led Jeff to suspect foul play and the burial of Lyn's body in the grounds. But Jeff added that he 'had a bit of a conscience' about the fact that he had not passed the information on to police at the time, three decades earlier.

These revelations floored me. Reading the transcript of the recorded interview Damian Loone had done in 1998 with Sue and Neville Johnston, it was obvious that the one thing Neville did not mention to the police was that Chris had asked, 'Where are you digging?'

The omission made sense. Neville and Sue had loved the house. They had raised children there. The idea of a corpse in the backyard must have horrified Neville. Perhaps he persuaded himself that Lyn was elsewhere, notwithstanding Chris's visits, his interest in walking over the land and his alarming question. By 1998, when they no longer lived at Bayview, Neville might have wanted to let sleeping dogs lie.

When I explained the strange turn of events to Sue Johnston, she told me that it made sense. Her husband had acted very strangely towards Chris on his impromptu visits. Sue did not understand why he was being so hostile and abrupt. With the benefit of hindsight,

Sue realised that Neville wanted to shield her from the spectre of a body buried in her backyard.

In 1991, the Homicide Squad detectives Paul Mayger and Stuart Wilkins did limited searching around the swimming pool with technicians using early ground-penetrating radar. They came up empty-handed. I told Sue that Jenny Carlson had said that an area of 'soft soil' outside the children's bedroom windows should have been searched by police the first time they came in the early 1990s, and after Damian Loone took up the investigation in 1998. Sue agreed that the area described by Jenny as 'soft soil' was not as hard as other parts of the block. It had been affected by water drainage. But it was no longer easily accessible because she and Neville had concreted over it.

Meeting Magistrate Linden confirmed my initial view of his motivations. He had been a judicial officer for about 30 years when he spoke to me. He did not do this lightly. The things he told me on the record were not helpful to his former client, friend and fellow Easts footballer, Chris.

I realised the highly regarded and softly spoken magistrate, who was 70 and nearing retirement, wanted to finally unburden himself of information he should have told police a very long time ago. His acknowledgment to me of his failure to speak up back then took courage.

He had also stayed silent when fellow magistrates Jan Stevenson and Carl Milovanovich ran the inquests into Lyn's presumed death. Perhaps his reticence was partly due to concern that his peers might regard it as inappropriate to volunteer information about his former client.

Jeff told me he felt very sorry at the time for Lyn's mother, Helena, whom he knew from his friendship with Lyn. Jeff had asked Helena whether Lyn had been in contact. It was a legal requirement to ensure that a husband and wife had every opportunity to appear in court and put their best foot forward. In a handwritten note, Helena emphatically scotched any suggestion she had seen or heard from her daughter.

She wrote to Jeff on 24 July 1984: 'I last saw my daughter on Jan 3, 1982 and last spoke to her over the phone on Jan 8, 1982, and up to this minute, neither her parents, brothers, sister or friends have had any contact from her.'

It must have been an awkward time for the young solicitor and the bereft woman in her late 60s. The divorce was rubber-stamped and the house at Bayview, no longer an asset over which Lyn could stake any claim, was sold to fund the next one, for Chris and Jenny.

In one of her diary entries, Helena wrote: 'Jeff Linden gave me the impression while speaking to him on a private basis, as he had upset me, that he would rather have not had anything to do with it. He and his wife knew Lyn & Chris and were at a loss to understand it.'

It tallied with the things Magistrate Linden was telling me in early 2018. He had smelled a rat for years.

In 1987, when Neville had told him of Chris's appearance and query about digging sites, Jeff was worried. 'That was quite chilling stuff. My reaction was, excuse the French, "Oh shit."'

I asked, 'And how sure are you that he used the word "digging" when he was describing what Chris asked him?'

'Probably one hundred per cent. Because that was the word that stuck in my mind. It's just something that I'll never forget.'

I asked him why he did not report the comment – 'where are you digging?' – straight away.

He replied, 'Probably, to me, it was hearsay, and I would have expected the police would have interviewed the owners about it. And that was about the time I was appointed and things were pretty bloody hectic. But a part of me didn't really want to get involved. I was happy to answer questions that anybody had for me but I didn't feel I had the carriage of the whole thing anyway. You're the first person that's contacted me.

'A young mother with a very young child. Very unusual, just to disappear. So, yeah, I've had my suspicions.'

I asked, 'If Chris Dawson contacted you again out of friendship, would you feel uneasy talking to him?'

Jeff replied, 'I wouldn't be terribly happy about it, to be honest. I have got sufficient concerns not to want anything to do with him.'

I showed him some pages of transcript from 1998, where Sue and Neville Johnston described to police the visits to the property by Chris Dawson.

Jeff told me, 'It makes me more suspicious.' He said it indicated that Chris had found out there was digging and landscaping work at his old house 'and he's gone to see where the work is'.

'Come to a conclusion from that,' he added sombrely. 'I . . . I don't want to say any more.'

'Are you happy for me to share all this with the police?' I asked.

'Yeah, absolutely. And if they need to talk to me, well, I'm always around.'

Jeff told me that about three years earlier, he had sent a letter to the Homicide Squad to disclose what he was telling me. But he had heard nothing back.

We finished our interview in a ground-floor waiting room of the old Lismore Courthouse and Magistrate Linden was due back in court. I took the elevator to Court 1 in time to see his firm but fair admonition and punishment of a wayward young offender.

On the drive back to Brisbane, I played the newly recorded audio on repeat. I was convinced the property needed to be thoroughly and professionally searched for Lyn's body.

'Lyn might still be there, buried in the ground at Bayview,' I told Ruth when my mobile phone's signal strengthened near Byron Bay. The twists in the case were doing my head in.

Ruth sounded oddly detached. I didn't realise until it was almost too late that my commitment to the case had put enormous strain on her, and on us.

On a Sunday morning, John-Paul Cashen called to talk through the legal landmines strewn through the podcast investigation.

There was always significant risk, John-Paul explained, in 'calling someone a murderer, especially someone like Dawson, who has no criminal record and presumably has some money'.

But, he added, I had assembled a great deal of evidence about Chris's actions.

'First, we have the generally grubby stuff about him sleeping with students, including Jenny. All of that would be considered sexual abuse today,' John-Paul advised. 'Then there is the stuff about him sharing girls with his brother and allegations he was violent and possessive. All of that makes it difficult for him to ever go before a jury.

'Second, we have the evidence against him that he committed the murder. We have the coroner findings, the hitman conversation, the motive with the affair, the timing of her going missing and his movements, the buried cardigan and his violent and possessive nature.'

John-Paul had a theory that our promotional video trailer, timed for release days before the first episode of the podcast, would probably make everything clearer.

'But we are testing the waters right now,' he cautioned. 'There is no doubt that we accuse Chris Dawson of murdering Lynette. This is not the type of publication where we can argue that we only convey the less serious meaning that there are reasonable grounds for suspecting he murdered her.

'We do say several times that he has always denied killing her – but ultimately, it doesn't do much to undo the overall sting of the publication which is, clearly, that he murdered Lyn.'

I weighed all the factors we would rely on to prove Chris murdered Lyn, including the findings of the two coroners; the many pieces of circumstantial evidence that Lyn must be dead; the fact Chris still claimed she was alive; the fact he had ample motive to murder Lyn; the witnesses who still had good recollections of events; the people like the investigating police officers who still had excellent knowledge of the case and whom we could call as witnesses.

John-Paul had done the same exercise.

'We also have witnesses who say that Chris was controlling, manipulative and abusive towards Lyn. Importantly, we have copies of the transcripts, police interviews and Coroners Court documents relating to these witnesses. This makes it harder for them to deviate from their stories. There is evidence from

Jenny that he tried to hire a hitman. We may have physical evidence from the house where Lyn's body is suspected to be buried.

'On top of that, even if we could not prove he murdered Lyn, we would reduce the damages to some degree because of the fact he was sleeping with his students. That is obviously not serious enough to overcome an allegation of murder but it lowers the overall amount he might be entitled to.

'Putting all of that together, if he did sue for defamation, I think we would mount a very strong case. Of course, it would not be cheap.

'I think there is a good chance we would prove, on the balance of probabilities, that he did commit the murder – even though police have decided they can't prove it beyond reasonable doubt.'

His reference to the balance of probabilities meant he was confident the jurors in a defamation case would believe it was more than 50 per cent likely that Chris had murdered Lyn. In a criminal trial, however, the burden of proof is beyond reasonable doubt, and it is necessarily higher at more than 90 per cent.

'On that basis,' John-Paul said, 'I think the overall podcast will be close to the line because, as I say, it's rare we accuse someone of murder without a conviction. But I think this is that sort of case.'

It was music to my ears. With this advice, Paul Whittaker, who had been calling me for regular updates, would not be risking his job for the story.

We went back and forth about the practical risk. Much had been written about Chris Dawson over the past 20 years and he had never sued. Usually, if someone has not previously sued, they would not sue now. Shanelle doubted her father would want to risk more scrutiny or significant legal bills. He would try to hunker down and wait for the storm to finish, as it always had before.

'That's great news,' replied the newspaper's deputy editor, Petra Rees, who had been reading my draft scripts.

The podcast had crossed a crucial hurdle. We were up for the fight. If John-Paul had gone the other way, if he had adopted the more conservative de-risking strategy favoured by many other defamation lawyers, our work would have been for nought.

Although Chris Dawson had known for months about my podcast series, he had not been contacted directly for an interview. For legal and ethical reasons, I would offer the opportunity.

Rebecca Hazel and I still speculated that Chris was ultimately behind the attempt to kill off her book with her friend Jenny. I believed that he had persuaded his youngest daughter to explain to her mother, Jenny, that it would only bring shame and hurt. I could see how Chris would envisage a scenario in which a withdrawal of Rebecca's book might halt the podcast as the author and the journalist had been working in tandem.

'What are the chances that he'll talk to us?' I asked her.

'Zero,' she replied. 'What do you think?'

Ever the optimist, I answered, 'Well, maybe if he believes that this is his last chance to have a say and it doesn't involve cameras, and we have a conversation, perhaps in front of his brother, Peter, the solicitor, perhaps he'll think, "Well, finally, I should do this." It could work.'

There were many questions I wanted to ask him. What did he do on the night of Saturday 9 January when Lyn was 'missing' and their two daughters were ensconced at Clovelly with their grandmother, Helena?

Chris moved Jenny into the house at Bayview one or two days later after he told her that Lyn was gone and 'not coming back'. At the same time, he was telling Lyn's mother that Lyn had said she wanted a little time away. Chris wanted Jenny to think the coast was permanently clear. He led Lyn's family to believe she might return after some quiet reflection on her own. I wanted to ask him why he was relaxed about the purported prospect of Lyn returning to Bayview any day and seeing a teenager running the home, bonding with Lyn's girls and sleeping with Chris in Lyn's bedroom.

Rebecca had been thinking about Chris for the past six years, yet she was still struggling to understand him. 'For me, he's almost a person with no personality. I'm unable to project much onto him because he's put so little of himself out there.'

Rebecca stopped herself and reconsidered. It couldn't be true, she said, that he had next to no personality. 'He's not a one-dimensional person. No one is, even people who do very, very bad things,' she said.

I believed his narcissism was the largest part of his character. It became more weird as a reflection of his identical twin brother. But unlike Paul, 'Cranky Chris' was as taut as piano wire. When things did not go right, he seethed and teetered on the edge of uncontrolled rage. He was controlling, manipulative, selfish and clinical.

Rebecca wished she could be there when I tried to talk to him.

I telephoned Chris from the kitchen at home. He must have been expecting a call.

My folders and files were haphazardly strewn across the family dining table. I had taken over the space and made it a mess. Outside, our chickens clucked contentedly. Ruth was working on the lawn, which I had not mowed or weeded for months. The neglect was obvious. Even the creek looked unkempt. There was no time.

I imagined something very different at Chris's house at Coolum. Everything would be ordered. Everything in its proper place.

He answered on the third ring.

'Chris speaking.'

'Oh, g'day Chris. My name's Hedley Thomas. I'm a journalist, and I—'

'Oh, Hedley. I know of you, yes.'

'Chris, I'd really like to have a chat to hear your views on this.'

'Hedley, I've spoken to journalists before. And articles and television shows and everything coming out have not been fair, in their interpretation of what I've said. Totally changed everything I have said. I'm sorry, I've lost all my faith in journalism.'

I tried to get a few words in, to let him know that if he agreed to be interviewed, he would not be edited. His insistence on his innocence would run in full. My offer was meant to overcome his concerns.

Surely it was better to put his side of the story out there? Even if he, correctly, believed that I saw him as a coldblooded killer.

He stuttered his reply, talking over me. 'So, so, so, so, sorry. My answer is no. I won't be speaking to you, sorry.'

Chris was courteous in his refusal. There was no abuse. No threats. No yelling.

I started to talk about how it would be audio with no filming – no cameras – but Chris had left the call.

'Are you there, Chris? Hello?'

The line was dead.

Chapter 28

Sue

As the launch for the podcast loomed, loose ends and missed opportunities played on my mind. Sue Strath's missing written complaint to the Ombudsman's office in 1985, about the failure of New South Wales Police to properly investigate the sudden disappearance of a loving wife and mother, was one of those loose ends.

The word 'ombudsman' is Swedish, and it means 'the citizens' defender'. What had happened to Sue's complaint after she lodged it with the defender of the people? Where were all the documents which must have been generated by police and public servants at the independent and impartial public watchdog during the investigation of citizen Sue's complaint?

According to a Sydney staff member from the Ombudsman's office who replied to Sue in late 2017, the documents arising from a complaint dating back three decades would have been destroyed long ago. It was dispiriting news. On the other hand, nobody could produce a record showing that, at a certain place and time, the file had been shredded. What if Sue's complaint file had been stored or archived somewhere?

I held a faint hope that the file still existed. This stemmed from an experience with another government bureaucracy, Queensland State Archives. In March 2013, while researching corruption allegations and gangsters going back decades, I drove 40 minutes south of the newspaper offices to the State Archives building in Runcorn. It was my first visit to this little-known repository of history.

I wanted to look at evidence from the 1980s, when a sweeping public inquiry had exposed endemic police corruption, aided and abetted by powerful politicians. The rottenness went to the highest levels. Even the police commissioner at the time, Terence Lewis, was found to have received hundreds of thousands of dollars in bribes and kickbacks from criminals and the operators of brothels and illegal casinos.

I was a cadet reporter at the *Gold Coast Bulletin* in 1987 when a brilliant lawyer, Tony Fitzgerald, had been appointed to head the public inquiry into the suspected corruption. Senior police had protected the illegal casinos for years. They insisted these places did not exist. They scoffed that the claims by journalists and their sources were wild fabrications.

In the opening days of the Fitzgerald Inquiry, I saw an opportunity to write a story about an illegal casino which I knew had been operating for years above a gelato bar in the heart of Surfers Paradise. My editor, John Burton, ran the story prominently. My friends were taken aback at my reporting. Les Green, Shayne Fergus and Darren Wilkes never let me forget it. We had started going to this dingy, exciting venue on Friday nights after school to wager our personal limits of $20 while taking advantage of the alcohol, which was worth much more. Sometimes we even won playing blackjack and roulette, though profitability was rare. More importantly, we always left merrily drunk and we reasoned that the free booze and entertainment made up for the disappearance of our cash. The doorman didn't mind that we were 16 and 17 years old. My revelatory story a few years later finally forced the hand of the bent and embarrassed local cops, who had to shut the joint down.

In 2013, when I went to State Archives, among the public documents I had requested were hundreds of files clearly labelled 'highly confidential'. Spilling across the viewing tables were extremely grave allegations and details of sensitive investigations which I knew had never before been disclosed. There were extraordinary claims about the purportedly corrupt conduct of well-known Queenslanders, from judges to politicians to business leaders. In a colossal bungle, I had been given access to the internal workings of years of investigation by the Fitzgerald Inquiry and its successor anti-corruption agency.

When I quietly revealed the stunning discovery to my close friend and colleague Matt Condon, he was astonished and replied, 'You've stubbed your toe on Lasseter's Reef!'

As I asked the public servant archivist for more and more documents, one of the staff flagged my interest with the Crime and Misconduct Commission. It started to dawn on senior investigators and lawyers that a large trove of highly confidential files had been accidentally made available – not just to me but to anyone who asked. This hugely embarrassing stuff-up triggered crisis meetings behind closed doors between bureaucrats, lawyers and investigators. The cat was out of the bag. Over several days, I had already copied dozens of these files with the help of a University of Queensland journalism student, Emma Hart.

We broke the story on the front page of *The Australian*: 'Thousands of sensitive files including secret National Crime Authority intelligence on suspects in unsolved murders, secret informants, undercover agents, drug operations and police corruption have been publicly available due to an error by Queensland's Crime and Misconduct Commission. The files, dozens of which have been reviewed at State Archives in Brisbane by *The Australian* in the past week, were the property of the Fitzgerald Inquiry in the late 1980s and meant to stay secret until about the year 2055.'

A public inquiry ensued. New laws were introduced to urgently block public access. Everything was put back into a vault.

The experience taught me that government agencies routinely keep thousands of documents for decades. Public servants have no idea what they've kept and what they've destroyed. So there was at least a slight chance that Sue Strath's file might be in the State Archives and Records NSW office.

Its website had an online search tool. When I typed in 'police' and 'ombudsman' and 'complaint', it delivered hits for numerous numbered files going back many years. It was encouraging and I kept looking. A helpful archivist in the office, Jenny Sloggett, suggested I put my request in writing.

In an email in late April, I wrote:

> The particular file we are seeking from NSW Archives relates to a complaint initiated with the Ombudsman's office about 33 years ago – in late 1984 or early 1985 – by a Sydney woman, Susan Browett. Susan's name now is Susan Strath.
>
> Under her then married name of Susan Browett, she complained to the NSW Ombudsman about a lack of activity by New South Wales Police in a missing person case. The missing person was Susan's colleague. Susan doesn't recall receiving the Ombudsman's report in 1985 arising from her complaint, nor any actual reply to her complaint.
>
> We can see that the NSW Ombudsman's office did do work on the complaint, as we have received correspondence from police showing they responded to the Ombudsman's queries. I mentioned the police correspondence on the telephone this morning, however, it doesn't reference a file number.

Three days later, Jenny Sloggett emailed me with astonishing news: 'NSW State Archives holds a file re Susan Browett's complaint.'

The file was in a batch called 'investigation files' for complaints which had been assessed by the Ombudsman as part of its duty to look at allegations of misconduct by police. Jenny Sloggett disclosed the file number and the number of the container in which the documents were kept.

But there was a snag. Jenny Sloggett explained that the government agency responsible for the documents, the Ombudsman's office, ultimately controlled all of the records in the investigation file.

'The Ombudsman's office has, under the State Records Act 1998, closed investigation files from general public access for 90 years to protect sensitive personal information,' she wrote.

I could scarcely believe it. Instinctively, I was sure there would be highly relevant evidence in the file, information we would be denied because of an arcane guideline that meant it would not be available until 2075. What was the point of archiving anything if those who might be interested in the documents were long-dead by the time the material became available for inspection? Or was that the point all along?

I again contacted the Ombudsman, my friend Michael Barnes, to let him know that Sue's complaint file had miraculously been rediscovered and that it could be released immediately with his authorisation.

A stickler for ethical conduct, Michael replied, 'In view of our friendship, I have declared a conflict of interest and requested that Deputy Ombudsman, Chris Wheeler, deal with your application.'

In an email sent to me a few days later, Chris Wheeler wrote, 'I don't recall the office receiving a request for a file that is this old before, so I am currently exploring the legal position about whether there are options available for enabling access to the file in question, and if so how such access can be arranged.'

The five-week wait was excruciating. Finally, Jenny called me with uplifting news.

'So, we've heard back from the Ombudsman. He's allowing access to that file,' she told me. 'What we're waiting on is for the file to come back from his office. It's kind of an unusual thing because he's opened that one file but none of his other files – the Ombudsman's investigation files.'

Jenny, a model of public service efficiency and courtesy, explained that I'd be facing a copying charge of $22 for the 44 pages and a further $26 in fees for photocopying and urgent delivery.

My anticipation was such that I would have agreed to pay the quote a hundred times over.

A few days later, she scanned the complete investigation file and sent it to me as a PDF. I saved and opened it with rising excitement and anticipation, and sent it straight to my home printer.

Sue's handwritten letter, in a file of more than 40 pages, was finally in my hands. It bore a stamp of the Office of the Ombudsman with a date of 5 February 1985.

Dear Sir,

It is three years since my friend Lyn Dawson of Bayview Heights was reported as a missing person by her husband Chris Dawson. Lyn was a devoted mother of two small children. I worked with her at Warriewood Children's Centre. It was known by all her workmates that she was having marital problems, we had all heard about Chris's affair with a then 16-year-old student of his, who was staying at the time with the Dawson family. Lyn – although she probably suspected – didn't want to believe this of her husband whom she idolised. She accepted her marriage was 'shaky' and on the Friday before she was last seen, she and her husband went to see a marriage psychologist. She and Chris came back to work excited about better understanding 'and working out problems together'. The next day, what happened????

Sue then described some of Chris Dawson's claims including that Lyn had 'packed a few things while he was out and just left without goodbyes to anyone'.

Chris has told another friend of mine that Lyn found he and his girlfriend in bed and just 'freaked' – sure, I can understand that but I don't believe she could walk out on her two girls and leave them for another woman to raise. She loved her home and was a very materialistic person. Why would she walk out on a home worth over 1/4 million dollars? Chris reported she left to join a religious group and is believed to be living on the north coast. As far as I know, she had no religious beliefs at all and didn't attend church. A person cannot become religious overnight and most religious groups are very family orientated so a woman with children would be acceptable rather than a woman without.

Her husband was so sure she would not return, his girlfriend was moved in the following week. He has now married his schoolgirl lover, has a beautiful house and established family. Everything seems too easy. He got exactly what he wanted and his wife, who wasn't up to standard, has vanished from the face of the earth, having no further contact with any family or friends. Chris has said he received a phone call but I put this down to the extended story.

It doesn't seem possible that a person can be swept under the rug and forgotten. I would like to know what the police have done in this matter. Why weren't her workmates interviewed as to her last 24 hours? Why were her husband's words used as sole evidence as to her whereabouts?

It appears to me the police have taken the view that Lyn left her husband, family and work friends of her own free will. I wonder if this is true. I'm concerned as I was one of the last to see her on the Friday, but was never questioned by the police.

Can a person just disappear and it be accepted, because she is over 16 years, that she did so willingly, when we only have her husband's word that this is what happened? Could you please throw a little bit of light on this mystery? I've seen her on the 'Missing Person' poster and just cannot accept the explanation of whereabouts.

Yours faithfully,

Susan Browett

Sue's letter was damning in its questioning tone and each time I read it, I was struck by its power. Sue had joined all the suspicious dots and was making out a case of foul play with this written plea for help, five years before Jenny raised her suspicions with police in Sydney, triggering the 1990 investigation.

I greedily read the other documents in the file, all of which were new to me. I was confident that Detective Damian Loone had never seen these documents. They had not featured in the inquests in 2001 and in 2003, or in any subsequent publicity about the case. This meant that the two coroners, who had separately recommended Dawson be prosecuted, had not seen the file either.

The next discovery was a document with the handwritten heading *Antecedent Report*, dated 16 August 1982. I was stunned to see the name of its author on the second page – C. Dawson. The formal and

legalistic word 'antecedent' threw me, so I called a lawyer friend, who
said the word was sometimes used by police in reports describing a
set of facts or events. It was probable that Chris Dawson had written
the document at a police station with the help of a detective.

In the document, Chris set out the actions he claimed to have
taken to find his wife, Lyn, who by then had not been seen or heard
from by her mother, siblings or work friends for seven months. Chris
wrote a dishonest version of what was going on in their marriage and
the circumstances of her supposedly leaving him without warning.

He stated that he had contacted all Lyn's girlfriends to try to find
her, without success. I knew it was a brazen lie. His focus had only
been on bringing Jenny back to the house at Bayview as quickly as
possible.

He wrote that he had called women's refuges at Manly and Dee
Why, the Salvation Army 'and all possible family connections'. For
their wedding anniversary of 26 March 1982, he said he had placed
an ad in *The Daily Telegraph*. He claimed to have driven to the Royal
North Shore Hospital to see if Lyn was working there. His father, Syd
Dawson, according to Chris, had called Lifeline.

'There was a slight possibility of contact with a religious organisation. Mrs Helena Simms, Lyn's mother, followed through on this
possibility,' Chris wrote.

Beneath an underlined heading titled *History*, Chris wrote: 'Lyn
and I had been having marital problems for approximately two years,
mainly over her Bankcard spending and financial matters in general.
I left home for three days over Christmas and travelled north to be
by myself. I returned home to Sydney, having missed my wife and
daughters and hoping to resolve differences.'

The lies and omissions in this paragraph were strikingly obvious.
The marital problems were due to Chris becoming infatuated with
a teenage student. He had been having sex with her and wanted to
spend the rest of his life with the girl.

Yes, he had 'travelled north' over Christmas but not for time
alone; he had walked out on Lyn and his daughters to start a new life
in Queensland with the babysitter. When Jenny anxiously regretted

the decision, they abandoned their plans and returned to Sydney. Chris's version to police made no mention whatsoever of the teenager in his life.

He wrote that he and Lyn had seen 'a marriage guidance counsellor/ psychiatrist' on Friday 8 January, adding that when he dropped her back to the childcare centre, 'we were both in particularly good spirits. We were holding hands and once again felt close'.

This was partly true. Sue Strath had witnessed the display of affection and she was pleasantly surprised, after months of hearing Lyn describe a marriage which appeared doomed. After Lyn disappeared, Sue suspected that Chris's display of post-counselling affection at the childcare centre was a manipulative ruse, lulling Lyn into a false sense of security. I believed it was also an attempt to deceive Sue and others at Lyn's workplace in the hours before he would kill his wife.

On the second page of his report, Chris sprinkled a few details which he must have hoped would convince police that his selfish, unstable wife had abandoned him and their children. He wrote that she had telephoned him at 3 pm on Saturday 9 January when he was at Northbridge Baths and 'she said she was with friends, not to worry, it was her turn and that she'd ring later that week'.

'She rang the following Saturday and said she needed more time and wouldn't return home until she felt happy to do so,' he wrote.

He added that Lyn had opened bank accounts and obtained a credit card in her name before Christmas, and that credit card statements – which were not included in the file – showed there were purchases at a women's fashion store on 12 January and at a jeans store on 27 January. He wrote that Lyn 'was reportedly seen' at Gosford by Sue Butlin, the wife of a footballing friend.

As I read the teacher's account of the marriage, Lyn's disappearance and his complete airbrushing from existence of his sexual relationship with a schoolgirl, I was struck by his audacity. He must have believed that he could get away with it. And, somehow, he had. Despite the many students, parents and teachers at the school and people in the wider community knowing about Jenny. Despite most of them knowing he had moved Jenny into the house immediately after Lyn vanished. Despite Jenny being paraded in public with Chris including at Belrose Eagles rugby league games on weekends. What was it about this time and place that afforded Chris his freedom after his terrible deeds? He not only had his freedom, he thrived. He was not inconvenienced in the slightest.

Barbara Cruise's precise summary when she talked to police in 1998 nailed it.

'He got all the money, whatever money they might have had. He got the children. He got the house. And he got the girlfriend. He didn't dip out in any way, shape or form. And it would appear that he did it without anyone questioning him.'

The last sentence in the report rang recognition bells for me: 'Sergeant Brian Gardner, Manly Detectives, has been advising me on procedure.'

Brian 'Smacka' Gardner, the well-connected senior detective and president of the Belrose Eagles Rugby League Club, the same cop who had persuaded Chris and Paul to be captain-coaches was, according to Chris, lending him a helping hand. It probably explained why Chris had called the document an antecedent report; the detective told him to head it up that way. Brian Gardner might have been terribly misled, an innocent dupe. Maybe even simply a product of the time – a macho cop who took the word of the celebrity footballer. But the inference that Chris was under the wing of a senior detective with a vested interest was hard to avoid. I remembered that Chris had also name-dropped Brian Gardner in his 1991 interview with the two detectives from the Homicide Squad.

Reading the rest of the file helped me understand some of what must have happened in the months after Sue's letter. Several senior police gathered any relevant Lyn Dawson files from the Missing Persons Bureau and the police stations on the Northern Beaches to try to satisfy the independent Ombudsman that Sue's complaint was not valid. A housewife alleging police inaction was not going to get the better of the senior brass of the New South Wales Police Force.

But when those senior police were preparing their self-serving response to the Ombudsman, crucial internal documents, including

Chris's antecedent report, were photocopied and included in the bundle. And now here they were, including this statement to police in which, in his own handwriting, Chris told blatant lies.

A strong prosecutor will almost always argue that an accused's lies are borne of 'a consciousness of guilt'. In other words, the lies were told because the accused was guilty and needed to divert suspicion to avoid being caught.

For the podcast, I briefed my friend Brian Jordan, a former barrister and retired judge, about the discovery of the antecedent report and asked if the lies in the statement written by Chris were 'evidence of a guilty mind and therefore possibly a powerful piece in a murder prosecution now?'

'They could be,' Brian replied in a tone which sounded pregnant with possibility. 'But there's another explanation. The lies could have been either to hide his killing of his wife, or they could have been to hide the fact that he went to Queensland with a former student.

'If I was defence counsel, I'd be saying, "Well, it's hardly surprising that he wasn't going to volunteer information about a suggestion that he'd had a relationship with a student." So it's not necessarily indicative of a guilty mind of a murderer. It can cut both ways.'

I called Peter Lavac, another lawyer friend who I'd met as a journalist at the *South China Morning Post* in Hong Kong in the 1990s, who believed the circumstantial case against Chris was 'overwhelming'.

Peter's criticisms of the Office of the DPP for its refusal to prosecute were scathing. 'I think a jury would have no problem whatsoever convicting him,' he told me.

Turning to the newly discovered statement written by Chris in August 1982, Peter added:

'That is gold. He is lying about his relationship with the girl and his relationship with the girl is his motive for murdering his wife. Lies can always be used in evidence in a prosecution against an accused to show a guilty mind.

'Defence-wise, of course, they'll say, "Well, he denied it and covered it up because he didn't want it to come out that he's having a relationship with a 16-year-old girl." But that's bullshit because everyone knew about that; it was common knowledge to everyone. He was seen by other students kissing and cuddling her on the football oval.

'That sort of evidence is absolutely crucial to a prosecution because it's just another nail in the coffin of his defence, namely that he's lying to the police about a very important material issue when he reports his wife missing.

'A mother does not just disappear overnight and abandon her kids never to be seen again. That's absolutely absurd. The fact that Chris Dawson was involved in this relationship with this young girl who is their babysitter provides a powerful motivation to get rid of his wife. The fact that he wanted to keep the house that they lived in provides powerful motivation for committing that murder and that's what in fact happened after the wife disappeared. He got to keep the house and he got to keep going with his relationship with this young girl. And when you put it all together with the other circumstantial evidence in this case, you've got a very powerful prosecution case which should go to trial and which, I'm pretty certain if it went to trial, would ultimately result in a conviction.'

When I asked Peter how he would be viewing the case if he were, hypothetically, a defence lawyer for Chris, he replied, 'I'd be very concerned. The evidence against him is extremely powerful. And I'm just amazed and puzzled and dismayed as to why the authorities haven't taken up the case and prosecuted it on the advice and findings of two very experienced and capable coroners.'

The Ombudsman's file from 1985 was a trove of secrets for other reasons too. I created a timeline to put the documents in context. I needed to better understand the internal machinations of police after Sue's complaint forced them to provide answers about how they had responded to Lyn's disappearance.

An internal file note written by Sue Thompson, investigation officer for the Ombudsman's office, states: 'This is a bit of a sensitive complaint. It's about the alleged disappearance of a woman some three years ago and [an] allegation that the police may have failed to properly investigate this matter. Should be allocated carefully.'

The officer's file note suggested that she understood the potential seriousness of the case. She understood that Lyn's friend from the child-care centre was obviously pointing the finger at Chris as a husband who had possibly murdered his wife. Sue Thompson went to the top of the police force, writing to then Commissioner of Police John Avery to ask him to comment on the allegations. From there, it was referred by the police chief to Inspector Geoff Shattles, who produced a two-page typed memo a fortnight later, which frustratingly recounted without challenge everything that Chris had disingenuously claimed since 1982. It was as if Chris had some brainwashing power over police, who must believe everything he uttered. Read in its proper context, which was as an internal response to the litany of suspicious actions in the complaint letter from Sue Strath, the document was even more troubling.

Inspector Shattles ended his memo with classic bureaucratic arse-covering: 'It might be noted that at no time has Mr or Mrs Simms ever hinted that there were any suspicious circumstances regarding the disappearance of their daughter or any foul play on behalf of Mr Dawson.'

As a result of the memo, a more senior officer, whose name was hard to read, stated on 20 March 1985: 'I am satisfied all avenues of investigation were covered at the time.'

There was one further step for police to take before they would close the file. It was decided that Sue Browett would be spoken to by police. A grand farce was in circular motion. Rather than going back to Sue, who had already laid out the facts in her complaint, detectives should have been interviewing teachers, students and neighbours about the relationship between Chris and the family's babysitter. Sue had told the police in writing that a teacher was having an affair with a 16-year-old student. This in and of itself would be a criminal offence called 'carnal knowledge'; it was unlawful for a teacher, being a person in authority, to have sex with a student under the age of 17. The lack of initiative was so poor it was offensive.

If just one cop involved in the paper chain had used a little commonsense, he would have quickly worked out what Sue was alleging: a teacher, dishonestly presenting himself as an abandoned husband with an unstable wife, wanted Lyn gone. And what happened? Lyn disappeared, replaced immediately by Jenny.

When Sue was visited by police in 1985, she had nothing further to add. Amazingly, that was as far as police took it. On 28 June 1985, an assistant commissioner of police wrote to the Ombudsman and advised that further inquiries 'have proved fruitless'.

Chris Wheeler, then a middle management public servant in the Ombudsman's office, was overseeing the file. It does not appear that the Ombudsman's office asked police why they had not attempted to talk to Chris or Jenny or Jenny's parents, her school friends or her teachers. The powerful implication of the offence of carnal knowledge went entirely unremarked.

In 1985, in correspondence and over the telephone, Sue was told by Chris Wheeler that police had no new leads. The file was then closed.

Coincidentally, the 2018 decision to release the file to me was made by the same Chris Wheeler, who had become Deputy Ombudsman in 1994.

Sue was moved to tears when I shared the file with her. She read her complaint for the first time since she wrote it as a young mum.

'I wrote it from my heart,' she told me. Her voice was breaking and the strong, now elderly woman needed to pause.

The police and the Ombudsman had utterly failed to investigate anything, despite the trail of clues left by Sue. It should have been obvious to investigators that Chris's 1982 statement held contradictions and omissions which needed to be carefully scrutinised. They never asked the obvious question: 'Why did Chris fail to mention Jenny?'

But there were more red flags which highlighted the hopelessness of the two well-resourced agencies. The file held a letter from Lyn's mother, in which she also raised the presence of Jenny and the related tensions in the marriage. On 21 August 1982, Helena described the events of 8 January and 9 January 1982 based partly on what Chris had told her and partly on what she observed herself.

She wrote: 'My daughter had become uptight and very tense over the latter months of last year. She and her husband had struck a bumpy patch in their marriage and partnership of 17 years, complicated by the taking in of a teenage student seeking help. She had babysat for them. My daughter offered her hospitality in good faith, which she later regretted when she caused her much anguish.'

The letter was another important discovery, and it corroborated what I had been told by Lyn's siblings. Helena, relying on the word of Chris, said the baby was disturbed on the night of 8 January 'and Lyn broke down, so Chris told me, took herself into a bed in the study, where I guess she stewed in her misery'.

Lyn had arranged to meet her mother at Northbridge Baths, where Chris worked part-time as a lifeguard, the next day, Saturday 9 January:

Chris said she woke early, did a load of washing, cut lunches for them to take to the pool, was very, very calm, apologised for her breakdown and asked to be driven down to the bus at 7 am to Chatswood.

She was to come back in time to have lunch with them at the pool. She was wearing shorts and carried three plastic shopping bags, saying she wanted to return some clothing at Chatswood and probably would go on to Paddy's Markets.

I arrived at the pool at 2 pm to have a swim with them and was met by an agitated Chris wanting to know if Lyn had contacted me. At 3 pm, he received a telephone call and came back to me and he was visibly affected. It was an STD call from Lyn saying she needed some days to think things out. Was on the Central Coast with friends – no idea who that could have been – and was alright.

In 1982, digital communications did not exist and mobile telephones were rare. Landline telephone calls between people who were not in the same district, or area code, were called 'long-distance calls' or

'STD' (subscriber trunk dialling) and they were distinct because of the pipping noise when the call went through.

Helena also described the purported telephone contact which, according to Chris, Lyn had with him over the ensuing days.

She emphasised Lyn's reliable nature and her love for her family, home and friends.

'She didn't drink or smoke, her only "vice" as such was to wander through shops and spend unwisely at times,' Helena wrote. 'She loved her children, her husband and home, family gatherings, going out as a family.'

Lyn was always the first to call on birthdays. There had been several birthdays since Helena last spoke to her daughter and nobody had heard a word from her – with the purported exception of Chris.

Helena wrote that on 15 January 1982 – seven days after she last spoke to her daughter – she received a call from Chris 'saying that he had had a call from Lyn' who had 'been north and needed more time'.

> He got annoyed with her and said, 'How much more bloody time do you need?' He asked her not to hang up as she said she wouldn't come home if he spoke like that. Chris said to 'ring your mum'. She said she would when she felt she could.
>
> He asked her to come home. He said we all needed her. She said, 'I can't.'
>
> That was the last time we had contact with her.

Helena was unknowingly describing a contemptible display of dishonesty by Chris. He had murdered his wife. To cover his tracks, he was feigning enthusiasm for her to come home and trying to appear the dutiful son-in-law with his claims that he had asked Lyn to 'ring your mum'. He tried to present as the responsible adult concerned for Helena. Cunningly, he was easing Helena's worries so that she did not raise the alarm when the trail was fresh. The truth was that by 15 January, Lyn had been dead for a week. Jenny was in the house, sleeping in Lyn's bed.

On the third page of her letter to police, Helena sprinkled a few important clues which nobody in the police force had the wit to appreciate.

Until recently I have held my son-in-law in high esteem and got along well with him, but my faith has been shaken when, for all his talk of wanting to look after his two little girls, Lyn 'goes' and he has introduced the teenager back into the home – as early as 6 February that I heard of it.

So if Lyn has been in the vicinity and seen them in the open together, she has cut herself off from us all totally and completely and I'm sure she can't be thinking straight.

Chapter 29

A Pack of Male Teachers

An extraordinary newsroom effort in the days around the launch of the podcast series encouraged Lyn's family and raised everyone's expectations.

There were many people involved in different ways, from advertising to public relations to reporting and production. Paul Whittaker had decided that *The Australian* would run daily news stories based largely on the revelations from each weekly episode. As I had little time for things other than the podcast, David Murray stepped up to scrutinise every script, work out the individual news angles and run the drafts past me. David organised photographs with the picture editor, Milan Scepanovic, and graphics were commissioned to accompany many of the yarns. We liaised closely with Petra Rees on the news desk as well as Kel Southan, who ensured the website was fresh and constantly updated. We wrote mini bios for everyone in the series, publishing each one as listeners heard their names in an episode.

Our resourceful photographer in Brisbane Lyndon Mechielsen went to Coolum to try to catch a glimpse of Chris Dawson.

'When he goes for a run along the beach, he walks out his driveway to where that street ends in a cul-de-sac, then he takes a walk through a sandy path that winds right to the beach, then he turns left to jog north towards the town of Coolum,' I told Lyndon.

A golfing friend who lived nearby knew of my interest and tipped me off.

Lyndon's patience and skill with a long lens were rewarded. Chris, tanned and bare-chested, was photographed on his front lawn, the image holding up the front page of *The Weekend Australian* news-paper with an accompanying story about what we were seeking to do with *The Teacher's Pet*.

Paul Whittaker described the podcast series as 'one of the biggest journalistic undertakings by *The Australian* in recent years'.

'This podcast is part investigation, part storytelling, with powerful voices in each episode,' he said. 'Hedley Thomas has spent six months tracking down all the key players in this case, and convinced many of them to speak for the first time about what they know, and in the process, he has unearthed compelling new information unknown to investigating police at the time.

'It is early days but we have some remarkable material in this series and we expect to gather momentum as people follow the story each week.'

Greg Simms had his eye on a potential outcome, adding that 'the best-case scenario is for us to convince the DPP and powers that be that there needs to be a court case'.

Pat Jenkins, apprehensive but hopeful, feared the DPP would be bloody-minded 'because they made a decision years ago and want to stick to it'.

'I hope they have an open mind, I'd like to think they've changed,' Pat said.

The first episode, 'Bayview', quickly went to number one on the podcast charts. Listeners began sharing positive reviews. My friend Katie Page, CEO of the massive retailer Harvey Norman, the first corporate sponsor of the podcast, gave it an immediate thumbs up. Katie predicted that the presentation of the story and its known facts would prompt authorities to review 'a case that was never solved'.

The top-rating Sydney radio presenter Ben Fordham, whose media-savvy father, John, supported me as a reporter in my early 20s, had become concerned about the absence of my byline from the pages of *The Australian* over the previous six months, though he stopped short of asking me if I'd been made redundant. When I explained what I had been working on, he immediately offered to help push the case and the podcast. After the launch, he texted me: 'Just finished Episode 1. Brilliant. I'm hooked.'

I was sitting at the dining table at home, my temporary office, and writing a draft chapter for a future episode when one of the most important early leads dropped into my inbox. Robyn Wheeler, who had seen Lyndon's photograph of Chris and read the accompanying story flagging the podcast, wanted to ensure that I didn't miss the wider picture about the exploitation of her fellow students at Cromer High.

'At the school during the period from, say, the late 1970s there was a "pack" of male teachers who were preying on female students,' Robyn wrote.

> It was like the elephant in the room. Everybody knew about it but nobody said anything, except, I believe, some of the girls' mothers, who confronted the teachers and threatened to destroy them.
>
> I guess my point is that, when you have a pack of twenty and thirty-something aged men preying on 15- and 16-year-old girls, and nobody stops them, they believe they can do anything. And they get away with it.
>
> Another point – Chris Dawson's twin and he acted in cahoots. They were known to have threesomes with young girls. They were football stars, after all. If anybody knows what happened to Lyn, it would likely be him.

Although she did not know me from a bar of soap, the former school vice-captain shared the names of other Cromer High teachers who were notorious offenders, telling me that they had ruined young lives.

She agreed to be interviewed and I sought the relative quiet of my car in the driveway to conduct the first telephone interview with a former Cromer student. As Robyn calmly and authoritatively talked about Chris, Jenny and a culture in which teachers pursued female students for sex, I realised that this was a piece which needed more emphasis and attention. Lyn's murder did not happen in isolation. I needed to widen the scope of the investigation so that it also dealt with a sick culture in the high schools.

Robyn was unwavering in her resolve to see the rot exposed. She had been disgusted for years by the conduct of Chris and the other teachers, and the institutional failure of authorities.

Robyn saw the podcast as a vehicle to potentially make Chris Dawson and all those other teachers accountable for the damage they had caused.

'I knew it was going on and many other people knew it was going on, not just with Chris Dawson and Jenny Carlson. It was going on with other teachers and students at the school.

'The culture at the school was such that there was a group of men, male teachers, in their 20s and 30s who preyed on young girls at the school, 15-, 16-, 17-year-old girls, usually not the Year 12s, they were a little bit old, and you would see them talking all the time, when there were sporting trips or school trips for whatever reason, they would be in the teacher's car, they would be babysitting for the teachers . . .

'I think Lyn's family deserve to know what happened to her, in particular her two daughters need to know. He needs to be exposed. There's been too [many] people not wanting to talk about it because it's not the done thing. If it had been discussed more openly from the outset, lives wouldn't have been ruined potentially and people would have answers to those questions now.

'In fact, the impacts of those relationships – and we're talking 35 years ago – still exist, and those girls are really quite damaged, and in some cases, the teachers left their wives and the first family of children and took off with the younger girls when they finished school.'

I asked how many Cromer High teachers including Chris were having sexual relations with students at the time.

Robyn replied, 'At least six. It was the same teachers pretty much year after year . . . Everybody knew. It was just common knowledge.

'This was a beach culture, where pretty much girls were judged on their appearance, their beach worthiness, and that's how we were brought up to value ourselves in that time and that place, so it was very misogynistic . . . it was a culture where the girls wouldn't argue; they were grateful for the attention.'

After naming the offending teachers, Robyn recalled Jenny Carlson, whom she described as a soft and easy target. She was not one of the 'in-crowd girls'. The teacher with a reputation as a sports star targeted a teenager unsure of herself and lacking confidence.

'This is what was allowed to happen because nobody said anything, nobody did anything. And the police didn't do anything. Why?'

With some fast writing, narration and editing, we made changes to include Robyn's interview in Episode 2, titled 'Cromer High'.

Robyn spread word to other former students from Cromer High, some of whom she had not heard from since the early 1980s. Soon they were group-chatting, sharing contact details and recalling the teachers who needed to be held accountable.

Robyn's courage in speaking out, and her leadership in rallying others to come forward, made a profound difference. The covers were being lifted off not just a probable murder but all the dirty secrets of a school where child sexual abuse was routinely perpetrated and ignored.

There was an easy rapport between Robyn and almost all the former students with whom she put me in touch. They each brought fresh perspectives, seemingly vivid recollections and the names of more students. We were about the same age and we had not gone to privileged private schools.

Having heard Robyn in the second episode, Phil Webster, a teacher himself and the father of a 15-year-old daughter, wanted to back up his high school friend.

'We always got on well and the way she speaks when I listen to her now, I mean, we're all much more wiser now, we're all parents,' Phil told me. 'It's starting to bring back a lot of memories for me.'

Phil described what he witnessed in the playground between his PE teacher, Mr Dawson, and Jenny as 'explicit'.

'It was almost like they advertised it. That was the culture at the time. I can actually say, and verify, that one of the teachers who was having an affair basically said, "Mate, they're 16, it's not illegal."'

Phil volunteered that his learning as a teenage boy was that girls 'are objects, you just fuck as many as you can. You get the best ones you can, you go after them and do what you can'.

'That's what I saw. And they weren't really trying hard to cover it up. The psychological damage those men caused . . . they were only after their own sexual conquests. And they should have known – they were PE teachers studying psychology – and yet they gave no regard for the welfare of the girls . . . it was just about the hedonistic pleasure of fucking young, good-looking girls.'

Chapter 30

Cromer High

Across the Northern Beaches, tens of thousands of people, many of whom had never listened to a podcast before, started hearing, sharing and talking about *The Teacher's Pet* with friends, family, colleagues and former schoolmates. The insular peninsular's dirty secrets were going viral.

I had written scripts for the first handful of weekly episodes prior to launching the first one. Slade Gibson was on top of production despite the significant demands of putting all the disparate pieces of audio together, pacing it delicately and composing and performing the many different music tracks to complement the storytelling. My interminable requests for changes, edits and tweaks would have sent a lesser audio engineer around the bend.

Shanelle Dawson offered ongoing encouragement. 'Don't stress, you're kicking arse, you've got this,' she texted me as Slade and I wrangled a redo of the third episode.

I had not planned for a rising flood of calls, emails and Facebook Messenger tip-offs from listeners who knew something, or knew someone who did. Every tip needed to be followed up. If the informant's credibility appeared solid and the details being imparted were new, Slade and I faced important decisions. A conventional, safer path would have been a new production at the end of the series – perhaps several bonus episodes to include the new information.

However, with Slade's unstinting support, I decided to take the riskier, more dynamic and potentially high-reward path of interviewing people as they came forward then restructuring already built episodes, sometimes last-minute before they went out.

It was crazy-brave and fraught with danger. We were creating new content in a high-profile investigation on the eve of its release.

Other media outlets started reporting on early disclosures in the series and its unprecedented popularity in Australia and around the world. Ben Fordham was an early mover and he stayed on it, giving a lot of airtime to the podcast, Lyn's family and me. His contribution and unwavering backing made an enormous difference. It gave early confidence to Lyn's relatives that something unusual in the competitive world of media might be unfolding; large media outlets, which would traditionally prefer to turn a blind eye to the stories of their competitors, were deeply interested in Lyn's case, and even promoting a rival outlet's story.

Renee Simms, who had explained to her parents, Greg and Merilyn, in late 2017 what a podcast might achieve, did a live television interview with Seven's *Weekend Sunrise* program. Responding to questions from hosts Basil Zempilas and Monique Wright, who spoke of revelations in the first two episodes of the podcast, Renee said her family strongly believed Chris had murdered Lyn.

Monique asked, 'Renee, we just heard he lives on the Sunshine Coast. There's every chance Chris Dawson is watching right now. If he is, what would you say to him?'

Renee, who bears an uncanny resemblance to her Aunty Lyn, replied, 'Just do what's right. Let us know where she is.'

Cocooned in Slade's studio at the end of his secluded driveway in Brisbane, we took opportunities like Renee's interview to reinforce the currency of the series. It meant taking out part of the third episode and replacing it with a new section featuring Renee talking about Chris, Lyn and the plea to her former uncle to 'do what's right'. Listeners realised that the episodes had not been sitting on the shelf for ages; they were taking form week to week. People with information could offer it knowing that what they had to say might air in the next episode, and therefore could make a real difference.

More former students of Cromer High started talking to each other and then to me. Former students from nearby Forest High, where Paul Dawson taught and was alleged to have groomed a trusting schoolgirl, Alice, for sex with himself and a pack of male teachers and footballers, were listening and wanted to disclose what they knew. It was the same for Beacon Hill High, where Chris taught after Lyn disappeared.

As the podcast topped charts in Australia and then internationally, I heard from hundreds of women. Many told me they had been damaged by domestic violence and sexual abuse. They would probably not seek justice for themselves, although some did. And although their abuser had not been Chris Dawson, they took comfort from a podcast exposing predatory sexual behaviour.

I waited for a contrarian to come up with evidence of a scenario which did not assume the worst. A witness to say, 'Hey! I know where Lyn went.' Nobody came forward. The reputations of Chris and many other teachers were dirt on the Northern Beaches long before this media scrutiny, yet nothing had happened. The failures of local police, school heads, teachers and community busybodies to blow an authoritative whistle on the predatory teachers had bottled everything up. Now, the early episodes of the podcast had picked up this time, place and behaviour and snowballed, gathering mass and speed each week. Nobody could predict where it would finish.

Robyn Wheeler and Phil Webster were conduits, passing on solid leads which emerged through the old school network. They put me in touch with Michelle Walsh, a talented gymnast two years below Jenny at Cromer High, who had a frightening run-in with Chris in late January 1982 after speaking to another PE teacher, Lesley Bush, affectionately known as 'Bushy'.

Throughout late 1980 and much of 1981, like most of the staff and students at Cromer High, Bushy had witnessed the closeness of Chris and Jenny. She was fiercely opposed to it. Bushy also knew and liked Lyn, and was alarmed by her disappearance.

Michelle Walsh was in the school gymnasium when she saw Bushy weeping.

'Her emotional state was bad. She was, like, crying and she sat me down in the gym and she was shaking and I can remember her telling me that Lyn had gone missing and no one had heard from her again,' Michelle told me. 'I was this 15-year-old kid and I've got a schoolteacher who was crying on my shoulders about this because she was quite good friends with Lyn and she was very good friends with Chris. And she had actually introduced me to Lyn at our end-of-year gym display.'

Michelle told me she sat and talked to the popular young teacher, consoling her near the staff office. A short time later, the usually bright and bubbly woman thanked her and walked away. Chris had seen them together. He summoned Michelle as she skipped over the quadrangle next to the canteen and he demanded that she disclose what Bushy had said.

Up to that point, Michelle had known Chris as a quiet teacher. Michelle said:

'I remember feeling awful. I didn't say anything to him about his wife leaving, because I remember thinking, "Oh God, like, I can't tell him I know his wife's left."'

'And then he told me to "keep my mouth shut" in a really aggressive way. I can remember just standing there, looking at him. I didn't even know what I was supposed to keep my mouth shut about . . .

'He never spoke to me again. I never went near him again. And then the next thing I knew, he just wasn't at school anymore and neither was Bushy. I have always said that somebody needed to contact her because she seemed to know whatever was going on and he was really concerned about what she had said to me. Without a doubt in my mind, she knew. His huge concern with what she told me would also indicate that she had to have known something. So where is Bushy?'

In January, before former students started contacting me, I had done a lengthy interview with the former deputy principal, Hylton Mace. The distinguished 90-year-old, a longtime member of the Manly Lawn Tennis Club and a keen badminton player, appeared as fit as a fiddle. His mind was still quick.

Hylton's wife, Phyllis, made us welcome in their home near Manly. In a sunny upstairs room, he freely admitted that he had been suspicious in early 1982, when Lyn vanished, that Chris 'could have been involved in her disappearance'.

He told me he had tried to rein in the obvious connection between Chris and his student. Chris rebuffed the older man, his boss, telling him, 'You've got a dirty mind.'

'I don't think it was too long before I started to feel that there was something amiss in her disappearance,' Hylton told me. 'And that wasn't just my feeling, it was a feeling of quite a few members of staff.'

I was incredulous at his matter-of-fact disclosure but did not want to alarm him with an overly pointed or accusatory question. 'And do you think that any of the teachers who were suspicious early in the piece would have gone to the police after Lyn disappeared and say, "Look, this doesn't add up, we don't think she would have left her daughters, there could be foul play here?"'

Hylton kept digging his own hole. 'I didn't feel it was the duty of any teacher to make an investigation or any statement in regard to what was going on,' he said. 'I thought, "Well, that's the police's job." And I feel strongly that now. And I was told the police were very, very slack in following up Lyn's disappearance. There was protection for Chris Dawson and his brother. Because his brother did have a bad reputation.'

Hylton revealed that other teachers at the time had told him they were fearful about speaking out.

'One of them in particular said that he would never say a word against the Dawson boys because, his words were, that he might end up under a slab of concrete,' Hylton said.

Hylton's bottom line was that without 'absolutely irrefutable evidence', it would have been dangerous to raise suspicions with police in 1982.

Hylton's failure to have Chris properly investigated over his grooming of Jenny and the powerful rumours of their sexual relationship – a criminal offence due to her being his student in 1980 – and the deputy head's subsequent failure to report his suspicions about Lyn falling victim to foul play were hard for Rebecca Hazel and me to fathom.

Hylton had become a good friend of Pat Jenkins, Lyn's sister. She had kindly asked him to talk to me and he duly agreed. His candour was appreciated, but his justifications for inaction when he was in a leadership position shocked and angered many listeners.

In my initial investigation, fully focused on Lyn's disappearance, I had failed to talk to students of Cromer High. I had not been thorough when it came to the school microcosm, which meant there was a big gap in the story. When the gap became too big to ignore, I worried about what else I could have missed. But with his distinctive voice and controversial remarks in just the second episode, Hylton unintentionally triggered former Cromer students to speak to me and to police. He was publicly criticised over what he said in the podcast and his self-confessed inaction. The responses must have distressed him.

Pat was grateful to Hylton and saddened when he died in April 2019.

'He was a very fine man and much troubled over his dealings with Monster Dawson, and what had happened to Lyn, and was always interested to hear any news,' Pat wrote to me. It was undoubtedly true but I wondered what might have happened if Hylton had blown the whistle on his concerns about teacher–student sex in the second half of 1980, or on his concerns about a probable murder in January 1982.

The podcast narrative's arc, and Slade's willingness to swap his expertly produced sections of our few completed episodes with fresh interviews from credible former students like Robyn, Phil and Michelle, ensured the story kept rolling and growing. The students became amateur sleuths, tracking down other potential informants and putting out the word that I wanted to talk to Bushy.

Lynda McCarthy, a former Cromer High student, said she had run into Miss Bush after moving to the New South Wales north coast. She had spoken to her both before and after the first inquest in 2001, and recalled the former PE teacher disclosing that police had never tried to talk to her.

Bushy told Lynda that she remembered Lyn coming to Cromer High one day and asking her, 'What's going on with my husband and these 16-year-old girls?'

In early March 2001, soon after Bushy recounted this conversation to Lynda, there were headlines in *The Daily Telegraph* about Chris being a suspect in Lyn's probable murder. It was the same burst of inquest-related publicity that had caught my attention.

Lynda told me that, after reading the story, she had called Bushy to tell her the fresh news from the inquest. She urged Miss Bush to go to police.

'And she said, "No. No, I won't,"' Lynda recalled. 'She didn't seem like she wanted to do any of that. She said, "They never asked me years ago."'

Looking back, Lynda believed that Bushy was probably intimidated or scared in 1982 and, years later, felt guilty about not having alerted police to her concerns. Her brother, Peter Bush, a prominent businessman, described her to me as 'a very naive young lady. She wasn't at all worldly'.

'She would have been quite horrified that that sort of thing was going on,' Peter added. 'I would find it very difficult to think that she could confront somebody like Dawson.'

Peter told me that Lesley had died some 15 years earlier after battling meningitis.

Lynda went rummaging through old paperwork, photos and memorabilia from her childhood for me. She had never been able to shake an uneasy memory: a dinner with Mr Dawson when she was 15.

'Remember how I said I had to sit next to him for the Year 10 formal dinner?' Lynda reminded me.

She had kept a Cromer High report with the autographs of her friends. It was dated 1979, soon after the dinner. His message was

Chris Dawson and Lynette Simms at a Greater Public Schools (GPS) Regatta when they were prefects at Sydney Boys High and Sydney Girls High in 1965.

Lyn Simms and Chris Dawson at a high school formal party, last year of high school.

Lyn on her wedding day, 1970.

Chris and Lyn leaving the wedding. Their friend Phil Day is in the background.

Chris Dawson (left) and Paul Dawson (right).

Chris Dawson (left) and Paul Dawson (right).

Chris Dawson (left) and Paul Dawson (right).

Chris Dawson (left) and Paul Dawson (right).

Lyn with her firstborn daughter, Shanelle, in early 1978 at the front of the house in Gilwinga Drive, Bayview.

Paul and his wife Marilyn (left) at lunch with Chris and Lyn in 1975 at their home in Cromer prior to building at Bayview.

Northbridge Baths where Chris worked as a part-time lifeguard on weekends.

© HEDLEY THOMAS

Classified advertisement placed by Chris in March 1982.

No.3318
00193708
LYN I love you, we all miss you Please ring. We want you home, Chris
00194343
MEG nearly 19 yrs. 5'1"

© GEMMA JONES

Driveway to the house at Gilwinga Drive.

© HEDLEY THOMAS

Chris and his newborn daughter with Jenny, Shanelle, and Lyn's other daughter, Amy.

Jenny with Lyn's two daughters, Amy and Shanelle (right).

RECEIVED
-5 FEB 1985
OFFICE OF THE
OMBUDSMAN

The Ombudsman's Office,
175 Pitt Street,
Sydney. 2000.

RE: MISSING PERSON—LYNETTE J. DAWSON

Dear Sir,
It is 3 years since my friend
Lyn Dawson of Bayview Heights was reported as
a missing person by her husband, Chris Dawson.
Lyn was a devoted mother of 2 small
children. I worked with her at Warriewood
Childrens Center. It was known by all her
workmates that she was having marital problems,
we had all heard about Chris' affair with a
(then) 16 year old student of his; who was
staying at the time with the Dawson family.
Lyn — although she probably suspected — didn't
want to believe this of her husband — whom
she idolized.
She accepted her marriage was "shaky" and
on the Friday before she was last seen, she

First page of a complaint letter by Lyn's
friend Sue in 1985 to the New South
Wales Ombudsman over the inaction
of police.

Sue Strath with Hedley Thomas
and Sue's daughter, Lulu.

From left: Barbara Cruise, Annette Leary, Sue Strath and Anna Grantham, all of whom worked with Lyn at the childcare centre.

Julie Andrew, Lyn's friend and neighbour at Gilwinga Drive from 1979 until 1982.

From left: Shaun Walsh, Bev McNally, Hedley Thomas, Abby Jeffery, her husband Phil Webster, and Shaun's wife Michelle Walsh. Bev, Phil and Michelle spoke out about their old school, Cromer High.

Ruth Mathewson, Shanelle Dawson and Hedley Thomas at Long Reef in September 2018 during a 'Walk for Lyn' to honour her.

Pat Jenkins with Shanelle Dawson in Hervey Bay in January 2018.

2GB broadcaster Ben Fordham.

Lynette Dawson

Aged 33 years old - Missing since 9th January 1982
from Bayview, Sydney NSW

Dearest Lynette,

For many, you are a mystery, a riddle unsolved for 35 years, a curiosity. For many, you are another missing person.

But to those you loved and those who loved you, to us you were (and are) so much more.

You were a mother, a daughter, a sister and an aunt. You were a colleague, a friend, a confidant.

You were a nurse, a carer for kids. You called Bayview home, after many years growing up by the beach at Clovelly. You were blonde-haired, blue-eyed, olive-skinned. You were 167cm tall, although you would have called it 5 foot 7

You were gentle, caring and kind. You were trusting. You were betrayed.

So much has happened without you. So many family events, both happy and sad. Birthdays, anniversaries, first days at school, seeing your daughters grow up. Who knows what celebrations never happened because you were gone.

You've got grandkids now, although you barely got started raising your own girls. But it was you who planted the seed, and they've grown into fine, strong women.

You've lost your own mum and dad Lyn, years after they lost you. I guess you are all together again now.

You should be 69, yet you are forever 33.

You have been so many things, and meant so much, to so many people. And you have been missed. You have been so missed. Your family has never stopped loving, caring, missing you. We never will.

We love you Lynette.

A one-page tribute to Lyn by her nephew, David Jenkins, in 2018.

Hedley Thomas with Northern Beaches author, lawyer and ocean swimmer, Rebecca Hazel.

From left: Greg Simms, his wife Merilyn, Hedley Thomas and Pat Jenkins at The Mint in Sydney in July 2018.

From left: Former Cromer High vice-captain Robyn Wheeler with Bev McNally, Greg Simms and Pat Jenkins, and a photograph of Lyn.

An aerial photograph of police diggings at the house at Gilwinga Drive in September 2018.

Chris Dawson, newly arrested for murder, getting into an unmarked police car at Sydney Airport after his extradition from Queensland in December 2018.

New South Wales Commissioner of Police Mick Fuller at a media conference in December 2018 announcing the arrest of Chris Dawson.

Slade Gibson, audio engineer and co-creator of *The Teacher's Pet* podcast, in his studio with Hedley Thomas after Chris Dawson's arrest.

Crown prosecutor Craig Everson SC on his way to the Supreme Court.

Criminal lawyer Pauline David who represented Chris Dawson at his 2022 murder trial and in his 1991 interview with homicide detectives.

From left: Rachel Young with her husband, former detective Damian Loone, Hedley Thomas, Merilyn Simms, lawyer John-Paul Cashen, Craig Simms and his father Greg Simms, arriving at court for the verdict of Justice Ian Harrison SC in August 2022.

Chris Dawson outside the New South Wales Supreme Court.

Homicide Squad Detective Senior Constable Daniel Poole, who led the reinvestigation of the murder from 2015.

TEACHER'S PET TRIAL: HUSBAND FOUND GUILTY

YOU DID MURDER LYN

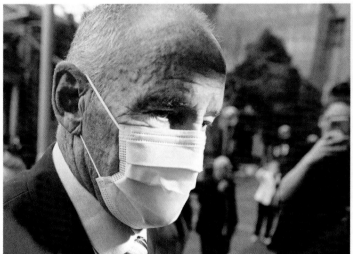

Former teacher and footballer Chris Dawson arrives at the NSW Supreme Court in Sydney on Tuesday to hear judge Ian Harrison declare him guilty of murdering his wife Lynette

Happy beginnings: Chris Dawson with his future wife Lynette Joy Simms in Sydney in the 1970s

At last, justice for gentle wife, mum

HEDLEY THOMAS
CREATOR, THE TEACHER'S PET

Lyn Dawson loved wearing pink. Her brother Greg Simms and sister Pat Jenkins treasure this vivid memory of her colour preference.

Even her scheming husband Chris knew at least this much about the personal choice of a wife he treated with contempt.

He claimed Lyn had pink shorts on 40 years ago when, he insists, she left him during a shopping outing - and stayed away. Lyn's love of pink was honoured by her loved ones in the Supreme Court in Sydney on Judgment Day, Tuesday, August 30, 2022.

Her family and friends - and even someone who had never met her yet remain deeply moved by her tragic story - came together in tribute.

Pink was Lyn's colour, but for fate, in early January 1982, jet black and white. Murdered in cold blood - that's the people's verdict.

And in his detailed judgment, Ian Harrison, the trial judge in Chris Dawson's murder trial, agreed.

Yet Lynette Joy Dawson's life, her marriage and her 40-year case are much more than anything Justice Harrison can summarise. They are now a touchstone for women who recognise domestic violence, grooming, coercive control and blame-shifting. It has been echoed around the world. Millions of people identify with something about Lyn. They acknowledge her experiences. Some of these people thank Lyn, a woman they never met, for helping them see a way out of their own destructive relationships.

Without reference to the judgment, here are some of the facts and circumstances that, finally, propelled the Office of the Director of Public Prosecutions in Sydney in December 2018 to change course, back police in a murder charge and take Dawson to trial.

Four years later, and four decades after her disappearance, here we are.

The extraordinary love shown by Lyn for her two children made the idea she would leave an absurdity to those who knew her.

Her bond with those little girls was stronger because of her desperation for several years when she was unable to conceive.

Surgery ended her heartbreak at being childless through much of her 20s.

The births of Shanelle and then her sister two years later changed Lyn's life. She wouldn't have left her children. And though it is not often said, she wouldn't have left Chris or ended their marriage, either, in my view.

Her constant forgiveness in the face of frequent humiliation must have contributed to her demise. If their marriage was going to fall apart formally, he'd have to be the one to take that decisive action.

Lyn just kept absorbing the pain. She wanted her little family to stay together, in spite of everything. The idea she would voluntarily take herself away - an action completely out of character - is extraordinary to all who remember her.

It becomes more extraordinary with such inconceivable layer: starting a new life with no job or money or car or capital assets, leaving no trace, not one

Continued on Page 4

Teen babysitter vindicated

MATTHEW CONDON

One of the Dawson trial's most maligned witnesses – JC – was on Tuesday vindicated in the conviction of the man who murdered her.

A former physical education teacher and rugby league player with the Newtown Jets, Dawson now faces spending the rest of his life in prison.

she had been mercilessly cross-examined by defence barrister Pauline David.

JC, who married Dawson after wife Lyn's disappearance in 1982 and had a child with him, was repeatedly accused at trial of being a liar, and of wishing to destroy Dawson because she was bitter about their marriage break-up.

Justice Harrison accepted her evidence on almost all counts.

FULL REPORT P3

Closure, custody and cuffs for Chris Dawson

DAVID MURRAY
NATIONAL CRIME CORRESPONDENT

Chris Dawson murdered his wife Lynette, disposed of her body and then lied for decades to conceal the crime, a judge has declared in a stunning vindication of her family's decade-long fight for justice.

Dawson was on Tuesday convicted of Lyn's murder by NSW Supreme Court judge Ian Harrison SC, who found the former teacher killed his wife because he feared losing a teenage girl he was "utterly obsessed" with.

"Lynette Dawson is dead. She died on or about 8 January 1982 and she did not voluntarily abandon her home," Justice Harrison said.

The judge was fortified in his decision by Dawson's lies, which he said were evidence of a consciousness of guilt. "Christopher Michael Dawson, on the charge that on or about 8 January, 1982, at Bayview or elsewhere in the state of NSW, you did murder Lynette Dawson. I find you guilty," he said.

That advanced him very significantly," Justice Harrison said, especially around the start of January 1982, when JC left to go to South West Rocks with friends.

She had by then communicated her desire to end her

CLAIRE HARVEY

After 40 years of lies, 10 weeks of trial, seven weeks of deliberation and four hours and 41 minutes of judge Ian Harrison reading out his reasons, finally the polite silence of Christopher Michael Dawson's life came to an end: not with a bang, but with the jingling of handcuffs.

The old man, straight-backed, masked, heard the judge say "I find you guilty", and turned to see two black-uniformed Corrective Services officers striding towards him

relationship with Dawson. It was clear Dawson did not want that to occur.

JC was "suddenly out of his physical reach and out of his control", the judge said. "I am satisfied that distressed, frustrated and ultimately overwhelmed and tortured by her absence up north, Mr Dawson resolved to kill his wife," he said.

Dawson shook his head and stood after the verdict, before being immediately handcuffed and led out of the court by armed security staff to gaps from the public gallery.

Lyn's tearful family embraced

through Court 13A. These friendly young men had until then been standing by the door, shepherding people in and out, glaring at the owners of buzzing mobile phones, relaxed, jovial.

And then suddenly they were standing by Dawson's sides, taking his hands and – still in silence – cuffing him, leading him in front of the bar table, taking him over to the far side of the court, to the glass-fronted dock and through the padded door, down to the cells deep below Macquarie Street, to the back of a prison van, and then to jail.

"Mr Dawson, it will be

after Justice Harrison left the room. Her brother Greg Simms hugged journalist Hedley Thomas, whose 2018 podcast The Teacher's Pet for The Australian ignited global interest in the unsolved case.

Outside court, the family, called for Dawson to reveal the location of Lyn's remains, and revealed that before the podcast they had doubted he would ever be charged.

Dawson's 10-week trial was held without a jury at his request to ensure proceedings could not be tainted by publicity, and to minimise the potential effect of

necessary for you to be taken into custody," Justice Harrison was saying, entirely impassively.

And he was gone.

Throughout the trial, Dawson had been afforded courtesies not usually allowed an accused murderer.

He didn't have to sit in the dock where ordinary accused people have to sit, instead sitting behind his legal counsel on the left-hand side of the court.

He wasn't held on remand like most others charged with murder.

He waited for this day at his

Covid delays. The prosecution presented a wholly circumstantial but powerful case, arguing Lyn would not have left her two young daughters, and were able to overcome the hurdle of her remains never being found. Lyn doted on the two little girls, aged four and two when she was murdered by their father.

Dawson's lawyer Greg Walsh said his client would appeal against his conviction and apply for bail.

"He's not well and he's been suffering from cognitive problems," Mr Walsh said. "He's obviously shocked, he's upset, he

lovely home in Mount Cootam, instead of in Silverwater or Long Bay, like any other accused.

He was allowed the company in court of his brother Peter, a solicitor, each day as the evidence proceeded.

It seemed to fit, for the man who had avoided any consequences for so many decades for the inexplicable disappearance of his lovely wife, the mother of his little daughters.

Chris Dawson gets special treatment. Chris Dawson is not an ordinary criminal.

Continued on Page 2

wanted me to ring his wife Sue." Dawson's twin brother Paul and older brother Peter were involved in scuffles with the media outside the Sydney court before and after the verdict.

Peter was sitting next to Chris as Justice Harrison read out a summary of his judgment, placing an arm over his brother's shoulder when it became clear the judge was about to declare him guilty of Lyn's murder.

The judge said he was satisfied Dawson lied when he claimed Lyn had phoned him after her disappearance, and dismissed "all alleged sightings of her.

Lyn was hopeful until the day of her disappearance that her marriage could be saved, the judge found. She "was not burdened by physical or mental health conditions" that would have compelled her to abandon her home and family. She packed no bags and no clothes, and even her contact lenses case was found when her belongings were returned to her family.

Continued on Page 5

INSIDE
» Bid for bail P3
» Day of legal drama P4
» What Dawson faces P4
» Timeline of a murder case P6
» Editorial P12

PODCAST
THE FRONT
Hedley Thomas
on the verdict

Front page of *The Australian* declaring the guilty verdict of Chris Dawson 40 years after Lyn's disappearance.

From left: Hedley Thomas, Craig Simms, Greg Simms, Damian Loone, Merilyn Simms and daughter Renee Simms.

Ruth Mathewson with Hedley Thomas and Damian Loone after the verdict.

Hedley Thomas with colleagues Mathew Condon, David Murray and Claire Harvey in the recording studio for a post-verdict episode of *The Teacher's Trial*.

penned in red ink, in his distinctive hand: 'Lynda, dinner was lovely. We should do it again some time. Love, Chris Dawson. X.'

The intimacy of this thinly veiled invitation from a teacher to a schoolgirl half his age made her cringe half a lifetime later. Lynda had been singled out a year before Jenny's grooming began.

'What a creep. I was only 15. Luckily, I wasn't interested in Chris Dawson at all or I might have been dumb enough to follow up on that offer,' Lynda told me.

The weekly episodes revolving around Cromer High were difficult for a number of the former students to hear. For decades, they had tried to forget memories of the conduct of the teachers and Lyn's disappearance. It was better to reflect on the good times.

'In our year at school, there was Jenny and Chris and all that infamous stuff – but we also had lots of famous people, like Evert Ploeg, who won an Archibald Prize for his art,' Lynda told me. 'And Jayson Brunsdon, who is a famous fashion designer with his own label. And Lisa Forrest, who won gold in the Commonwealth Games in swimming.'

Robyn, Lynda and their growing group of informants were alerted by Peter McEntyre to the experiences of another former student, Bev McNally, and they soon put her in touch with me. Our first recorded interview spanned an hour and 40 minutes on the telephone, as Bev told me of her time as the Dawson family's babysitter, when Chris had repeatedly quizzed her about a strikingly attractive schoolgirl he had seen in the playground, Jenny. Bev, who had been secretary of the student council for three years, was not a fan of the younger girl.

By the time she knew Chris, Bev was a vulnerable teenager who had already endured a lot of trauma. She described him taking her 'under his wing'. Lyn knew that Bev was trying to get into nursing, and they talked about the caring profession a lot.

Seven minutes into the conversation with me, Bev volunteered, 'I adored him. I felt he was a wonderful person. So I defended him for a long, long time. But I knew that Lyn was very unhappy. She confided in me a few times. I actually saw him hit her, once with a tea towel and once a shove, on two separate occasions.'

Bev told me that 'if there was anything out of place, it would throw him – from his wardrobe to the girls' room – everything had to be perfect, especially his clothes'. She described an obsessiveness with his wardrobe, with everything colour-matched and neatly lined up. It was the same at Paul's house. The twin brothers needed to be perfectly colour-coordinated. Paul wore what Chris wore at the same time 'and if something would get mismatched, he would get angry'.

'It was weird that they couldn't even leave their house without figuring what the other person was wearing. It was almost like they didn't even have to speak, they'd just think it and they knew what the other one was thinking. It was little nods and stuff.'

I was more interested in the two incidents of apparent violence against Lyn which, according to Bev, she had witnessed. In all of the police brief of evidence, there was no direct evidence of violence from someone who could say, 'I saw him hit her.' Bev would be a valuable witness if the two incidents stacked up.

'So the tea towel incident – what do you mean? Like, he flicked it at her, or he whipped her with it? What?' I asked.

'Yeah, he whipped her with it,' she answered. 'In the kitchen. But then they tried to cover it up because they didn't realise I was walking in. He walked out the other side and she tried to pretend she wasn't crying. It hurt her, plus he upset her. She had her back to him, putting a glass in the cupboard. It was just the fact he was so vicious towards her over a dirty glass.'

The shove, she told me, was in one of the girls' rooms. Bev was looking down the hall when she saw Chris roughly push Lyn into a doorframe when they were 'having words'.

'They didn't want me to see it. He stormed off again into his bedroom and neither of them would talk about it.'

Bev's descriptions of Lyn were poignant. 'I remember her being sad but I can't remember her being angry. It was almost like she was defeated. She adored those kids and when she was with them, she was happy. It was like she shrunk an inch when he walked in the room.'

She recounted Chris being obsessed with sex. He talked about it often.

'I can tell you that one of the first dates he and Lynette went on was to the zoo and all the animals were having sex including the turtles because he used to tell that story all the time. He used to say he was surrounded by sex. I believe he was grooming me. I took the moral high ground so he backed off and looked elsewhere. I stopped babysitting and that was when Jenny took over.'

Lesley Bush was concerned for Bev and started 'steering me away from him', particularly after Chris had offered her the spare room at his house because of the troubles in her family home. For a short but uncomfortable time, senior staff, including Hylton Mace, believed that Chris was having sex with Bev, who strenuously denied it.

Bushy, Bev added, tried to protect her. 'When I was in the office with Chris and she walked in, she started screaming and said, "We've been told the door isn't to be closed!" She got angry when she thought that her girls were in danger, and I was one of her girls.'

As she remembered the early 1980s and talked of the little girls she had babysat, their adoring mother, the bizarre twin brothers, the culture of teachers bedding schoolgirls and her own destructive childhood, Bev began to cry. She was deep in the pain of that time; of its consequences.

'I feel stupid that I didn't say anything or do anything to help prevent it,' she said. 'I feel guilty that I didn't step in, that I didn't defend her, that I didn't stop Jenny from going. There's a lot of guilt there. People would close a door and go, "Right, whatever happens behind that door is no one's business."'

By speaking up now, in the podcast, Bev told me, someone who knew other pieces of the story might come forward and help the case.

'I've got no proof of anything,' she said. 'I just know that if anyone did anything to Lyn, it was him.'

Chapter 31

The Mint

It was hard to know whether detectives in the Homicide Squad and lawyers in the Office of the Director of Public Prosecutions were completely ambivalent or cursing as successive podcast episodes aired fresh interviews with former police and inquest witnesses, prompting new ones to come forward. I initially expected indifference; then, as more details and evidence emerged, anger from police – potentially up to commissioner level – at the intrusion on their murder investigation. But how would they deal with it?

The revelations in the episodes of historical failures of police in Lyn's case meant there was already a public trust deficit. If the cops came out swinging hard against a new podcast investigation that had the full backing of Lyn's family, her friends and the former students of Cromer High, the police would surely struggle to win public sympathy.

The quietly effective but naturally guarded Detective Senior Constable Dan Poole, who was leading the cold-case review, had not built close relationships with key people.

'It's a job and he's probably doing it well,' Pat Jenkins said to me at the time, 'but I don't think he's emotionally in there like Damian was.'

Dan had done things by the book and deliberately not shared information about his leads or breakthroughs with Lyn's family. They knew very little of what he had done since 2015. Accordingly, they doubted that the brief had changed much since Damian Loone handed it over. When the discovery of Chris's 1982 antecedent report with his lies to police came out in the podcast, Lyn's loved ones were shocked.

Greg Simms got another surprise when he tried to telephone Dan Poole to talk about it. The detective had been transferred to another part of the Homicide Squad but nobody had told the family.

'We were informed of this after calling the Unsolved Homicide Branch when we were wanting to speak to you,' Greg wrote in a text message to Dan.

Greg and Merilyn were not happy. They feared that once again, Lyn's loved ones were being relegated. Kept in the dark. They were learning much more about Lyn's case from the podcast.

'We have just listened to Episode 5 of *The Teacher's Pet* podcast,' Greg texted the detective. 'Are you aware of a handwritten statement made by Chris Dawson in August 1982? If so, do you have a copy? We have no prior knowledge of this statement being in existence. Have you been listening to the podcast or made contact with Hedley Thomas?'

Dan replied: 'Yes we have the note. I spoke about it with you the last time we all met at Pat's house. I've been following the podcast with interest. No haven't contacted Hedley.'

Greg was perplexed. Merilyn said they would have remembered or made a note of something so significant.

'We have no recollection of you mentioning the note or statement or any of the details in it,' Greg wrote. 'Has this been included in the brief?'

Dan allayed their biggest concern. 'Yes it's in the brief. I would have mentioned it when going through some of the additional enquiries we had made but it may not have been clear what I was referring to.'

It raised tensions in Lyn's family but on the positive side, it was new evidence in the police brief and it was in front of the DPP. Perhaps it would tip the case over in favour of prosecution.

Damian Loone could scarcely believe it when he heard about the antecedent report while driving. 'I've never seen that handwritten document from Dawson. Just letting you know,' he texted me.

He told me that if this damning evidence had been uncovered by him when he had control of the case, he would have immediately charged Chris with murder.

It was inconceivable that Dan Poole would disclose anything about his investigation to me. But, as our episodes broke listenership records and more people contacted me and *The Australian* with information or requests to talk confidentially, I toyed with the idea of turning over some of their intel to police. It would reduce the risk that a lead of vital importance would fall between the cracks.

Ruth was worried about the toll on us. I was sleeping when exhaustion overcame me around midnight, then rising again, my head buzzing with details, about 4.30 am. Dinners went cold on the table as I mulled over aspects of the case or interviewed new leads, pacing the house and backyard with my overheated iPhone constantly against my ear.

David Murray maintained a cracking pace, writing thousands of words a week for the newspaper, re-interviewing people who had spoken to the podcast and others who were coming forward, and organising photographs. His partner Catriona Mathewson, Ruth's sister, generously put off her own work to help me with mine.

Slade was simply heroic.

We were stretched thin and could not do much more. When fatigue was acute and tempers frayed, our loyal friend and editor, John Lehmann, came to the rescue with an urgent approval of funds to have many hours of relatively fresh audio transcribed by someone whom I knew and trusted, bean counters be damned.

Sandra and Joe Cimino, who bought 6 Gilwinga Drive, the original home of Paul and Marilyn Dawson, came forward. Sandra recalled the Cimino family's dog one day returning from the bush with a strange-looking bone.

'The second time he brought me back this bone, I thought I should take it down to Mona Vale police station, so I wandered in there,' Sandra told me. 'I told them where I lived and said, "That lady is missing, so could you identify this?" Because you think that maybe she's there.' Sandra eventually heard from an officer, who said, 'I'm just ringing to tell you it was a lamb bone, it's not a human bone.'

Before he worked for the Cimino family concreting business, Joe was a former student of Paul Dawson. He recalled that during the many weeks of concreting and paving work he did in the late 1980s for the new owners of 2 Gilwinga Drive, Sue and Neville Johnston, they noted anomalies in the soil. It did not look or feel normal to Joe. At that time, the police were still treating Lyn as a missing person, not a possible victim of homicide, so Joe had no reason to connect the ground anomalies to the disappearance of Lyn.

He pulled his work diaries from 1988 and sent copies to me. Every job he did with the family business was described and dated. 'We did the garage floor, we did behind the house, a retaining wall and we did some pathways,' Joe told me.

Joe recalled digging out the earth down to about a metre beside the swimming pool wall. 'I remember pulling out quite a few children's toys. And it was really soft. It wasn't compacted virgin ground. Which either tells you it's been disturbed or there's been some bad soft filling thrown in there. And I can remember this clear as today that the shovel was just going into the dirt like I was cutting a cheesecake.'

I learned from Joe that when a pool is being constructed, the ground is usually over-excavated and once the concrete shell is finished, there would be a 'void' of up to two metres from the pool's edge. The void would then be backfilled, which meant soft soil.

'So it is an easy area to dig up and refill, if you understand what I mean,' Joe said.

Joe's theory about Lyn having been possibly buried in this void made macabre sense. The official police video from 2000 showed Detective Damian Loone and forensics officers digging in one area around the pool and unearthing what they described as a woman's cardigan with multiple cuts. In the video, they hold the garment up.

Joe's theory had more force after Bob Gibbs, one of the crime scene investigation officers from the 2000 dig, got in touch. He told me they had searched only a 'small area' as the budget was tight.

'And those marks on the cardigan, the stabbing, the holes in the cardigan, are very consistent with knife marks in a domestic sort of stabbing situation,' he told me.

'I wanted to go further and I think Damo [Detective Loone] did too, of course but they didn't want us to dig up a whole pool area, basically. I'm sure Damo was pulling his hair out, he probably couldn't say too much about that. I reckon she's still there.'

The retired cop's matter-of-fact acknowledgment that the 2000 search had been completely inadequate, despite it finding what appeared to have been a garment from a possible knife attack, fitted with what Joe Cimino had told me.

I had been contacted around this time by Matt Fordham, the former police prosecutor who had made a convincing case for the 2001 and 2003 inquests. Inquest transcripts depict Matt expertly questioning witnesses and drawing out Jenny's devastating testimony. Near the end of her evidence, Peter Dawson, acting as solicitor for his younger twin brothers, put to Jenny that as she 'had never in ten years mentioned this alleged conversation with Chris about a hitman', she was not telling the truth.

Her retort was menacing. 'There are many things I haven't mentioned even to this day.'

I asked Matt what Jenny might have been suggesting there. He had no idea. Neither Matt nor Peter Dawson asked follow-up questions during the inquest proceedings. Matt told me that Jenny's truthfulness was obvious to him, adding that he had no doubt she would have been an exceptionally strong Crown witness if the DPP at the time, Nicholas Cowdery, had not rejected the recommendations of two coroners that Chris be prosecuted.

Matt had a chilling theory about Lyn's remains. He believed she had been buried near the pool immediately after she was killed and, sometime later, Chris had dug up the body and moved it to a new location well away from the property. It would explain the cardigan; in his haste and probably in darkness, Chris had overlooked it. Matt's offer of background help with the podcast investigation was generous and gave me confidence we were on the right track.

Another former police officer spoke knowledgeably about the local garbage depot, the base for the trucks on which Chris and Paul had part-time jobs in the early 1980s. He said it would have been easy for an insider to visit the depot on a Saturday in January 1982, when few if any people were around. There was scant security and no CCTV. A body could easily be concealed in a sheet or rolled-up carpet and sent west in a garbage truck to one of the major landfill sites.

Some locals suspected an alleged contract killer, who had reputedly used his half-cabin cruiser to dump bodies encased in concrete kilometres offshore in the Pacific Ocean. Although far too speculative to publish in the absence of evidence, his name kept coming up. His reputation for violence, and a clean despatch of the remains of the dead, was chilling. I opted to leave that line of enquiry to police.

Leigh Maloney introduced herself and became a big help as a go-between to a rich store of information from a former Olympian, Shelley Oates-Wilding. As a young mother on the Northern Beaches in the early 1980s, Leigh went to aerobics exercise classes run by Chris and Paul and she witnessed their grooming and obvious close contact with schoolgirls.

One of those girls, Shelley, had remained in touch with Leigh over the decades and, after gentle lobbying by the older woman, she agreed to speak to me. I had previously talked to Greg about Shelley because her name jumped out in her Forest High schoolfriend Alice's harrowing 1998 statement to police.

Detectives should have interviewed Shelley at the same time back in 1998. For two decades they had overlooked a key witness who had spent a lot of private time with Paul, Chris and Jenny.

Shelley told me: 'I must admit there's been so many times I've asked, "why hasn't anybody asked me anything?"

'Chris obviously was madly in love with Jenny. When we would be together, Chris was always complaining about Lyn and he painted her out to be an absolute bitch. And then I do remember when it was like, "well, we don't need to worry about her anymore."'

As a student, Shelley said she was pursued by Paul, who initially groomed her as the family babysitter. She did what he asked of her. Chris and Jenny at this time were inseparable. The four of them went to the beach and on drives together. Shelley recalled conversations in which Chris and Paul spoke extremely disparagingly of Lyn.

From her home in Hawaii in 2018, Shelley told me that close to the time Lyn disappeared, Paul said to her that something 'terrible' had happened. He said he had to stop seeing Shelley.

Shelley and I talked about her Forest High friend, Alice, too. They got back in touch during the podcast. Alice was anxious.

I had written to Alice a few months before the first episode to explain what I intended to do. I offered a sensitively handled interview in which she would not be identified – unless she expressly wanted to be named. She politely declined and I let it go.

After remaining silent and unknown to police for 36 years, Shelley now wanted to try to help Alice and Jenny. Three teenagers from 1982 reconnecting in 2018, recalling the wrongs of the past, and possibly joining to seek justice.

When Sydney businesswoman Kay Sinclair got in touch to relate a conversation she had with the Dawson twins about Lyn in 2007, the file went straight to the bulging folder of audio for urgent use in an upcoming episode. Kay's husband had been friends with Chris and Paul at Sydney Boys High. At first, Kay was tentative as we talked about what she heard and saw when she met the twins at the 'living wake' of a close mutual friend, Phil Day, who was dying of cancer.

'People who are listening to the podcasts are actually finding their own voice, people who know things, having been silent for a long time,' I told Kay when we spoke. 'And they're hearing other people talk about this and then coming forward to me, because they do have a great sense that there's been a terrible injustice here, and it's wrong.'

Kay replied, 'Since that night, that's what I've felt. I've felt that guilt. I should have told someone, I should have rung the police. So I totally relate to people who are coming forward to you. And I now feel a lot better.'

Everyone liked Phil Day, a single man with firm religious beliefs. Not having been in touch with Phil for some time, Chris rang his wedding groomsman a few days before that fateful Saturday 9 January 1982 to let him know there had been marriage problems. He asked Phil to meet him, Lyn and their little girls at Northbridge Baths. Phil was close to Lyn, too, and they spoke on the telephone on the Friday afternoon when he called to confirm the impromptu catch-up. In his 2003 inquest evidence, Phil recalled Lyn sounding 'very calm and relaxed, she was warm and friendly'. Lyn told Phil they had just come back from marriage counselling. She expressed confidence about their relationship and future.

The next day at the baths, Phil and Lyn's mother Helena were chatting when they saw Chris returning from the public kiosk. He told them that Lyn had just phoned to say she would not be coming; she needed a few days away to think things over. Helena was very surprised. Chris asked Phil to take his girls and his mother-in-law from the baths to Helena's house at Clovelly, near Phil's place at Coogee. It conveniently gave Chris time to clean up at Bayview, and perhaps to dispose of Lyn's body. I had long suspected that Chris had used Phil as an unwitting dupe that day. They had been mates since 1961.

Recalling her 2007 conversation with Chris about their respective former marriages, Kay told me:

> 'I asked "When did you get divorced?" And he said, "She joined a commune in the Blue Mountains."
>
> 'I said, "Really? Did you have any children?"
>
> 'And he said, "Yeah we had two." I said, "What sort of mother would leave their kids?" And he said, "Yeah, well, we don't know. She's joined a commune in the Blue Mountains."
>
> 'It was one of those very unusual things. But I think I was more thrown by the fact that Paul left the people he was with and sat down next to Chris. You know how your instinct kicks in? There was just something creepy about it. Paul was the one who wanted to make sure Chris didn't say anything that was going to come back.'

Paul's sudden intervention spoke volumes to Kay, who immediately suspected deception and deflection. For me, the more relevant feature was Chris having changed his story about where Lyn went. Previously, he had told people that Lyn went north to the Central Coast, possibly with a cult.

By this stage of the podcast investigation, I found it difficult to give Chris the benefit of the doubt about much at all. In my mind, Kay Sinclair's direct questions exposed a killer who could not accurately remember his own past lies.

New information from Kay and others needed to be worked into the episodes. There was so much of it and getting it right took up a lot of time. It meant that the comfort of our buffer of completed episodes disappeared. Interviewing, writing and narrating many thousands of words of audio in the days and hours before deadline left Slade a tiny window for production, music and editing. This had never been part of the plan. It was a bit like releasing a bestselling audiobook to the market before half of it had even been drafted, let alone narrated and produced. I constantly feared being unable to keep up. If Slade or I fell over from illness or accident, we would be in huge strife.

When Ben Fordham, who wanted to ensure his 2GB Radio audience was kept up to speed with developments, asked me about my ties to and cooperation with New South Wales Police, I explained the reality: they had brushed me off months earlier and appeared determined to avoid contact with me.

Their reluctance must have been due in part to the Homicide Squad's head, Scott Cook, having sent a new police brief of evidence to the Office of the DPP in April, about five weeks before the podcast's first episode came out. The cops wanted to remain at arm's length but in the meantime, as I told Ben, many listeners were coming forward with solid information. These people were unaware that there might still be active police interest.

'You're getting closer and closer to nailing a murderer, you know,' Ben texted me after a handful of episodes had been aired. 'Bloody riveting stuff. I couldn't sleep at 2 am so I was up listening in.'

Without disclosing names, I confided to Ben that several sources clearly knew things that were new, highly credible and held such promise that police should investigate, urgently, and ahead of me. Shelley was one of those.

Some of these informants didn't trust the police or wouldn't go to the police unless pushed. I believed that a one-way channel of information would work. If the sources contacting me consented to it, I would hand their details to the cops. I would not ask the police for anything, not even to ask whether the information had been helpful.

In 2010, when New South Wales Police had announced a $100,000 reward for information about Lyn's suspected murder, the official police line stated: 'Hopefully we can harness the power of social media to assist police with this case'. The reward doubled to $200,000 in 2014 as another publicity campaign unfolded. Greg Simms used it to deliver a special message to Chris: 'You can only run and lie for so long.' But in mid-2018 when police had every opportunity to harness the power of a widely heard podcast about Lyn's case, those in charge tried to look the other way.

Ben had good relationships at the highest levels of New South Wales Police. He was trusted by Commissioner Mick Fuller and the force's media manager, Grant Williams.

'Leave it with me,' Ben said.

At the same time, Michelle Walsh, who had been in direct contact with Detective Poole, was not going to remain silent about what she perceived to be a lack of urgency from police.

'This is actually getting a ball rolling now, in a big way, and that hasn't happened before,' Michelle told me in one of our numerous evening phone calls. 'People are coming out and talking about their bad experiences at the school and what we grew up with and that it's not okay.'

Michelle was livid, too, about lethargy in the NSW Department of Education.

'There's so much that's damning and there's so many different angles and injustices that have gone on, but the Department of Education – why are they not being taken to task over this?' she asked crossly.

Back in 1990, after Jenny had fled Chris and returned to the Northern Beaches, she attended a catch-up for some of the ex-Cromer girls, then in their mid-20s. Michelle also went and recalled Jenny's disclosures and the determination of the newly estranged single mother to try to put things right.

'Her mission that night was that she was going to get Chris thrown in jail. She was furious with him, she hated him. It was serious. She was definitely accusing him of murdering Lyn. She wasn't saying, "I think he did." She was saying, "He did." And I said, "Well, aren't you scared?" And she was like, "Well, this is why I'm doing this. He won't be able to come near me. I'm going to pursue this and I'm protected by doing this."

'She told us how he'd basically started dating girls up there from school. She became Lyn. She was being pushed around by him. He had all these high school girls in the pool. And she was basically getting out before he killed her. She just hated him and wanted him to go to jail. And I'll never forget it.

'Why does Chris have so much power? It seems to be everywhere. It seems to be with the system, with the police, with the girls. Everyone in his life seems to be protecting him. What is it with him that he is able to do that?'

At the time of the 1990 catch-up, Michelle thought about Miss Bush's hysteria over Lyn's disappearance, and the menace in Chris's voice when he subsequently told Michelle to keep her mouth shut. She thought her experiences were insignificant compared with what Jenny was describing.

'Which is why I didn't really feel the need to go to the police then,' Michelle said.

Michelle was also angry with a schoolfriend who had been in Jenny's clique, and was becoming increasingly anxious as *The Teacher's Pet* episodes aired.

'She kept saying to me, "Just be careful" and "I can't get involved in this." And I'm like, "What am I being careful of?" And she just said, "Well, you know, there's like six teachers that can go to jail."'

Michelle told me she felt sick at having so easily accepted for years the idea that Lyn had been killed and buried near the house. Her friend had reminded her in a recent conversation.

'She said, "Remember we used to all talk about it? How she was buried under the tennis court?" She said, "I can't believe we used to just talk about it like it was just normal." She said, "That was some-one's mother."'

The Australian's marketing head, Alice Bradbury, had organised a public event at Sydney's The Mint, the city's oldest surviving building. It dated back to 1816 when it was built, originally, as a general hospital at a cost of 45,000 gallons of rum. Alice wanted the newspaper's subscribers to meet and ask questions of editor-in-chief Paul Whit-taker, crime reporter David Murray, Lyn's siblings Greg Simms and Pat Jenkins, Lyn's friend Julie Andrew and me.

Paul opened the event by recalling that I had proposed the story eight months earlier because of 'the lingering feeling that the police in New South Wales and the Office of the Director of Public Prosecu-tions had not gone as far as they could have and as they should have in this case' and that, if we re-examined everything, there would be 'new leads which might make a difference, perhaps even bring a killer to justice'.

'Then he had to convince people to trust him, starting with me agreeing to give him six months to work on one story,' Paul added.

'What has been truly unique about this investigative podcast series is that this is a story that is literally unfolding day-to-day as more and more people come out of the woodwork, sometimes within hours of the deadline for the next episode. The podcast has created its own momentum that is making it a constantly evolving story.'

Greg Simms told the audience, 'I hope the DPP are listening.'

He described how a senior lawyer in the Office of the DPP had told his sister Pat and their cousin, Wendy Jennings, that one of the reasons why there had not been a prosecution was because Lyn's mother 'saw her after she disappeared'.

There it was again. Michelle had recently heard Dan Poole make this claim to her. Years earlier, it had been asserted as if fact by a lawyer in the DPP to Lyn's sister and her cousin, according to Pat and Wendy, who made notes at the time. It could not have been a coinci-dence. But it could not have been more wrong.

That night, we all witnessed something I had not seen in journalism before: a large room filled with people, mostly unknown to each other, united in commitment and anger over the injustice of a very old and unsolved case.

Michelle Walsh shared with the public meeting her exchange with Detective Dan Poole. 'I asked him directly if Chris wasn't in jail because there wasn't a body. I got an answer that, yes, that was the case.

'He said, "You can prosecute without a body." I said, "Well, why not Chris?" And he said, "Because someone that knew her very well had sighted her." And that was said to me three weeks ago. And that's why they're not pursuing it.'

There were audible groans and sighs. Greg looked shocked. It seemed that the DPP or police – or both – were still relying on a hearsay report stemming from a long-deceased woman at a Central Coast fruit barn.

'And he actually told me to keep it confidential. Not that I am, as I don't think there's really anything confidential about this,' Michelle added to noisy cheering. 'And I was quite shocked that he told me to keep that confidential. But he certainly said that was the reason why Chris was not in jail.'

I would later learn that, while Detective Poole acknowledged having talked to Michelle about a so-called sighting of Lyn, he believed he had been misunderstood about its credibility. He assured Greg Simms that he was aware of the dubious standing of the sighting claims.

I had read Ray Butlin's evidence to the 2003 inquest when he was asked about his wife Sue's purported sighting of Lyn at a fruit barn near Gosford.

Ray told the inquest that if Sue 'had seen somebody that may have been of like appearance to Lyn – and she knew Lyn extremely well – then she may have wanted herself to see Lyn, it would put her in a situation where she would be at the centre of attention'. Sue 'didn't have a lot', Ray added, and 'Chris and Paul to Sue were more or less stars. She looked up to them quite a bit'.

Delicately, respectfully, Ray was suggesting to the courtroom in 2003 that Sue could exaggerate things. They got 'distorted' by her.

Inexplicably, her unverified sighting claim was given a lot of currency by police in the 1980s and 1990s, before Sue Butlin died, despite no police officer having questioned her about it.

I asked the Office of the DPP about it but they declined to comment. When I reached the solicitor named by Pat and Wendy for having stated that Lyn had been seen by her mother, she replied: 'If you or anyone else defames me I will take the appropriate proceedings.'

Mark and Faye Leveson, the parents of Matthew Leveson, a 20-year-old who had disappeared in September 2007, were quietly watching from their seats in The Mint. After a decade with no answers and no body, their son's remains were finally found in May 2017, following an immunity deal with Matthew's suspected killer. Mark Leveson, unprompted, asked for the microphone.

'We had about a dozen sightings of Matt during the course of our investigation,' Mark Leveson said.

The claims of the witnesses who told police they had seen Matthew, according to his father, 'were given some weight in the investigation'. It was only when the witnesses were tested under oath that their claims were exposed as rubbish.

Six episodes, each one documenting allegations of teachers preying on underage schoolgirls for sex, had been aired before *The Australian*'s subscriber event at The Mint. Yet not one investigator or bureaucrat from the NSW Department of Education had called or emailed me.

It was lamentable that, while the nation was responding to child sex abuse exposed by a national royal commission, the revelations about the sordid conduct of teachers on the Northern Beaches did not appear to ring alarm bells.

There was resounding disgust also about the inadequacy of the previously low-budget searches at Chris and Lyn's former Bayview property, over which Chris had claimed sole ownership after Lyn disappeared.

Magistrate Jeff Linden's disclosures, with the suspicions of Jenny and others, had prompted offers from wealthy listeners to help purchase the property to ensure every square centimetre could be searched. When I spoke to the new owner, Susan Saul, about the idea, she sounded shocked; everything to do with Lyn and the house's history was news to Susan and her family, and curious listeners had started parking outside.

The energy, ideas and exasperation on display at The Mint that night were powerful. It was a critical turning point. Ben Fordham stood up near the end and addressed everyone: 'You spoke about media muscle. I give you my word that I'll increase that as of tomorrow.'

Ben promoted a public petition calling for action and he turned up the pressure on air, telling 2GB's listeners:

'There's a lot of history here, including accusations that, back in the 1980s, local police were too close to Chris Dawson and too quick to believe his story. The past can't be changed. We need to focus on the here and now. Everyone who has the power to bring justice to the family of Lynette needs to get off their arses and start delivering. That means a high-energy approach from New South Wales Police, which should include sitting down with Hedley Thomas and analysing all of his new evidence, and police should consider digging for Lynette's body at the old family home at Bayview.

'It also means the Director of Public Prosecutions, Lloyd Babb, giving his personal attention to this matter and considering whether there's enough new evidence to bring a charge of murder against Chris Dawson.

'There's only ever been one suspect. And right now, he's a free man.'

As Pat was leaving The Mint, the people sitting next to her asked if they could have a quiet word.

'The man started by saying he knew of two hitmen in Manly police,' Pat told me. 'He said they would meet in a room at the back of the Ivanhoe Hotel in Manly.'

Pat did not sleep well that night.

Chapter 32

The Commissioner

In a private room above Verde, a longtime favourite restaurant of the Fordham family, we must have looked an unlikely quartet: the most powerful cop in the country, his senior adviser, a leading Sydney radio broadcaster and me, an investigative reporter from Brisbane with a true crime podcast, all putting aside differences at a meeting in Darlinghurst. We came together to talk about a woman who disappeared on the Northern Beaches in 1982.

Ben Fordham was sure the confidential lunch was the best chance for a breakthrough; that it would build trust and possibly result in a beneficial agreement so that all leads and evidence were followed. I went because of my regard for his judgment and, I hoped, anything was possible. If Lyn's disappearance was ever going to lead to a criminal charge, it would need to be in 2018, during this unprecedented media, public, police and prosecutorial focus on the case. The public clamour would not last indefinitely. Every story, even this one, eventually runs out of puff. Some other scandal would come along sooner or later and, I feared, Chris would once again walk away from it all.

Before we sat down to eat, Mick Fuller challenged me to tell him what I was trying to do with *The Teacher's Pet*. The officer in charge of Australia's largest police force with almost 20,000 police looked nonplussed. The podcast had been a searing indictment of a system which had failed to deliver justice. Public anger was spreading and growing. Listeners were appalled that nothing at all had been done about the exploitation of students by their teachers.

The evidence of police inaction or even corruption was also deeply troubling. The discovery in State Archives of Chris's 1982 lying statement to police sowed suspicion about why this had not come out before. Suggestions from Magistrate Jeff Linden, Joe Cimino, Jenny Carlson and others that Lyn's body might still be in the ground near the house at Bayview highlighted the inadequacy of the limited digging around the pool in 2000. Criticisms levelled by former Cromer High students Michelle Walsh and Bev McNally had cast the current investigation as flat-footed and unresponsive.

All of these things annoyed the Homicide Squad's Detective Superintendent Scott Cook and his detectives in Sydney. They didn't want to talk about what they had up their sleeve for the DPP. They didn't like being second-guessed by outsiders or questioned by a Brisbane journalist with a microphone. They weren't to blame for the failures of police from an era before Dan Poole was born. And their information was that a reef of subterranean rock meant the ground at Gilwinga Drive was almost impenetrable; too hard for a grave.

Within a few minutes of meeting Mick Fuller, I worried that my decision to leave Slade Gibson in the studio was a poor one. The police chief started sternly, delivering a thinly veiled warning that he and his officers could cut *The Australian*'s reporters and me out of the loop of all police briefings about this case and other crimes. Mick Fuller didn't use the words 'you should play by our rules or face the consequences' but that was how I interpreted his opening gambit. It was an aggressive play.

I told him it wouldn't change the way the podcast was going, apart from the fact I would also need to report that the police chief had decided to retaliate against the national daily newspaper. He was left in no doubt that any 'shoot the messenger' approach would not be well received by Lyn's family, friends and other media outlets.

These were a few awkward moments while Mick Fuller and I stood our ground. Tensions eased when we found things on which we agreed.

As Grant Williams chatted a few metres away with Ben Fordham, his friend from their time in TV current affairs, Fuller spoke about the findings of the two coroners who had recommended a prosecution of Chris Dawson for murder. I agreed, adding that we had only got to this point because of the persistence of a cop: Damian Loone.

I wasn't trying to smear police in the podcast, I told the police commissioner. However, the failures of the 1980s were inescapable and impossible to airbrush from the narrative. I said my objective went beyond the storytelling; I wanted to do whatever was journalistically possible to achieve a trial. It would then be up to a jury to determine if Chris was guilty.

Mick Fuller's instincts were to protect his detectives, protect the force's bruised reputation and produce the strongest brief of evidence to improve the chances of the DPP green-lighting a murder charge against the only suspect. He went to Verde on 13 July in part because of his respect for Ben and John Fordham, both of whom had warned him privately that the police strategy to date was likely to end badly for police with the public and the media. And, in turn, badly for the police and their prospects of getting a result in their investigation.

The commissioner knew, too, that even key members of Lyn's mild-mannered family had lost confidence and were for the first time publicly criticising police. A week before the Verde meeting, Lyn's cousin, Wendy Jennings, a longtime campaigner for justice for Lyn, wrote a scathing letter of complaint to Mick Fuller about what she called 'the appalling manner in which this murder investigation has been handled at various periods over the past 36 years'.

'There is no justice system when people who swear an oath to uphold the law choose not to carry out their duties in a manner required of them but decide to collude or possibly engage in corruption to protect a murderer,' Wendy wrote.

Wendy demanded to know 'why was there no investigation done' into the evidence of Cromer High teachers having sex with their students, which had been available for decades. She told him she was

'staggered' at the volume of damning evidence in the podcast and
The Australian's articles and baffled by what she perceived to be the
inertia of police.

Detective Superintendent Scott Cook promptly replied. 'I am
sorry for your loss and that this matter has not yet been resolved.
I understand why you and Lyn's family are angry and I would be
happy to meet privately with you or other members of Lyn's family
to discuss the investigation and answer any questions. It is important for police to ensure the security and integrity of evidence in
criminal matters and it is neither normal practice nor appropriate
that such evidence is publicly debated prior to the trial of an individual. The Homicide Squad will remain focused on getting the best
outcome for Lyn without entering into debates in the media about
particular cases.'

Greg Simms and his wife Merilyn were also angry. The complaint
letter they wrote to police and the DPP on 6 July made Wendy's
diatribe look tame.

'What a debacle! We feel incensed, frustrated and hugely let
down. As a family, we are too trusting, accepting and compliant in
relation to Chris, the police and the DPP. Due to the overwhelming information that has come forward through the podcast, the
mounting and strong public support, and the astounding support of
some very high-profile journalists, we now want to demand answers
and action. We will no longer be fobbed off, swept under the carpet
or ignored! We have waited too long for justice. It is time for the
DPP and the police to admit to their mistakes because we have been
treated abominably.'

The Simms letter urged Mick Fuller 'to personally look into the
historic bumbling of this case and report back to us of his findings'.
Greg and Merilyn also criticised the 'very slow progress since the
case was moved' in 2015 to the Homicide Squad.

'While appreciating the huge amount of work involved in gathering new evidence and fine-tuning the brief for the DPP, we are
extremely frustrated and annoyed it has taken the best part of three
years to complete it,' they wrote.

Pat Jenkins was trying to be positive. However, she told me 'the injustice surrounding Lyn's case, her loss and thoughts of her reduce me unexpectedly at times to spontaneous and deep emotion'.

When we sat down to eat at Verde, Ben argued that as we were all on the same page in wanting to achieve justice for Lyn, it would be crazy for police to not be afforded every opportunity to investigate leads which listeners and informants had shared with me. I was prepared to share under certain conditions. It would have been the height of hypocrisy for an investigative journalist, particularly one criticising police over failures in the case, to withhold information from detectives who might be able to use it to far greater effect. The exceptions were sources who would not permit their names and information to be disclosed to police. They would remain confidential.

All the work of Dan Poole had received scant public attention since the Homicide Squad assigned him to reinvestigate the cold case in 2015. His natural instinct to go under the radar aligned with the police policy to say as little as possible, particularly with the DPP reviewing the brief of evidence.

Over pasta and a bottle of red wine, the way forward looked obvious. The goodwill of Mick Fuller, mediating skills of Ben Fordham and Grant Williams, and my willingness to share promising information resulted in broad agreement. It put the police and the podcast on a unity ticket while we continued to do our jobs independently. Mick Fuller would leave Verde with a no-strings-attached agreement to receive information which could be more valuable in the hands of his Homicide Squad detectives.

In a follow-up note immediately after lunch, I emailed him: 'Let me stress that I'm not seeking any on- or off-the-record interview for this. The information is offered unconditionally.'

He replied: 'In light of the enormous interest your story has generated and the potential for new evidence to be obtained, I'm keen to connect the investigating police with you. Solving this case is extremely important to me and the New South Wales Police. Secondly, identifying and bringing to justice the men who engaged in horrendous acts of organised pedophilia.'

*

Greg and Merilyn Simms rode an emotional roller-coaster. One day they were on a high, the next a gut-wrenching low. I had not disclosed the Verde meeting to them at that stage.

The day after it, Greg brightened with a few omen tips for the racetrack. 'Try a trifecta. Sword of Justice by ten lengths, followed by Ombudsman, and Wallowing Copper a poor third!'

But he was pessimistic again a few days later when he wrote to me: 'Hey Hedley, had a call from Daniel Poole that DPP are looking at brief.'

I was confused. 'But you knew that already, right? He told you ages ago, didn't he?' I replied.

'Yeah, it was with them,' Greg texted back. 'But now they are looking at it, if that makes any sense.'

If Greg's understanding was right, the brief had been sitting for three months awaiting a prosecutor's availability to examine it.

Mick Fuller was true to his word. I flew back to Sydney, this time with David Murray, and went directly to Verde to meet the Homicide Squad's head, Detective Superintendent Scott Cook, State Crime Commander Mal Lanyon, Grant Williams and Dan Poole. We got along well. The detectives heard some things about the Dawsons they didn't previously know. Thanks to the efforts of Leigh Maloney, former Forest High schoolgirl Shelley Oates-Wilding agreed I should share her details and our recorded conversations with Dan Poole.

I had withheld the well-known kayaker's connection and her recollections from the podcast.

Her information was of significant interest to Dan who promptly made contact with Shelley in Hawaii. Detectives would subsequently meet Shelley in Sydney in late 2018 and interview her at length for a formal statement.

Five years later, in August 2023, Shelley revealed herself more publicly on *60 Minutes* and repeated some of what she had told me and police in 2018, including that Paul Dawson groomed her for sex.

'It was intimate,' she said, adding that she was 15 or 16 at the time.

'There would be times at the fitness classes where we'd be in the store room together, or there'd be times in the pool where we'd be intimate.'

She repeated the story of Paul's worried reaction after Lyn's disappearance.

'At the beginning of school, I vividly remember going to see him,' she said. 'He said to me with this extremely pained look on his face that something terrible has happened and he can't see me anymore.'

Paul, still with Marilyn on the Gold Coast, emphatically denied Shelley's assertions on national television. 'You'd have to ask her why she made it up,' he said.

At Verde in 2018, we worked out a protocol for Dan Poole to request select audio files, the contact details of cooperative sources and other documentation which might help, and for me to alert him to probative information which had not been published due to its sensitivity.

Over the ensuing months, Dan Poole asked for numerous files and contacts, which I sent electronically and sometimes handed over in person, including the details of several important witnesses who had not been known to police and their hours of audio which provided further leads and evidence.

I was on my way to the airport on 20 July when Mick Fuller texted: 'Hope meeting went well.'

He must have already had feedback from his detectives. 'It could not have been more constructive,' I replied. 'Dan stayed on and we had a good talk. I can see why you rate him highly as an investigator. He's smart and he's measured. We had a good landing with Mal and Scott too.'

In this new spirit of goodwill, Fuller mentioned a horse running on Saturday in the second race at Brisbane's Doomben racetrack, Miss Quaintly.

'Got a tip from an old trainer,' he told me.

The two meetings at Verde made a profoundly positive difference. There were risks but Mick Fuller gambled on them being manageable.

He harnessed the podcast and instructed his detectives to take an advantage from it instead of being defensively annoyed by it. It wasn't a competition. Having abandoned the 'no comment' position, he agreed to be interviewed by Ben on 2GB.

Ben Fordham briefed his audience: 'Well, the New South Wales Police Commissioner Mick Fuller admits that police dropped the ball investigating the disappearance of a Sydney mum in the 1980s. After a six-month investigation, *The Australian*'s national chief correspondent Hedley Thomas has released an episode a week of his record-breaking podcast, *The Teacher's Pet*, which gives new details about this case. And the evidence is mounting up and the pressure is building on the DPP to consider all the new information and whether or not there's enough evidence to bring a charge of murder against Chris Dawson. It is my opinion that Chris Dawson got away with murder. Mick Fuller joins us on the line. Why do you say that police dropped the ball?'

'Even if you only read the coronial reports handed down in 2001 and 2003, clearly police had taken a view very early in the piece that it was a missing persons case,' Fuller replied. 'Police and there were lots of other people, Ben, made an assumption, a pretty poor one, that Lyn had made a decision to leave the family home. There is much, much more to this case.'

The commissioner publicly apologised to Lyn Dawson's family for the failings of police in the past.

'There's a whole range of things that I'm sorry for. And at the end of the day, it's our job to protect the community. We can't stop every crime from happening. But when they do, it's our responsibility to ethically and diligently investigate them. Our Unsolved Homicide Unit started investigating this matter again a few years back, working back through the evidence. Trying to piece it together with modern technology, modern methods of trying to solve crime. Detective Senior Constable Dan Poole, who has worked extremely hard on this case – and he is a qualified, well-respected young police officer – in my opinion, is doing a very good job.

'It's a new style of journalism, the podcasts, it's unusual that these happen and run over the top of a current investigation and a brief that is before the DPP. Some unforeseen challenges in such a popular podcast is that there's people in the community scratching their heads, thinking that police are sitting on their hands. But I can assure people that we haven't.

'The positive point is that New South Wales Police, Hedley and of course the family and neighbours and people who are invested in this all want the same thing and that's justice for Lyn Dawson. And Hedley is meeting with their homicide detectives and they will work through any fresh leads that may only assist the DPP in their decision.

'I think it's a wonderful thing that people are coming forward. We need to collect that evidence in an admissible way, Ben.'

Up to this point, the Verde meeting and my contact with senior police had not been on the public record. I had withheld it from Lyn's family too, not wanting to get their hopes up until things had fallen into place. Ben took the cue to disclose.

'Commissioner, in the interest of transparency, it's just occurred to me that I should probably declare to my audience, because I'd hate for people to find out later on, that I had a small role in bringing you and Hedley Thomas together. And hopefully deliver that justice for Lynette's family that they've been waiting for so long.'

'It was a good connection, Ben,' Fuller replied. 'If there's evidence that comes out of Hedley's discussion with the police that helps us get a prosecution, then everyone's going to be happy.'

Mick Fuller had a slip-up, inadvertently saying on live radio that he had put me 'in charge' of his detectives; he meant to say 'in contact' with them. Ben jumped on it to correct the public record. He called me afterwards, giggling at the notion of the Homicide Squad's cops answering to a hack from Brisbane.

Asked if there would be more digging at Bayview, the commissioner said, 'One hundred per cent, Ben. It goes without saying. From our perspective, we've spent two or nearly three years re-investigating this tirelessly. It is important to us.'

He assured anyone with information, including the former students of Cromer High and the other schools on the Northern Beaches, that the police would run down every lead.

Pat Jenkins, Greg and Merilyn Simms and Wendy Jennings were jubilant about everything they heard. Their doubts and antagonism towards police fell away. Dan Poole spoke to the family and undertook to be more open with them and to keep them informed without compromising the case in any way.

A week later, Mick Fuller established Strike Force Southwood to investigate the allegations of unlawful student–teacher relationships at Cromer High and elsewhere. For the first time, there would be a serious investigation into the sex offences of a number of Northern Beaches teachers.

'This is a timely reminder to victims – it's never too late to make a report to police. We will investigate it whether it happened yesterday, last year, or 40 years ago,' a police spokeswoman said.

I remembered to place a bet on Miss Quaintly.

After stalking the early leaders for most of the race, jockey Jeff Lloyd steered the filly to the outside. She savaged the line, winning easily.

Chapter 33

Terry's Balancing Act

Amid the daily escalation of public interest, numerous listeners found Dawson family Facebook profiles and fired unsolicited messages, many of them angry and accusatory. Reporters turned up unannounced at the homes of Dawson relatives to seek an interview and, when turned away, they knocked on the doors of the neighbours. The *Gold Coast Bulletin* splashed its front page with the headline 'It's a witch-hunt' after Shanelle's younger sister, Amy, spoke in her driveway to the newspaper's local reporter, Sally Coates, telling her 'my dad's getting hounded because there's all these people that have got it in for him'.

Sally persisted, and Amy added, 'I don't trust the media, it's a witch-hunt. And I'm over it.'

Like her father, Amy blamed Jenny as well as the journalists. She wanted the Homicide Squad's detectives to question her former babysitter and stepmother, not her father.

'Stepmother was a bitch,' she told Sally in response to a question about her childhood and Jenny. 'She made up all these false lies, and then she screwed my dad over. She's got to live with that. I don't want to be around all this negativity and this falseness.'

Shanelle was caught in the middle, still privately encouraging my investigations for the podcast which, she hoped, would lead to her father being exposed and made accountable for the murder she strongly suspected him of carrying out.

Shanelle was haunted by a possible fragment of memory which, she feared, was from the night her mother was killed: an image of her father. He held a shovel. It was dark. He was digging.

Despite Amy's certainty that her innocent father was being mercilessly hunted by a rabid media, Shanelle believed she could maintain a closeness with her.

She was moved by the goodwill directed at her from listeners. Shanelle resolved to write a book to honour her mother.

'When I realised the truth about my dad and was really fucked up for a bit, it was the true stories I read of people overcoming challenging circumstances that helped pull me through,' Shanelle told me.

In Dee Why, a crew from the Nine Network's *A Current Affair* followed Jenny. They cornered her while she tried to walk outside and peppered her with questions. One of *The Australian*'s photographers surreptitiously snapped a picture of Jenny as she went to work in the half-light of dawn. She looked inconsolably sad. I urged the editors to stamp it 'not for publication'. It never saw the light of day.

Near Chris Dawson's investment property at Runaway Bay on the Gold Coast, my reporter friend Chris Allen and a crew from *A Current Affair* filmed the twin brothers out walking. Paul became incensed as pint-sized Chris Allen asked questions and tried to stay out of harm's way. It was dramatic television.

In the footage, Chris looks to Paul for guidance and help.

'Can we ask you some questions about what happened to your wife Lyn?' Chris Allen asked Chris Dawson.

A terse reply. 'She left.'

He appeared unperturbed about the DPP's consideration of a new brief of evidence. 'Good. Good. I'm very pleased that they do it,' he said defiantly.

'They're obviously still very much in one another's pockets,' the veteran TV reporter told me from his car some hours later. 'Paul was clearly defending his brother and running interference and pushing the camera out of the way, claiming that we were assaulting them and all that sort of rubbish. It was quite bizarre. At one point I stood on Paul's thong, accidentally. And he said "Oh!" And he pulled out of his thong and he said, "if I did that to you, you'd charge me with assault!"'

The adult children of Chris's brother Gary distanced themselves from their infamous uncles, telling curious friends they weren't related.

The growing pressure on Chris and Paul Dawson and their respective wives, Susan and Marilyn, must have been unbearable as millions of people heard their bizarre stories.

In the podcast series, I had reconstructed large sections of interviews Marilyn and Paul had done in 1999 with Damian Loone and his more senior colleague, Detective Sergeant John Pendergast.

Marilyn had said in her police interview that Lyn was not fighting to save her marriage.

'I wanted Lyn to fight for Chris and her marriage and her children and she didn't, she just kept making opportunities for him and Jenny to be together. She seemed to be meek when I wanted her to be strong.

'I would fight, I would've fought, and in a way I did fight for my marriage because my husband was his twin, and you know, whatever Chris was doing my husband may have been doing too.'

Two decades later, the comment infuriated listeners, some of whom contacted me to ask what more could Lyn do when her own sister-in-law had secretly taken Jenny in so that she could continue having sex with Chris?

An unofficial Facebook site for *The Teacher's Pet* became another online forum for thousands of people, mostly women, who speculated over what had happened to Lyn. Listeners were increasingly angry that authorities had been lax and unresponsive for so long; their fierce comments needed careful moderation by volunteers, who worked around the clock to catch the most defamatory accusations and theories.

The legal and editorial challenges for *The Australian* and its editors were more serious. Weekend Editor Michelle Gunn took these in her stride and ensured that breaking news from the podcast episodes would splash the newspaper's front page. The affirmation Michelle was receiving outside the newsroom from old schoolfriends who would not usually talk to her about our journalism was 'just incredible'.

'It has made me realise what a powerful storytelling medium it can be,' Michelle told me in a note. 'You should be very proud. x'

Back in May, when I first spoke to Chris a fortnight before the podcast series began, I had sent a follow-up note with another offer of an unedited interview; he did not reply. The same offer was extended to Paul and their solicitor brother, Peter, from whom I also heard nothing. He had been given his chance. If Chris didn't want to defend himself, I couldn't force him.

A few months before the podcast started, I had interviewed the rugby league great, former Penrith Panthers player Scott Sattler in my car outside his house. He'd had a strong and positive connection with the Dawson twins as teachers and coaches at Coombabah State High on the Gold Coast. Fat raindrops falling onto the car's roof meant the audio raised Slade Gibson's blood pressure, though he polished it into shape. Scott's thoughtful praise of the twins still featured prominently in an episode but his was one of very few voices of support.

If members of Dawson's family or his former footballing mates had come forward with positive anecdotes about him, I would have published those in successive episodes. Nobody with a good word to say about Chris had stepped up since the episodes began.

In the media maelstrom, Terry Martin, newly retired Queensland District Court judge, former top criminal defence lawyer and a wise and close personal friend, became concerned about what he saw as a campaign which was powerfully vilifying Chris. The public frenzy surrounding the podcast amplified everything. Terry heard the thunderous regular pronouncements about the case by Ben Fordham on 2GB and the senior broadcaster Peta Credlin on Sky News. Terry suspected that if Chris Dawson were charged, he and his lawyers would rely on the podcasts and the bandwagoning media condemnations of the accused to argue that he could never get a fair trial.

Terry gave constructive advice then made a generous offer: he would write a legal opinion reflecting some of the arguments a competent criminal defence lawyer would frame to put a different and innocent light on Chris. In this way, Terry saw an opportunity to put forward Chris's side of the story in the podcast and make it appear less biased.

He didn't pull his punches with the document he produced and emailed.

> The podcast has generated overwhelming bias against Chris Dawson and has done so not by relying upon relevant allegations of fact, but by reliance upon irrelevant allegations of fact as well as entirely worthless expressions of opinion that Chris Dawson is guilty.
>
> The podcast has a life of its own. It publishes the useless opinions of persons which in turn induces others to come forward to share their useless opinions. Ensuring an even wider publication of purely prejudicial material, Ms Credlin on television and Mr Fordham on radio have expressed their worthless opinions as to Mr Dawson's guilt.
>
> Notwithstanding that there has been no trial, no proper scrutiny of assertions made, no full and proper cross-examination of potential witnesses and no impartial assessment of the whole of the admissible evidence, all of these persons stridently announce to the world Chris Dawson's guilt. The outcome of a trial will result from the proper assessment of facts, not from giddy hysteria whipped up by the podcast, including the gratuitous opinions of some, seemingly keen to attract ratings or celebrity.

Fellow journalist Paul Larter used his most authoritative baritone to give voice to Terry's anonymous analysis, particularly regarding Jenny Carlson's claims that Chris told her he had intended to hire a hitman to kill Lyn before changing his mind in late 1981:

> 'She asserts that Lyn disappeared very shortly after this conversation and that Dawson told her that Lyn was never coming back. These allegations were first made by her during her

divorce proceedings with Chris Dawson. No doubt, as she saw it, the allegations were to give her a substantial advantage in the proceedings. However, Jenny also asserts that notwithstanding the circumstances she alleges, it did not occur to her, at a time proximate to Lyn's disappearance, that Chris Dawson may have killed Lyn. That is an absurdity.

'Either her allegations against Chris Dawson are fabricated, or, if true, Jenny could not have failed to know that Chris Dawson likely killed Lyn. Moreover, if true, Jenny not only concealed this evidence from police, but she stayed with a known wife-murderer, married him and bore him a child. One must have grave doubts about the veracity of her allegations.'

Terry's analysis also attacked the credibility of Julie Andrew for having said that she had suspected domestic violence against Lyn and strongly believed since 1982 that Lyn was murdered but waited until 1999 to make a statement to police.

'One must ask, if Ms Andrew's evidence is truthful, how could she not go to police? It would be a nonsense to suggest that her failure to do so was because of an inadequate investigation in that police failed to knock on her door to specifically invite information. Ms Andrew's allegations lack credibility.

'Further impacting adversely on her credibility, Ms Andrew is one of the persons who has loudly, vehemently and often pronounced that Chris Dawson is guilty. Any assertion of fact made by her against Chris Dawson must be seen as reflecting her entrenched bias against him.'

Terry took the damning evidence of Chris's hasty installation of Jenny in the Bayview house within a couple of days of Lyn's 'departure' and recast it as an indication of his innocence.

'He made no secret of the fact, and it seems that family and friends were well aware within a very short time, that his lover was sharing the matrimonial bed. If, as seems to be asserted in the podcast, the motive for the murder was to be with Jenny and to retain the house and children, one would think that the very last thing he would do would be to immediately and openly move his lover into Lyn's bed. Óf the many criticisms levelled at Chris Dawson in the podcast, being a complete fool is not one of them.'

Finally, the analysis dealt with Lyn's family and how they had accepted for the first eight years that she had left voluntarily.

'Despite efforts in the podcast to suggest otherwise, the family's acceptance that Lyn was capable of abandoning the family can hardly depend upon Chris Dawson's renowned charisma.

'The fact is, whatever it was about Lyn and Chris, those closest to them, including Lyn's brother the police officer, accepted that Lyn was capable of walking away and that Chris was entirely incapable of her murder. And this is so in the full knowledge of his relationship with Jenny.

'Over time, things have changed. It is obvious that Lyn's family grew to resent Chris Dawson. This is hardly surprising. He moved Jenny into Lyn's house and bed, married her, using the wedding rings that he and Lyn had used for their wedding, divorced Lyn, took the whole of the interest in the house and failed to repay a loan associated with the house to Lyn's parents. Further, as the resentment continued to grow, Chris Dawson made it difficult for Lyn's parents to have access to Lyn's children. Chris Dawson's behaviour is undoubtedly worthy of condemnation. It explains why Lyn's family and friends now have such a toxic attitude towards him. But it also explains why history is being re-written, reconstructed.'

In the years since two coroners had separately studied the brief of evidence and recommended a prosecution, Lyn's family had lost confidence in the prosecuting agency and its then head, Nicholas Cowdery, for repeatedly refusing to take the case to trial. But in 2011, Pat Jenkins and Wendy Jennings, who were doing most of the letter-writing to the DPP, got their hopes up. Nicholas Cowdery was retiring. A younger lawyer, Lloyd Babb, was appointed to head the office.

But they were soon disappointed. Wendy alternated between furiously blaming the DPP and police. She blasted both in a February 2012 letter to then Police Minister Mike Gallacher.

'It is a disgrace and when time permits, I am going to expose this unjust system and lack of support to the media,' Wendy wrote. 'I do not believe that all murders are treated equally, but the families suffer immeasurably.'

'It was another period of optimism, you know, a change of the guard – [we thought] maybe they'll look at it with fresh eyes,' Pat told me. 'And then nothing changed. That was another letdown and it just went on as before. As if Cowdery was still there.

'I'm optimistic now Hedley, but then I think, "Oh DPP, that's what we're dealing with". And they're just a law unto themselves. So you don't know which way they're going to go.'

Strange coincidences and bizarre curveballs were part and parcel of the case, the story and the podcast, but I was still taken aback at a tip-off from a listener, Adrian (not his real name). He remembered two likeable physical education teachers, Chris and Paul Dawson, from his time at Asquith Boys High. With their lofty reputations as first-grade rugby league players, the twins also coached the school rugby league team.

A year after Lyn's disappearance, the Education Department's transfer of the Dawson brothers must have seemed like a convenient solution to an embarrassing problem: move two popular men with reputations for grooming schoolgirls to the all-boys high school at Hornsby, west of the beaches. It would be their last two years of teaching in Sydney before moving to Queensland.

But until hearing from Adrian, when the podcast still had several episodes to go, I was oblivious to the fact that the Director of Public Prosecutions, Lloyd Babb, also went to Asquith Boys High. He was school captain while the Dawson brothers taught there. He played rugby league in 1983 for the Asquith Boys High team; Chris and Paul Dawson had coached the future NSW Director of Public Prosecutions.

'We saw more of them. Being our coaches as well as our teachers,' Adrian told me.

He recalled that many years after he and Lloyd Babb had left Asquith Boys High, they caught up at a social event.

'I saw Lloyd there and I ended up bringing up the subject of the Dawson twins and, knowing that Lloyd was head of the DPP, I said sort of half-heartedly, "When are you going to bring the Dawson case to a head?"

'And he said, "Oh I've got to be careful there because I've had a past" – don't quote me word for word but there was the fact that he knew the Dawson twins and he would have to disclose that. The way I took his conversation was, he couldn't be the one sort of pushing that issue.'

The school connection was news to me. Lloyd Babb had been DPP since 2011. It was known that the Office of the DPP had received the new police brief of evidence provided by Dan Poole and the Homicide Squad's head Scott Cook in April 2018, but the former link between Lloyd Babb and the Dawson brothers was a tightly held secret as far as the general public was concerned.

When I spoke to Pat Jenkins about the connection, she was flabbergasted and sounded shaken. Neither Lloyd Babb nor anyone in his office had disclosed the old school tie to the family or the public. The Dawson brothers, of course, had known since 2011 that a boy they had coached was in charge of the office which had repeatedly refused to prosecute Chris.

'Oh my goodness. Unbelievable. Unbelievable. I'm going to have to digest this,' Pat said. 'We should have been told. I don't think it's good that he's got that past association. He probably respected Chris, he probably thought he was a great teacher. Because he probably got along very well with the young men. It's a real complication, isn't it?'

If Adrian's memory of their catch-up was correct, Lloyd Babb clearly understood that the connection with the Dawsons was a potential problem and he had rightly determined that he should not be involved in any of the decision-making around the case.

I told Pat that if Lloyd Babb had disclosed the connection to senior lawyers in his office and effectively quarantined himself from the Dawson case, there would not be a legal problem, putting aside the fact that Lyn's family had been treated like mushrooms. I assured Pat I was 'confident that he would have been very professional', probably telling his office about the past association. But in such a high-profile case, it struck me as foolhardy that the association had not been disclosed to the public.

Lloyd Babb responded to our detailed questions in writing:

> I played rugby league and had contact with both men in that context. I was not taught by Chris Dawson or Paul Dawson.
>
> I had no involvement with either man in activities outside of school.
>
> Upon my becoming aware of this matter I immediately indicated my conflict of interest to the Deputy Directors in 2015 and again to current Deputy Directors in 2018. The matter was referred to them, and those referrals, and the registration of my declaration of a conflict of interest, was formally acknowledged. The correct procedure in declaring a conflict of interest and ensuring that I have no involvement in the review has been followed. That conflict would prevent me from any involvement, including contact with the family.

These answers begged more questions.

Lloyd Babb had been DPP since 2011 and I had copies of a letter he was sent by Lyn's family in that year. Yet he was telling us that he raised his conflict of interest four years later, in 2015.

I wrote again to Lloyd Babb via his media adviser, Anna Cooper, with background information for context and a number of new questions:

> [Lyn's family] say they have been treated 'abysmally' in relation to the current brief before you – and that your decision to withhold from them your conflict of interest shows a lack of courtesy, compassion and respect. Pat Jenkins wrote to you almost four weeks ago on 10 July 2018. When she wrote she was unaware of your past association with the Dawson brothers and your

disqualification since 2015 from contact with the brief of evidence. She has not received a reply.

In a note to me on the weekend, Mrs Jenkins stated that in her opinion 'it is without question obligatory that he (Mr Babb) should have contacted us and explained any implications and safeguards for the integrity of Lyn's case'.

Inexplicably, four days after we received his first written answers to our questions, a new statement was posted on the website of the Office of the DPP. It had a different date for the timing of Lloyd Babb's disclosure.

The newer statement said Lloyd Babb wrote to the then Attorney-General Greg Smith SC on 14 October 2011 and told him, 'I have found it necessary not to play any part in the consideration of the matter myself for the reason that I am acquainted with the suspect in that he was a teacher at my high school and my rugby league coach in about 1983. For this reason the matter has been considered by Mr Chris Maxwell QC, Acting Deputy Director.'

The conflicting versions made it difficult to understand who knew what and when in relation to Lloyd Babb's old connection with Chris Dawson. But his office pulled the shutters down and refused our attempts to clarify things. We saved and printed the statement on the DPP's website, which was fortunate as the statement soon disappeared.

Pat Jenkins remembered Chris Maxwell from the letter she had received from him in 2011. In his 5 August 2011 letter, Mr Maxwell stated: 'I note that you have sought my advice as to why this office has declined to have a meeting with police in this matter. In this case, this office has, on a number of occasions, carefully considered the evidence that has been provided. The further material recently provided by Detective Sergeant Loone has also been carefully considered. However, based on the presently available evidence, this office is of the view that there is insufficient evidence to satisfy a jury, properly instructed, that a particular person was responsible for the disappearance and/or death of Mrs Lynette Dawson.'

The disclosures in the podcast and in *The Australian* of Lloyd Babb's conflict of interest were carefully handled. We made no suggestion of wrongdoing but I said that he should have been open about the Asquith Boys connection with Lyn's family. Withholding such things only encourages suspicion and conspiracy theories.

I discovered that the Homicide Squad's detectives were stunned. They were, effectively, the client of the Office of the DPP, yet had no idea about the association.

Police Commissioner Mick Fuller could scarcely believe what he was hearing, even though Lloyd Babb had confirmed it in writing.

'You couldn't write this in a book, people would think it's fiction,' Fuller told me. 'When you started it, you wouldn't have imagined that you would have gone on this journey.'

On a lighter note, he added, 'The good news is, I went to Engadine High School. For the record, I didn't visit northern suburbs, and I wouldn't have played rugby league at any standard that would have got me anywhere close.'

Chapter 34

Helena

Within hours of meeting Ruth at the opening of a bar called Ric's in Fortitude Valley, then whisking her away for an Indian curry and impromptu takeaway dinner, I willed a future with her. At my *Courier-Mail* desk the next morning, I told my journalist friend Neil Breen that I wanted to marry a thoughtful, beautiful, funny and highly intelligent young reporter, Ruth Mathewson. I wanted to spend the rest of my life with her.

Our happy marriage was painfully stress-tested several times over ensuing years. The shooting at our Brookfield home in 2002 triggered a particularly rocky time. A near-fatal illness which seized our daughter for several years was traumatic. But our bonds seemed stronger after we had fought and overcome each family crisis. In our busy and demanding careers, we had always tried hard to find time and show kindness, respect and unconditional love for each other and our two children.

But our relationship went alarmingly awry during the creation and delivery of *The Teacher's Pet*. The injustice in Lyn's case had made me righteously angry and increasingly difficult to live with. I was distracted and obsessively determined to try to put things right. My disinterest and lack of time for just about everything at home was acute.

After a handful of episodes, I had assured Lyn's sister: 'Pat, I do believe the DPP will prosecute him this time. The evidence is overwhelming. If they don't, there is something very wrong in the system.'

Firm predictions such as this to those people most affected by Lyn's fate were unfair. I should have been more circumspect and not raised their hopes to this level. I had gone a long way out on a limb with the podcast investigation and the storytelling. There was no way back. Success, which meant the realisation of my prediction to Pat, might come only by working harder for longer; finding more leads and witnesses; breaking more stories; provoking more public anger at the injustice of it all. Whatever it took to tip the balance and prompt the DPP to tell Police Commissioner Mick Fuller: 'Yes, charge him.'

There was something else driving me. Unseen. At the time, I believed, erroneously, that Ruth had identified the invisible influence from her hotel room in Copenhagen.

She went there to help our son settle as a university exchange student on the other side of the world. Alexander at 19 was coping well, studying chemical engineering and more than capable on his own. But Ruth and I needed some distance. Our marriage had come under enormous strain amid the rollout of the episodes. We were in perpetual disagreement. Ruth was increasingly sad and wanted things to return to how they were before the podcast took over. I couldn't stop the work until the story was finished, and while she was in Copenhagen I saw an opportunity to do more without feeling guilty or neglectful.

Ruth went to the Maritime Museum of Denmark where Dad, an avid yachtsman, would have loved to wander, study and learn for days about the seafaring Danes and their history under sail. He was captivated by all things maritime. He had sailed solo from San Francisco to Brisbane, just before he turned 70.

'I spent the time thinking of your father. He would have found it fascinating,' Ruth told me.

'Dad would have been absolutely riveted by it,' I replied. 'That's the secret to my commitment, I think. Dad's mum, the Northern Beaches. Eerie in a way. I'm dazed from fatigue but close to the finish line now.'

She was talking about the museum. But I was too blinkered by the podcast to grasp her point; I immediately believed that Ruth meant he would have been fascinated by the murder investigation. The case had taken over my thinking. It was even featuring often in my dreams.

The brunette ghost of my grandmother was always there, too, on my mind and in invisible ink on every page of my notes for *The Teacher's Pet*. Her ethereal presence nudged me to take bigger risks and fight harder than I had in any other story. I wondered about her when I looked at photographs of my father as a little boy, dressed smartly and holding her hand.

What happened to her at 35? Dad was just 16. I worked overtime in my mind to banish thoughts of possible foul play. She was probably depressed at the time; her siblings did not, to my knowledge, have suspicion over her disappearance; police didn't suspect anything sinister as far as I was aware. Her husband, my grandfather, never remarried. On one level, all of those accepted facts were reassuring, and the circumstances of her disappearance being a suicide lined up with the tragic pattern of suicides of two of her siblings. I pictured her walking purposefully into the Pacific Ocean at Dee Why, ten kilometres south of Bayview, and turning to have one last wistful look at the shoreline of life and the safe sand and the post-war cottages, sheltering seemingly happy families, then putting her head down and swimming, strongly, effortlessly, through a foamy shorebreak, past distant breakers and into the deep blue. Swimming until she was ready to succumb and slip beneath the surface. Never to be seen again. That was the never-discussed family version of events, and I wanted to lean into it. On another level – the one I didn't want to go to – some of the similarities with the facts of Lyn's case were unavoidable. I had acquitted my grandfather, also named Hedley, of wrongdoing.

But I was journalistically convicting Chris of murder; I had become relentlessly invested in ensuring he faced a trial, which might confirm guilt. It was a labyrinth of psychological, criminal and familial tensions.

A perceptive Queensland writer and insomniac, Archie Butter-fly, would somehow subsequently discover the link from his own research, and publish on his website details about my grandmother's disappearance along with his speculation about my commitment to Lyn's case.

He wrote:

> The 16-year-old boy that she turned her back on as she took that last lonely walk across the sand into nothingness was Hedley Robert Thomas, in one of those awful ironies at the time a New South Wales state champion swimmer. He went on to be a war hero, a pilot in the Vietnam War. Later he became a flight instructor, an Order of Australia medallist and the father of four children of his own. One of them was the modern day Hedley Thomas, author of *The Teacher's Pet* . . .

Using online genealogical information and details from obituaries, Archie had keyword-searched the digital archives of newspapers and found something I didn't have and had never seen before: a brief article published in the late edition of *The Sydney Morning Herald* on 5 October 1956, under the headline: 'Clothes find: Woman sought'.

The snippet from six decades ago was published on his blog:

> Police are searching for a woman whose clothes were found on Deewhy Beach [sic] early yesterday morning.
>
> Footprints led from the clothes to the water's edge.
>
> The missing woman is Mrs Gladys Olga Thomas, 35, of Pacific Parade, Deewhy. Police Sergeant R. Gunnyon, of Manly, is in charge of inquiries.

Archie wrote:

> Rivers run deep but the ocean floor is deeper. Hedley Robert Thomas took his final flight on 14 March 2017. His son began the award-winning *The Teacher's Pet* series of podcasts just months

after. Was it a paean of love to those he'd lost, a vicarious exorcism of the ghosts of the author's own family's past, haunted by the pain wrought by water, and the swallowing vortex of the sea? We are all formed as adults from our experiences as a child, but even more – consciously or unconsciously – from our deeper family experiences long, long before. You just couldn't have made this story up if you tried.

Ruth messaged me again from Copenhagen after listening to the new episode: 'I know how hard you're working. You and Slade are doing something extraordinary.'

But Slade was exhausted. When I joked that he would soon be hiding under the bed when he heard the rumble of my car's diesel engine in his long driveway, he brightened at the idea. He was dealing with an almost impossible number of audio grabs from my interviews, growing in number each week when new leads came in. He was still writing all the music, recording and chopping up my clumsy narration with its abrupt stops and expletives when I couldn't get the words out right, then he was processing it and standing by to make dozens of difficult changes after my listens to the first and second drafts.

In a bid to make things easier, I had started taking flash drives of my interview audio files to a university share house on the other side of the city. I would make the delivery in the early morning, and Zachary Womal, my son's friend since they were small boys, would wake up and retrieve the flash drives from the drop-off point: inside his running shoes, on the house's deck. When Zac was fully awake, he'd chop up the time-coded pieces that I had set out in episode scripts.

These efforts eased Slade's load temporarily. But we were both running on empty, and we didn't know whether more help would even be available from Sydney with the commitments of the busy staff there. When Slade had first quoted a price for the podcast, he unknowingly but seriously under-estimated the time he would need to spend on it. For the time it took him to produce, he was being paid a relative pittance. But budgets in Sydney were tight. Rather than ask work, I gave him the winnings from a bet on a racehorse and hoped we could both keep up with the workload to the end.

Before our series had launched in May with the first episode and a simultaneous text from Slade who cheerfully asked me 'Is he in jail yet?', the gifted musician and sound engineer would deliver a draft episode for my review. We would spend a couple of days working out an improved structure and tone, kicking around ideas after multiple listens, and determining numerous itty-bitty edits. But this luxury was impossible by July. We were cutting things too fine with deadlines.

Our credibility would be shattered if we got something fundamentally wrong. *The Teacher's Pet* had been riding a wave of good press with other media outlets but it could go the other way in a heartbeat. It was little wonder that Slade looked pale most days. He barely had time to leave his studio. He had worsening pain in his hands from repetitive movement and his head was spinning with all the tasks he was trying to juggle, mostly on his own. He was also voice-acting the evidence of Chris, Paul and Peter Dawson, and guiding the voice-acting of Brisbane friends, including Tim Lunn, who voiced Damian Loone, and his wife Amanda Emmerson, who had the role of the first coroner from 2001, Jan Stevenson.

I was dropping into the houses and workplaces of friends and colleagues to record them voice-acting the written evidence of former witnesses who were now dead or unavailable.

Ruth voiced part of the 1998 police statement of Jenny's mother who had supported her daughter moving into the Dawson house in late 1981 as it meant fewer arguments and tensions at home, particularly with Jenny's step-father.

'If Jenny wanted to have a relationship with her teacher there was nothing that I could do to stop it because she was young and determined,' she said.

Chris and Jenny stayed with Jenny's mother on visits from their new home on the Gold Coast after 1985. 'During the stay, he would often go to the house at Bayview twice in a week. He used to say that he just wanted to have a look at the house and see how it was going.'

Her daughter burst into tears during a visit over Christmas 1989. 'Jenny told me that she was scared of Chris and the marriage was strained. Jenny was crying uncontrollably and I sensed that something terrible must have happened as I've never seen Jenny like this before.'

On another occasion, gifts to her daughter of plain cottontail underwear had angered Chris who 'cut the underwear up with scissors'.

'I don't know why Chris did this but I do recall Jenny not being allowed to wear a two-piece costume and not being allowed to go to the beach by herself,' she said.

Slade's father voiced Jenny's dad. He told Damian Loone that he saw what was going on and told his schoolgirl daughter he would cut all contact with her unless she ended things with Chris.

'And she told me point blank that she wasn't going to stop seeing him. I said to her "What you're doing is bloody wrong", you know "you don't do these things", you know "you get right out of there". The bloke's a married man.

'She was in her last year. And her marks were abysmal. I told her that I thought he was a bloody disgrace to the teaching profession to have committed this or got involved in this way with her.

'She subsequently got married and I took no part in the proceedings at all. She was prevented by him from developing relationships with other people.

'But Jenny told me that some little time after Lyn's disappearance, they had some concreting done around the pool. I would have said something like, "that's where she is, she's under that bloody concrete. I'll bet my balls you'll find her."'

Graham remembered being telephoned by Lyn 'a matter of months' before her disappearance. She told him that 'Jenny was playing up'.

'And I said, "Oh, no, Lyn, no, cut it out." I said, "That's not fair." I said, "My daughter wouldn't do that." I can recall the inference was that my daughter should be spoken to . . . she was pretty upset about it. I would say that Lyn was very aware that Jenny was doing the wrong thing.'

Lyn visited Jenny's mother, too, and said she was 'worried about Chris being unfaithful and concerned about Jenny's apparent relationship . . .'

These disclosures to the divorced parents of a schoolgirl must have been incredibly humiliating for Lyn. She was desperate for help. She needed an intervention. But Graham and Ann were in denial.

At my request, Pat Jenkins was still going through dozens of her mother Helena's letters and diary jottings. It was taking an emotional toll. Her mother had nightmares after Lyn's disappearance; Helena would not sleep well again for the two decades she had left.

'I found myself saying, "Poor, poor Lyn," or "Poor, poor Mum,"' Pat told me. 'I have been left feeling so very sad and yesterday quite teary but I will move on . . . thinking of the many kind words of support and hope has been a great help.'

Pat told me that her mother found out about Chris and Jenny moving to Queensland with Lyn's daughters in late 1984 by chance after bumping into one of Lyn and Chris's old friends.

'When Dad died, there was no way to let Amy know,' Pat said.

'Isn't that so sad that Chris had denied Amy contact with her grandparents for all of those years and she had to find out about her grandfather's death through Mum's chance encounter with a friend? I think that was disgraceful.'

Helena's hand writing was small and difficult to read and I relied on Pat to accurately transcribe every word. She would email me in batches. Some of it was prescient; other notes were heartbreaking. On 6 October 1981, when Helena visited the home in Bayview three months before her daughter's disappearance, she noted: 'Jenny there, too. Lyn shopping. Chris comforting Jenny on bed in study!'

Two days later on 8 October, Helena wrote: 'Lyn not going to tennis – upset. Chris had to drive Jenny down to work late night shopping, then pick her up. Think it's an imposition and unfair on Chris and Lyn to be put in this situation. Lyn seems to feel it's ok.'

Thirteen days after her last conversation with her daughter, Helena wrote on 21 January 1982:

Dear Pat and Ron . . .

The long and short of it is, Lyn took herself off on the 9th and after three phone calls to Chris and none to me, as promised, we now haven't heard for well over a week. Won't state where she is, only once it was Central Coast, and now north. I was with Chris at Northbridge pool when he had the first call and he was obviously very much affected and emotional. She says she is with friends but nobody knows who they would be. She was very affected with Chris leaving her and the girls right on Xmas but Chris assures me they were 'coming good'.

Whether she has cracked under the strain or is being vindictive or what the answer is I don't know.

As she told me, at one stage she had said to Chris, 'you give all your love to your two girls, your companionship to your twin brother, where do I come in'?

Pat sent me some of her mother's jottings of things Lyn's daughters had said after Lyn disappeared.

'Mummy is lost! Daddy has Jenny now. Daddy will marry Jenny when she becomes a mother!! We hope they don't find Mummy in the holidays – Jenny wants to marry Daddy. We have to call Jenny "Mum" now. Jenny doesn't like Nanna! Mummy didn't love Daddy anymore!'

Pat's concerns about revisiting these letters and diaries for my benefit stemmed from a sense of disloyalty; she knew Helena had wanted her private papers destroyed on her death. Pat stored them instead, but now she was sharing them with a podcast and listeners around the world. They were, however, a treasure trove of clues and evidence that had not been seen by the DPP until Dan Poole collated it all and put it in the brief.

Helena's diary note about a classified advertisement that Chris had placed in Sydney's *The Daily Telegraph* on 27 March 1982, a day after his wedding anniversary, prompted my colleague Gemma Jones, *The Australian*'s chief of staff at the time, and her deputy James Madden to go hunting for the archived edition of that day's *Tele*.

'James found it!!' Gemma texted me.

The tiny two-line advertisement stated: 'Lyn, I love you. We all miss you. Please ring. We want you home, Chris.'

This was another wretched lie. If we were all wrong about Chris having murdered her, and if she had seen and responded to the ad, what was she going to walk back into? Even all of Lyn's clothes had been taken from her wardrobe and stuffed into green garbage bags. The dishonesty of Chris's message in the paper was shameless.

My Brisbane journalist friend Susan Hocking Mackie voiced Helena's words evocatively. Susan's voice made a strong impact on listeners. The letters and diary notes were always extremely relevant to the case, and they should have been part of the original briefs of evidence the DPP had reviewed. Chris's story that Lyn simply left, voluntarily, and never returned seemed even more absurd with the benefit of an old woman's writings about her daughter's responsible nature and her son in law's fast work to replace her with a teenager.

On 1 February 1982, Helena, who had turned 66 and was to have been the subject of a surprise party being organised by Lyn, reflected: 'What a sad birthday. No ring from Lyn.'

7 March 1982: 'To footy. Shocking day. Chris brought Jenny. Nobody spoke. Chris ignored me.'

One of the most moving letters from Helena was dated 20 August 1984. Helena, who had heard one of Lyn's daughters refer to their absent Mum as their 'pretend mother', wrote:

> Dear Chris, it grieves and saddens me that you would issue an edict that, should I come to the school, I was not to see my grandchildren. It would seem that you have achieved what you have set out to do, rid yourself of Lyn, to whom you said 'I don't love you anymore, I hate you!', and 'I have no feeling for you!', and 'I don't want to be married to Lyn anymore'. And that's enough to break anyone's spirit. I've never condoned mothers leaving their children, I don't know how they could, but by the same token I do not condone a father either who takes off, instead of facing up to the problem. You've wielded the big stick and cut me out of yours and Lyn's children's lives. I love my granddaughters and don't you

ever tell them differently, Chris. Now they are lost to me as well as
to their 'pretend' mother, the burden is great.

Despite her own distress, Pat still thought to write notes of encouragement to me. They were uplifting when I was drowning in detail and
worrying about getting the weekly episodes finished. She would go
back to early episodes and listen again to 'cheer' herself up. Reading
and transcribing all her mother's letters and diaries had convinced
Pat of something.

> I truly believe Chris hated Lyn at the end as she stood between him
> and all he wanted – the children, the house and Jenny, and he got
> the lot. So much sadness and grief, lives changed irrevocably, the
> children deprived of their loving mother, Lyn lost, and all for what?
> All for that man's ego and his belief that whatever he wanted, he
> should have, without the kindest thought to anyone. I'm off my
> soapbox now.

I told Pat: 'When this is all over, hopefully with some resolution after
all these years of being cruelly denied justice, we will sit down and
reflect on it all as having been painful but mostly worthwhile.'

Rebecca Hazel, who continued working on her book, stayed in
touch, sending fond messages of support. She had been sadly cut off
by Jenny since January 2018. A month before the abrupt termination of their friendship, Rebecca had told me: 'We've got a very, very
strong bond and enormous respect. I have a feeling for her that's quite
unique; a kind of love that I have for her, for someone who has just
kind of opened herself up and said, "This is all the dirty stuff inside
me, ask me whatever you want". I think that's an incredibly brave
thing to do. And it's not just me. I mean, she did it at the inquest.
All of Sydney read about it. She's a very, very brave person. It's not
something she enjoys talking about. But if you ask her the question,
she'll tell you the truth.'

Although I had not given up on Jenny agreeing to talk to me,
it seemed unlikely. Women who knew her were coming forward

instead. Karen Cook, who was Jenny's friend during her lonely years living in what she called 'the compound' – the house and acreage near Dreamworld on the Gold Coast – likened the younger woman's lifestyle to that of the perfect specimens in *The Stepford Wives*. In the science-fiction black comedy, Nicole Kidman plays the role of a beautiful young wife, Joanna, as she first conforms and then rebels against a secretive, sociopathic and controlling husband who has tried to mould her into an artificial form of perverse perfection.

Karen Cook described Chris 'hovering' like a dark menace over everything Jenny did, watching her, checking she was doing everything correctly, and resenting that her friends had come to the house to spend time with her.

'He had control entirely over what she did, and I remember thinking it was quite unusual that she was even allowed to spend time with us. That's why I said, almost *Stepford Wife*. He didn't want her to be grown up. We just felt so worldly compared with her, she just seemed like a kid.'

The older woman recalled being surprised at Jenny's disclosures of what Karen regarded in the late 1980s as 'kinky sexual innuendo . . . he made demands that she dress up and perform certain ways'. One such demand that Chris made of Jenny, Karen told me, was to dress as a schoolgirl.

'I think she did, yes, which I thought was strange. Jenny confided to us that she was frightened of Chris. She was given a very small amount each week to keep the house and provide for the children,' Karen said.

'He was critical of her in our presence, belittling her, which was uncomfortable. Everyone including the children seemed to be walking on eggshells. She said she had to do everything that was asked of her or there was trouble in the house. She talked of Chris having a voracious sexual appetite and she could not say no to him.'

Karen told me that she recalled being told by Jenny that 'his previous wife had died'. If Karen's recollection 30 years later was correct, it seemed that Jenny had come to a view by the late 1980s that Lyn was dead. Or perhaps Jenny's suspicions were still forming.

Either way, the disclosure aligned with her going to police soon after she had left Chris in early 1990.

When I was flagging as the podcast series lengthened, I would be heartened by poignant notes and messages like the one from Lulu, daughter of Lyn's loyal work friend Sue Strath.

Lulu told me that when the United States *Serial* podcast came out in 2014, Sue wanted her journalist daughter to do a similar podcast but about Lyn. Lulu was worried she would not be able to do the vast story justice. I understood exactly where she was coming from.

'I do know that all these years later, people have heard Lyn's story and they have heard Mum's questions and they're asking the same ones,' Lulu said. 'The onus wasn't on Lyn's family, or Mum, to lead the investigators to water. It wasn't their responsibility to know who to ask what, and where to push for answers. It was that of the police and, obviously, they failed Lyn and her daughters and family and friends too. Regardless of whether Chris Dawson faces legal ramifications for any of the myriad things you have exposed, I do know he would not be able to swagger into his local coffee shop and comfortably sip on his regular latte. That brings me comfort. Millions of people have heard Lyn's story and millions of people now know more of the truth.

'This story resonates with me for so many reasons other than that I grew up with Mum talking of her friend. Without ever spelling it out, by listening to Mum over these many years, I learned the importance of friendship and loyalty and persistence. It makes me incredibly proud that others have seen those qualities in my mother now, too. I thank you so much for that – for honouring Lyn, of course, but for honouring my Mum too.'

Chapter 35

Hedley, You're a Fucking Wanker

The major highway from Brisbane, the M1, had never looked so inviting. Driving 900 kilometres to Sydney meant temporary freedom from a punishing cycle of pursuing people, interviewing, writing, narrating, editing and producing, with little let-up. The drive was an escape from domestic tension. Ruth's return from Copenhagen had not fixed things; we were, briefly, under the same roof again but in every other way we were far apart. She remained in Brisbane while I went to Sydney. The trip revolved around work but the silver lining was that after 14 weekly episodes, Slade and I were pausing the podcast. It had become the most downloaded story in Australia, the United States, Canada, the United Kingdom and New Zealand and was simultaneously entertaining and mortifying millions, many of whom willed it to help catch a suspected murderer.

The series was not over, I assured Pat, Greg and Merilyn, it would be merely resting while we caught our breath in the interval. In the meantime the Office of the DPP could continue its closed-door review of the police brief of evidence.

As Julie Andrew, Lyn's former neighbour and good friend, said: 'It's almost to the stage where everyone just has to settle and allow it to all sink in. The reason you came to this in the first place and the reason most of us have been involved with you in it is to seek the final justice for Lyn. We've all done what we can do and it really is up to the authorities. I feel the weight of public opinion will be such that they cannot afford not to press charges. Politically it would be very dangerous.'

Julie identified an unprecedented public clamour for action. For a prosecution. After everything that had come out, surely the Office of the DPP would soon recommend a murder charge. On the other hand, the agency prided itself on its fierce independence; its immunity from public and media pressure. Admissible evidence, not public fury, should drive every decision to prosecute. I believed that the public interest had become so great that if the office once again refused to take Chris to trial, it would need to share its detailed reasons. They would need to be very solid to withstand scrutiny because the alternative was a collapse in public confidence. Too many people were angered by the criminal justice system's handling of the case since the early 1980s.

By the 14th episode, Carl Milovanovich, the former deputy state coroner who had invited Rebecca and me to his home to hear his candid assessment of the case back in December 2017, was more confident than he had been when he pressed for a prosecution in 2003.

The additional evidence and witnesses in the podcast had bolstered the case, Carl concluded. The lies in the antecedent report written by Chris for police in 1982, and recovered from archives decades later, was a game-changer. A former New South Wales detective, Paul Curby, who examined the statement, told me its deceptions went beyond the obvious. He singled out phrasing which in his opinion belied more dishonesty around the concealment of a violent crime.

Carl agreed to a second interview in which he described the lies as 'another stitch in the overall fabric of this particular case, this circumstantial case, that tends to get stronger and stronger as more additional pieces of evidence are put together'. He heard Bev McNally's description of Chris shoving Lyn into a door frame, and of whipping her with a tea towel; instances of domestic violence, Carl opined, which raised 'the possibility that he was capable of committing violence towards her and possibly even committing a homicide'.

In our first formal interview, the Police Commissioner Mick Fuller told me: 'The officers are looking into some potential new opportunities of gaining evidence that we've identified through the podcast. It's obviously had enormous interest and that has generated some potential fresh leads. We will continue to investigate and, if necessary, continue to dig to get justice for Lyn Dawson. The challenge for the homicide unit and the advice that they provide me is that we need to be absolutely sure that Lyn Dawson is not buried there. I'll go on record in saying that cost has nothing to do with this. There's a perception piece as well that, if we don't dig again – and don't dig in the areas of concern – it will be an open wound for lots of people.'

The files of evidence that had gone missing or been destroyed while under police control; the failure of police through the 1980s; their pigheadedness in 1985 when a formal complaint by Lyn's work colleague Sue Strath set out all the key suspicious facts pointing to a possible murder – all these weird occurrences raised the possibility of police wrongdoing back then. Mick Fuller agreed the circumstances were troubling. In this day and age, he stressed, the notion of a mum being innocently 'missing' would not be accepted by police.

'If it wasn't corruption, then there were some officers who clearly got this case extremely wrong,' he said. 'One thing I will say is that there are plenty of good detectives in the last 150 years of policing that did take reports of missing people and did solve them as homicides. So there's something not right about this case. But the problem is, it took ten years for us to get on that front foot (and determine) that something's wrong. And obviously in ten years, so much evidence was lost.'

Separate to the murder investigation, expanded since the brief of evidence went to the Office of the DPP some four months earlier in April 2018, the probe known as Strike Force Southwood into historical sexual offences was, Mick said, 'progressing extremely well, much thanks to victims that you identified during your investigation and your podcast'.

'It's a case, Hedley, that's captured so many people because the stories almost don't seem believable around teachers sleeping with schoolgirls, taking them to the school dances and the whole issue around Cromer and the community. Now the benefit of that is that you have generated so many fresh leads for us. At the end of the day, all I can do for Lyn Dawson and the family is deliver justice for her, and that has to be my focus.'

Mick Fuller asked whether the podcast series would restart after its break. As I started to explain why we were putting it on hold, he chimed in: 'Because your wife's going to divorce you.'

He was joking and I laughed, uneasily. He was, unknowingly, close to the truth. We spoke about how far we had come since our meeting at Verde.

'If there's any criticism, even if it's in two years time . . . we can both say, hand on heart, that your interest was only ever like mine was, which was justice for Lyn, and you gave us everything,' he said.

The 14th consecutive weekly episode, which included these new interviews with Carl and Mick, was overly long at two hours, but we released it anyway. The alternative was chopping it in two and running the second chunk as a separate episode the following week. But the idea of any more time on the tools left Slade and me cold. We needed it to pause immediately. It would give me time to reply to hundreds of people who were emailing me and pursue some of their promising leads.

I had talked for some time to John Cox, a prolific goal-kicker and Eastern Suburbs rugby union legend who'd been a teammate of Chris Dawson and his brother Paul before the twins switched to rugby league with the Newtown Jets. John was focused on Jenny's story to police of going with Chris in late 1981 to a building on the southern side of the Sydney Harbour Bridge. John believed she had accurately described the old clubhouse of the Newtown Jets, where the contract killer Arthur 'Neddy' Smith and his brother-in-law, Paul Hayward, were once regulars.

'Lesley and I had been to that particular club a few years before and sat at a table with the Dawsons and a lot of our friends from Easts as well . . . and from the people we saw in the club that night, I wouldn't be surprised if that would be a good place to go and look for a hitman. Paul Hayward! He was Neddy Smith's brother-in-law. He was sitting at the table that we were on.'

John's wife, Lesley, had been frowned upon by some of the Eastern Suburbs rugby crowd because of her outspoken opinions for years about Lyn's fate and Chris's hand in it. Lesley hated what she saw as the club's misplaced loyalty. She recalled being unnerved when she went with John and two other friends to a lunch at the house at Bayview, when Lyn was newly gone. A teenager, Jenny, was hosting.

'I was suspicious even then. I felt so uncomfortable going up there that day. I had a really, really horrible feeling even then, being at the house. And at that time, myself and another wife both saw the ring she was wearing.'

The women believed at the time that it looked familiar. It looked like Lyn's ring and they were confused. When I told Lesley that she had seen Lyn's diamond ring, albeit refashioned into a ring which Jenny wore, she gasped.

'Well, I hate him actually, I hate him for what he's got away with; I can't believe that he hasn't been prosecuted,' she said. 'I mean, we looked at him as a friend, as a good person, as an upstanding citizen and yet he's had this mask on all these years. It's just terribly unnerving that he's done this. And he obviously has. It's obvious to all of us.'

I drove south and stopped over for a few days in a rented cottage in foothills near Byron Bay. This gave me time to listen more closely to interviews of recent weeks and to consider options for the two or three episodes which, I hoped, would finish *The Teacher's Pet* series.

I also needed to get my head around a plethora of approaches from smooth-talking executives who said they had listened to the podcast and wanted to turn it into a scripted drama, preferably a TV series. In emails filled with flatter they wrote of the potential for an international blockbuster; a dark story of misogyny and schoolgirl exploitation; domestic violence and the powerlessness of Lyn living with a sociopath in the 1980s; a murder and a failure of the criminal justice system; and journalism and a controversial podcast. The pitches from leading studios, agencies and streaming platforms in

London, New York, Los Angeles and Sydney promised authenticity and respect for Lyn and Jenny.

The Australian acting legend Hugh Jackman contacted me through the footballer Matthew Johns, apologised for the interruption and proceeded to tell me he and a number of his friends had been at the Toronto International Film Festival, listening to Lyn's story. Hugh's questions and observations were well informed; he had followed the Dawson twins through their footballing career and was clearly fascinated by Lyn's case and the sprawling story around murder and the teachers having sex with students. He cautioned me to prepare for an avalanche of schmoozing from interests in Hollywood, as the podcast was getting a lot of attention. Hugh was right.

Over the ensuing weeks, the interest became unmanageable without the efforts of my colleague, *The Australian*'s CEO Nicholas Gray. He and Hugh became my trusted confidantes on the film side. Their advice was invaluable. Hugh wasn't pushing his own barrow or trying to steer me into any arrangement tailored for his needs. His motives revolved purely around wanting to help me ensure that Lyn's story, if it should ever become a scripted drama, would be sensitively handled by professionals with integrity and a deep understanding of the big touchstones in this case.

I knew from the little online research I had done that Hugh understood some of these touchstones. As an eight-year-old living in Sydney, he had come home one day to discover his mother had suddenly gone and moved to England, leaving him to be raised by his father. One day she was there, the next she was up and gone. This abrupt loss must have cut deeply. Hugh was a bit of a junkie about journalism and he had once wanted to be an investigative reporter; it would have been his focus if he had not become a successful actor. Hugh had also seen in others the impacts of teacher–student sexual abuse. Three years before the podcast's release, he closely followed a public inquiry into child sexual abuse by teachers at his old school, the prestigious Knox Grammar where he was school captain in 1986. Some of the abuse was occurring during his schooling there. Three decades later, his former headmaster, the feared and once-revered Dr Ian Paterson, gave evidence at the Royal Commission into Institutional Responses to Child Sexual Abuse and admitted that he had impeded a police investigation into serious allegations of abuse by teachers at Knox Grammar. It was unsurprising that Hugh found parts of Lyn's case, her disappearance, and Cromer High's scandal so relatable.

Pat Jenkins sounded rapt when I told her of Hugh's interest and belief in Lyn's story.

'People have always said, "Oh, if it was a movie, no one would believe it,"' she said.

On arriving in Sydney, where I found another rental cottage a short walk from Chris and Lyn's old home, I met 'Damo'. In January 1982 he was a teenager with a new driving licence and he would go hooning with friends over the school holidays on isolated, unlit McCarrs Creek Road, which snaked through the bushland behind Bayview. It was a haunt for newbie drivers of the Northern Beaches. Damo and his friends favoured Friday nights.

He told me they stopped when they saw a taxi parked on the side of the road. It was between 11 pm and 1 am. When they went to see if the driver was okay, he suddenly walked out of the bush. His shirt was ripped and, in the beam from the headlights, Damo said he and his friends saw scratches on his face and neck. Before angrily telling the boys to get lost, he asked: 'Can't a man have a midnight swim?'

He was a long walk from Pittwater and he hadn't been swimming. Two decades later, Damo started to dwell on the incident when he first heard about the disappearance of Lyn, and the suspicions of police and coroners. By working out when he gained his driving licence, Damo put the date at a time close to Lyn's disappearance. He contacted me during the podcast as he believed the man he saw that night looked like Chris Dawson in photographs from that time. Damo said he once went to police as he feared that in 1982 he had chanced on Chris disposing of Lyn's body in the bush. The police weren't interested.

He remembered the location: a bend in the road near Crystal Creek.

After first hearing from him, I emailed Pat and Greg and asked: 'Do you recall whether Chris ever had any connection with a taxi? Such as driving part-time or having a friend with a taxi?'

They were unaware of any link. But Lyn's cousin Allyson Jennings told me that back in January 2014, a guy called 'Damo' had written in to the Facebook page for Lyn. Allyson forwarded his email. Damo told the same story then as he was telling me in 2018. The consistency counted for something.

It was a long shot but stranger things had happened. We drove there and spent several hours traipsing in the bush. He wielded a metal detector while I did some shallow digging. A friend and supervising producer for the ABC's *Australian Story*, Rebecca Latham, was intrigued when I told her about Damo while she was organising filming for an upcoming program. We went back to McCarrs Creek Road with a spade from her shed. There were literally millions of locations in which a body could be concealed. The chances of success were infinitesimal in the absence of rock-solid information, but this tiniest possibility spurred us forward.

In the meantime, Dan Poole had obtained a secret warrant to capture increasingly agitated telephone conversations of Chris and Paul Dawson. Their exchanges were carefully transcribed for the police brief of evidence.

The twin brothers were furious on 9 September 2018 after the Nine Network's *60 Minutes* program. I had told the reporter Allison Langdon as we walked on the beach of Pittwater at low tide that Chris was, in my opinion 'a despicable person ... severely narcissistic ... lying to himself, lying to his daughters, his friends, his family and he has been for a long time'.

Bev McNally, the former Cromer High student who had talked to me in an earlier episode about her babysitting in 1980 and seeing Chris being violent towards Lyn, was also interviewed by *60 Minutes*. The telephone conversation revealed:

Paul: 'Hedley Thomas has set himself up as prosecutor, judge and jury; didn't mention anything about the evidence that Lyn left of her own accord. That Bev McNally is a fucking idiot.'

Chris: 'Yeah, we didn't get her back because she was a bloody hopeless babysitter.'

Paul: 'How can Hedley Thomas go on TV there and just lie? He goes on TV and says how you should be charged . . .'

Chris: 'He thinks there's enough proof of it. And there's contradictions in my statements, or something.'

Paul: 'So he knows more than the DPP?'

Chris: 'Yeah. Do you reckon I should ring Peter now?'

Paul: 'Yeah. Yep.'

Chris: 'Jeez, they keep photos of me, don't they?'

Paul: 'Chris, Hedley Thomas has decided you're guilty.'

Chris: 'Yeah.'

Paul: 'He's going to have you convicted by the media.'

Chris: 'The guy's never met me. He's never sat down and talked to me, you know.'

Paul: 'Yeah.'

Chris: 'So what's he judging me on?'

The twins talked again that night after Chris called his brother Peter, the solicitor.

Paul: 'How can a fucking journalist, Chris, go on national television and basically say that you're a murderer and you should be charged?'

Chris: 'Yeah.'

Paul: 'That . . . the DPP has got it wrong?'

Chris: 'Yeah.'

Paul: 'How can he say they've got it wrong, when they've got the whole – all of the facts, and they're – they look at all the facts.'

Chris: 'Yes. Yeah.'

A short time later, after they acknowledged the call was probably being intercepted, Chris sent me a special message.

Chris: 'Hedley, you, you're a fucking wanker. If they want to, the police want to pass that on to Hedley Thomas.'

Paul: 'Yeah.'

Chris: 'You're a wanker.'

Paul: 'The way that they present the truth, yeah.'

Chris: 'Tried to get me to be a part of his podcast, telling me he'd give me a fair hearing and all the rest of it. Total bullshit.'

Paul: 'Yeah.'

Chris: 'He's come to his own conclusion I'm narcissistic. They keep bloody using the word "narcissistic". Bloody hell.'

In another intercepted call, Chris mentioned the support he was receiving from three key women in his life: his daughter with Jenny, his youngest daughter with Lyn, and the adult daughter of his third wife, Susan. But Chris had not heard from Shanelle. Paul mentioned ABC TV's promotion of its imminent program, which Rebecca Latham was still busy producing.

Paul: 'I've just brought the *Australian Story* thing up on the TV guide. It's called "The Teacher's Wife – The case of missing Sydney mother, Lyn Dawson, has captivated audiences around the world since the release of the new podcast".'

Chris: 'He's just got a real machinery behind him, hasn't he, promoting his bloody podcast?'

Paul: 'All these different channels and everything else, all wanting to jump on the bandwagon and show everybody. But they don't want to talk about both sides.'

Some of the phone-tapped conversations must have sounded funny to the detectives when they heard the clear audio. Chris complained to a hapless tradesman: 'I get more publicity than bloody Karl Stefanovic's marriage break up. What's his name? The poor old politician? Barnaby Joyce! I get more bloody concentration than those two together.'

Tradesman: 'So, well, Chris, I gather they're trying to convict you, obviously?'

Chris: 'Yeah, that's what they've been trying to do, because, look, what happened was my, the wife who left was a really nice person to me, and it seemed out of character for her to just take off and not have contact with people.'

After accusing Jenny of lying to police about his conduct, Chris took aim at *The Teacher's Pet* again.

Chris: 'Mate, there's a whole podcast out at present, 14 episodes, this guy's made a friggin' fortune . . . all you people buying this stuff, you're just buying a bloody fiction. This guy has embellished and . . . his whole motivation is to make more money and make it as sensational and as sex-scandal as he can make it.'

Tradesman: 'Yeah. No, it's not good. It's not good mate.'

In a call with his brother Gary, they spoke of strains on family and the harassment by journalists. Chris 'felt responsible for all the shit' his siblings and their loved ones were going through.

Chris told Gary: 'Why should the whole family be penalised for my stupid . . . 'cause I had a fucking affair, but married the bitch.'

Back in police headquarters, Mick Fuller had strongly hinted at the inevitability of a dig. Rumours were flying in the community. I saw Dan Poole at the Avalon Beach surf club where he wanted to meet for another handover of more audio files. Dan had said nothing of a pending search. No surprises there.

Two days after the *60 Minutes* program aired, a convoy of vehicles with heavy equipment rolled into Gilwinga Drive. It was early morning on 12 September.

The ABC's most prominent current affairs anchor, Leigh Sales, summarised the breaking news: 'There's been a major development in the case of a Sydney woman who has been missing for 36 years. Police are now digging up the former property owned by Lyn Dawson and her husband Chris.'

Residents of Gilwinga Drive were pleasantly surprised. Finally, a proper and extensive dig at Chris and Lyn's old house was starting.

'And everyone's just really hoping,' Sarah Bunning, who lived a few doors down, told me. 'Everyone's convinced he's done it. They're just hoping they'll find something.'

In the weeks before the official dig, a multi-millionaire listener wanted the house's owners to sell it to him for the market price. He wanted to turn over the entire block to look for Lyn. There were high public expectations of her body being there.

As the story of the dig went to the top of news websites and radio and TV bulletins, journalists crowded around the head of the Homicide Squad, Scott Cook. He was sharply dressed in a blue suit and striped tie. Scott would not be getting his hands dirty at the dig, but his words cut through: 'We're here today conducting a police operation in regards to the Lynette Dawson murder. We're here for approximately five days. We're searching a number of areas around the property.'

Scott's language was unequivocal. He had dispensed with the usual key words – 'alleged' and 'suspected' – when referring to a possible murder. The sound of jack-hammers and rock-cutting machinery reverberated down the driveway. Even the mating cicadas went unheard for a while. Scott described four areas which would be searched; three in the backyard, and the fourth around the pool. The dig would, he pledged, be more extensive than the previous effort. It would rely on new technologies to revisit 'a number of anomalies in the ground'.

'This is all about getting justice for Lyn and we need to put our best foot forward,' he said. 'We've got a good understanding of this particular property. It is a complex block of land but it's largely rock and so digging is not easy.'

Our defamation lawyer John-Paul Cashen texted me in the afternoon: 'Were you at the dig today? I presumed you were operating the bobcat (digging machine).'

But I had deliberately stayed away from Bayview. Journalists were not permitted to walk onto the property. Sarah Bunning and her neighbour friend Peter Selge kept me informed. Another neighbour used a drone over Lyn and Chris's house and shared the footage with me.

When David Murray spoke to Pat Jenkins that morning, she said she was feeling 'very anxious'.

'My mind's always out at Bayview,' Pat said. 'I'm staying in all day, just in case.'

Sue Strath, trekking in Italy's Dolomite Alps, texted: 'Fingers and toes crossed on the Bayview dig. Sure they will find her.'

Chapter 36

Digging

Before and after the dig people in Sydney who were teenagers when Lyn disappeared had become determined to do whatever they could to help me. A former part-time 'trolley boy' at Dee Why Coles supermarket told me he vividly recalled having been roughly accosted at the age of 16 by a jealous Chris in a dimly lit car park for having asked his young co-worker, Jenny, on an innocent date to a disco.

'And he shoved me against the wall and said words to the effect of "just stay away from her", and I was sort of looking at him going "stay away from who?", and I had no connection as to who he was in relation to Jenny, but I did by the time I'd got over the shock . . . because his brother taught me at Manly Boys High.'

He was intimidated and scared by the confrontation with the muscular, towering Chris. There would be no more teenage flirting with her.

A swimmer, Maya Sydney, who lived near Northbridge Baths and swam there often, proved to be a brilliant amateur sleuth. She not only remembered the Dawson twins during their days as part-time lifesavers there, she had found a woman, Janet, who once worked in the kiosk and would have been present for a phone call from someone purporting to be Lyn on the afternoon of Saturday, 9 January. About 3 pm on that day, Chris had walked from the kiosk to tell his visiting friend, Phil Day, and Lyn's mother, Helena, that Lyn had phoned the kiosk and told Chris she needed some time away and wouldn't be back for several days.

'It's weird that I've still got this diary,' Janet, who was a teenager back then, told me. 'I think I'm just so embarrassed that I have to shred it because it's got all the boys that I had crushes on. But how bizarre, I must be some weird anal hoarder that I've still got the damn thing.'

I urged her to keep the diary intact and in a safe place. Janet read to me her handwritten entry from Saturday, 9 January 1982.

'Worked in the shop. 8 to 5.30. Didn't get any money because Col (the manager) left at 12 and as usual Chris never pays.'

Unsurprisingly, Janet didn't remember any phone call she answered at the baths. She was annoyed that police didn't ask her back in 1982 when she might have remembered such a call. I agreed with the police view: if there was a call for Chris, it was from someone other than Lyn as she was already dead.

Listening to the podcast episodes had affected Janet in other ways. She started thinking about Northbridge Baths as a possible burial site and went back to take photographs in sandy areas where digging would not have been difficult. It was not an unusual phenomenon in this case; people were strangely attracted to the idea of Lyn being buried in the areas they knew well.

An artist, Kristin Hardiman, had been in touch to describe meeting a doting Lyn when she commissioned portraits of her two daughters in late 1981. When Kristin's artwork was completed in mid-January 1982, she called the house and Chris answered.

'He said that he was Lyn's husband and she'd gone away and didn't want them anymore, and I asked him if he'd like to see them and he said, "No. Don't want to see them",' she told me. 'I remember it so clearly because she was really excited about having them done.'

My escape to Sydney was meaningful for a more important reason than fresh interviews. It put Ruth and me back on track. When Ruth flew to Sydney, we went to the Northern Beaches for a stay in a bungalow near the waves at Avalon Beach of a few days, followed by a trip to the Blue Mountains with two longtime friends

Martin and Alison Leonard. Bush walking, talking and avoiding the commitments of the podcast helped a lot. We were taking tentative but positive steps to get our marriage back on track.

Hours after Ruth flew home, the news we were most dreading after six days of police digging at Bayview came. I had just cleared Sydney's outskirts for the drive back to Brisbane when Grant Williams, the NSW Police media manager, told me the search was a bust. A formal police statement noted: 'Police have not located Lynette's remains or any items of interest to the investigation.'

The 'soft soil' outside bedroom windows turned out to be soft only close to the surface. There was too much rock beneath it for a grave. On the house's other side, the ground was excavated the length of the pool to about two metres. As a result of a relatively superficial dig around the pool 18 years earlier, the ground there produced a garment described by police forensics experts at that time as a cardigan that had been slashed multiple times with a knife. There were high hopes in 2000 that it was Lyn's; police speculated she had been wearing it when stabbed to death. Damian Loone even took it to the United States for DNA testing in a specialised forensics laboratory, however, the results were inconclusive. But in the far more extensive and deeper dig spanning six days of September 2018 and costing more than $1 million, the earth around the pool yielded only dirt and rocks. We were gutted by the outcome.

Reflecting on the depressing news, I took a turn-off on a whim to Lake Munmorah, the place where Paul and Marilyn Dawson said they were holidaying in a caravan with their girls on 8 and 9 January 1982. It was an easy and short detour from the Pacific Highway, which Chris had driven on his way to and from South West Rocks to collect Jenny and bring her to Bayview within a couple of days of Lyn's disappearance.

Chris had never been questioned about whether he had also detoured into the caravan park. It would have been normal for him to see his twin brother. While cruising slowly around the few public facilities of Lake Munmorah, on the edge of huge and uninhabited conservation areas, swamp and wetlands, I imagined Chris in his

Corona station wagon, driving through the night. I wondered whether he would have risked having Lyn's body wrapped up in something in the car, pending rural burial. At this pivotal high-stakes point in his life, would he have driven the short distance to see Paul?

My next stop was Greg and Merilyn's house near Newcastle. As Merilyn put the kettle on, detective Dan Poole thoughtfully telephoned them with news of the dig being called off. He sounded genuinely disappointed. We all were, bitterly, but Greg and Merilyn put on brave faces.

It was another three and a half hours on the road to South West Rocks. Another must-see locale, circled in red highlighter on a sketchy murder map in my mind. It was Chris's destination, too; the holiday spot he sped to, to whisk Jenny away from her surprised school friends and back to Bayview. One of those friends who knew Chris from school had told police in her statement in 1998 that she saw the teacher arrive in the morning.

'Chris appeared nervous being around us . . . he appeared strange and agitated. He certainly wasn't his charming flirtatious self that I remembered him to be,' she said.

In a cottage which was once home to the warden of the historic Trial Bay Gaol, I opened one of the saddest emails. Pat Jenkins seemed broken by the failure of the dig.

'I was so exhausted last night I could hardly walk up the stairs,' she wrote. 'Today I am just immensely sad . . . with the realisation and acceptance that we will most likely now never know where Lyn is. How fitting it would have been to have finally been able to lay her to rest.'

Pat never wavered in her certainty that Chris killed Lyn. She was appalled that Nicholas Cowdery, the retired DPP who oversaw the repeated decisions to not prosecute, had suggested on the ABC's *Australian Story* just days earlier that Lyn was alive. Two experienced coroners had already found that Lyn had died. In 2001, a formal death certificate had been issued.

But Nicholas Cowdery told the program: 'Without a body, without knowing first of all whether in fact she is dead, without knowing secondly, if she is dead, how she died, it's very hard to mount a case of a reasonable prospect of conviction just on motive and the undefined existence of means and opportunity. That makes it very weak. Lyn Dawson disappeared and that really is as far as I can take it in my own mind. In mounting the discussion, very little consideration has been given to Chris Dawson and his position. He is either somebody responsible for his wife's death – or somebody who was deserted by his wife.'

Pat told me that in a meeting with Shanelle before the program, her father looked her "dead-straight in the eye".

'He didn't fidget and he said, "I have never harmed your mother or laid a finger on your mother". He's a very accomplished liar.'

From a high part of South West Rocks overlooking the northern reach of the Macleay River, Pat told me, I would see a dwelling perched above Stuart's Point. It was where she had lived happily with her late husband, Ron, and their toddler son, David.

'Just a couple of houses in the distance, surrounded by bush,' Pat added.

This was another odd connection. I realised for the first time that Pat was close when Chris arrived at South West Rocks to pluck Jenny from a camp site. Lyn must have been dead. Chris had told Pat and her mother that Lyn said she just needed some time away, on the Central Coast, with friends. As I walked in bushland near secluded beaches and sandy ground, easy for digging, I wondered whether Chris's claims about Lyn having gone to the Central Coast were true. Had he buried her body within a short distance of where he would meet Jenny? Out with the old and in with the new.

'I didn't know until I read your note how close to South West Rocks you were – just a few kilometres from where Jenny was holidaying and where Chris came,' I told Pat.

Pat preferred not to dwell aloud on the days either side of her sister's disappearance. She had happier memories of going with Ron to the town's local motel for the chef's lunch special, freshly caught lobster, as David devoured a Vegemite sandwich in a highchair.

Chapter 37

Arrested

Rebecca Hazel steered her car on a beachside road through Dee Why. The sun shone on mothers pushing prams on their way to breakfast cafes. We were driving north to meet Lyn's family and friends at Long Reef Golf Club near the start of a walk in honour of her life. Ruth had come to Sydney with me and Rebecca had kindly picked us up near the Manly Ferry stop on the last Sunday in September.

'We're coming up to Jen's favourite cafe,' Rebecca said. She was still deeply distressed at the breakdown of their friendship.

'I wonder if she'll be at the walk today,' Ruth added.

We turned in unison and, for the first time in real life, I saw the other woman in this tragic case, Jenny, the teacher's pet. She was standing at the takeaway counter and smiling with the guy serving her. Rebecca decided soon after that she would be unable to do the walk. She was suffering a migraine.

Bev McNally had worked like a trojan to organise the dignified event. Hundreds of people who turned up to walk together wore pink and chatted easily with whoever shuffled alongside.

Greg Simms told the throng: 'Lyn would have been 70 last week so this is a fitting tribute to her for her 70th birthday. I know if she was here, she would be here – but we all know the truth.'

Shanelle, who came with her daughter, witnessed a public outpouring of goodwill and compassion from strangers for her, the

Simms family and her mother. The trail to Long Reef Headland lookout was green and picturesque; a zephyr of wind came off the adjacent Pacific Ocean.

The Seven News Reporter Robert Ovadia in his piece to camera spoke of 'a sea of pink', and said: 'It is somewhat appalling to say a person's entire life slipped through the cracks but obviously that is exactly what happened to Lyn Dawson all those years ago. Police acknowledge a shoddy investigation played its part and they are doing everything they can today to make up for it.'

The presence of Ben Fordham, who brought his little boy, demonstrated a personal commitment he had shown Lyn with the microphone at 2GB; this was bigger than work. His colleague Chris Smith found and interviewed Judy Brown and her husband, Ray, whose disclosures were insightful.

'And one of the most interesting people I've met on this walk is actually Chris Dawson's cousin, Judy,' Chris said.

'Give me an idea of Lyn's devotion to those two little girls,' Chris asked her.

She replied: 'Okay, we knew Lyn very well growing up and I knew how much trouble she and Chris had to go to, to have those two little girls, and I knew that she was absolutely devoted to them and would never have left them for a day. Finally, I think we'll get justice for her, I'm very confident. And I think we'll see that for the family, yes.'

When I recorded an interview with Judy and Ray Brown some days later, they revealed that they suspected foul play in the beginning, when Chris told his cousin Judy that Lyn had left. Judy was closer to Chris and Paul than any of the other cousins. They were only 11 months apart in age and they went to teachers' college together, and Judy regularly went to watch them play football.

She and Ray exchanged Christmas cards with the twin brothers, and Paul would write a poem once a year to acknowledge everyone in the extended family. Going on the walk to acknowledge Lyn, and then talking to Chris Smith and me about their longtime suspicions, was courageous because it meant they were severing all ties with Team Dawson.

Judy told me: 'I do remember Marilyn, and Peter's then wife Lynelle, talking together, and I was there, and I remember Marilyn saying to Lynelle, "You know, Chris has had Jenny at home sitting on his lap while Lyn is there."'

Ray said: 'When we heard that Jenny had moved in, we said, "What's happened to Lyn?" And straight away, we knew something had happened.'

For the umpteenth time in the investigation of Lyn's case I realised that many people with suspicions of foul play do not go to police. I asked Judy if she found it difficult to go to police about her cousin in the 1980s, when she knew there was no serious investigation on foot.

'I couldn't really see that I had any evidence to offer, I suppose,' Judy said.

'We thought, "Well, why isn't anything being done about it?" We always wondered. I thought her family surely have told them everything.'

Judy and her sister, Patricia, told me that Chris Dawson's mother, Joan, had quietly asked her nieces, "You don't think Chris has done it, do you?"

These were very rare and private conversations. Lyn's disappearance was usually unmentionable; a taboo subject across the extended clan. Everyone trod warily around it.

Two further episodes would complete the podcast series. I wrote the chapters from an apartment on the sand at the Gold Coast's Main Beach. The building was a stone's throw from where I had lived with my mother, Diana, and my three sisters in the early 1980s. A dedicated supporter and friend, Katie Page, who owned the property, wanted me to rest and recuperate in this familiar place near the waves.

Katie's generous offer made a rejuvenating difference. Her financial support as CEO of Harvey Norman, the original sponsor of the podcast, made this costly project financially viable; and now she was trying to prevent its journalist from unravelling before the end.

The crashing of waves outside the apartment made it easy to sleep, but the symphony of ocean noise presented more problems for Slade Gibson when he got the audio files of the new interviews I was doing, including with more former schoolgirls who had come forward, from Sydney and the Gold Coast.

The news cycle returned again to Nicholas Cowdery, but this time it was for a program featuring his role in the controversial prosecution of Keli Lane in 2010 for killing her baby. The Crown's case was wholly circumstantial. There was no body. The alleged murder had occurred 14 years before she was charged. To Lyn's family, police and me, Lyn's case was significantly stronger. Keli Lane was convicted.

In Keli Lane's 2010 trial, there was evidence of her sex life on the Northern Beaches before, aged 21, she delivered her fourth baby. Nicholas Cowdery remarked upon her sexual activity in an ABC TV interview in October 2018. He opined that while Keli Lane was not a threat to the general community, 'she seemed to be a bit of a risk to the virile young male portion of the community'. The former DPP, who had twice rejected coroners' recommendations to prosecute Chris Dawson, then chuckled at casting her as a sex maniac.

'Not acceptable, no excuses for it. Apologies to Keli Lane particularly and women everywhere,' Tracey McLeod Howe, the CEO of White Ribbon Australia, immediately responded.

Nicholas Cowdery apologised and resigned as chairman of the anti–domestic violence organisation.

I was checking in and talking regularly with Pat, Greg and Merilyn. They were intrigued by the ongoing interest of TV and film studios who were still pitching to be chosen to dramatise Lyn's life and death. Pat and Greg were supportive of the idea as long as it would be done tastefully, and *The Australian*'s CEO Nicholas Gray asked me to take a week out to meet the shortlisted parties in Hollywood, London and New York. Lyn wasn't a celebrity or a politician or a movie star or a sports champion.

The medium of the podcast had taken her story around the world, touching millions of people. Pat said her sister, a humble woman, 'would never have believed it'.

'We were a very ordinary family growing up in the 50s and 60s without a thought that anything evil could affect our lives, and yet it did, so dramatically and tragically with the loss of Lyn,' Pat told me. 'I'm sure even though her private life is being so exposed she would be pleased if the telling of what happened to her helps young people at risk from sexual predators, and helps women who are the victims of domestic violence to seek help. The consequences of not doing so are all too terrible.'

On Tuesday, 4 December, I told Pat the 16th and final episode of *The Teacher's Pet* was well advanced. My partner in crime, Slade, had been working wonders in the studio.

But Pat was impatient. She willed the Office of the DPP to finish reviewing the police brief of evidence which had been provided back in April 2018. It had been with the DPP's lawyers for eight months. It had bulged as new leads and witnesses emerged during the series.

'They can't be much longer, surely,' Pat told me with a note of exasperation.

'They've had it for so long. It's our last chance.'

Ruth and I were at home in Brookfield the following morning, Wednesday, 5 December 2018 when everything changed.

I was, typically, running late to get to Slade's studio to record more narration in his padded booth for the final episode. I had heard nothing for weeks from Mick Fuller or Dan Poole or Grant Williams.

My mobile lit up. It was David Murray. But his voice had changed. Instead of a jocular "Hi mate, how's it going?", my close friend, tireless colleague and brother-in-law sounded strained. Worryingly serious. I now realise it was a reaction to shock.

'Chris Dawson has just been arrested by police for the murder of Lyn,' he said.

Part 4

Trials

Chapter 38

Best Defence is Offence

December 2018 to June 2019

Merilyn and Greg were ebullient after *The Betoota Advocate*, a satirical news website, reported on the arrest: 'Paul Dawson, twin brother of Chris Dawson, has arrested himself today so he can be with his brother once again.

'Not wanting to be away from his brother or risk people forgetting that he is the alpha-twin, Paul Dawson has now handed himself in and in return, hopes to be able to share a cell with his twin brother.'

The story went viral and was shared thousands of times by Australians who had become invested in the saga and now appreciated some light relief after a roller-coaster with a podcast and months of frustration over the injustices they heard.

Merilyn told me, 'Hope you are laughing. We are just picking ourselves up off the floor from rolling around laughing!'

Shanelle and I had built a trusting relationship since we first met in Hervey Bay in January 2018. We spent hours on the telephone, often as her delightful daughter Lala played nearby. But Shanelle had forfeited her privacy. Everyone wanted a piece of her. She had navigated a path through a media maelstrom when TV networks were hounding her for interviews. Shanelle continued to honour her mother while refusing to say publicly if she regarded her father as a murderer. When *60 Minutes* journalist Allison Langdon asked the hard questions, Shanelle deflected. But the unspoken truth was that Shanelle had been very confident, before we met, that her father had murdered her mother, and she became certain of his guilt as she heard the mounting evidence.

Her stepbrother was furious with her for talking to me for the podcast and stories in *The Australian*. She forwarded me the scathing message he had sent her. 'Reporters aren't going to go out and solve the case based on the shoddy memory of people from 40 years ago and outdated and archaic 70s police work.'

Shanelle was cut off by her sister too, and almost all of the Dawson side of the family. She told me she wanted her father's guilt to be confirmed by the criminal justice system although that was never going to mend things.

After her father's arrest, Shanelle said she was 'feeling quite strong . . . sad for my dad but knowing it's necessary for progress'. She envisaged freedom 'as a result of dissolving lies and the heavy burdens I've been carrying for 37 years'. Shanelle warmly thanked me for for tackling the case, and she thanked Ruth for being the 'wonder woman by your side'.

Shanelle held out hope that someone who knew her father's secrets 'will crack and we can find where my mum is buried'.

I told her that I had just finished watching the evening TV news reports and, for the first time, felt sorry for her father. 'He looks stoic and very alone. Susan and Paul are nowhere to be seen. That's sad.'

Ten days after Dawson was charged with murder, Ruth and I headed away with Alexander and Sarah for a long-planned family holiday in Europe. On the second flight, I constantly refreshed my laptop's internet browser for up-to-the-minute news and emailed an update to Shanelle.

'Greetings from 36,000 feet over China. Your dad has just been granted bail. And the magistrate said, "I consider that the crown case is not a weak case." Okay, back to the family holiday.'

I did not know the lawyer responsible for Chris Dawson's success-ful application for bail but Peter Lavac, who had decades of trial experience in defending and prosecuting murderers, warned me that Greg Walsh would fight tooth-and-nail.

Immensely experienced and highly respected by judges and other lawyers for his commitment to criminal law, Walsh projected an unshakeable belief in the innocence of every client who darkened his doorstep, from alleged pedophile priests to coldblooded wife-killers who exploited schoolgirls for sex, as good criminal defence lawyers must do.

In front of a media throng outside a Sydney court in December 2018 immediately after a bail hearing, Walsh smoothly posited the theory that Lyn had started a new life and was living happily in some unknown hideaway.

'Can I just say this. Whilst it seems most unusual that a lady, with the greatest respect for Lyn Dawson, would disappear and not have any contact with her children, I mean that's obviously a live issue, [but] it has happened. I am aware of another case where a woman disappeared for 60 years and her daughter only found out that she'd gone to New Zealand, had married and had had a family, after she died in 2002. And her daughter did not know where her mother had gone for over 60 years. It does happen.'

A journalist asked, 'So does Mr Dawson believe his wife is still alive?'

Walsh responded, 'I haven't particularly asked him that question and he doesn't know. He's naturally, I think, anxious and stressed about the situation. He seems quite a reserved sort of man to me but he's doing the best in these circumstances, holding up.'

The solicitor had worked through the night to prepare for the hearing. He was well known to reporters for his personable style and they accorded him due respect.

'One of the things that concerns me is that this man, Chris Dawson, is entitled to the presumption of innocence. He will plead not guilty, he strenuously asserts his innocence. He should be afforded that fundamental right.'

When asked if it would be difficult for Dawson to get a fair trial, Walsh, who had heard none of the podcast at that stage, replied, 'It is of concern that some of that reporting, with respect, is rather perva- sive and it's coming from an ideological perspective that he must be guilty. That is a worry because it can distort peoples' memories. There are genuine concerns that the media have a particular ideological view that the man must be guilty. That's just not right.'

He highlighted the significant delays in the case and the inadequacies in the investigation by police, adding that after Lyn's disappearance, 'she was observed by a number of people. Unfortunately, two of those people are deceased.'

He then raised what I regarded as another red herring – supposed Bankcard transactions of which there was no record, purportedly made by Lyn in retail stores on the Northern Beaches in January 1982 after her disappearance. The illogicality was always obvious; if, for argument's sake, Lyn had been alive and visiting friends on the Central Coast, as Chris claimed she told him, why would she return to buy a couple of items of clothing, contact nobody and then never use the credit card again? She couldn't drive. If she had been alive and needed clothing, why wouldn't she use her credit card to make purchases in stores on the Central Coast?

But Walsh hammered the point. 'Those transactions, regrettably, were never investigated by the police. So there were aspects of the investigation that have prejudiced Mr Dawson and the police should've conducted proper investigations and got witness statements at the time, which would've indicated probably she was alive.'

He disclosed that when he played rugby for Wests as a young man, he had come up against the flashy blond twins, Chris and Paul Dawson, when they were with Easts.

'They were obviously very talented. It's just ironic. Six degrees of separation,' he told my colleague from *The Australian*, Sam Buckingham-Jones.

Greg Walsh must have given confidence to almost everyone he represented. His sacred belief in a presumption of innocence for everyone to avoid miscarriages of justice is admirable, and one I agreed with. But privately, I wished Dawson would roll over. I willed him to plead guilty and go quietly to spend the rest of his life in prison, sparing everyone the challenge of proving his guilt in a legal fight which could take years and exact a heavy toll.

We would learn later that the case Greg cited of the mother who had disappeared voluntarily to start a new life in New Zealand was well known to the Dawson family; she was the mother of Peter Dawson's first wife and had vanished in the 1960s. Cynically, I suspected that Chris's knowledge of it possibly contributed to the story I believed he had concocted about Lyn.

'She did not contact her family, did not contact the kids, did not contact her husband,' Peter Dawson told a journalist for a story about his mother-in-law, a woman he has never known.

'We don't know where Lyn is,' he concluded. 'I hope she is living happily somewhere in the world.'

Greg Walsh added, 'It happens all the time.'

Every time I took a call from Peter Lavac after the arrest, he passed on some new tidbit or warning which left me cold. Avoiding him became tempting. 'Your podcast got Dawson charged over Lyn's murder,' Peter told me, 'but it's your podcast, with all the interviews and research that you did, which will be used by Walsh to set him free.

'Greg Walsh is a killer. He'll want every audio recording, text message, email and document you've generated. When he's across the detail in all of them, he'll have you cross-examined in court by a top silk who will set out to show how you destroyed the reputation of an innocent man. He's going to put your journalism on trial and try to avoid a murder trial altogether.'

When I could put aside Peter's warnings, it was tempting to feel good about things. Not smug but satisfied. We had scaled a mountain and contributed to something few people would have thought possible after 37 years and no body.

While in Berlin in the days before Christmas 2018, Rebecca Hazel gave me a heads-up about some of the decisive steps police were taking now that the case was before the court.

Rebecca was out buying ingredients for a festive fruit cake when two detectives paid a surprise visit to her Northern Beaches home to ask for the handover of all her working files. They sought paper and electronic drafts of the manuscripts for her unpublished book, jottings and interview notes, emails and text messages with me and others, and material she had collected in her research into the Dawson case over the previous seven years. I should not have been surprised, given all of the feedback from Peter Lavac.

Michael Barnes had also told me over a few beers that I should anticipate such an action by the police, adding that if he were the lawyer defending Dawson, he would want everything. The ramifications of such a sweeping disclosure troubled me greatly as an investigative journalist who strived to protect sources.

My files included unsolicited, deeply private messages from women confiding stories of the abuse and domestic violence they had suffered. They shared these experiences to help me better understand what they believed Lyn and Jenny had also suffered. I believed they would have been distraught about it ending up in the hands of police, administrative staff and Dawson's lawyers. Indeed, I had assured listeners at the end of each episode that they could contact me 'confidentially'. I had wanted members of the public to come forward with information which might help the podcast's murder investigation.

My appeal in the podcast for help had worked too well. The disclosures of many people about their own experiences, which had no direct relationship with anything concerning Lyn and Chris, had poured into my email inbox and the Messenger function of my Facebook profile. They were irrelevant to the police charge that Chris had killed Lyn in January 1982. The preliminary view of John-Paul Cashen was that as they were not, strictly speaking, confidential sources for something I had reported, I could not rely on the journalist's rule to withhold information which might identify them.

After the initial euphoria following Dawson's arrest and his extradition to Sydney to be charged with murder, I intuited subtle changes in some of the key people with whom I had enjoyed an easy and candid rapport over the previous 12 months work on Lyn's case.

There was an unexpected coolness. I couldn't put my finger on why I was feeling slightly distanced. The penny dropped when Shanelle texted 'to let you know that apparently you're a witness now and that's why people including myself have been requested not to talk with you'.

On my return from holidays in January 2019, we decided to handle the demands from police, Dawson's legal team and the Office of the DPP in stages. The audio files would be provided first on flash drives, which we handed to Detective Senior Constable Heath Silvester and Detective Senior Constable Rowena Clancy, who had crossed the border to meet John-Paul and me at the Southport Police Station in February 2019. Heath, clean-cut and supremely fit, bore an uncanny likeness to a much younger Chris Dawson, and Rowena momentarily got the giggles when I mentioned it.

The officer who had led the reinvestigation of Chris Dawson, Detective Senior Constable Dan Poole, sought a statement from me, as well as a document with 'the details of persons spoken to, date or approximate date, reference to the audio file, reference to any documents received from or given to the person'.

Listening again to some of the interviews and conversations I had recorded, I berated myself for my candour. These files would, I knew, be transcribed by police and copied to the defence team, in accordance with the Crown's obligations for disclosure to an accused.

Nobody, except me, Slade and my interviewee, had heard the audio not used in the podcast.

While talking to Pat Jenkins on the telephone, for example, I had described the former DPP for New South Wales, Nicholas Cowdery, as 'a knucklehead' for having seriously suggested that Lyn might still be alive, somewhere. My cavalier remark about him, though never published, would give Dawson's legal team an easy line of courtroom attack to characterise me as a journalist who showed disdain for a very senior lawyer, a pillar of the criminal justice system.

In another call, I had mentioned to Pat that I was getting a lot of details and leads from my interviews with her and others because my conversations were significantly longer than those the witnesses had had with detectives many years earlier. I was trying to reassure Pat about the thoroughness of the podcast investigation and my hope that it would make a difference but the remark would be used as evidence of my disdain for the police.

When Dawson returned to Sydney for another court appearance in mid-February 2019, there was another impromptu media conference in which Greg Walsh's comments made the legal defence's strategy crystal-clear.

'There will be an application in this case to examine at a committal hearing certain witnesses, and in particular, Mr Hedley Thomas,' Walsh told journalists outside court. 'I require proper disclosure by the Crown as to all the interviews, including the raw material such as audio recordings and transcripts of all the persons, potential witnesses and witnesses that he interviewed. They're vital in this case.'

The Seven Network's crack reporter Chris Reason asked, 'How significant is it, Greg, that Mr Thomas will be called in this case?'

Walsh replied, 'I think it is very significant. I think he has played a very central role in the circumstances in which Christopher Dawson is charged. He well knew that police were investigating this very serious matter. And he interviewed witnesses in the full knowledge that they had previously been actual witnesses at the inquest. And he knew the risk of contaminating them and affecting the reliability of the evidence. As a very experienced journalist, that was the forensic judgment that he undertook in this case.'

Reason asked, 'So he could have jeopardised your client's case?'

'Not only the accused's case,' Walsh said, 'but the prosecution case, because what he's done, in my understanding, has been to impact upon the reliability of witnesses. Now, when you discuss what a particular witness's memory is and then do it on multiple occasions and then give them access to what other witnesses are saying in the very same case, I think it's a matter of common sense that the risk of contamination and collusion is a very real one in the context of modern communications as well, here.'

Watching the footage of the media conference, and seeing how Walsh was managing the journalists and creating a new narrative about the purported poison of the podcast, my hopes for an early result were dashed. Although I had no direct connection to the events of 1982, the case was being cast as the journalist versus the alleged killer. Peter Lavac's early predictions were on the money.

Greg Walsh also took the opportunity to paint Chris as a blameless victim. A model father and husband. 'He's very apprehensive at times. He's a very quiet and very reserved man. A good family man. It's a very daunting thing to know that you've got a huge team of investigators and Crown prosecutors against you. I think he's a bit overwhelmed by that. I have a strong belief in his innocence, and I'm determined to achieve justice for him.'

Walsh genuinely believed that Chris had a pathway to success, and his relationships with journalists saw some of them run legitimate stories which were good for his client, even after seven months of overwhelmingly bad publicity.

Having handed over 100 gigabytes of audio in January 2019, I spent months sorting and copying thousands of emails, text messages and communications over WhatsApp and Facebook with people who had provided information for the podcast. Everything that had passed between me and Lyn's relations, Lyn's friends, and even the writings of listeners who had random theories but no connection to anyone in the case, were captured in the big sweep.

Revisiting it highlighted my failure to include in the podcast the insightful disclosures of people such as Virginia Raison, partner in the 70s and 80s of the twins' friend from their early teens, Phil Day. Virginia had reached out to tell me that Lyn confided, when they first met, 'her desire to have children. Over the next few years it became obvious this was affecting Lyn and Chris's relationship'.

'Lyn rang me one day and asked if she and Chris could come and talk to Phil and me,' Virginia said. 'I invited them to dinner at Phil's unit in Coogee. We were delighted when they asked us to be referees as they were applying to adopt a child. Several months later, Lyn rang to say they had been successful – and would be getting a baby shortly. Not long after this, Chris rang Phil to tell us the adoption was off as Lyn was pregnant.'

Virginia went travelling in Europe and on returning in late 1982 she was told by Phil of Lyn's disappearance. He had unwittingly played a role for Chris by going to Northbridge Baths on 9 January 1982.

'I shared with Phil and still hold absolute commitment to the belief that Lyn would never have left her very precious girls. It is Chris's biggest lie to suggest this,' Virginia said. 'Eventually, Phil told me he couldn't continue the friendship as he didn't understand why [Chris didn't seem] too concerned about Lyn's disappearance.'

Chris and Paul went to Phil's 'living wake' in 2007. The dying, widely respected man believed in forgiveness. Virginia said it was 'in keeping with his character to invite them despite his revulsion at their behaviours with school students'.

In April, following a request from the NSW Office of the DPP, we removed *The Teacher's Pet* podcast series from platforms in Australia. It became clear that by leaving the series online, we would make ourselves a bigger target for the defence and the DPP. The argument that Dawson might not be able to get a fair trial would strengthen if the podcast, with its 16 episodes of detailed evidence and the opinions of many people about Dawson's guilt, remained available to potential jurors and witnesses.

It was a wrench. Just five months earlier, Slade and I had won a Gold Walkley for our efforts.

The podcast's removal in Australia caught many late listeners by surprise; many thousands were only part-way through listening to it. The frustrations and annoyance of those in Australia who were abruptly denied access to the podcast were only partly smoothed by a brief update episode, the 17th, in which I explained what we were doing and included audio of Greg Walsh's criticisms, and Peter Lavac's view that taking the series down was appropriate.

Outside Australia, listeners retained unfettered access to *The Teacher's Pet*. It continued to enjoy hundreds of thousands of downloads a week as people around the world caught up with a story which had made global headlines with the arrest.

Chapter 39

Black Blotting Pens

Greg Walsh's efforts to try to make the case as much about journalism as it was about his client ratcheted up again in May 2019, on a day Greg and Merilyn Simms were visiting Brisbane and coming to see me in Brookfield.

The online reports by journalists at the court hearing quoted Walsh's statements to Chief Magistrate Graeme Henson: 'Mr Walsh told Sydney's Downing Centre Local Court that Thomas hadn't disclosed all relevant material to investigators and may have "shredded" some.'

Outside the court, he told the waiting journalists that his assertion about me having destroyed evidence was underpinned by comments I had made at a public event in Brisbane in 2018, when the podcast series was still unfolding. Walsh quoted me as having said at the event that some of the material for Episode 7 'must be shredded or otherwise we'll all go to jail'.

'And I think it's essential that this material be disclosed, and as the chief magistrate said, you would hope that Mr Thomas, in effect, would cooperate with the administration of justice and ensure that this material is produced,' Greg Walsh said.

Chris Reason asked, 'When he says that "people will go to jail", do you think that he's talking about the witnesses he's speaking to, or is he talking about himself?'

Walsh replied, 'Chris, I honestly can't answer that question because I don't know, and that's why there'll be an application that he give evidence at a committal hearing. We've got to get to the bottom of this because Chris Dawson's entitlement to a fair trial, in my respectful opinion, has been seriously prejudiced by the conduct of Mr Thomas and others, and it's been a deliberate course of conduct. This is about a man facing the most serious of charges, murder, in very, very unusual circumstances. And whilst there was an ongoing police investigation, a very senior journalist has taken it upon himself to interview all of the relevant witnesses on multiple occasions. We depend upon the police to be allowed to do their job of investigating crime. To suggest that Mr Thomas was not aware of the implications is just not tenable.'

When a reporter asked Walsh if he was suggesting that I had 'somehow shaped the podcast to get a result', the solicitor became emphatic.

'Absolutely. It's the most biased piece of journalism I've ever come across, seriously. And the target was to influence New South Wales Police, consistent with the theory that Chris Dawson was guilty of murder, nothing more and nothing less. And he did everything possible to shape witnesses' memory and to distort their memory. There is just something that's seriously wrong here. And why is he taking so long to produce this material? It should have been produced months ago.'

I was astonished at the claims. Greg and Merilyn, sitting with me at the Brookfield General Store, were loyally furious.

It was soon obvious that the solicitor's claim about me having 'shredded' material came from an audio recording I had handed to police. It came from one of *The Australian*'s public subscriber events. A member of the Brisbane audience had asked me about legal implications and the advice we were getting for each podcast episode, and I spoke openly about it in the context of a small part of one episode being withheld on advice.

My exact words to the audience at the public event were: 'The legal aspects, I know they're expensive. We're getting weekly legal advice, so last night at about 11 pm, I sent the draft of Episode 7 to the lawyers. And it was about 11 and a half thousand words so it took them a while to read it. But they got back to me today and said, "We, ah, we think Chapter 5 of Episode 7 needs to be significantly shredded, cut out", and I was like, "Oh, why?" And they said, "Well, you'll go to jail if it stays." So that was the most dramatic advice we've had so far.'

There was never any suggestion that any underlying document, such as an audio file or crucial evidence, had been destroyed. I was describing the legal advice from the newspaper's diligent lawyer Tom Otter to cut a chunk from the script of one of my draft chapters. It quoted Family Court documents about the divorce proceedings between Dawson and Lyn and, eight years later, Dawson and Jenny. I had mistakenly believed that I could quote parts of the documents at length, as they were part of the police brief I had obtained from Greg Simms, arising from the first inquest.

Shortly before it was due to be aired, Tom Otter realised the grave risk; it is an offence punishable by imprisonment to publish Family Court documents. I was factually wrong for believing that they were public exhibits as a result of the 2001 and 2003 inquests. Before urging me to cut the chapter out, Tom wanted a second opinion to be doubly sure. He went to a senior barrister, who quickly reached the same view: delete the draft section or risk imprisonment.

The action we took to 'shred' that section of Episode 7 was ethical and responsible. Ironically, its deletion was also good for Chris Dawson as it omitted evidence from his divorce proceedings. But when Greg Walsh saw the transcript of what I had candidly volunteered to the event audience, he interpreted something altogether different.

John-Paul Cashen was protective of me, describing Walsh's claim as 'an outrageous allegation'. We worked on a hard-hitting statement to set out the facts.

'Chris Dawson's lawyer is distorting the truth in comments he made today regarding Hedley Thomas,' the statement said. 'The statements made by Mr Walsh in court and outside court today, in claiming there had been document destruction or shredding, entirely misrepresent public statements made by Mr Thomas last year at a *Teacher's Pet* event held for subscribers to *The Australian*. They appear to have been made for the purpose of smearing the reputation of Mr Thomas.'

A reporter from a rival media outlet called amid the fuss to share his sense of what he had seen unfolding in and outside the courtroom. He told me Greg Walsh was a top lawyer in front of judges, and very adept in the public arena in front of journalists, adding, 'His agenda is clear – it's about shaping the media message'. The story about my alleged conduct would briefly spike in the news cycle.

Over the ensuing weeks, the many written communications that had passed between me and hundreds of people – from family members to unrelated listeners, many of whom connected with Lyn's story and shared poignant accounts of their own abuse and escape from dangerous relationships – were tagged, pending handover to police. I seethed at the intrusion and urged our legal team to push back.

In John-Paul's view, I would be unable to run an argument that in order to protect 'confidential sources', I needed to withhold hundreds of these documents from police, the court and Dawson's lawyers.

But his analysis of the predicament gave me comfort. 'Our job is to help guide you through the process and to protect your legal interests and to assist you to resist any attempts by the DPP or Dawson's legal team to force you to disclose material you feel ethically bound not to disclose,' he assured me in June 2019.

Although we were lawfully compelled to comply with the court's directions, I made several trips to an obscure stationery store in Sydney, the one place that sold a particular brand of foolproof black blotting pen. I ended up buying a box of them. It would ensure that the identities of people whose stories were completely irrelevant to the alleged murder of Lyn in 1982 were redacted, and not visible when the printouts were magnified.

Where I believed I owed an ethical obligation of confidentiality to a source, there was a different scenario. Fortunately, the interviews I had done and the information I had received for the podcast investigation predominately came from family and friends of Lyn and other people who would have no difficulty with our communications being handed over.

After a lot of debate, John-Paul and I agreed that the best way was for me to contact everyone whose confidentiality might be an issue, explain the thorny problem and seek their permission. If they opposed release of their communications, the fallback position was to redact details which would identify them. John-Paul and I hoped that when the police detectives, prosecutors and Dawson's defence team received the numerous bulging folders and read the thousands of printed documents – which had been individually collated and, in many cases, part-redacted by me and Miriam Sproule, a longtime trusted editorial assistant in the newspaper's Brisbane office – they would appreciate that there was nothing to be gained from forcing full disclosure.

A journalist's obligation to protect confidential sources is enshrined in the craft but it is interpreted differently. My position has been rigid: a journalist must not disclose his or her confidential source to anyone. Period. This meant that my colleagues, from reporters all the way up the chain to the editor-in-chief, would be told, 'Sorry, no,' if they said they needed to know the identity of a source. I counselled cadet reporters to stand their ground if asked by an editor the identity of a confidential informant. It was understandable that some editors would want to know before putting their own job and the masthead's reputation on the line with a story based on a source known only to the reporter but in my view, the risk had to be taken. A secret cannot stay a secret when it is shared with someone outside the original pact. Confidential sources who trust an individual journalist to keep their identities a secret would not anticipate the journalist telling anyone.

In my experience, lawyers and judges in Australia care infuriatingly little for journalism's duty of confidentiality. Lawyers and judges who immediately and irrevocably uphold lawyer–client confidentiality display a disturbing double-standard about the same important principle in journalism. Several of my colleagues have been led away to prison for refusing court orders to reveal a source. It was a fate

I narrowly avoided during a political corruption trial some weeks after the shooting at our house in late 2002.

Raymond Bonner, a veteran former investigative journalist for *The New York Times* and a friend in whom I confided our predicament, told me that we should not hand over anything at all; that we should fight the official demands for my journalistic workings.

In 2019, however, John-Paul Cashen and I were weighing a number of competing factors. As he summarised, we needed to cooperate with the homicide investigation and prosecution as much as possible, and this meant handing over files. It was a strategy which denied Chris Dawson and his lawyers the ability to claim that I had withheld evidence that could have shown that he had not murdered Lyn. Of course, I held no such evidence, and doubted that it existed anywhere, but that was beside the point.

The downside to handing over boxes of documents in addition to all the audio was it gave Chris more material with which to run an argument about me having made it impossible for him to get a fair trial.

We landed on the position John-Paul had recommended: disclosing everything which would not breach my ethical duty. 'Source issues are always complex and this approach is not entirely risk-free,' said John-Paul.

> 'It involves careful consideration of each obligation of confidentiality and careful redaction of material in order to honour that obligation. It is important we get that right. However, in our view, it is the best way of protecting your ethical position and your legal position. You may be criticised by Dawson for applying redactions to the documents. However, he will probably criticise you no matter what you do.
>
> 'Due to the sensitivity of the information concerned, and the importance of you upholding your obligations of confidence, you have quite rightly been very protective with the documents involved in this matter. That does make the process somewhat slower and more cumbersome than it would have been if we had

felt free to scan all of the documents, email them around, save them on our desktops, make printed copies and highlighted copies and apply the redactions on a computer. Of course, doing those things increases the risk of your sources being outed and was not something you were willing to do in this case.'

John-Paul agreed that the presumption of listeners who had contacted me was that they had been given 'a promise of confidentiality', particularly when they were disclosing highly sensitive personal information. We took special care with all of them, and John-Paul urged me to consider 'the source's cooperation or otherwise with police; whether the person's identity or story has previously been in the public domain; and your impressions of the person's personal circumstances and demeanour'.

There were many communications in which former students and some former teachers had named others from different schools as having been involved in underage sex. All of it required the utmost discretion and sensitivity.

John-Paul cautioned that 'in due course', a judge might not agree with me should I assert that I had a confidential source about whom I would say nothing whatsoever. We agreed it was a challenge we would deal with later, if it became necessary. The most important task at hand was to talk to sensitive contacts – I was concerned about several – and get their blessing.

Matt Fordham, the former police prosecutor who had done a remarkable job in the coronial proceedings in 2001 and 2003, immediately consented to me releasing emails we had exchanged when he contacted me as the podcast episodes were being released. Other sources were similarly unperturbed. There was a narrow path to transparency. With each call and email I sent to people explaining our situation, the more confident I became.

By mid-June, we had handed over about a dozen ring-binder folders of copies of emails and documents going all the way back to 2001, when I first took notes about the case. It had taken an enormous amount of time and effort, and had so far cost *The Australian* a small fortune because of the legal vetting and advice. As the police had requested it, there was even a sample folder of what we called 'fan mail' – correspondence via email and Facebook Messenger from people, many of whom lived in North America, Europe and the United Kingdom, who had no actual link to the case and no knowledge of anyone in it. They merely wanted to pass on their ideas about things such as where Chris had buried his wife's body. I pictured him and his brothers reading the one-way email traffic and being surprised and angered by the condemnatory responses.

John-Paul explained to police that the large number of redactions were necessary for reasons including compliance with laws to prevent identification of persons involved in sexual offences and family law proceedings, to honour confidential source obligations and to prevent naming women who had disclosed to me highly sensitive personal details, mostly relating to domestic violence or sexual exploitation and abuse. We did not want to needlessly disclose any things which could cause distress.

Several days after the handover of the files, Chris Dawson was back in court. He was silent. Greg Walsh, however, spoke freely outside the court, speaking to journalists about his concerns over my professionalism, my purported faith in clairvoyants and my grandmother.

I did not travel to Sydney for these appearances. After months spent collecting and preparing the thousands of documents to hand over to police, prosecutors and Chris Dawson's legal team, I went to visit my sister Peta on Paros, and then to Mykonos, where our friend Jackie Cross was throwing a significant birthday party.

I woke to a flurry of emails, text messages and missed calls.

Perry Duffin, a reporter for Australian Associated Press, wrote, 'Hey mate, was just at Dawson. Walsh made a big deal inside and outside court about potential contamination of evidence – cited impact of your podcast. He also said a clairvoyant that worked with you and cops could have impacted on witnesses. Called it bizarre. Finally – something I haven't filed on but need to ask you about – he gave out an email you wrote to Rebecca Hazel about your grandmother vanishing.'

My heart sank. It was the private email I had written to Rebecca in late October 2017 about my father's mother. Until Walsh's disclosure, there had not been a word uttered publicly by anyone about the unusual coincidence. I had disclosed it privately to very few people.

Perry added a paraphrase of Walsh's comment: 'When Mr Thomas has had that emotional difficulty in his life and where repeated assertions are made a woman cannot simply disappear – truth is stranger than fiction'.

'Not quite sure what he was driving at but he seemed to think it was relevant,' Perry wrote.

It was good of him to give me a heads-up. I thanked him and let him know we would not be making a comment.

Perry replied, 'No worries, mate, totally understand and appreciate the response while on holiday. I'm sure you're all over it now but we just ran down to Surry Hills to see he's been charged with carnal knowledge.'

Police had hit Chris with a charge relating to alleged underage sex with a girl from Cromer High. It was one of the outcomes of the Strike Force Southwood, the team of specialist detectives established by Police Commissioner Mick Fuller in July 2018 as a result of the disclosures in the podcast episodes to that point.

While in court for what was meant to be an administrative purpose – for police to formally certify the charge of murder – Deputy Chief Magistrate Michael Allen was told by Greg Walsh that what he described as my 'contamination' of witnesses would be explored in future hearings. I would need to be a witness in proceedings the following year.

'For example, it's now apparent that a clairvoyant has undertaken a very active role in helping Mr Thomas,' Walsh told the court.

The claim was absurd. I have always regarded clairvoyants with contempt for the false hope they gave people. It was clear from the podcast that it was the police, not me, who had direct contact with clairvoyants. In my email communications, I was scornful of them. Greg Walsh must not have seen these emails from me.

When the deputy chief magistrate said the murder trial was in 'uncharted waters', the Crown's senior prosecutor Craig Everson agreed, adding, 'It's unprecedented, Your Honour.'

Walsh had printed copies of the email I wrote about my grandmother. He provided these to some of the reporters. Of the hundreds of communications, I tried to fathom why he was highlighting this one. It had no direct relevance to Chris's case. A decade before my birth, a young woman with two siblings who had taken their own lives walked into the Pacific Ocean at Dee Why and, we believed, swam until she vanished. It had no connection to the events of 1982 except for the coincidental circumstances, none of which would be admissible as evidence in a trial. The most that could be said was that it had helped to motivate me during the podcast investigation. Did Chris's side even know this fact by June 2019?

The release of this email by Greg Walsh, and his comment about me and my father's mother seemed calculated to be personal.

John-Paul Cashen, who went to court and then briefed me and *The Australian*'s executives, confirmed everything I had already been told by Perry Duffin. He believed we should play a straight bat, adding, 'we don't want to start a game where we respond to each and every allegation Walsh makes'.

'There seems little point in responding to the email about Hedley's grandmother. At some stage, Hedley can speak about that if and when he wants to,' John-Paul said. 'The clairvoyant allegations are wrong. I think we need to start getting used to the idea that Hedley will be asked to give evidence at some stage.'

As I mulled things from afar and drank Greek beer to make everything seem better, another email from someone I had never met dropped in. The fellow had 'dreams and premonitions' about Lyn, adding, 'I continue to see a pale blue big waste bin on wheels near a wharf.'

I allowed myself a sardonic sigh.

Chapter 40

Podcast on Trial

'Well, let's not beat about the bush. You believed that in all probability, Mr Dawson killed Mrs Dawson, right?'

After ten minutes of legal footwork on the morning of Thursday, 16 July 2020, Phillip Boulten SC, a leading criminal defence lawyer, was punching towards his key points and assertions: that I was recklessly indifferent to justice and his client's presumption of innocence and, having a preconceived view of him as guilty when I first heard of the case in 2001, I used every device and innuendo at my disposal in a 2018 podcast to falsely smear Chris as a killer and a sex predator, across Australia and the world, while ratcheting up pressure on the DPP and police for an oppressive prosecution.

Exactly two years earlier, during the rollout of episodes of *The Teacher's Pet*, I had flown to Sydney for a lunch meeting with the Commissioner of Police, Mick Fuller, culminating in an agreement that saw the Homicide Squad receive my relevant information from potential new witnesses and sources.

The scenario in the Supreme Court in Sydney could not have been more different. Christopher Michael Dawson had instructed his lawyers Greg Walsh and Phillip Boulten SC to run a costly and determined bid for a 'permanent stay'. He wanted Justice Elizabeth Fullerton to permanently block his prosecution for alleged murder. The former high school teacher would not go into the witness box to

409

answer questions in his stay application. The accused always enjoys a right to silence. The six subpoenaed witnesses, however, had no choice. We were compelled to give evidence.

Chris's lawyers had another advantage. Since May 2019 they had been leafing through thick folders with hundreds of documents – my notes, emails, texts, WhatsApp and Facebook Messenger exchanges with Lyn's family and friends, police, former students and teachers and others. They must have read tens of thousands of words.

Team Dawson had also received many dozens of audio files from my recorded interviews and random conversations for *The Teacher's Pet*. In addition, they had identified – and planned to tender as evidence – interviews that I had done for media outlets including *60 Minutes*, where I described Chris as a dangerous narcissist who had been lying to his daughters and Lyn's family for years.

With all of this material, as well as by questioning me and other witnesses in these unreported stay proceedings in 2020, Phillip Boulten would try to persuade Justice Fullerton that Chris could not get a fair trial. Greg Walsh had already told journalists that my podcast and opinions had probably 'contaminated' witnesses. Although Phillip Boulten did not suggest to me that there were factual inaccuracies in the podcast, he would argue it had been so detailed, biased and widely heard that listeners strongly believed Chris killed Lyn.

Furthermore, according to the defence claims, the podcast was too pervasive for its poison to be cured by a trial judge who would ordinarily instruct jurors and witnesses to focus only on evidence in a courtroom.

The podcast was not the only target. It would also be argued that detective Damian Loone ran a slapdash and biased investigation for 17 years, since 1998. And that the failure by police in the 1980s to investigate properly at an early stage, combined with their loss or destruction of evidence, greatly disadvantaged Chris, a victim of their incompetence. If evidence such as Bankcard statements had been recovered by police in 1982, the legal argument went, Chris might have been able to show that Lyn had used it and that she obviously was not dead, as the police and prosecutors and coroners would subsequently believe. I looked at it the other way: if police had done their jobs properly in the 80s, Chris would have been convicted of Lyn's murder back then. He had enjoyed four decades of freedom because of the incompetence. Or the corruption. Or was it both?

Opposing Chris and his lawyers in their bold bid was Craig Everson, the prosecutor from the Office of the DPP. I had met Craig and his junior counsel, Emma Blizard, when I was asked to attend a conference in the Crown's Sydney offices in late 2019 where I was put through a line of questioning in advance of being put in the witness box. It became clear to me after this meeting that the strategy of the defence was to attack. To put the journalism on trial.

Terry Martin SC, the former top criminal defence lawyer and newly retired District Court judge in Brisbane, told me he believed the stay application was futile. While the High Court had made it clear that in an appropriate case pre-trial publicity could result in a permanent stay of a murder trial, 'an appropriate case' would very rarely, if ever, exist. The trial courts take all necessary steps to ensure a fair trial, including by questioning potential jurors. On the other hand, *The Teacher's Pet* had been downloaded 50 million times by that stage. It had generated thousands of related stories across the media. None were good for Chris. I feared that, despite the evidence against him, he might win.

Terry's view was that my lack of direct knowledge of the events of 1982, when I would have been 14 and living far from the northern beaches of Sydney, made me 'completely irrelevant' in a murder trial. A bid for a permanent stay, however, was different. Team Dawson would roll out a showcase of shame in which the podcast, my interviews and my methods would be closely examined by the lawyers and the judge, all of whom were, I suspected, tut-tutting about journalism's role despite the criminal justice system's failure for all the previous years.

Terry had a high regard for Phillip Boulten. He had been junior counsel to Terry in a criminal defence case years earlier. He was neither shouty nor overly aggressive. He was forensic, clever, determined and bitterly sarcastic at times. He had an air of superiority. He had to be taken very seriously.

In July 2020, Australia was gripped by COVID-19 and many courts were using video conferencing technology for witnesses, particularly those living interstate who risked catching the deadly virus on unnecessary flights. There was still no vaccine and communities were in lockdown amid widespread fear. There were travel restrictions as hospitals risked being overwhelmed. Ruth's elderly parents, Iain and Mary, who lived with us, were frail and their immune systems were compromised. The Homicide Squad's Dan Poole, who had been methodically going through my files and following up leads, assured me I should be able to give evidence via a video link in Brisbane to the Supreme Court's hearing in Sydney.

When Ruth's father took a serious turn and needed an emergency admission to hospital, it seemed a foregone conclusion that Ruth and I would not be made to travel. We feared Iain was dying and would not get out of hospital. Our family GP, who was gravely worried about his condition, wrote a letter stressing the risks and imploring us to not travel. Going to Sydney could mean returning with the virus.

My barrister retained by *The Australian*, Dauid Sibtain, set out the medical position in preliminary hearings as the pandemic rippled across Sydney. My strong preference to testify from Brisbane was firmly rejected. Justice Fullerton required me in her courtroom in Sydney.

I opted to drive the 900 kilometres with Ruth to lower the risks of contracting COVID-19 on an aircraft or in airports. I used the 11 hours in the car to re-read files and join telephone conferences with the lawyers. It had been 19 months since the podcast series had ended, with a 16th episode being updated and produced by Slade and me on the day Chris was arrested for alleged murder. I had spent more time meeting the demands of police, the Office of the DPP, the defence, and *The Australian*'s lawyers than I had investigating Lyn's case and writing *The Teacher's Pet*.

If Chris succeeded in his bid for a permanent stay, fallout for Lyn's family and friends, journalism, *The Australian* and me would be disastrous. I had been acknowledged as the reporter who single-mindedly, perhaps obsessively, drove the story. It was cast in a positive light during the series and soon after the arrest. But if the pendulum should go the other way with the termination of a murder prosecution *because* of the podcast, severe criticism and blame would undoubtedly come our way. My editors and colleagues would be tarred with the same broad brush. The potential financial costs for the newspaper and me could have been calamitous. Lyn's family would be inconsolable. Their last chance dashed.

Peter Lavac, former prosecutor and criminal defence lawyer, struck an optimistic tone with a mid-morning call as Ruth crossed the Queensland border and gunned our Audi into Tenterfield.

'Mate, they're only going after you because Dawson would not have even been charged if it hadn't been for the podcast,' Peter said in his slow and husky drawl.

'It's not something you should be apologetic or defensive about. I'm proud of what you did. The DPP should have run the case years ago. The podcast forced them to do the right thing.'

In his interviews with me two years earlier, Peter had expressed bafflement that Chris had not been prosecuted after the recommendations by coroners in 2001 and 2003.

We spoke of revelations in the podcast about Lloyd Babb, the Director of Public Prosecutions since 2011, having been coached in rugby league by the Dawson twins in 1983 when they were teaching at Asquith Boys High where Lloyd would go on to be school captain in 1984. Lloyd's office had told David Murray and me that he had declared his conflict of interest at all relevant times. It had been two years since we broke the story. In anticipation of being questioned about it I went through all the documents again to refresh my memory about who said what and when.

Peter Lavac added, unhelpfully, that Greg Walsh and Phillip Boulten, both of whom he knew professionally, made 'a brilliant combination'.

'They're killers and they're the best thing Chris has going for him,' he said. He predicted they would pull every legal lever.

In my suitcase, a medication known colloquially as 'beta blockers', was at the ready after a recommendation from a friend who swore by them to quell stress and nervousness in unusual situations. A couple of hours from Sydney in the gloom of a winter's early evening, Ruth slept soundly in the passenger seat while I spoke on the phone to Rebecca Hazel, who had also been subpoenaed to give evidence. My stomach was in knots and my head throbbed.

Tired from driving after little sleep and long days preparing for a courtroom interrogation, I had become irrationally convinced that the malevolence of Chris Dawson could bring down those who posed a serious threat.

Rebecca, usually inclined to pessimism, became soothingly reassuring. She predicted the prosecution would go ahead as we had done nothing wrong. 'And Chris did evil,' she added.

But my despondency was hard to shake. *The Australian*'s new editor-in-chief Christopher Dore called to wish me well as I drove into the hotel car park. We had been friends for many years. I knew he would back me, double down and run a powerful new campaign if an alleged killer ultimately achieved prosecutorial immunity. But it would still leave an ugly stain on the newspaper and our journalism.

The next day, after early-morning coffee with Dauid Sibtain in his chambers and the borrowing of one of his ties, we entered the courtroom. Ruth was anxiously clenching and unclenching her fists. Chris's lawyers had been granted a blackout on all publicity, a sensible position with a murder trial pending. The reporters who were present could not publish anything. Chris sat staring. Glaring. His solicitor Greg Walsh came over with a friendly greeting and offered me a glass of water. Over the preceding months, Greg had presented as a mortal enemy. His retaliatory statements in court and to journalists outside got under my skin. But when we met face to face on the day that he and a leading barrister intended to try to expose me in the witness box, he was disarmingly courteous. It messed with my head.

Phillip Boulten started by asking about my original interest in Lyn's disappearance. He took me back to newspaper reports I had read of the coronial hearing in early 2001 and my trip to Sydney; a meeting with Damian Loone in a Northern Beaches police station, and my reading of witness statements and evidence there before I wrote 'Looking For Lyn' for *The Courier-Mail*.

'What attracted you to this case in the first place? A national broadsheet daily doesn't normally delve into the proceedings at the Coroners Court at Glebe, does it?' he asked.

The Australian is a national broadsheet daily. But *The Courier-Mail* is a local newspaper with negligible circulation outside Queensland. Phillip Boulten had made a small error. It gave me an early and meaningful boost in confidence.

'It seems that your interest in the case continued off and on over years, is that right?'

'Yes.'

He established that while I met Pat Jenkins in 2001 and exchanged emails with her over the years, I did not go to Sydney for the second inquest in 2003, did not stay in touch with Damian, and did not meet Greg Simms until 2017.

He asked 'what had happened between 2003 and October 2017' that strengthened my view that the decisions of the DPP over several years to not prosecute Chris were incorrect.

'I had some experience of seeing – and being a reporter in cases – that seemed to me to be, and were found to be, miscarriages or travesties of justice where an accused hadn't gone to trial,' I replied.

He wanted examples. I raised the case of a swimming coach who had been accused of indecently touching several girls in his training squad in Brisbane. The answer appeared to surprise him. Four months earlier, he had been successful in the District Court in Queensland in obtaining a permanent stay for the disgraced coach, though not because of adverse publicity; the stay was granted mostly because of the unreasonable delay since the alleged offences in the 1980s. I knew one of the alleged victims, a highly credible woman called Julie Gilbert. I met her in 2003 when I investigated and reported on it. We remained in contact.

Experienced lawyers were appalled then and now at the shambolic handling and botching of the case by prosecutors. The Royal Commission into Institutional Responses to Child Sexual Abuse in 2015 and Queensland's then Crime and Misconduct Commission in 2003 had investigated and reported on the defects in the prosecutorial process in Sydney and Brisbane. The alleged offender always emphatically denied wrongdoing. The royal commission's 2015 report into what happened in the case found much that was wrong, and stated that an independent Office of the DPP which 'cannot be subject to any external reviews, is at risk of failure in its decision making processes'. Phillip Boulten had a more current stake in this saga. He questioned me about it. We could not have been farther apart about where the injustice lay.

Boulten: 'What are the other cases that have shaped your opinion about this particular case, this Dawson case, leading into the development of the podcast?'

The killing of Lynette Daley, who was repeatedly sexually assaulted and bled to death in 2011, sprang to mind. Two men who had committed the attacks were finally prosecuted in 2017 by the New South Wales DPP but only after robust findings of the then coroner Michael Barnes, a public outcry and powerful journalism by reporters at *The Daily Telegraph* and the ABC. The jury needed only about 30 minutes to reach its verdict of guilty. The DPP, Lloyd Babb, whose office had repeatedly refused to prosecute, publicly apologised afterwards. The trial judge was, ironically, Elizabeth Fullerton. She condemned the actions of the two perpetrators as 'extremely serious, reflecting a very high level of moral culpability'. It was another classic case study of prosecutors getting things hopelessly wrong.

'There was a terrible rape and unlawful killing of a woman called Lynette Daley, and that went to trial after being repeatedly refused by the New South Wales DPP,' I told Chris's defence lawyer.

Boulten: 'Any others?'

Me: 'I have been involved in other cases in Queensland involving the fallibility of prosecuting authorities.'

I had seen the administration of justice in Queensland shown up as useless amid serious official corruption over many years. I was a cadet reporter in the 1980s when journalists Phil Dickie and Chris Masters exposed the state's bent system, triggering a public inquiry, far-reaching reforms and life-long lessons for young reporters to always push, prod and ask tough questions.

Boulten: 'I suggest to you that to choose this case as the subject of your first podcast, you had a firm view that the DPP had made the wrong decision a number of times when they refused to prosecute Chris Dawson?'

Me: 'I would agree with that.'

His early cross-examination put on the record what he already knew: I had been investigating Lyn's case for the podcast since late October 2017, and in April 2018 I learned that an updated brief of police evidence had been provided by the Homicide Squad to the Office of the DPP to review, and I released the first episode of the podcast the following month, May. None of this should have been controversial in my view. The DPP had repeatedly declined to prosecute Chris after reviewing all the updated police briefs in the past. Greg Simms and Pat Jenkins had no expectations of anything different in April–May 2018. The mere fact of a brief being considered by prosecutors has never been any barrier to reporting by journalists. Many reporters would never know that an unsolved crime was in review. It's not something routinely publicised by the system.

Boulten: 'You joined with Lyn Dawson's family and friends who believed that Mr Dawson had murdered her and you wanted that view, which you shared, publicly known, right?'

Me: 'Yes.'

Boulten: 'You didn't trust the Office of the DPP to reach the conclusion that Mr Dawson be prosecuted, did you?'

Me: 'It was not my call, and I didn't know what they would do. I was trying to do a story that would possibly make a difference.'

Boulten: 'And you wanted to develop the podcast in an endeavour to convince them in part to prosecute Mr Dawson?'

Me: 'I wanted to try to find new material that could make a difference and if that had an impact, then so be it.'

Boulten: 'Yes, but you wanted to change the DPP's approach, didn't you?'

Me: 'I wanted to tell the story, and if it changed the DPP's [thinking], that would follow.'

Boulten: 'A central reason you broadcast the podcast was to see justice, right?'

Me: 'Yes.'

Boulten: 'And by that, you mean justice is Chris Dawson charged, convicted and sentenced for murdering Lynette Dawson, right?'

Me: 'No.'

Boulten: 'What do you think?'

Me: 'Charged and prosecuted.'

He and his instructing solicitors had selected snippets from podcast episodes and parts of my recorded interviews to play in court. I expected only one-star reviews.

'I want to be clear to you that I will be submitting that this was done deliberately to whip up views in the community that Chris Dawson murdered his wife. That's what you did,' Boulten said.

He went to the intro of every episode. A snippet of Jenny, in her own voice in her 1998 police interview, says 'he said he was going to get a hitman to kill Lyn'. I was asked why the quote was there when I didn't know what had really happened.

'I can speculate that it appealed to myself and the audio producer as an interesting grab,' I said.

Boulten: 'You were trying to win listeners when you were producing the podcast week by week, weren't you?'

Me: 'That was not what I was trying to do, I was trying to tell a story.'

Boulten: 'You were trying to make it a success, weren't you?'

Me: 'Well, I didn't want it to be a failure.'

Boulten: 'You intended to put pressure on the DPP, didn't you?'

Me: 'No, I intended to expose inadequacies and if that caused them to look at it in a more forensic way, then that would be a good thing.'

Justice Fullerton chimed in after hearing an excerpt from the Nine Network's *60 Minutes* in which I expressed strong adverse views of Chris and his conduct.

'At the time you volunteered your opinions of Mr Dawson, were you then, at that time, alive to the possibility that potential jurors and witnesses would pay attention to what you said were your views about the type of person he was?'

Me: 'Your Honour, because I didn't know whether there would ever be a trial, I don't know how to answer that.'

Judge: 'Well, you have agreed with Mr Boulten that you were alive to the possibility that potential jurors would pay attention, and potential witnesses would pay attention, to your opinion that in your view he was, as you described him in unflattering terms, a despicable, severely narcissistic and dangerous person?'

Me: 'Yes.'

Boulten: 'You didn't care at all about Mr Dawson's interests in the course of justice, did you?'

Me: 'I did care about those. I had hoped that he would be interviewed in a podcast and put his side of the story.'

Boulten: 'Was it your belief that the police investigation throughout the 1980s was one involving wilful blindness or worse?'

Me: 'Yes, in the 1980s.'

Boulten: 'Did you intend the viewer to understand that Chris Dawson was a member of a sex ring of teachers preying on schoolgirls?'

Me: 'I don't know what I intended, but I believe that he was part of that sex ring.'

The lawyer suggested that in August 2018, I 'knew that Mr Babb had no personal involvement in considering any aspect of the Dawson matter' in the Office of the DPP.

Me: 'Well, I'm not in his office. How could I know?'

The lack of certainty, for me, was due to the different statements which had been sent by Lloyd Babb's office in response to our detailed questions in 2018. The responses with their different dates about his disclosure muddied the water.

Boulten: 'You formed the view during the course of your reinvestigation that Mr Dawson had a corrupt relationship with police officers who were interfering with the course of the murder investigation, didn't you?'

Me: 'I thought it was possible in the 1980s that that would have been the case . . .'

Justice Fullerton took up the questioning again, and I felt the conde-
scension: 'So at the time that you were conducting – and I'll grace you
with the description 'investigation as a journalist' – you knew that the
agents appointed by the State to investigate criminal conduct, and, ultimately a member of the executive who would decide whether criminal
charges would be laid, were current and continuing?'

The answer was an emphatic 'yes', of course I knew. But, so what?
It was surprising to me that Phillip Boulten and the judge seemed
invested in the fact that my work for the podcast continued to unfold
in 2018 at the same time police were still investigating and lawyers in
the DPP were still reviewing. Unsolved murders and other serious
crimes are always regarded as under investigation. Journalists have
never been restricted in investigating and reporting on these crimes.
In the Dawson case, a perfect example was the ABC's 2003 hard-
hitting episode of *Australian Story*, featuring interviews with key
witnesses from the inquests during a much earlier investigation and
while the DPP was considering a new brief of evidence.

A review by the DPP's lawyers of an updated brief of evidence was
of no consequence; it must happen all the time.

The one barrier to ongoing investigating and reporting by journalists would be a criminal charge. If Chris had been charged in May
2018, I would have stopped digging and we could not have released
episodes of the podcast.

Justice Fullerton sounded indignant when she asked whether I knew
of 'any journalist who would publicly venture a view about the guilt of a
person suspected of homicide', during a review by a DPP and an active
police investigation. I said I didn't know of journalists who wouldn't.

Phillip Boulten read aloud from emails exchanged with Police
Commissioner Mick Fuller after the lunch meeting at Verde.

Boulten: 'So you knew from that time on that you could provide
information to the police?'

Me: 'Yes, and they could seek information if they heard something they thought would be helpful.'

Boulten: 'Did they say anything at all about how the podcast
might help them?'

Me: 'No, I think we were both a bit defensive.'

He circled back to more questions relating to Lloyd Babb. Justice Fullerton weighed in again.

Judge: 'Were you aware that Mr Babb had made a media statement to quell any question that he may, in any decision-making, be confronted with a conflict of interest?'

Me: 'I was aware, Your Honour, that Mr Babb made two statements and they were in distinct conflict with each other, days apart.'

Boulten: 'Mr Thomas, I want to tackle your assertions that you were even-handed in the way in which you conducted the podcast, and play a tape for your consideration.'

The defence lawyer played a snippet of one of my recorded conversations with my friend in Brisbane, Brian Jordan, a retired Family Court judge who had generously offered his time and expertise for the podcast investigation in 2018.

Brian had commented to me that 'many people who behave badly should not be regarded as being capable of heinous crimes; it's a matter of whether you can be satisfied beyond reasonable doubt that he should be convicted of a serious crime'. And in response, I had jokingly said, 'Well, that fucking bit is not going to make it [into the podcast], let me tell you'.

We both laughed and the courtroom in Sydney heard it all.

Boulten: 'And he's a friend of yours apparently, by the sound of it?'

Me: 'Yeah, we have a very good sense of humour together. It's just banter.'

I suppressed a smile at the memory of our exchange, so typical of the sarcasm and joking between us. But in the Supreme Court, its omission was being put as evidence of my awful bias despite the fact that I had, instead, expanded on Brian's point by using Terry Martin's longer analysis in the podcast.

The questioning moved to my knowledge of mothers who abandon their children and never contact them again. I sensed it was imminent. He was going to ask about my grandmother's disappearance on the Northern Beaches 64 years earlier.

Boulten: 'You have woven into your narrative in public your own experience in this regard, have you not?'

Me: 'I don't think so.'

Boulten: 'Haven't you talked about your own grandmother?'

Me: 'Not in public.'

Boulten: 'Well, tell us about your grandmother?'

Me: 'Well, I've never met her, I don't know anything about her.'

Boulten: 'What happened to her?'

Crown Prosecutor Craig Everson stood up, interrupting before I could answer.

'Can I raise a matter?' he asked Justice Fullerton.

Phillip Boulten said he would not raise it further. At that time, Ruth noted that Chris Dawson appeared agitated. He must have instructed his barrister to question the circumstances of my grandmother going missing. He had worked out that it meant something to me.

The linking in the podcast of the Newtown Jets rugby league club with dangerous criminals was scrutinised. It was put to me that I was 'trying to get everybody to understand that Mr Dawson had criminal contacts, like [contract killer] Neddy Smith and [drugs trafficker Paul] Hayward . . . and that he was in a position to contract his wife's murder because of those connections'.

Justice Fullerton described such links to Chris as 'a whisper on a hunch on a nudge on nothing much more'. It was a vivid word-play and I made a mental note to use it one day.

Shortly before the end of the first day of my cross-examination, Phillip Boulten asked about Carl Milovanovich, the former deputy state coroner who had agreed to be interviewed at his home for the podcast. The defence lawyer's questioning had a tone of incredulity that Carl had made himself available and been so candid about his disappointment that Chris was not prosecuted in 2003. Again, Phillip Boulten and I were poles apart. Carl's openness in his interviews with me was courageous. He was free to say whatever he liked about an unsolved probable murder that troubled him greatly.

Early on the second day, another part of my many recorded chats with Pat Jenkins was played. I cringed this time. Her Honour would surely not be pleased.

Boulten: 'You were telling [Pat] that judges are too rigid, they don't apply as much common sense as they do legal principle, and that they can get caught up in technical legal principle, and that's a long way from what's pragmatic, practical, commonsense thinking. Right?'

'No, I didn't say the first thing – that they're too rigid. She said that. I said the other things.'

'Too true, but you agreed with her?' Phillip Boulten added.

'Yes.'

'And what you were doing was basically saying, "Trust me, Pat Jenkins. The legal system can't be trusted." Right?'

Me: 'No.'

Boulten: 'Why am I wrong in putting that to you?'

Me: 'Well, it's putting words in my mouth.'

Boulten: 'Well, why is it wrong?'

Me: 'Because that's not what I said.'

There were slip-ups and misstatements about events, witnesses and the timing of things but, to be fair, Phillip Boulten had not lived the case for several years. Neither he nor the judge could be expected to know all of it. Inaccurately framing some circumstances in their questions was fine. Trying to be helpful, I pointed it out each time. For the record.

He went back to the intrigue about the disappearance of the evidence gathered by the detectives Paul Mayger and Stuart Wilkins in the Homicide Squad's first probe in 1990 and 1991.

'The whole Homicide Squad file, brief, evidence, statements, has gone missing and when Mr Loone took over the investigation, he got a box that had tape recordings of Mr Mayger's interview with Mr Dawson and nothing else,' Boulten said.

He wanted to know whether I was suggesting 'that Mr Dawson has spirited this evidence away because of his connections with apparently corrupt police . . .?'

Me: 'I am not suggesting Mr Dawson spirited anything away. I believe that because of an extraordinary loss of apparently important documents, police documents concerning a footballer who had apparently good police contacts, that I didn't know what had happened but it seemed highly irregular.'

My voice from another bit of awkward audio filled the courtroom. It was the unpublished conversation with Pat in which I had called the former DPP Nicholas Cowdery 'a knucklehead' for presuming that Lyn might still be alive. It seemed like a fairly tame label at the time in conversation with a dignified woman.

Phillip Boulten's question dripped with sarcasm: 'How ridiculous would that be, that the Director of Public Prosecutions was publicly suggesting that Lynette might still be alive? What a ridiculous proposition, Mr Thomas, don't you think?'

Me: 'Yes.'

Boulten: 'And he is a knucklehead, isn't he?'

Me: 'Mr Boulten, in conversations people have, that they don't expect to be the subject of forensic examination like this, we all make comments that sometimes are a bit flippant and cavalier.'

For the third time, the cross-examination returned to the interest we had shown in 2018 in Lloyd Babb having been coached in the rugby league team by Chris and Paul Dawson; a fact which neither Lyn's family nor the New South Wales Police even knew until a former student told me, and I told them. David Murray and I had subsequently asked the DPP a number of legitimate questions about it. In about 20 hours of audio across 16 episodes, a mere six minutes were spent on Lloyd Babb's old link with the Dawsons. His statement about his disclosure took up a good part of it.

'We actually tried to play the straightest bat possible in everything that was published on this, and I think we played it down,' I said.

For Justice Fullerton, however, the matter assumed greater importance. Perhaps one of the reasons lay in Phillip Boulten's suggestion to me that I had 'formed the view that the Lloyd Babb issue was a good way to press for a favourable outcome on the DPP's consideration of the brief'. Was the defence going to argue that we muscled the DPP to prosecute off the back of our knowledge of Lloyd Babb's old association with the Dawsons at Asquith Boys High?

'The DPP is an independent office, they are not going to be influenced by a journalist's questions,' I said.

We went from the arcane business of Lloyd Babb's disclosure to the frippery of Hollywood screen drama. The interest of film and TV studios in *The Teacher's Pet* throughout 2018, and even Simms family speculation with me and others over acting roles for Nicole Kidman and Margot Robbie, got a colourful run.

Boulten: 'But who did you think might be you?'

Another unavoidable cringe moment was imminent. Best to take it head-on.

Me: 'Well, I didn't know who that could be until I had a contact out of the blue from Hugh Jackman, who . . .'

Boulten: 'You like that idea, Mr Jackman being you?'

Me: 'I think he's a great guy.'

Boulten: 'He's a great actor.'

Me: 'Brilliant.'

Boulten: 'He's a great man, a great Australian, and here he was showing interest in you and your . . .'

Me: 'No, he was showing interest initially in the story.'

Boulten: 'Yes, and you could see him playing you?'

Me: 'No, not at that time. He saw that.'

After testy exchanges late on the second day of cross-examination, he put forward the proposition: 'You were trying to manipulate the whole set of circumstances so that there would be maximum pressure on the authorities, both the police and the DPP, to charge Mr Dawson with murder, weren't you? Just about everything you did with this podcast was done in the hope and with the intention that eventually you would sit in a courtroom when the jury came in and said to Mr Dawson that he is guilty of murder. Isn't that right?'

Justice Fullerton: 'Did you not have a personal wish that he would be convicted?'

'Your Honour, I had a personal wish that there would be a prosecution, and if I had found – or if someone had come forward with – evidence showing that Mr Dawson had done nothing wrong in this, that would have become a big part of the podcast. I also had regard for a highly experienced, former Deputy State Coroner, who gave me extensive interview time to tell me why he believed this was one [case] that really troubled him that it wasn't prosecuted, after his own finding. So it wasn't as if I was going off [with] my own fantasy; there were learned or skilled people saying "I have looked at this, this was unfair".'

The second full day in the witness box ended anti-climactically. There were no further questions about my grandmother. I put this down to Dauid Sibtain and Craig Everson having explained the circumstances to Phillip Boulten outside court. The glaring from Chris and the ongoing charm offensive by his solicitor, Greg Walsh, who had been calling me 'mate' and cheerily asking how I was going, were behind me. I would need to give evidence for part of a third day, but Justice Fullerton kindly agreed this could be done from Brisbane. Ruth and I would not need to stay in Sydney over the weekend. We could not get home soon enough.

Some lawyers and judges are, in my experience, often very reluctant to publicly criticise fellow lawyers and judges. On the other hand, they're prolific and unflinching in finding fault with the methods and output of journalists. In *The Teacher's Pet*, my on-the-record interviews with two magistrates, Jeff Linden and Carl Milovanovich, and a former judge, Brian Jordan, provided gravitas and credibility, along with the critique by another former judge Terry Martin SC; they were significant voices in the series about an alleged killer. But these interviews and contributions became contentious in the stay proceeding.

Anyone in the courtroom would have surmised that Justice Fullerton did not approve of the intrusion by a journalist and podcast in the criminal justice system, at least not in the way I had done it. She seemed, to me, dismissive of the notion that there had been system failure; and that a journalist might find or understand evidence that had been missed or misunderstood by prosecutors. I was very confident she would criticise me in her findings, and perhaps even let Chris off the hook, but if I had done the wrong thing did it follow that the judicial officers had too, and would be similarly criticised?

By Monday morning, Ruth and I were ensconced in a government office in Brisbane, watching the judge and Phillip Boulten on a TV monitor look increasingly agitated in the Sydney courtroom because of repeated transmission failures and technology snafus.

The defence lawyer asked about my interview with Magistrate Jeff Linden, who spoke to me in the Lismore Courthouse. Jeff's suspicions about his former football teammate Chris being possibly involved in killing Lyn were plain. As Jeff had acted as a solicitor for Chris in his divorce from Lyn in 1983, his decision to share sensitive information with me about a former client's possible role in foul play was interesting. On the other hand, Jeff didn't go into detail about the legal work he did for Chris. He did not breach any confidences. He was much more concerned about a subsequent suggestion that Lyn's body might be buried near the Bayview house, because Chris asked the new owner 'where are you digging?'

Boulten: 'It's a question for others, perhaps, but did you think it was appropriate to be having this discussion with Mr Dawson's solicitor, ex or former solicitor?'

Magistrate Linden was not on the witness list for the stay proceeding.

'Yes, I believed it was appropriate for me to inform myself as much as I could – and if he believed it was inappropriate he would have cut it off,' I replied.

Phillip Boulten suggested I 'used the fact that Chris Dawson's own lawyer had concerns to underscore' my own concerns. He put to me that I was 'proactive in endeavours to seek evidence of Mr Dawson's violence towards Mrs Dawson'. He chided me for not accepting what he called 'Mrs Dawson's assurances to her family that she was not being hurt or that the minor injuries [bruises] that her brother saw were innocent'.

'I believed that it was a common explanation of battered wives to cover up for their abusive husbands,' I answered.

When Phillip Boulten called it quits and finally passed the baton to the Crown prosecutor, Craig Everson, I expected a smooth ride and exit. But after a soft start, he appeared to be against me too. I believe that part of his strategy was directed at scotching any possible suggestion in the stay proceeding that any pressure from me and the podcast had influenced the Office of the DPP to prosecute after it had repeatedly refused to do so.

Everson: 'What effect did you think that any public pressure from you or the family of Lynette Dawson would have on the decision makers at the DPP?'

Me: 'That it might cause the DPP to look at something properly. I was well aware the DPP had publicly apologised for failing to prosecute Lynette Daley just a short time before my podcast started. It's not unusual for officers of the DPP to be fallible.'

Judge: 'And you really thought that your way of looking at things was going to be the overwhelming source of influencing the director's decision, did you?'

Me: 'No, Your Honour, I haven't said that.'

My view and my answers were that if the podcast caused people in the DPP to hear relevant new things, and if it caused them to look at it more forensically, well and good.

Craig Everson told me: 'Guideline 7 is the one that says "a decision that's been made won't be revisited unless there's been an error, fraud or change in circumstances".'

In the overwhelming majority of reviews of cases, the Office of the DPP would not reverse a previous decision to not prosecute.

Craig Everson's questions and statements were, I believed, purposefully crafted to show that the Office of the DPP's consideration was independent and had no regard for anything in the podcast. I didn't oppose him. All I knew was that during the podcast and over two years from July 2018, I had been providing police with information and contact details for witnesses, and a number of these became part of the police brief of evidence for the DPP and, in turn, the Crown's case.

Justice Fullerton put to me that 'you thought your way of looking at it was better than the way they were looking at it', and asked 'why wouldn't I divine from what you have said there in evidence, again leaving journalistic hubris to one side, that you thought you knew better than anyone?'

Me: 'My view and my answer was that if the publication of the podcast caused people in the DPP to hear things they hadn't heard or to look at it more forensically, then well and good. I was very aware that Lyn's family had completely lost confidence and trust in the Office of the DPP because of the communications they had had from DPP officers, which strongly indicated to them the DPP had a view about some of the evidence that was just wrong. And you can refer to my journalistic hubris, I think that some practitioners also have legal hubris and believe that their view is the view that should be accepted and . . .'

Judge: 'Let me interrupt you, Mr Thomas. The difference between your views, as a journalist, of evidence sufficient to put somebody on their trial for murder is a wayside different, and if you'd read the director's guidelines you might know the reason why it's a wayside different, to the obligations statutorily imposed on the director's office to look, consider carefully, evaluate forensically, and make a legal decision about the sufficiency of evidence to prosecute a person for murder.'

And for the fourth time, the DPP Lloyd Babb's schoolboy connection with the Dawson twins became the subject of more questioning. A very small part of the podcast was still getting an inordinate amount of attention. Craig Everson seemed to be suggesting that Lloyd Babb didn't need to tell his office that he had a conflict of interest; and that it would have sufficed for him to step aside from any consideration of it and leave it to another independent officer. In my view, a position such as that would fall short of full and open disclosure. Justice Fullerton, sounding cross with me again, stated 'you are the one through the podcast who, if I can be so blunt as to say it, has stirred the pot of doubt and suspicion over the director's independence'.

Me: 'Your Honour, I strongly disagree in relation to our handling of Mr Babb's involvement, or no involvement, that we have been stirring the pot, and I believe, Your Honour, when you listen to that section, you will agree that we haven't done that. We have played a very straight bat on that. It was used and ventilated very briefly and then we moved on.'

We all moved on soon afterwards, too. Excused from giving evidence, I got on with work for a new podcast series, *The Night Driver*, about the unsolved murder of young Bathurst woman Janine Vaughan.

Seven weeks later, my reporter colleague Emily Ritchie prepared a draft news article. Emily did not know what the findings would be. But by having something already written in the event that the judge sided with Chris, Emily would be first with the breaking news.

I swallowed hard on reading her first speculative sentence: 'Christopher Dawson will avoid facing trial over the murder of his missing wife Lynette after successfully arguing the proceedings would be "unfair" and having them quashed in the NSW Supreme Court.'

Emily's draft included a quote she heard during courtroom legal argument: 'Justice Fullerton at one point agreed with Mr Boulten, saying it was her view that "nothing short of an order of the court would have stopped Mr Thomas from doing what he considered was his right and principled purpose – however misguided that might be – to bring the wheels of justice to a full stop at Mr Dawson's doorstep".'

The next day, on 11 September 2020, her findings were provided to our lawyers and the other key parties. The 176-page document included a detailed encapsulation of the evidence in the police brief, and Justice Fullerton issued strict orders that her judgment must not be released while a trial was pending. Instead, the public and journalists received a summary of her findings, and it was made plain by our lawyers that even the words 'The Teacher's Pet' should not be published for now. The title of one of the world's most downloaded podcasts was unmentionable.

The breaking news was that Justice Fullerton had rejected the stay application. Although she had determined that Chris Dawson could, and would, get a fair trial, her annoyance with me and the podcast was made plain in her summary in which she said that while 'skilled investigative journalists have been responsible for the public exposure of incompetent or corrupt behaviour of public officials and private entrepreneurs, and the public exposure of serious sexual and other misconduct within institutions of church and state . . . the risk that an overzealous investigative journalist poses to a fair trial of a person who might ultimately be charged with an historic murder – or another historic criminal offence or offences – is self-evident'.

'The new genre of podcasting and the popularity of the so-called "true crime" podcast, providing as it does a new platform for the investigative journalist to attract a wide and diverse listening audience, highlights the need for both the journalist and the broadcaster to apply restraint if that new medium is to coexist with the fundamental right of a person accused of a serious crime to be tried in a court of law, not in a court of public opinion,' Justice Fullerton stated. 'Her Honour was left in no doubt that the adverse publicity in this case or, more accurately, the unrestrained and uncensored public commentary about Lynette Dawson's suspected murder, is the most egregious example of media interference with a criminal trial process which this Court has had to consider in deciding whether to take the extraordinary step of permanently staying a criminal prosecution.'

It went on to state that 'a journalist who assumes the role of an investigative journalist, or the role of a narrator of a podcast, and who either ignores the potential impact of that commentary on the integrity of a police investigation or the impact of that commentary on a future trial in a case where a person is ultimately charged, will do so at their peril'.

'The particular, perhaps even novel, challenge presented by "podcasters" and broadcasters of podcasts who, in the legitimate pursuit of their journalistic and commercial endeavours undertake research, conduct "investigations" and comment upon so-called "cold case murders", needs to be the subject of reflection and restraint,' she added.

In my opinion, Justice Fullerton's criticisms of me and *The Teacher's Pet* were one-sided and went too far. Her Honour's findings covered a lot of evidence. As they ran to 176 pages and were released just five and a half weeks after the hearings concluded, the factual errors in the published findings were understandable. I was perfectly entitled to express strong opinions about Chris Dawson, who had not been charged at that point and might never have been charged. All journalists and citizens in our democracy with its underpinnings of free speech have the same rights, and of course they could be sued for defamation by their targets. I believe we are on a slippery slope if we yield over something as vital as free speech. Thomas Jefferson's famous words ring true, always: 'Our liberty depends on the freedom of the press, and that cannot be limited without being lost.'

Justice Fullerton stated that 'ultimately there was no submission advanced [by Phillip Boulten] that there was any evidence of actual collusion or contamination of witnesses because of Mr Thomas's association with any of the Crown witnesses he interviewed for the podcast'.

She quoted from Detective Dan Poole's evidence, which was that he did not approve of me having contact with potential prosecution witnesses, although he had 'no concern' that those who had already given evidence in witness statements and to the inquests would be contaminated or influenced.

'Anyone who appeared on the podcast and we spoke to subsequently, obviously we were cautious in relation to the reliability of their evidence but you have to take what people say as what they saw,' Dan Poole had told the judge.

Justice Fullerton said that having listened herself to the podcast, she found that I had paid 'passing lip service to [Chris Dawson's] denials and the presumption of innocence and then, only rarely'. My interviews with judicial officers and Damian Loone's former boss, Paul Hulme, were singled out.

'The implication of [his] guilt by his former solicitor, Mr Linden, is more subtle, but the publicised views of Mr Milovanovich, the coroner who presided over the second inquest, are, as with Inspector Hulme, simply declaratory of [his] guilt,' she found.

Justice Fullerton described Magistrate Linden's decision to be interviewed by me as 'surprising to say the very least', however, she rejected Phillip Boulten's argument that it was 'egregious', and should result in the stay being granted. I was the egregious one.

She found: 'At repeated intervals in the podcast Mr Thomas also paints [Chris] as a sexual predator with accompanying lurid accounts of his and his twin brother's sexual misconduct with underage girls and their membership in a "sex ring".'

She made it clear that Lloyd Babb had acted professionally and ethically at all times whereas I had 'raised the false spectre of impropriety', and that my motive was to apply pressure to the decision-makers in his office. There were serious questions, she suggested, 'as to whether the Commissioner of Police was misled [by me] into believing that

Mr Thomas had information that would be of great significance to police'.

She found that 'the narrative that links each of the successive episodes of the podcast is one which was, at all times, firmly tethered to Mr Thomas's personal belief that [Chris] murdered Lynette Dawson; that he has succeeded in avoiding being tried for her murder, either because of corrupt or incompetent police, and that those failures were in turn reinforced by the timidity of the . . . prosecuting authority'.

'It is, in my view, eloquent of a lack of ethical responsibility as a journalist,' she said.

The other significant part of the defence's stay application was the long delay in bringing the prosecution, however, Justice Fullerton found that the new evidence meant the brief of evidence was materially different to the earlier versions. Her findings referenced and footnoted the details of many witnesses and the dates of their statements to police. I went through them one by one. Although her listing was not exhaustive, it was a helpful guide. By working through all the mentions by name of these witnesses, and drawing on my knowledge of several who were not referenced in the findings, I calculated that detectives took statements from at least sixteen additional witnesses after the podcast episodes began coming out in May 2018. I doubt that police would have known of most of these individuals if it were not for the podcast and associated publicity.

Of the sixteen, I counted twelve who had come forward to me with information or been found by me, having not previously given any statement to police or been known to police. Some of the twelve I had interviewed for the podcast; some I relied on as sources. I helped police get in contact with a number of them. At least four witnesses who had no direct contact with me and no earlier contact with police, would give statements to detectives after the podcast started. These are just the ones I knew of. The relevance and importance of their evidence to the murder case varied. Some would be called to the trial; some were relied upon in the separate carnal knowledge case against Dawson. The podcast had loosened the lips of people who were hitherto silent. Mick Fuller called it 'the most powerful investigative tool I've ever seen'.

Although Justice Fullerton disapproved of Commissioner Mick Fuller's 'ill-advised' decisions to engage with me, she was 'unable to find that he deliberately, or even recklessly, joined forces with Mr Thomas to ensure that the applicant was tried for murder'.

She concluded there was no evidence my 'deliberate efforts' to force a murder trial had influenced anyone in Lloyd Babb's Office of the DPP in their decision to prosecute Chris.

In my view, after the criminal justice system had hopelessly failed a young mother of two for 36 years, a podcast highlighting the debacle attracted new witnesses who helped tip a 'no' case into a 'yes' for the DPP.

One of many who came out of the woodwork due to the podcast was a career criminal and Newtown Jets teammate of Chris, who alleged in a statement to police on 9 November 2018 that Chris asked him about getting a 'hitman' to kill Lyn in 1975, seven years before her disappearance. Three and a half weeks after he came forward, Dawson was arrested.

The system had been embarrassed by *The Teacher's Pet*. It hated it. But would the Office of the DPP have reversed its earlier decisions going all the way back to 2001 and recommended the prosecution of Chris Dawson in 2018 if there had been no podcast and, in turn, no new witnesses coming forward? Many believed the system was shamed into action by the ensuing public outcry.

Justice Fullerton's findings did shed fascinating light on the timing of several key events during the Homicide Squad's cold case reinvestigation from 2015. A major breakthrough occurred when the antecedent report, the 1982 handwritten statement of Chris Dawson with its big lies, was 'retrieved by Detective Poole in an archived folder from the Parramatta Records Repository in September 2015'. This piece of evidence was damning. Damian Loone had told me he would have immediately charged Chris with murder if Damian had found it during his earlier investigation.

But it took another 19 months, according to Justice Fullerton's findings, for New South Wales Police to forward the brief of evidence on 20 April 2017 to the police force's internal legal section 'with a request for advice as to the sufficiency of the brief of evidence to charge the applicant with murder'. Remarkably, it then took another year for the legal section of the police force on 4 April 2018 to provide its view, which was not disclosed by police to the court.

Finally, on 9 April 2018, the Homicide Squad's head Detective Superintendent Scott Cook, who knew at that time that my podcast series was imminent, sent the updated brief of evidence to the Office of the DPP for its consideration. In his covering letter, Scott Cook wrote: 'This was a murder which attracted, and continues to attract, significant public interest.'

It seems extraordinary that two years and seven months *after* finding the very serious evidence – the long-lost Dawson antecedent report – and just five weeks before *The Australian*'s May 2018 release of *The Teacher's Pet* after months of my investigation, police finally told the DPP words to the effect, 'We found new evidence and want to know if we can charge Dawson with murder.'

Why did it take so long in a case in which many witnesses were old and some were in ill health or dying?

Justice Fullerton's judgment meant Chris would definitely face a murder trial after all. His attempt to overturn her decision was rejected by the Court of Criminal Appeal in New South Wales in June 2021. The High Court of Australia rejected his bid for special leave in April 2022.

Although they had no insight into the workings of the Office of the DPP in the case, Lyn's family and many of my legal and police sources were confident Chris Dawson would not have been charged and prosecuted if it were not for *The Teacher's Pet*. Justice Fullerton could not know; the office didn't need to disclose its sensitive workings. I did not know. Speculation was pointless. It was time to look ahead to the murder trial.

A Note from the Author

After receiving a subpoena requiring me to give evidence at Chris Dawson's murder trial, I was under strict instructions to stay away for most of the hearing days.

My colleagues Matthew Condon, Claire Harvey, David Murray and Kristen Amiet covered the trial for *The Australian*.

Matthew, who went every day, wrote about the remarkable trial's ebb and flow for the Epilogue of *The Teacher's Pet*.

Epilogue

The Murder Trial

By Matthew Condon

At 8.41am on Monday 16 May 2022, Chris Dawson, 73, crossed pretty Queen's Square into the Law Courts of NSW building for the first day of evidence in his Supreme Court murder trial.

A massive media pack was waiting.

Dawson said nothing, though the day before at the Sunshine Coast Airport, he had offered a few words to a local news crew. 'I'm looking forward to justice being served and the truth coming in the next few weeks. I just want the truth to come out.'

The Law Courts building, at 30-storeys, had been officially opened in 1977 and refurbished in 2013. It is a far cry from many of Sydney's old sandstone and timber theatres of justice. It is so plain and utilitarian that you wonder if history could possibly attach itself to it.

Just after 9.30 am – three years and five months since Dawson's arrest for murder – His Honour Justice Ian Harrison SC entered the courtroom to commence proceedings in this judge-alone trial.

Harrison, appointed a Supreme Court judge in 2007 following an already distinguished career, was eloquent and no-nonsense. He had what some would consider eccentric interests: fast cars – in particular his classic yellow Holden Monaro – and he was an avid twitcher, drawn specifically to the Yellow Wattle bird, the nation's largest honeyeater.

Harrison also had a reputation for being gregarious, a bit of a practical joker with a formidable wit. On occasion throughout the trial, he would tilt his head slightly as he listened to court proceedings, his eyes beady behind wire-rimmed spectacles carrying the countenance of one of his beloved Yellow Wattles.

The stocky Craig Everson SC, deputy senior Crown prosecutor for the Office of the DPP, would display throughout the trial a quietly ruthless efficiency and an almost encyclopedic knowledge of the law.

Also under the horsehair was Dawson's defence counsel, barrister Pauline David, a specialist in criminal law. During the course of this hearing, a videotaped interview between Dawson and police on the Gold Coast in 1991 would be played to the court. Sitting beside Dawson in that video, through the dull-edged wash of old-fashioned magnetic cassette tape, was his then legal representative, a young Pauline David. She and Dawson went back a long way.

David brought an entirely different temperament to Court 9D. She appeared at times as a varying conglomerate of annoyance, frustration and occasionally exasperation. She seemed unsettled, which was not surprising. She had a tough case to run.

She was assisted by respected Sydney solicitor Greg Walsh. In his 60s, he was highly affable and proficient, although the trial would ultimately test his patience.

Another fixture in the Dawson camp was his older brother, Peter. Tall, slightly stooped, his skull shaved and polished and with dark sunglasses permanently affixed to his face, he was distinctive for his daily suits and overcoats of funereal black. Indeed, he garnered a nickname among some members of the public gallery – The Undertaker.

He took a seat behind the bar table, constantly studied his mobile phone and, as a trained lawyer, regularly passed notes up to Pauline David and her team.

Everson, in his opening address, offered an almost dot-point infrastructure of the Crown's case to come. It focused primarily on the early 1980s, when Dawson, married to Lynette and working as a physical education teacher at Cromer High School, developed a sexual interest in the schoolgirl who would become known as JC.

'He was infatuated with her,' Everson told the court.

It was this lust – for a student half his age – that triggered a caval-cade of events that the Crown said led to Lynette Dawson's murder at his hands. The Crown case would venture into the criminal under-world surrounding the Newtown Jets first-grade rugby league team, which Chris and his twin brother, Paul, played for in the 1970s. It would probe Dawson's early queries about hiring a hitman to eliminate his wife and unveil a surprise witness to come – Robert Silkman – a crim-inally connected Newtown Jets player. It would encompass allegations of domestic violence against Lyn, sexual liaisons with JC in parked cars and even in his own home up on Gilwinga Drive at Bayview.

Most importantly, it would answer the question, why did Chris Dawson do it?

'He was motivated to kill his wife Lynette by his desire to have an unfettered relationship with JC,' Everson said.

The Crown contended that Lynette had been murdered by Chris, possibly with the involvement of another 'person or persons', on or around Friday 8 January 1982.

It was an opening address that had it all – sex, a teenage lover, a hitman, shady dealings on the fringe of Sydney's underworld and a devoted mother who had vanished off the face of the earth.

Seated at a long table behind the Crown were members of Lynette's family – her brother Greg Simms, a tall, kindly former police officer, his wife Merilyn and their daughter Renee. With them was Pat Jenkins's son, David.

Resting on the table was a single sheet of white A4 copy paper, printed with: SIMMS FAMILY. It would remain there for the duration of the trial. They sat, patiently, just metres from Dawson. It was impossible not to see them as the beating heart of this tragedy.

At 9.46 am, barrister Pauline David rose to deliver a summary of the defence's case. Dawson sat at the far end of the row behind her, just below the courtroom's white-faced clock, a small black backpack at his feet.

Mr Dawson did not kill his wife Lynette, David said flatly. He may have failed her as a husband, but he did not kill her.

'It is entirely understandable that her family and those that love her would like an answer,' David told the court. 'The answer . . . does not lie in the prosecution of Christopher Dawson, and that suggestion that he has murdered his wife is the wrong answer.'

She pointed out that during the four decades Lynette had been missing, witnesses had died, other important witnesses had been ignored, police investigations had failed, there had been unexplained delays, records had been lost and there appeared to have been a reluctance by authorities to follow significant leads of 'signs of life' in relation to Lyn Dawson. There had been 'wilful' disregard by 'some' police, she added.

To come was another defence plank – that Hedley Thomas's podcast, the global phenomenon *The Teacher's Pet*, had somehow 'contaminated' the evidence of trial witnesses. That Christopher Dawson had in fact been tried and convicted by Thomas and by millions of podcast listeners before the retired teacher had even set foot in Court 9D. It was this proposition that would hover about the trial for its duration like a distant, unrecognisable scent that might announce itself at any moment.

At 10.30 am on that first day, Julie May Andrew was called as the first witness. She also happened to be the first interviewee on *The Teacher's Pet* podcast.

She entered the court with a brisk, compact step. Andrew was petite, almost impish, dressed in a black and red patterned outfit, black stockings, black shoes and a black Covid face mask. Her hair was dark and cropped short.

Before she'd even completed the short walk from the courtroom door to the witness stand, you could feel an energy that thrummed off her. A sense of purpose. That she had waited four decades for this and her moment had arrived.

Julie Andrew was a neighbour of the Dawsons in Bayview. Her property shared a fence line with Lyn's. Once they became friends, the pair established a shortcut to each other's houses through a stand of she-oaks.

Both women had young children, and Ms Andrew's evidence evoked a vanished Australian era. A time when neighbours slipped over and into each other's kitchens for a cup of a tea and a gossip. Long, hot summers with children squealing in the pool. Women who stayed at home to look after the kids and lived on tight household budgets controlled by their husbands. Buying things on your Bankcard. Decorating your home with massive ferns spilling from pots hanging from the ceiling.

Through Andrew's recollections, the court travelled back in time and was now peering behind the curtains of a deeply suburban and salacious human drama.

Andrew said she had witnessed, from her own yard, a fight between Lyn and Chris out by their kids' trampoline one weekday morning. She said she heard a 'wail' and alleged that Chris Dawson was towering over his wife, screaming at her. Ms Andrew said she heard Lyn say to one of her children immediately after the fight, 'God' or 'gosh, what's Daddy doing to us?'

Andrew said she later popped over to make sure Lyn was alright.

'She was putting on a brave front and put the kettle on for a cup of tea,' Andrew told the court. Lyn told her neighbour she was upset because JC was moving permanently into the house.

'I said, "You've got to get rid of her,"' Andrew said from the stand. 'I'm not a woman prone to swearing but I said, "Lyn, you can't have her move in here, he's [Chris] fucking the babysitter."'

Andrew jousted with Pauline David during cross-examination.

'You are incapable of coming to this court and giving impartial evidence,' said Ms David.

'No' was the reply.

'You've come here to portray Chris Dawson as a monster,' David suggested.

'I've come here to tell the truth,' Andrew shot back.

Crown prosecutor Craig Everson SC later asked Andrew why, when she realised perhaps something was amiss with Lyn, she didn't go knock on the Dawson front door to check on her welfare, or leave a note in the letterbox, or even call the police.

Andrew replied, 'Forty years ago was a very different time for women. Women were disenfranchised. I had no experience of family breakdown or domestic violence or police, for that matter. I waited for someone to knock at my door . . . No one asked me. To my great regret and shame, I didn't do anything about it.'

Justice Harrison asked her directly if she was able to put her prejudices aside and offer the court impartial evidence.

'I see myself as a person who gives people the benefit of the doubt,' she replied. 'I do believe Chris Dawson murdered his wife. I'd be lying to you if I said otherwise.'

By this stage, Chris Dawson, after a long day, was leaning slightly forward in his chair, his hands clasped together in his lap.

For anyone familiar with *The Teacher's Pet* podcast, the trial henceforth became a roll call of characters. Witness after witness would be summoned, these characters you'd grown to know through the podcast, rendered incarnate on the stage of this dreary, stained-wood courtroom.

Lyn's older sister, Pat Jenkins, shared with the court a thumbnail sketch of their childhood in the seaside suburb of Clovelly.

She spoke of Lyn's gentleness, but also of her determination to stand up for what was right wherever she saw an injustice. Lyn was opinionated and not afraid to express herself.

Pat, an elderly, kindly-faced woman in a blouse and lavender cardigan, appeared via audio-visual link from a police station 'somewhere in NSW'. She had a cloud of short grey hair that covered her ears. She spoke with the reserved solemnity of the emotionally wounded.

Pat recalled speaking to Lyn on the telephone just prior to Christmas 1981 and that Lyn had arrived home to find that Chris had gone. He'd taken his clothes, his pillow and had left her a note. It said not to 'paint too dark a picture' of him to his daughters.

'She was speaking very quickly, she was upset, she was breathing heavily . . . from the note she said she didn't know if Chris was coming home again or not,' Pat said.

At this moment in her evidence, Pat retrieved a tissue from a box out of sight of the camera and dabbed at her eyes.

'She said to me he was always so angry with her all the time,' Pat said ' . . . his black eyes flashing . . . she thought he needed to go and see a doctor.'

This was followed by an unexpected passage of evidence that would echo throughout the remainder of the trial: the letters and diary entries of Pat, Greg and Lyn's mother, the late Helena Simms.

'I am holding up three small diaries,' Everson said. 'Have you seen them before?'

'Yes, I have,' Pat replied.

'When did you see them?'

'I saw them in a group of old diaries. Mum took me into the bedroom before she died and said, "These are my diaries." She asked me to destroy them. When she passed away, I took them home. I didn't read them.'

Later, the family decided there might be some useful information in the diaries and they took them to the police and Hedley Thomas.

Some diaries are written with an eye to posterity. Others to help a disordered mind keep track of life. Many are the by-product of a compulsion – a record that tethers you to the here and now. The majority mean nothing beyond the orbit of the author, these volumes filled with life's daily minutiae – groceries purchased, records of phone calls and encounters, trips to the beach, urgent household repairs.

Mrs Simms's diaries, the quaint product of a pre-digital era, belonged to the latter category. Until her daughter Lyn went missing. At trial, those diary entries evolved to become a real-time record of events surrounding a possible murder.

Prosecutor Everson read several dozen extracts from Mrs Simms's diaries and letters into the court record, beginning in October 1981, when Mrs Simms wrote of the Dawsons' babysitter, the schoolgirl JC, and how the young woman was 'C's [Chris's] shadow'. Lyn was 'very unhappy, almost in tears about Chris'.

Then the entry of 6 December 1981, at a Christmas party in the Simms family home in Clovelly. 'Chris said, "I only want to look after my two little girls." I said, "What about Lyn?" He said, "She can get in the bloody kitchen where she belongs."'

The diaries note a phone call Mrs Simms made to Lyn – shortly before her daughter disappeared – on the evening of Friday 8 January 1982: 'Rang Lyn. Sounded half sozzled.'

Then it was the turn of Lyn's little brother, Charles Gregory Simms. Greg entered the witness stand still with the bearing and quiet authority of the NSW policeman he had once been. He served for 27 years. Throughout his evidence, Greg only referred to Dawson as 'the accused'.

Dawson remained blank-faced. Chris had been Greg's best man at his wedding to Merilyn in 1976.

'He [Chris] was a very colourful character,' Greg said. 'To have a first-grade footballer as best man, it was good to have that.'

Greg said he was at the Clovelly house when Lyn's belongings were dropped off, a moment captured in Helena Simms's diary. Greg later went through those garbage bags.

He told the court the bags were filled with 'a pair of gardening gloves with dirt still on them. There were clothes, Lyn's nurse's badges. One was a circular one. A badge nurses wore when they were on duty to show they were sisters. There was a small blue container with contact lenses in it.'

There was jewellery. And underwear.

Defence barrister Pauline David asked Greg Simms if Lyn was under a lot of pressure at the end of 1981, and if she was distressed about the state of her marriage. He agreed.

'You also said Lyn Dawson loved Chris Dawson with all her heart and soul,' Ms David said.

'That is correct.'

Greg returned to the stand the following day. Pauline David, in cross-examination, again introduced *The Teacher's Pet* podcast, dancing around the potential issue of cross-contamination of witnesses and suggesting the podcast was filled with rumours.

'What is your attitude to Mr Dawson today?' she asked pointedly.

'I wouldn't want to speak to him,' he said.

At which Justice Harrison briefly excused Greg Simms from the stand for legal argument. It would be the first of innumerable times the judge would call a temporary halt to the defence's proceedings for clarification and direction.

'Ms David,' Justice Harrison said, 'you've asked Mr Simms what his attitude is today and he says he wouldn't want to speak to him. There could be a thousand reasons why he doesn't want to speak to him. I'm not suggesting you should take up my suggestion if it's not one you . . . want to embrace.'

Greg Simms returned to the stand.

And David rattled the same cup.

'Mr Simms, as you sit here today it's the case isn't it that you feel great animosity towards Mr Dawson, don't you?'

'Great animosity?'

'Yes,' David said.

'Not great animosity.'

'You've taken the view that Mr Dawson is guilty,' David asserted.

'I believe so, yes.'

'You have a fixed view.'

'I have a fixed view but it's up to the court to decide that,' Greg said.

'The view of the podcast was that Mr Dawson was a murderer and he had gotten away with it for some decades.'

The Crown objected and Justice Harrison again interjected.

'I think what Ms David wants to know is whether or not any evidence you are able to give from your own observations might have been . . . tainted or influenced by other information that came to you, being part of the podcast,' His Honour clarified.

'A lot of information did come in, but I rely on my integrity,' Greg responded. 'In this case I wasn't influenced by Mr Thomas's podcast.'

He later added, 'I would like an answer to my sister's disappearance.'

She walked into a hushed Supreme Court 9D at 2.51 pm on the first Wednesday of the trial.

Walked is not totally accurate. She entered with just short of a heavy-footed stride, as you might if you were late for an appointment you did not want to keep.

She wore black shoes, black slacks and a white and navy floral printed blouse. Her light brown hair fell away from a central part. Now approaching her late 50s, she looked young for her age.

This was JC, the teacher's pet.

It took some moments as a court observer to register that she was real and not just a signature at the bottom of some police statement.

Dawson had glanced towards the courtroom door several times before she first entered, watched her take the stand, then ever so slightly shook his head, there in his seat beneath the ticking clock.

It was a tense scenario, former teacher and his student in the same room. Here was Dawson a few metres away from his ex-wife, breathing the same air-conditioned air. And, to offer a completely non-legal term, facing off.

JC would respond to questions from Everson and David across several days.

Everson initially took her through her family life from the late 1970s and into the early 1980s and her teenage years, socially and as a school student. She had a part-time job at Coles in Dee Why. She had a settled group of friends.

The more you heard JC, the more you knew this – her delivery was confident, not hard but firm, driven not just by the recollections she produced but something else, something far deeper. Her speech had a resolve that seemed tempered by her teenage experiences. Something horrible had happened to her that had pulled her away from her true nature and given rise to an understandable bitterness that had shifted her alignment in the world.

Listening to her in court, you got the sense that it had taken her years to truly comprehend what she had been submitted to at the hands of Dawson, that she had waited an age for maturity and wisdom to be able to make sense of her early life. The sense in court was that she was up for a fight. That here, at least, was her opportunity to set the record straight.

In her evidence, she repeated the word 'grooming': Dawson had groomed her. It was a part of his grooming process.

This older JC was looking back and commenting on her younger self as if they were two very different people, leaving the impression that she pitied the teenage JC. Was concerned for her safety. That she wanted to shout some common sense into the girl that had been her.

At the edge of it all, too, was a sense that her obvious strength and courage could fall apart with the pull of a single thread.

Everson took JC through the frayed-edged and foxed ephemera of her teenage affair with Dawson – the Christmas, birthday and Valentine's Day cards he presented to her, presumedly picked up at a local newsagency at the time, now kept in plastic sleeves as exhibits in a murder trial.

On another card Dawson wrote, . . . *love always, GOD*.

'He wanted to disguise himself and that's what he called himself,' JC told the court.

The court heard that Dawson offered JC a room in the house on Gilwinga Drive so she could study away from the tumult of her own family life. JC's mother and new husband were drinking heavily and fighting. Dawson wanted to provide her with a safe haven at a critical moment in her life. A place close to him. Besides, she had been the family babysitter now for several months.

Was the topic of you moving into the house at Bayview ever discussed between you and Lyn? Everson asked.

'No.'

'You moved in?'

'Yes.'

It was October 1981.

'Lyn was very welcoming,' JC remembered. 'Chris Dawson was very distant with her. He'd sing songs that were cruel, put her down. Songs with double meanings.

'He used to call her fatso. He referred to her while I was living there as fatso. He didn't call her Lyn. He called her fatso and laughed about it. The songs were about her unattractiveness.'

JC said that while she was at the house, she saw Lyn occasionally drinking alcohol.

'Where did the drinks come from?' Everson asked.

'Chris Dawson made them for her.'

'How many would she have?'

'Maybe one or two.'

'What happened after the drinks?'

'She would fall asleep,' JC said. 'Sometimes in the chair. Sometimes she'd excuse herself to go to bed.'

'What happened in the house after Lyn Dawson would fall asleep?'

'Chris Dawson would want to have sex with me.'

'Did it happen?'

'Yes.'

'Where?' Everson asked.

'In the bedroom I was designated.'

At this point in JC's evidence, Dawson had his head down, scribbling notes on a large writing pad.

Everson asked about her modest wedding in January 1984 in Lyn's old home.

JC: 'After all the people were leaving, all the guests, we were on the driveway and everyone had disappeared. And he turned to me and grabbed me about the neck with his hand, two hands, and I don't know why that happened, and it was frightening. For no good reason.'

On JC's second day in the witness box, Everson guided the narrative closer to the ultimate commission of murder. It was transfixing.

JC said that before she moved into the Bayview home, Dawson drove her into the western suburbs of the city, parked the car near a building and told her to wait.

JC said, 'I asked what was that about and he said, "I went inside to get a hitman to kill Lyn then I decided I wouldn't do it because innocent people could be killed, could be hurt."'

The court also heard of Dawson and JC's drive north to Queensland on 23 December 1981. The plan was to start a life together and never return to Sydney but she felt unwell and was unsure she wanted to run away with the schoolteacher and leave her family and friends behind.

A photograph appeared on the court's television monitors. It was a picture of JC in front of Dawson's car, packed with their belongings, on the brink of that great Queensland adventure. It could have been a snap of a teenager setting out on a Christmas road trip with Dad.

No questions were asked in court about why a man aged 33, with a wife and two small children, might wish to memorialise this cowardly moment – the instant he intended to abandon his family. Through the lens of forty years, it defied logic.

There were several such moments, and a fuller understanding of Dawson began to take shape, like a photographic image appearing on paper in a chemical bath.

It showed a golden child, born naturally beautiful and athletically gifted, who had transcended from ordinary circumstances to a position of not so much worship (despite his nomenclature as GOD) but adoration in the late 1970s and early 1980s as a young father, a member of the Newtown Jets rugby league team (he had his image on a football card), an occasional fashion model, a fitness instructor and a teacher.

Dawson understood the power of his attractiveness. And within a few years of his marriage to Lyn, it was this self-awareness, this rampant narcissism, that continued to grow, leaving his high school sweetheart in his wake.

By the time he became infatuated with JC, he had seemingly reached his personal apotheosis as a virile young male and remained there, intellectually and emotionally stunted as a man-child.

As Everson went to her trip to South West Rocks in early January 1982 with two of her sisters and friends from Cromer High, you could feel the air contract.

'There was a public phone box near where the caravan park was and I called Chris Dawson on the phone,' JC said.

'Why?' asked Everson.

'Because he asked me to.'

'What number did you call?'

'His home phone number.'

'What did he say to you in those phone calls?' Everson asked.

'That he missed me, that he had hives and gastric problems, the same as I had . . . that he missed me terribly and couldn't live without me, that kind of thing . . . he wanted to know exactly what I was doing.'

'What other people came up during the phone calls?'

'He asked what I was doing with other people. He didn't talk about himself.'

'What was said about Lyn?'

'Only one time he brought up Lyn Dawson.'

'What did he say?'

'"Lyn's gone and she's not coming back. Come back to Sydney and help me look after the children, be with me."'

Then Dawson drove all the way from Sydney and picked her up at South West Rocks. It was into the second week of January 1982.

Dawson, according to JC, then returned directly to Gilwinga Drive.

Everson asked, 'When you got there, what did you do?'

'Walked through the door.'

'What did you see?'

'The place exactly as last time,' JC said.

'Who did you see?'

'Nobody.'

'What time of the day or night did you arrive back at 2 Gilwinga Drive?'

'I don't remember if it was night or day.'

'When you went to sleep after arriving back there from South West Rocks, where did you sleep?'

'In Lyn's bed,' JC said flatly.

'And the night that followed?'

'In that same bed.'

'How many more nights did you sleep in that bed?'

'Every night.'

'What else was in the room apart from the bed?' Everson asked.

'A walk-in wardrobe and drawers.'

'What was inside?'

'Lots of clothes that belonged to Chris on one side and Lyn on the other.'

'What did you see in the drawers?'

'Lyn's underwear,' JC said.

She said she also noticed a basket of jewellery. 'Two diamond rings. Various costume jewellery as well. I think there was her nursing badge. Definitely the diamond rings were there.'

In the days and weeks that followed, she said, Lyn's clothes were put in garbage bags to be taken to Lyn's mother Helena's place at Clovelly.

'I was allowed to go through Lyn's clothes and keep anything I wanted.'

JC told the court she wondered when Lyn was coming back to look after the Dawson children.

'I was a child,' JC said. 'I couldn't look after two children.'

She said she had to look up a cookbook to find out how to make mashed potatoes. She had gone from a babysitter to the mother of two small children. And Dawson's 'sex slave'.

'Did you have an expectation you'd see Lyn Dawson again?' asked Everson.

'I didn't have one.'

David began her cross-examination in a quiet, almost motherly manner. But things quickly heated up, and JC held her ground.

The picture David quickly painted, and which JC repeatedly spoiled, was that Dawson had been a caring, thoughtful, respectful and personable teacher who only had his students' interests and well-being at heart.

JC, she suggested, had misinterpreted Mr Dawson's pastoral care as sexual advancements. David said Dawson has behaved respectfully towards her.

JC: 'He was behaving inappropriately by favouring me, by brushing up against me, by deliberately seeking me out in front of the class. That's disrespectful, isn't it?'

David: 'You've given evidence he treated you differently to other students. You wouldn't know how he treated other students.'

JC: 'The grooming process started early, very early on in 1980.'

David: 'You may characterise it as grooming, I'm simply asking you to talk about what was said and done in that time.'

JC: 'I told you. Special attention. Sought me out. Brushed up against me in classroom. That's grooming.'

The court heard that JC and Dawson had married in January 1984, precisely two years after Lyn Dawson disappeared in January 1982, had a child together and parted in 1990.

David questioned JC about Dawson calling his wife 'fatso' and suggested he did no such thing.

JC: 'He did, often.'

David: 'You're saying it in your mission to destroy Mr Dawson.'

JC: 'No.'

David: 'I also want to suggest he never said anything demeaning about the appearance of Lyn Dawson to you.'

JC: 'That's a lie.'

David again suggested JC was trying to destroy Dawson.

'I'm not trying to destroy him,' she said. 'He'll destroy himself from what he's done to other people, to Lyn, to me. It's the truth.'

While David's strategy appeared haphazard on the surface, it had an underlying design. Her style, repeated over and over with the rest of the trial's witnesses, was to ask a question in the form of a suggestion.

David suggested JC had misinterpreted her schoolgirl relationship with Dawson. She suggested that JC had invented the narrative surrounding her moving into the house at Bayview after Lyn had disappeared. David suggested that JC was a liar and that her previous statements to police over the decades were inconsistent.

David: 'Did you ever say to Lynette Dawson on any occasion that you wanted to get rid of her?'

JC: 'No.'

David: 'Did you convey to Lynette Dawson that you wanted to have her out of the way?'

JC: 'Absolutely not. I respected her. As a mother, she was a terrific mother. She was respectful of me. I didn't want the responsibility of cooking, cleaning, and looking after Lyn's children whom she loved. I wondered where she was. I wanted her to come back so I could go and live my life as a 17-year-old. Mr Dawson was a very explosive person, and I did everything I could to avoid that by complying with every request he made. I think I resigned myself to the fact that I was not going to get away from him, because I'd tried. And he had pursued me down the street, rapped on the door. I didn't feel as though I had a choice.'

David: 'I suggest to you that Mr Dawson was never violent towards you?'

JC: 'A lie.'

Prosecutor Craig Everson SC briefly stood for re-examination. He asked JC about the jewellery she was photographed wearing on her wedding day to Chris Dawson.

A bangle. An engagement ring. A wedding ring she had received that day.

'The wedding ring was made from scratch to match his [Chris's] one from his first marriage,' JC said. 'The diamond ring was made using the diamonds from Lyn's engagement ring and eternity ring. That she left.'

Some in the public gallery simply shook their heads; Chris had broken down and repurposed Lyn's own rings for his new bride.

When JC was excused, she rose and walked straight out of the court. She did not pause by the door and bow to His Honour, as is custom.

Everson now informed the court, 'There is an expectation that we'll move at a cracking pace from now on in this trial.'

He was true to his word.

*

If the babysitter's evidence was the core plotline, then what followed was a non-chronological sequence of cameos; tranches of men and women who had bloomed at various points along the timeline of this tragedy and, in turn, lowered their own tiles into the mosaic of the trial.

The courtroom travelled back in time to Saturday 9 January 1982, the day Dawson took his children to the Northbridge Baths, where he worked part-time as a lifesaver. Dawson claimed that Lyn had told him she was going to the markets that morning.

At the baths, Dawson claimed he received a telephone call from Lyn, telling him she needed a break from their relationship and was off to see friends. Young employees at the baths who were there on that crucial day, now middle-aged women, were called to the stand.

Then came several women who worked with Lyn at a Warriewood childcare centre. Barbara Cruise. Annette Leary. Anna Grantham and Sue Strath. They offered their observations on Lyn's state of mind at the time. Here, the defence once again raised its nebulous theory – had the testimony of these women been 'contaminated' by their engagement with the podcast *The Teacher's Pet*?

JC's sisters appeared as witnesses. The younger remembered being taunted by her fellow students with the then popular song 'Don't Stand So Close to Me' sung by Sting of the British pop group The Police. The lyrics involved teachers being the subject of school-girl fantasies.

Justice Harrison added in a moment of levity, 'I hate to admit it, but I know the lyrics.'

Everson replied, 'So does the Crown.'

Defence lawyer Greg Walsh seemed nonplussed. 'It's beyond my knowledge.'

Next were a slew of former Cromer alumni who had seen the PE teacher Dawson being flirtatious with JC on numerous occasions.

They were followed by the then teenagers who had been on that caravan holiday at South West Rocks with JC in January 1982. They were witnesses to the girl's last moments of freedom beyond Dawson's orbit. He would soon be chaperoning her back to Gilwinga Drive and installing her as his new partner and mother to his children.

Chris's older brother Peter Dawson was called to the stand. His deep, rattly cough had regularly entered the landscape of the trial like moments of firm punctuation. He had the women in the public gallery quietly shaking their heads when he described Lyn as 'a competent mother'.

As the trial turned the corner on the run for home, the outer world finally, and emphatically, insinuated itself.

'Have you heard what's happened?' asked Greg Walsh on his way to the bar table. 'Crown. Covid.'

Craig Everson SC had been struck down by the virus. The trial was adjourned for a week.

Identical twin brother Paul Anthony Dawson appeared as a witness via audio-visual link. It was a peculiar double-take situation. The only difference between the Dawson on the TV screen and the Dawson sitting near the courtroom wall clock was that one faced the rest of his life behind bars if found guilty of murder.

And metaphorical mirrors were suddenly everywhere.

Paul Dawson was asked if he had ever spent a lot of time in the car with his own teenage babysitter. And had he ever been in a swimming pool at a Sydney suburban school at the same time as Chris and JC? 'Not to my knowledge,' he said.

Paul Dawson said Lyn was not 'overly affectionate' and that she 'felt her children didn't need her as much' as those at the local child-care centre where she worked as a nurse.

This assessment provoked a shocked reaction from some of Lyn's relatives observing proceedings, and sent a murmur through the back half of the court.

Then, another ripple.

Paul Dawson exited left from the video link and up popped his former babysitter herself, beamed in from her home. Only hours earlier, she'd been a nameless figure. Now here she was, looking down, albeit virtually, on the court.

Paul's babysitter, blonde and tanned, vividly recalled her younger self on Sydney's Northern Beaches. Yes, she told the court, she had driven around in a car with Paul and Chris Dawson in the front seat, and she and JC in the back.

The recovered Everson asked, 'What did Chris Dawson say if anything about Lyn Dawson in those drives in the car to and from the Lindfield school?'

'Things like . . . that she was a bitch.'

'A what, sorry?'

'A bitch.'

Another court room tremor.

Defence barrister Pauline David said this assertion was a total fabrication.

The witness carousel continued for days, then weeks. People came forward and swore that they or someone they knew before the person died, had caught a glimpse of Lyn in various locations after she was allegedly murdered. In Gladesville in Sydney's inner-west. In Macquarie Street, the city, during the royal visit of then Prince Charles and wife, Lady Diana, in 1983. At a fruit barn on the Central Coast. The defence was pushing the question: if she'd been seen, how could she have been killed by Chris?

At this point, several weeks into the trial, the supposition that Lyn Dawson had been seen alive in various locations but only by friends and relatives of Chris Dawson, did not just stretch credulity but suggested that proceedings had gone off the rails.

It brought to mind the great writer Helen Garner's query in her classic courtroom drama, *This House of Grief*: 'Was there a form of madness called court fatigue?'

The next witness seemed to confirm that madness.

In his opening address several weeks prior, Crown prosecutor Everson had said off the top: 'On the first of October 1975, Muhammad Ali fought Joe Frazier in the Philippines. That fight was watched by members of the Newtown rugby league team, who had travelled to the Gold Coast for an end of season holiday as it were.

'On the return flight, seated in an aisle seat was Robert Silkman, a man with some admitted criminal connections. He was approached by Chris Dawson, the accused. The two of them were well known to each other having played together in the second-grade side at Newtown.

'And the Crown alleges that the accused asked Mr Silkman if he knew someone who could get rid of his wife. That is a matter that went no further.'

The clear imputation was that Dawson had sought a hitman to eliminate his wife Lyn and had attempted to tap the connections of a man with tendrils in the underworld. In October 1975, Lyn and Chris had been told she would be unable to bear children; Lyn had plans to adopt.

The court heard that Silkman had recently sustained a spine injury in a fall down a set of stairs, and legal debate centred on whether he should give evidence at a local police station or courthouse, or be permitted to speak from his suburban heart of darkness due to his pain and discomfort.

The following day, Silkman stepped out of the shadows and into the light of a police interview room in western Sydney and was beamed into the trial.

Silkman's evidence was to be repeatedly potholed by objections from David. Between the stoppages, though, a faint picture of a mid-70s rough-and-tumble world of the Newtown Jets rugby league team and after-game drinking at the Henson Park Hotel in Marrickville with Silkman's criminal associates emerged.

Silkman was asked about his rugby league playing history, the training schedule of the Newtown Jets and the players downing a few drinks at 'the pub in the next street'.

During Silkman's sporadic evidence, he admitted that he couldn't recall if Chris or Paul Dawson ever came to the hotel and socialised with the other players.

Then the Crown asked, 'In addition to going to the Henson Park Hotel after training sometimes, and Newtown Leagues Club, who else was in your social circle at that time in 1975?'

Silkman said one of his friends, and a fellow Jets player, was a man called Paul Hayward.

Paul Cecil Hayward played 73 first-grade games for the Newtown Jets (14 tries; 43 goals), but was arrested in Thailand and charged with trying to import more than eight kilograms of heroin into Australia in 1978. He ultimately died of a heroin overdose.

Hayward's brother-in-law was convicted murderer Arthur 'Neddy' Smith, one of Australia's most feared gangsters in his day. Smith died in jail in 2021.

Defence barrister David strongly objected to what she described as the Crown's backdoor attempt to imply that Chris Dawson was somehow associated with this criminal milieu.

The following day, the extensive criminal history of Silkman was aired. It was perhaps David's finest moment in the trial. She disembowelled Silkman's character, running him through his criminal past which extended from alleged arson to fraud.

David said he was lying about Dawson approaching him and seeking a hitman.

'Incorrect,' Silkman said.

And with that, the audio-visual link was cut off and Robert Silkman was terminated.

Sometimes it's possible to study a person's bearing and guess, with a degree of accuracy, their higher calling. Damian Loone is one such person. You only needed to take one look at Loone and a single word came to mind: detective.

The disappearance of Lynette Dawson had hovered around almost the entirety of his career (he joined the force in 1986 and retired in 2021). As the case's leading detective for years, he had interviewed the bulk of the major and minor players, hunted for documents, produced briefs, marshalled material for inquests and, finally, here he was as a witness in a trial that had his fingerprints all over it.

Tall, ruddy-faced and with studied patience, he was used to the occasional rough and tumble of court, and the uppercuts the defence might throw at him. He entered the witness box with the sort of easy manner that said he had been in the same position many, many times before.

It was irrefutable that Loone was the first detective to gain genuine traction in the case of Lyn's disappearance. When he read the transcript of the 1991 interview between Chris Dawson and Loone's predecessor, Detective Sergeant Paul Mayger, he felt that 'something gravely suspicious had happened' to Lyn.

When David asked him directly if he believed then that Chris was responsible for his wife's death, Loone simply replied, 'Yes.'

David would later share with the court her deep concerns about Loone's early investigation, saying that he and his police colleagues were 'uninterested with Lynette Dawson being alive . . . that wasn't a lead worth following up.' She said the police investigations were wilfully 'improper'.

Former homicide squad detective Paul Mayger was called to the stand and quizzed at length about his 1990–91 investigation and why police did not follow up the purported sighting by Sue Butlin of the missing mother outside a fruit barn soon after she supposedly vanished.

Mayger said that he did not interview Sue Butlin, who allegedly saw Lyn. Sue, the wife of Ray Butlin, a Gosford football friend of the Dawson twins, died in the 1990s and never made a police statement.

'It may have been it was something we had intended to do, but you have to remember . . . being in the homicide squad and being on call . . . the workload often meant that matters such as this that weren't fresh, weren't alive so to speak, got pushed to the back,' Mayger told the court.

This supposed sighting, conveniently conveyed in 1991 by the then murder suspect Dawson while being formally questioned by the homicide detective, was the key claim which terminated the police investigation at the time. Mayger said he had raised the purported sighting with the DPP and the Coroner, and he was advised that 'unless we could refute that evidence, then the investigation probably shouldn't proceed'. Sue Butlin went unquestioned; yet the murder probe was still terminated.

The decision to give up on a murder investigation because of this unverified claim by Dawson was a turning point, three decades before the trial.

Then on Monday 27 June, during the trial's late morning tea break, a haunting snippet of music accidentally leaked through the courtroom's speakers: the opening soundtrack to *The Teacher's Pet* podcast.

This slippage of sound – presumably from a defence counsel computer – heralded the imminent arrival of podcast creator and multi-Walkley Award-winning national chief correspondent for *The Australian*, Hedley Thomas. He was one of the final star witnesses as this trial entered its eighth week.

At 11.41 am, the journalist, attired in a navy suit and a blue shirt and tie, was called by the Crown and went to the witness stand.

It was fascinating to watch Thomas in court. I had first met him on the Gold Coast in the early 1980s when I worked as a cadet reporter on the *Gold Coast Bulletin*. Thomas, then just 16, came by chance to our home at Nerang for a barbecue with some friends of my parents. He indicated to my mother that he too wished to have a career in journalism. Before long, my mother contacted *Bulletin* editor John Burton and said there was a young lad at Keebra Park State High School who had his heart set on being a journalist. An interview with Burton was arranged. Thomas left school and started as a copyboy at the *Bulletin*'s offices at the back of Southport at the end of 1984. At that moment, Chris Dawson and his new wife, JC, were packing up the house at Gilwinga Drive, Bayview, for their new life in Queensland. And at the start of 1985 Dawson began his new job – as physical education teacher at Keebra Park State High School. The young copyboy and the teacher had missed each other by a matter of weeks.

Tall, bespectacled and with a rich voice that barely needed artificial amplification, Thomas was asked his full name by the prosecution and a few questions about a list of people he had interviewed. Then the floor was opened to defence barrister David.

It was logical to assume that Thomas would have been one of the defence's primary focuses for two reasons. First, it was *The Teacher's Pet* that had brought Lyn's cold case roaring back to life, offering the sort of granular focus on Chris Dawson that had never been applied before. And it had dragged fresh facts to the table about what really might have happened to Lyn.

Second, it had done so via the relatively new communication platform of the podcast, a form of audio journalism that could dive deeper and more quickly reach an infinitely larger audience than the traditional legacy media.

The rise and impact of podcasts had been so meteoric that the law had yet to catch up. This was the target of the defence's witness 'contamination' argument. If Pauline David was to bring home this argument, she would have to explore it in depth in her cross-examination of Thomas.

Instead, she took the analytical low road. And it was here that the courtroom, already heated to mildly sweltering, got warmer.

David declared that the podcast was from the outset an exercise in condemning Christopher Dawson.

'No, I disagree,' said Thomas. If as a journalist he had uncovered or received information that disrupted or changed the narrative, that disputed the findings of the two coronial inquests into Lyn's disappearance, then that would have become a 'very significant part of the podcast'.

'When you were embarking on the podcast, you'd formed the view that Christopher Dawson was guilty of murder?' David asked.

'No,' said Thomas. He said that at the start he thought it was quite likely, and as his investigation developed he became very sure Dawson was his wife's killer.

'Or the probable murderer as you refer to in the podcast . . . so it was premised on the basis that he had committed the murder.'

'I don't think it was premised on that basis. I think there had been a failure of police to properly investigate. And that led into a failure of the system to put the matter before the court.'

'You also included Mr Dawson in accusations about sex rings of teachers on the Northern Beaches, didn't you?'

'Yes.'

David continued. 'When you talked about the podcast, the message you conveyed to Lyn Dawson's family was you would assist them to seek justice for Lyn.'

'Yes.'

'So justice for Lyn meant the prosecution of Christopher Dawson.'

'Yes, I think that's a fair call.'

Thomas was also subjected to the defence's now familiar grilling-by-audio-excerpt, an almost tortuous method of cross-examination whereby audio grabs were played to the court and the witness was then questioned on the ins and outs of the content. Then they were taken to another bite of sound. And another. And yet another.

The music of the podcast started again as Pauline David played a snippet of Hedley Thomas narrating a piece about purported sightings of Lyn at a fruit barn and elsewhere.

'Any suggestion of a confirmed sighting of Lyn Dawson after 8 January 1982 is a cruel hoax. And yet over the years it's been put to Lyn's family by lawyers representing the Office of the DPP that there had in fact been such a sighting, possibly by Lyn's own mother, and that this was one of the reasons there has not been a prosecution.

'It's absolutely wrong. But if it's true that the DPP has baulked at prosecuting because of this completely misguided belief about a so-called sighting of Lyn, heads in there should roll.'

Pauline David suggested, 'Do you agree that that is the message that was conveyed throughout the podcast? That any sighting was a false sighting?'

The journalist countered that he had clearly stated every suggestion of a 'confirmed sighting' was a cruel hoax.

'Confirmed means, for me, corroborated and definite, not a fleeting glimpse where the person doesn't even say, "Hi, I'm Lyn Dawson, you've found me,"' Thomas said.

On more than one occasion, David shifted from asking questions to her now familiar suggestive declarations. She said to Thomas that at no stage in *The Teacher's Pet* podcast did he ever give Dawson the benefit of the doubt.

'I don't know if I gave him the benefit of doubt ...' Thomas responded. 'I formed the view, which got stronger, that he'd gotten away with murder.'

'You continued to talk to people, witnesses, about what other witnesses had said ... [you weren't] concerned at all by the fact you may have contaminated those witnesses by telling them what other witnesses had said?'

'The case was 36 years old ... there'd been no prosecution for 36 years,' Thomas replied.

'Your hope was to bring one about, wasn't it?'

'I hoped to flush out new witnesses that might make the difference.'

Much of the repartee that followed seemed to hover around an elusive conundrum: the function of journalism in society. What it can and can't do, what its responsibility is and where the craft is even permitted to tread in the context of the law. This was the elephant in the room. Potentially, it was a huge point of debate, one that would require an entire symposium to unpick.

There was little point in simply declaring that the podcast had contaminated witness statements. The critical issue left unexplained by the defence was simple. How? How had that legal biohazard occurred on a micro-level, or on any level?

The defence never produced an answer. And in the absence of that answer, Thomas was by proxy drawn into having to defend journalism itself.

He was forthright in trying to explain his work. He wanted to make a difference in an important case that had been cold for decades. He was seeking justice for Lyn.

The defence, however, seemed to be looking down the opposite end of the telescope. David accused Thomas of undermining public confidence in important institutions involved in the criminal justice process.

'My job is not to uphold confidence in these institutions,' Thomas said, 'it's to question whether something's gone wrong.'

It was as powerful and memorable a statement as the trial had produced to date. And the defence, again, had no answer.

Then, just when you thought this lengthy court ordeal was limping to a close, something miraculous happened: everyone in Court 9D got to meet Lynette Joy Dawson, missing since 8 January 1982.

The defence team decided to play an episode of the ABC's television documentary series *Chequerboard*, about the nature of twins, featuring Chris and Paul Dawson. The episode, titled 'Heckle and Jeckle, Bib and Bub', went to air in late 1975. In it, the Dawson boys, in their prime, were extensively interviewed. So too were Paul's wife, Marilyn, and Chris's wife, Lynette.

To suddenly see her up on the court's four television monitors – manifested, tangible, incarnate after a seemingly unending blizzard of words and documents and photographs – was astonishing.

It was difficult to ascertain the defence's motive in playing the ancient clip. Was it to show Chris Dawson and his family as an average, loving, all-Australian household?

What it in fact did show, and profoundly so, was the opposite. We got to see Lyn as a three-dimensional human being. We understood with indisputable clarity what had been lost in this case, and the future life she'd been denied.

It was only when the episode was over and the screens switched off that you noticed the long tables just behind the Crown prosecutor and his team near the middle of the court. For eight weeks, that space has been occupied by the Simms family. Now, it sat empty except for Greg's jacket, hanging over the back of a chair.

The defence had one last card up its sleeve: a Paul Stephen Cooper, 60, from the Gold Coast.

Cooper, dressed in a pale grey suit, cream shirt without tie and black runners with white trimming, entered the court and walked to the witness stand on the balls of his feet, his style of perambulation giving him a half-swagger. His darkish hair was swept straight back from his forehead, and he sported a grey Caballero-style sawn-off moustache that contrasted to his head hair.

Cooper, who said he had never met Chris Dawson nor any members of the Dawson family, told the court that back in the early months of 1982, he popped into the Warners Bay Hotel on Lake Macquarie, south-west of Newcastle, for a drink with friends and relatives, and caught the eye of an attractive young woman sitting alone at a table. She was nursing a tumbler of water.

Then just 20, Cooper sidled over to the table and started talking to this woman he believed was in her late 20s, possibly early 30s.

And what a story she had to tell.

In no time, she started relaying how she had recently left her husband after discovering that he had been unfaithful. She had children and had walked out on them too.

She explained to young Cooper that she had no ID and had 'left everything behind'. She had some cash because she'd sold a personal item. She was waiting for her passport to come through so she could travel to Bali and beyond.

The mysterious woman, wearing a scarf, also said that she was on the way to her sister's place but was still building up the courage. She believed her sister might try and talk her into returning to her husband and family.

She told Cooper she wasn't going back.

On the witness stand, Cooper said, 'I said, "What about the children? It's not fair to them." We had a conversation about that . . . I grew up without me parents . . . I said it's not fair to them without their mother . . . I told her how hard it is and how hard it was for me . . . I tried to drill into her to get it across to her.'

Cooper told the court he bought her a glass of white wine and he sipped on Jim Beam and Coca-Cola.

He said the woman asked him if he could book a motel room for her under his name, and he said he 'thought the obvious, you know, it's for me and her', but was quickly put in his place.

Then, with a couple of bourbons on board, she shocked him.

'I did say to her by her leaving all her belongings, her purse and everything else at home, there was a good chance people might think her husband had done something to her, that he'd knocked her . . . when I looked back at her, she had a different demeanour.'

Had he stumbled across some sinister criminal plot in a tradies' watering hole?

It wasn't until Cooper saw a television current affairs program decades later that he realised the woman at the heart of this unforgettable moment was none other than Lyn Dawson.

The defence had found its own version of Robert Silkman.

It was unusual and unexpected evidence on which the defence rested its case. A shadowy sighting. A scheme by Lyn Dawson to set up her husband for murder. A witness with an extensive criminal history whose life had been salvaged by God.

If the case had not been about a murder, and if the stakes hadn't been so high, it would have been comical.

For the duration of his trial, Chris Dawson kept to his routine with the focus of an athlete.

He and his legal team met each morning in an anteroom off Court 9D. At morning tea or lunch, Dawson often had a can of Coca-Cola.

In court, he sat in his chair beneath the clock, rarely paying any meaningful attention to the witnesses, despite a cursory glance as they came and went from the witness stand. (JC was different. Though even then, the occasional shake of his head amounted to little.)

Dawson came. And he went.

In the final days of the trial, His Honour had come down with a sniffle. 'I'm not well,' he said. He reported that he was Covid negative. 'You can all relax. Okay, we're back on air.'

Craig Everson's final submission was sleek and logical.

Pauline David's was harder to follow. Everson took the court back to Saturday, 9 January and the hours after Lyn's no-show at Northbridge Baths. Paul Dawson said he was staying at that time at Lake Munmorah with Marilyn and their daughters in 'Aunty Audrey's caravan'.

Lyn's two daughters and their grandmother Helena had been driven from the baths by Phil Day to stay at the Simms family home at Clovelly.

Dawson 'had his dominoes all lined up and they were ready to fall', the prosecutor charged, adding 'this engineered window of quiet seclusion gave the accused the opportunity to dispose of a body before he started making his way north to collect JC'.

Pauline David meandered across her material. At one point, she told the court that the defence did not know what happened to Lyn Dawson after she was, according to Chris, dropped off at suburban Mona Vale on the morning of Saturday 9 January 1982. Maybe she had since passed away. Maybe there was the 'deeply unpleasant possibility' that she had committed suicide.

Justice Harrison interjected. 'But there'd be a body, wouldn't there? You can't dispose of your own body after you've taken your own life.'

David cited the case of former prime minister Harold Holt, lost at sea off Portsea, Victoria in 1967. It was an incongruous observation that briefly jolted the court, like a bum note played in a symphony.

As David continued, Justice Harrison repeatedly intervened. 'I want you to help me,' he said. He needed her to elucidate what was wrong with the Crown's case. 'I'm in your hands, really,' he added.

After four days, the defence finally brought its submission to a close. It was Monday 11 July.

The discussion then turned to Dawson's bail conditions. He was subject to an order to report to police every Monday, Wednesday and Friday and he was not permitted to travel beyond a set kilometre radius from his place of residence at Coolum, Queensland. Justice Harrison relaxed Dawson's reporting conditions to every Friday and told the court he would come to judgment soon. 'Not by tomorrow, I can assure you, but relatively quickly.'

The clock hit 12.09 pm.

'Alright. Thank you for your assistance,' Justice Harrison said in his husky, flu-struck voice. 'I'll reserve my decision and adjourn.'

With that, he stood, walked to the door at the rear of the room, issued one final cough, and was gone.

Just after 8.30 am on 30 August, Dawson, Greg Walsh and Peter Dawson entered the southern end of historic Queen's Square. The square had for hours been populated with media crews.

As Dawson and his team made their way to the court building entrance, a media scrum engulfed them. Walking at the edge of the scrimmage was Chris's twin, Paul. Paul hadn't attended a day of the trial and gave evidence via video link, but here he was, supporting his brother on this critical day of judgment.

As the phalanx slowly progressed across the square, Paul flanked it all the way to the courthouse steps when he was accidentally bumped by an oblivious television cameraman. Paul Dawson immediately lashed out and shoved the cameraman in the back. The melee quickly dissipated.

Dawson's verdict hearing was no longer scheduled for Court 9D, but 13A, four levels up. The newly assigned courtroom allowed for additional interested spectators who came from far and wide to view proceedings via audio-visual link in the adjacent, spacious Banco Court.

Team Dawson gathered casually on the western side of the court. They were relaxed. Peter Dawson led a conversation that elicited laughter from those around him. It could have been a weekend summer barbecue. Were they anticipating a 'not guilty' verdict?

A reporter approached the group and both Peter and Chris Dawson shook his hand warmly. They had a yarn. Solicitor Greg Walsh sat alone on a chair to the side of the group, writing feverishly in a notebook.

At 9.30 am, the court opened its doors and many of the public spectators, the majority of them female, edged their way in. Nearly all of these women were festooned in pink scarves and pink blouses and pink ribbons – even pink anti-Covid surgical masks – in honour of Lyn Dawson. For a moment, in that dreary court, it appeared spring had already sprung.

Justice Harrison took his seat on the stroke of 10 am. He had a monologue of great gravity to deliver, along with a decision that might instantly change the life of a fellow human being. His tone this time was flat; there were no quips.

'The Crown case is wholly circumstantial,' he informed the court.

As Justice Harrison read his verdict, it was impossible to detect his decision. One moment, he rejected a tranche of witness evidence that would have been favourable to the Crown. The next he gave no weight to allegations that Dawson had inflicted domestic violence against his missing wife. Then he rejected claims that people had seen Lyn Dawson weeks, months and years after her alleged murder.

At around 3 pm, Harrison's reading pace demonstrably slowed. There was a tangible sense in the room that a verdict was imminent.

The genius of Harrison's reasoning was the way it stripped back the forty-year detritus. It removed, by reason of logic and human experience, Dawson's version of events offered through the years, as well as that proposed through his defence counsel.

In the end, with everything removed, Dawson was left alone on a stage of his own making.

At precisely 3.11 pm, after over four hours, Justice Ian Harrison looked up at Christopher Michael Dawson and proclaimed, 'I find you guilty.'

Some in the public gallery emitted throaty gasps of shock; others started weeping.

Dawson was standing at the rear bar table. He briefly turned to his brother Peter and for all the world looked like he expected to go back home, that perhaps this small matter of murder could be sorted out some other time.

Justice Harrison informed Dawson that it would now be necessary to take him into custody. Two prison officers made their way towards Dawson. It was now clear why the venue for the verdict had been changed: Court 13A had a prisoner's dock.

Dawson was quickly handcuffed then bundled unceremoniously to the right of the court, towards the glass-panelled dock. As the guards, one on each side of Dawson and gripping his arms, marched him into that small space, the convicted murderer listed sideways, his limp impeding him. His feet were almost dragged across the carpet.

It was a pathetic sight, a final glimpse of a wounded animal being led to his fate.

Dawson could not know that spontaneous applause and cheers and hooting had erupted from more than one hundred spectators gathered in the nearby Banco Court.

Downstairs, in Queen's Square, a massive media pack waited. There were dozens of television crews. Media choppers buzzed overhead. It felt like a moment that had stopped the nation.

Lyn's brother Greg eventually appeared on the steps of the Law Courts building, overlooking the square, alongside his wife Merilyn, daughter Renee and son Craig. Pat Jenkins's son David was there. So too was former detective, Damian Loone, and his wife Rachel Young. And journalist Hedley Thomas and his wife Ruth. Ben Fordham stood nearby.

It wasn't entirely sombre, this impromptu press conference, but it was far from a celebration.

First off, Greg reclaimed his sister's name. She would now be known as Lynette Joy Simms.

He added: 'The journey is not complete. She's still missing. We still need to bring her home. We would ask Chris Dawson to find it in himself to finally do the decent thing and allow us to bring Lyn home to a peaceful rest. Finally showing her some dignity she deserves.'

Hedley paid tribute to Lyn's family, Damian, Dan Poole, the prosecution team led by Craig Everson, and to JC for having disclosed things to Lyn's family and police in 1990.

One of the most emotional moments in this epic saga came on Thursday, 10 November when the Supreme Court heard the victim impact statements during Dawson's sentencing hearing.

The most profound, and moving, was delivered by his oldest daughter, Shanelle.

After hearing from Lyn's brother Greg and sister Pat Jenkins, Shanelle entered the witness stand, directly across from her father in the dock, at 12.34 pm. Women in the public gallery variously whispered, 'Good girl', 'Dear girl', and 'Breathe, darling'.

Dawson looked down at his shoes.

'The night you removed our mother from our lives was the night you destroyed my sense of safety and belonging in this world for many decades to come,' Shanelle said. 'Almost all of the love, nurturing and kindness vanished from my life.

'Because of your selfish actions, we will never see her again, we will never hear her tell us she loves us, feel her hold us or hear her laugh.

'There are not enough words in the English language to describe the impact of 41 years of deceit, trauma, being silenced and gas-lighted, the absence of a loving mother–grandmother, abusive-unloving replacements, emotional and psychological abuse. The fact that the father I love and trusted is capable of such a heart-wrenchingly selfish, brutal and misogynistic act – she's no longer any use to you, a hindrance with no value, you can coldly dispose of her in such utter disrespect . . . this has affected my trust in men and subconsciously, every relationship I've had.

'For many years I worked through abandonment issues, believing that our beautiful Mother left of her own accord and I had believed what you said, because she didn't love us anymore. Most, if not every day I feel the absence of her from our lives.'

Shanelle continued, clear and strong. The court was completely hushed.

'No mother to cuddle me when I'm hurt or sad,' she said of her loss. 'No mother to love, help or advise me. No mother to be a role model for my own mothering. No weekly home-cooked meals to return home to, no family gatherings, birthdays, Christmas to look forward to.

'You took that away and so much more and you had no right to. You are not God.'

It was a heart-breaking scene. Shanelle, who was just four years old when her mother was murdered, faced her father, the convicted killer. And still he couldn't look his daughter in the eye.

'It hurts me deeply to think of you in jail for the rest of your life,' she concluded. 'But I also choose not to carry your burdens anymore. I need my life back. My daughter needs me back and not overwhelmed by grief anymore.

'This is how I will honour my beautiful mother. The torture of not knowing what happened, or what you did with her body, please tell us where she is.

'I hope you will finally admit the truth to yourself and give us the last bit of closure we need, to make at least partial peace with this horrible tragedy.'

Dawson was back in Court 13A on Friday 2 December 2022 for sentencing.

Prison officials were seated nearby. Dawson was in the dock, dressed in prison greens. He looked older. Jowly. Miserable.

The public gallery was packed – there had even been some minor jostling for seats – and tense. The day had finally come for Dawson to be held accountable for his actions. He had lived a full forty years of life beyond that of his first wife, Lyn, and there was a tangible sense that people were in the public gallery to see him suffer.

Justice Harrison entered the court and got down to business. His Honour said Dawson had good prospects of rehabilitation. Some in the gallery laughed. When the judge said that at 74 and with his various health issues, Dawson would find the conditions of incarceration more 'onerous' than most other inmates, one of Lyn's childhood friends whispered, 'Bad luck.' Justice Harrison then pointed out that Dawson would likely not live to see out the end of his non-parole period; someone in the gallery snapped, 'Good.'

'Lynette Dawson was faultless and undeserving of her fate,' Justice Harrison said.

'Despite the deteriorating state of her marriage to Mr Dawson she was undoubtedly also completely unsuspecting.'

Finally, when His Honour sentenced Dawson to 24 years in jail, with a non-parole period of 18 years, another in the gallery turned and asked, 'Are we allowed to cheer?'

Dawson remained stone-faced. His older brother Peter, seated within touching distance of the dock with legal counsel Greg Walsh, was similarly unmoved. Twin Paul wasn't at the sentencing.

'Mr Dawson,' Justice Harrison said, 'would you please go with the officers now.'

It was 12.26 pm. Dawson had been in court for exactly 30 minutes, and lost 24 years of his life.

Justice Harrison then departed.

For the first time since the trial began in May, there were smiles in court. Smiles on the faces of Lyn's family. A smile on the face of prosecutor Craig Everson SC.

'Are you happy?' he was asked.

'I'm never happy,' he said. Then he winked.

Smiles from the police, including former detective Damian Loone, and current cold case Homicide Squad detectives.

Solicitor Greg Walsh left the court quietly. 'This is my last day, I'm out of it now,' he said.

'You did your best,' someone said by way of consolation.

'I did my best,' he said flatly.

The sense of relief was no greater held than by Lyn's family.

'I'll never have to see Christopher Michael Dawson again,' Greg Simms said without malice. 'This has been hanging over us for so long.'

Greg later told the media on the steps of the court building that from this day forward, he wanted his sister to be known as Lynette Joy Simms.

Soon after, the bells of St Mary's Cathedral began to ring. The chiming washed through the northern end of Hyde Park, in and about the great fig trees, the sound spilling across Macquarie Street and into the square beside the courts.

The media left. As did the Simms family. And all the lawyers and police and public spectators.

And those cathedral bells rang and rang and rang.

Postscript

On the outskirts of Orange, birthplace of my father, Hedley Robert Thomas, a narrow road uphill leads to a rusty gate and a long row of pine trees soaring high above the fields. Loewenthal Lane was named after Les Loewenthal, an eccentric orchardist who grew apples and pears, railed against bureaucrats and wrote hundreds of letters for publication in the town's local newspapers.

My close friend and cousin, Rob Loewenthal, and his father, Darrell, brought me here in April 2017. My visit was prompted by sadness and longing.

One month earlier, in a hospital bed on the Gold Coast, my father was taking his final breaths and saying goodbye.

'I'm so proud of you, Dad,' I told him.

'I'm proud of you too, pal,' he replied.

My loyal stepmother, Donna, held him in a loving embrace. Dad went peacefully soon afterwards.

Dad had talked to me about Loewenthal Lane, the pine trees, orchards and family farmhouse. He had been to this place – his mother's childhood home – many times as a boy. There were happy memories.

Rob and I walked to the house with its broken timber flooring. Abandoned relics from another farming era were strewn in the fields, which had long been cleared of fruit trees. We met a friendly young woman who had recently started to renovate. She kindly invited us to come in and look around.

I stood in each room and stared at the empty spaces where the beds went and the dressing tables stood and the pictures hung. When I closed my eyes, I saw my grandmother here. As a girl. A teenager. And a young mother, holding my father.

I looked wistfully for too long at an ancient stone sink where clothes were once handwashed. I saw a baby boy being lovingly bathed in this sink. I saw my father. It was eerie and comforting at the same time.

Where do stories that affect us start? Where do they end? I was deeply moved in the house on Loewenthal Lane. It gave me a connection – through blood, grief and nostalgia – to my father. And to his mother. A woman who would disappear from the Northern Beaches in 1956. Never to be seen again.

'The missing woman is Mrs Gladys Olga Thomas, 35, of Pacific Parade, Deewhy,' the *Sydney Morning Herald* had reported.

Rob had been suggesting for ages before our journey to Orange that I should try to tell a big story in a podcast series. For a long time, I was not ready. When I was ready, I knew it needed to be a story that would make a difference. A story with which I felt a unique connection. A story that might help answer difficult questions.

Lyn's case, the story that became *The Teacher's Pet*, met these needs.

I reflected on some of the unusual coincidences and karmic happenings, while standing outside the Supreme Court in Sydney after Justice Ian Harrison pronounced Christopher Michael Dawson guilty of murder in August 2022. Strangers randomly approached to hug me, shake my hand and thank me. Many women who embraced me were teary. I reflected again in June 2023, while holidaying in Italy with Ruth, after Judge Sarah Huggett in the District Court found Dawson guilty of underage sex with a schoolgirl. He has been sentenced for life and is likely to die behind bars at Long Bay Correctional Centre near his childhood home in Sydney.

An investigation inspired by something intangible drove me in unusual ways. I pursued a killer after he had enjoyed 36 years of freedom. No other story had affected me this way. It would not have happened if not for Gladys Thomas (nee Loewenthal).

Acknowledgements

The many people who helped me create *The Teacher's Pet* podcast are permanently tethered to Chris Dawson's conviction for Lyn's murder and to this book, *The Teacher's Pet*.

Many of you are named in the pages. Thank you. It is impossible to acknowledge everyone, however, I am forever indebted to Lyn's amazingly loyal and trusting family, particularly Pat Jenkins, Greg Simms, Merilyn Simms and Shanelle Dawson. They have lost so much yet they still deliver light and guidance in difficult times.

My own family and my wife Ruth Mathewson are wonderfully supportive and loving. In early March 2001 when Ruth was heavily pregnant with our daughter, we knew Lyn's case demanded justice. Thank you, Ruth, for standing with me as we expose the wrongs.

My employer, *The Australian*, and colleagues and friends, particularly Paul Whittaker, David Murray, Matthew Condon, Michelle Gunn, Nicholas Gray, Claire Harvey, Trent Dalton, Petra Rees, John Lehmann, Gemma Jones, Christopher Dore, Kristen Amiet and Zac Skulander, are exceptional. We did this. Together.

In late 2017 when I decided to reinvestigate Lyn's murder, Rebecca Hazel told me 'I think we might be able to do something very special'. My talented second cousin, Rob Loewenthal, agreed. And Slade Gibson, peerless audio guru and gifted musician, made it happen with heart, soul and great dedication. Thank you.

I am incredibly grateful to Lyn's awesome friends, particularly Julie Andrew and Sue Strath, and the whistle-blowing former students of Cromer High, led by the amazing Robyn Wheeler. Legends, one and all, along with my own friends who pitched in and looked out for me.

I thank our highly skilled lawyers, especially John-Paul Cashen and Dauid Sibtain SC, my broadcast friend from 2GB, Ben Fordham, my Brisbane legal duo friends, Brian Jordan and Terry Martin SC, and my mate from another era in Hong Kong, Peter Lavac. I am grateful to the ABC's podcast-savvy Leigh Sales for listening in 2018 – and then reading the manuscript and sharing her kind words five years later.

Pan Macmillan's Ingrid Ohlsson, Danielle Walker, Libby Turner and the rest of the publishing team are magnificent. We talked about a book in September 2018, however, I did not write a chapter for four and a half years as we awaited Chris Dawson's 2022 murder trial and 2023 carnal knowledge trial. Thank you, Ingrid, for your patience, professionalism and care.

I hope our book will be a fitting tribute to Lynette Joy Simms.

The Timeline

26 March 1970: High school sweethearts Lynette Simms and Chris Dawson are wed at St Jude's Anglican Church, Randwick.

1971: Chris and Lyn build their first house at Toronto Avenue, Cromer.

1972 to early 1977: Lyn works as a nurse and Chris plays rugby for Easts, then rugby league for the Newtown Jets.

1975–76: Chris and Lyn build their house at Gilwinga Drive, Bayview.

1977: After surgery to make it possible for her to have children, Lyn and Chris welcome the birth of Shanelle.

1979: Chris begins working as a physical education teacher at Cromer High. He notices Jenny Carlson while she's in Year 10.

1980: Chris teaches Jenny in Year 11 physical education. Chris becomes her confidante and she babysits Chris and Lyn's two daughters. Chris and Jenny start having sex. She is 16.

1980–81: Lyn begins working as a casual then goes permanent part-time at a childcare centre. She tells her friend, Anna, that Chris had been violent towards her.

1980–81: Chris and Lyn's marriage deteriorates as Lyn is upset that he is often angry and spends time with Jenny.

October 1981: Chris insists that Jenny moves into the spare room at Bayview as his infatuation grows amid trouble at Jenny's home.

Late 1981: Jenny recalls driving with Chris to a building where he said he went to see a 'hitman' about getting rid of Lyn.

November 1981: Jenny moves in to Paul Dawson's house, after Lyn discovers Jenny is having sex with Chris. Chris puts a deposit down on a unit in Manly for himself and Jenny.

December 1981: Lyn's friend, Ros, notices bruising on Lyn.

23 December 1981: Chris and Jenny set out for Queensland to start new lives together, but Jenny changes her mind.

8 January 1982: Chris and Lyn attend marriage counselling. That evening, Lyn speaks to her mother and tells her Chris has made Lyn 'a lovely drink'.

9 January 1982: Chris says he drove Lyn to a Mona Vale bus stop so she could go shopping. He takes his daughters swimming at Northbridge Baths, where Lyn is scheduled to meet them. She never arrives. Chris claims he took a phone call in the kiosk from Lyn who said she needed time away.

10 January 1982: Chris asks Jenny to move in to the Bayview house.

10–11 January 1982: Chris drives to South West Rocks to collect Jenny from a camping holiday with her school friends and brings her back to Bayview to replace Lyn.

January 1982: Two purported purchases on Lyn's Bankcard statement after she disappeared.

mid-January 1982: Chris continues to tell Lyn's mother, Helena, that Lyn is calling him saying she needs more time away.

18 February 1982: Chris files a missing person's report.

27 March 1982: Chris places a newspaper ad: 'Lyn, I love you, we all miss you. Please ring. We want you home. Chris.'

April 1982: Unsubstantiated sightings of Lyn.

1982–83: Chris briefs a solicitor to initiate divorce proceedings, which culminate in him owning the house and continuing to raise his two children.

October 1982: Chris takes Lyn's belongings to her mother's house.

1984: Chris and Jenny marry and move to the Gold Coast. All of Lyn's assets are transferred to Chris's name. He sells the Bayview house.

1985: Jenny gives birth to a daughter. Lyn's friend Sue Strath makes a formal complaint of police inaction to the Ombudsman.

1985–90: Jenny calls her Gold Coast home 'the compound' and says Chris is coercive and controlling. Their relationship deteriorates. In 1987 or 1988, the new owners of the Bayview house say Chris visited the home and asked, 'Where are you digging?'

1990: Jenny fears Chris and flees back to Sydney, starts divorce proceedings, meets Lyn's family and goes to the police. Police conduct a survey of the Bayview house but nothing is found.

15 January 1991: Chris is interviewed in Queensland by detectives from NSW Homicide Squad. The probe stops after Chris tells them of an unverified 1982 'sighting' of Lyn at a fruit barn.

1998: Investigation into Lyn's disappearance is officially reopened by Detective Senior Constable Damian Loone after urgings by Lyn's friend Sue Strath.

2000: Police conduct a limited excavation around the pool at the Bayview house and find a suspected slashed woman's cardigan and a popper container with a 1981 expiry date. Forensic testing is inconclusive.

February 2001: A coronial inquest is held. State Coroner Jan Stevenson finds that Lyn is dead, terminates inquest and refers case to the Office of the DPP, recommending a 'known person' be charged over the alleged murder.

March 2001: Newspaper journalist Hedley Thomas meets Damian Loone and Lyn's sister Pat, reads brief of evidence and writes feature and news articles about case.

February 2003: A second inquest, this time run by Deputy State Coroner Carl Milovanovich, also finds that a jury could find that a 'known person' killed Lyn, and recommends a prosecution of Chris. DPP Nicholas Cowdery refuses to prosecute, citing lack of evidence.

2003–18: The DPP repeatedly refuses requests from police and Lyn's family to launch a prosecution.

2015: Homicide Squad Detective Senior Constable Daniel Poole takes over from Damian Loone for a reinvestigation of Lyn's case.

October 2017: Lyn's loved ones agree to help Hedley Thomas in a podcast investigation into Lyn's probable murder.

April 2018: Police submit new brief of evidence to the DPP.

May 2018: After investigating for six months, Hedley Thomas launches *The Teacher's Pet* podcast. It finds new evidence and witnesses.

September 2018: Police dig in the backyard of the Bayview house, but don't find Lyn's body.

early December 2018: DPP advise police there is sufficient evidence to charge Chris Dawson with murder.

5 December 2018: Chris Dawson is arrested as the 16th and final episode of *The Teacher's Pet* is being produced.

April 2019: *The Teacher's Pet* podcast is withdrawn in Australia to ensure Chris Dawson can get a fair trial.

mid-2019 to April 2022: Chris Dawson tries to persuade judges to terminate the murder case. His lawyers argue the podcast ruined his prospects of justice. Judges refuse his applications.

May 2022: Chris Dawson's trial begins.

30 August 2022: Chris Dawson is found guilty of Lyn's murder.

May to June 2023: Chris Dawson faces a separate new trial and is found guilty of carnal knowledge of a schoolgirl.

The People

Simms Family

Lynette Simms (Dawson): A nurse, loving wife and adoring mother of two little girls, Lyn grew up near the beach at Clovelly and disappeared, aged 33, from Bayview on 8 or 9 January 1982.

Helena Simms (Lyn's mother): A mother of four, Helena was about to turn 66 when her daughter vanished. She would spend the next two decades looking for her until Helena's death in 2001.

Len Simms (Lyn's father): A retired naval officer and school mathematics teacher, Len immediately suspected foul play over his daughter's disappearance. He died in 2001.

Greg Simms (Lyn's brother): A former police officer and the youngest of the Simms children, Greg pushed police and prosecutors to act after initially believing Chris's claims about Lyn's absence.

Merilyn Simms (Greg's wife): A former music teacher, Merilyn's influence resulted in a meeting with Jenny in 1990 and the Simms family's realisation that Lyn was possibly murdered.

Pat Jenkins (Lyn's sister): A former radiographer and mother of four, Pat repeatedly pushed the DPP to act, and helped Hedley Thomas in 2001 and during *The Teacher's Pet* podcast in 2017–18.

Phil Simms (Lyn's brother): A former engineer and the eldest of the Simms children, Phil suspected that Lyn's remains were buried on the Bayview property. He died in 2021.

Lynda Simms (Phil's wife): Lynda never liked Chris since first meeting him in the late 1960s, and recalled that he was a bully who cruelly teased Lyn's younger brother, Greg.

Shanelle Dawson (Lyn and Chris's daughter): Aged four when Lyn disappeared, Shanelle helped police investigations and Hedley Thomas and has pleaded with her father to tell the truth.

Wendy Jennings (Lyn's cousin): A staunch advocate for a prosecution since 2001, Wendy wrote numerous letters to the DPP, politicians and senior police to seek justice for Lyn.

Dawson Family

Amy (pseudonym, Lyn and Chris's youngest daughter): Aged two when Lyn disappeared, Amy severed all ties in 2001 with the Simms family whom she accused of persecuting her 'innocent' father.

Chris Dawson (murderer): Identical twin with Paul and former Newtown Jets footballer, Chris groomed schoolgirls on the Northern Beaches. In August 2022, he was found guilty of Lyn's murder, and in June 2023 he was found guilty of underage sex with a schoolgirl.

Paul Dawson (Chris's twin): Also a schoolteacher, Paul was the dominant twin who overshadowed Chris in sports, teaching and relationships. Paul and Chris were renowned for their exceptional closeness and mirroring of each other throughout their lives.

Marilyn Dawson (Paul's wife): A mother of three girls who lived down the road from Lyn and Chris at Bayview, Marilyn told police that Lyn had not 'fought' for her marriage when Jenny came on the scene.

Peter Dawson (Chris's older brother and lawyer): A solicitor, Peter represented his brothers at inquests in 2001 and 2003, and he was closely involved in the legal team after Chris's arrest in late 2018.

Susan Dawson (Chris's third wife): A former teacher with twins from her first marriage, Susan met Chris at Coombabah State High and loyally stood behind him during media and police investigations.

Students of Cromer High

Jenny Carlson (pseudonym, Chris's second wife): A vulnerable school-girl in 1980, Jenny was 16 when groomed in Year 11. Chris moved Jenny into the house within a couple of days of Lyn's disappearance. She fled from him in 1990 and went to police and Lyn's family.

Lynda McCarthy: An early target of Chris when she received a 'creepy' note from him as a 15-year-old in 1979, Lynda came forward for the podcast and shed important light on the culture and contacts at the time.

Bev McNally: A babysitter in the house at Bayview before Jenny was groomed and installed, Bev came forward for the podcast and spoke of seeing Chris whip Lyn with a tea-towel and violently shove her.

Michelle Walsh: A talented schoolgirl gymnast, Michelle came forward for the podcast and spoke of being ordered by Chris to say nothing about his wife's disappearance in the days afterwards.

Phil Webster: An aspiring basketballer and schoolteacher, Phil came forward for the podcast and disclosed details about the charisma at school of Chris, his grooming of Jenny, and the conduct of other teachers.

Robyn Wheeler: A former vice captain of the school, Robyn was the first of its students to come forward for the podcast and lift the lid on the pred-atory conduct by Chris and other teachers with girls.

Students of Forest High

Alice (pseudonym, babysitter): A 15-year-old when she was allegedly groomed by schoolteacher Paul Dawson and persuaded to have sex with him, other teachers, Paul's friends and Chris, Alice spoke to police in 1998.

Shelley Oates-Wilding (babysitter): A future champion kayaker, Shelley was a babysitter for Paul and Marilyn Dawson's children and would drive around with Chris and Jenny, however, she was overlooked for 36 years by police.

Police

Geoff Shattles (police officer, author of report to Ombudsman): Geoff cleared police after a 1985 complaint to the Ombudsman by one of

Lyn's friends that police had failed to do proper investigations in the early 1980s.

Brian 'Smacka' Gardner (detective sergeant, Manly): A president of the Belrose Eagles football club at the time Chris and Paul Dawson played there in the early 1980s, Brian was named by Chris as an officer who helped him with 'procedure' after Lyn's disappearance.

Paul Mayger (Homicide Squad detective 1990–91 investigation): A seasoned detective, Paul interviewed witnesses for the first murder probe but all the files were lost. He went to the Gold Coast in 1991 for a video-taped interview with Chris – and this file survived.

Stuart Wilkins (Homicide Squad detective 1990–91 investigation): A relatively new Homicide detective at the time of the first murder probe, Stuart worked with Paul Mayger, and in late 2017 he talked to Hedley Thomas about the evidence and his suspicions.

Bob Gibbs (crime scene investigator): With expertise in crime scene analysis, Bob was at the 2000 dig which he criticised as inadequate as he believed it missed Lyn's body at Bayview.

Damian Loone (Dee Why detective): A dogged investigator, Damian started investigating in 1998 and interviewed key witnesses, triggering inquests in 2001 and 2003. His investigation files went to the Homicide Squad in 2015. Damian shared evidence with Hedley Thomas in 2001 after the first inquest had ended.

John Pendergast (detective): A more senior officer working with Damian Loone, John helped with investigations and led the formal police interviews of Paul and Marilyn Dawson in 1999.

Matt Fordham (police prosecutor): A strong believer in Chris's guilt, Matt took Damian Loone's evidence forward for the inquests in 2001 and 2003. He questioned key witnesses under oath in an effort to persuade the Office of the DPP to run a prosecution.

Paul Hulme (police officer, 1998 investigation): A longtime friend of one of Lyn's friends, Sue Strath, Paul directed Damian Loone in 1998 to re-open an investigation into Lyn's 1982 disappearance.

Daniel 'Dan' Poole (Homicide Squad detective): A quietly effective investigator, Dan received Damian Loone's evidence files in 2015, found fresh evidence and witnesses, liaised with Hedley Thomas and stayed on the case until the guilty verdict in 2022.

Mick Fuller (Police Commissioner): A staunch defender of his detectives, Mick acknowledged that Lyn's case was poorly handled in the past and intervened to establish a beneficial relationship between the Homicide Squad and Hedley Thomas during his podcast.

Scott Cook (2018 head of Homicide Squad): A senior officer who wrote to the DPP in April 2018 to urge a prosecution, Scott oversaw a proper search at the Bayview house in September 2018.

Coroners

Jan Stevenson (State Coroner): After examining the brief of evidence and hearing detective Loone give evidence under oath, Jan terminated her inquest in 2001 and referred it to the DPP with her finding that a jury could find 'a known person' guilty of murder.

Carl Milovanovich (Deputy State Coroner): After hearing from witnesses in public hearings in 2003 and seeing how they stood up during cross-examination, Carl terminated his inquest and recommended a murder prosecution.

Lyn's Friends

Julie Andrew: A young mum and neighbour who enjoyed regular coffee catch-ups with her good friend. Julie warned Lyn in late 1981 that Chris was 'fucking the babysitter'.

Anna Grantham: In the months before Lyn disappeared, Lyn's coworker Anna was shocked when Lyn told her that Chris had pushed her face into the mud around the pool.

Annette Leary: Another worried coworker, Annette remembered Lyn saying that Chris had put his hands around her throat and squeezed on their way to marriage counselling.

Barbara Cruise: The head of the childcare centre where Lyn worked, Barbara was impressed with Lyn's reliability and shocked when Chris called her to say Lyn had suddenly decided to go away.

Sue Strath: A persistent advocate for Lyn, Sue set out a strong case for possible foul play in her 1985 complaint to the Ombudsman about the lack of investigation by police, and kept pushing police for years to look at the case as a probable murder.

Roslyn McLoughlin: A tennis-playing mum, Ros was concerned about Lyn's large bruises and her pleas for someone to go back to her house with her before Christmas 1981.

Northern Beaches Schoolteachers

Bev Balkind (PE teacher): After transferring to Cromer High to replace Chris Dawson in PE classes in early 1982, Bev heard from students who witnessed Chris and Jenny's close liaison at school.

David Clarke (PE teacher): Husband of Bev, David taught at Beacon Hill High and knew Chris there and heard stories of teachers having sex with students in a number of schools at which he taught.

Hylton Mace (deputy principal): After challenging Chris about Jenny leading up to Lyn's disappearance, Hylton suspected she had been murdered but he did not act as he said he had no direct evidence.

Others

Brian Jordan (legal expert): A former judge and criminal defence lawyer, Brian examined evidence provided by Hedley Thomas and gave considered opinions of the strength of the police case.

Jeff Linden (magistrate): A former rugby teammate of Chris at Eastern Suburbs and a friend of Lyn and her family, Jeff acted as the schoolteacher's solicitor in his divorce from Lyn.

Kate Erwin (former student of Chris): As a St Ursula's College boarder in Yeppoon, Queensland, Kate became concerned at the conduct of Chris when he was teaching at the all-girls' school.

Kay Sinclair (wife of Chris's schoolfriend): After questioning Chris at a social event about the disappearance of his wife many years later, Kay became convinced he was lying.

Lorraine Watson (Lyn's dressmaker): After watching ABC's *Australian Story* about Lyn in 2003, Lorraine told police Lyn was covered in bruises and had said she lived with a violent man.

Michael Barnes (NSW Ombudsman): A former coroner, lawyer and newspaper reporter, Michael's forensic investigations of cold cases during inquests led to successful prosecutions of killers.

Neville Johnston (1980s owner of the Bayview house): Annoyed by Chris Dawson's visits to his old house to inspect landscaping and ask 'where are you digging?', Neville gave him short shrift.

Sue Johnston (1980s owner of the Bayview house): Wife of Neville, Sue remembered the unusual visits by Chris to his old house but Sue doubted Lyn's body was buried in the block's rocky ground.

Pam Eckford (friend of Jenny's mother): A social worker who helped women fleeing violent relationships, Pam helped Jenny contact and meet Lyn's family in 1990 to share her concerns of foul play.

Rebecca Hazel (author and Jenny's friend): An ocean swimmer and former lawyer, Rebecca befriended Hedley Thomas, shared ideas with him and joined him in a number of key podcast interviews.

Sandra and Joe Cimino (later owners of Paul Dawson's house): A former high school student of Paul Dawson, Joe saw anomalies in the soil during work at Chris and Lyn's old house. When Sandra's dog brought a bone home from the bush, she took it to police.

Scott Sattler (former student): A schoolboy rugby league star, Scott appreciated the encouragement and coaching he got from Chris and Paul Dawson at Coombabah State High.

Slade Gibson (audio engineer): A musician and former guitarist for Savage Garden, Slade was the co-creator of the podcast series, writing and performing all the music, overseeing audio production and advising Hedley on structure and tone.

Terry Martin (legal expert): A former judge and criminal defence lawyer in Brisbane, Terry wrote legal points which were strongly in favour of Chris and designed to provide balance to the podcast.

Peter Lavac (barrister): A former criminal defence lawyer and prosecutor in the 1990s in Hong Kong where he befriended Hedley Thomas, Peter shared his legal analysis with the journalist and slammed the DPP for its failure to prosecute Chris.

Journalists

Ben Fordham (broadcaster): A prominent 2GB radio presenter, Ben became riveted by the podcast and worked behind the scenes in 2018 to persuade police to work with Hedley Thomas and be co-operative.

Ruth Mathewson (Hedley's wife): A journalist and registered nurse, Ruth befriended Lyn's family and supported Hedley through the podcast investigation and five years of legal proceedings.

Michael McKenna (journalist): As head of the Queensland office of *The Australian*, Michael supported the podcast investigation from late October 2017.

Paul Whittaker (editor-in-chief): A twin himself who had met the Dawson twins in 1989 for a human interest story, Paul took legal, editorial and financial risks at *The Australian* to fully back the podcast investigation from its inception to its conclusion.

David Murray (journalist): An early mover on podcasts, David supported Hedley, followed up leads and interviewed people for 2018 newspaper stories, and covered the murder trial and carnal knowledge trial with colleagues, Claire Harvey, Matthew Condon, Hedley Thomas and Kristen Amiet.

Matthew Condon: A widely published author, podcaster and senior writer at *The Australian*, Matthew has been a colleague, friend and professional mentor to Hedley Thomas for many years. He attended every day of Chris Dawson's murder trial, wrote the Epilogue for this book and has been integral in sequel podcasts since the original *The Teacher's Pet* series.

Charles Miranda: A former London correspondent for News Corp newspapers in Australia, Charles Miranda is a senior reporter who wrote the original 2001 stories for Sydney's *The Daily Telegraph* after attending the first inquest for Lyn Dawson.

Defence Proceedings and Murder Trial

Greg Walsh (Chris's solicitor): A veteran of hundreds of criminal trials, Greg attacked the podcast as so biased and detailed that it made it impossible for his client Chris to get a fair trial.

Phillip Boulten SC (Chris's barrister before murder trial): A leading lawyer, Phillip tried unsuccessfully in the Supreme Court, Court of Appeal and High Court to have the case against Chris terminated.

Pauline David (Chris's barrister in murder trial): A former solicitor on the Gold Coast who acted for Chris in his 1991 interview with Homicide Squad detectives, Pauline defended him at relatively short notice in his murder trial.

Craig Everson SC (Crown prosecutor): A quiet and methodical lawyer with vast trial experience, Craig appeared in court against Chris on numerous occasions from 2019 and laid out a powerful circumstantial case in the trial to ensure a guilty verdict for murder.

Justice Elizabeth Fullerton SC (Supreme Court judge): A former schoolteacher, Elizabeth held hearings in 2020 to determine whether the murder proceedings should be terminated due to the podcast and the conduct of police.

Justice Ian Harrison SC (trial judge): Managing the trial without a jury at the request of Chris, Ian's extensive experience as a senior judge was called upon in a murder trial in which emotions ran high and witnesses recalled 40-year-old memories.

John-Paul Cashen (newspaper lawyer): Legal adviser to Hedley Thomas and *The Australian,* John-Paul was on the case from 2018 and also dealt with police, prosecutors and Chris's defence team.

Endnotes

Chapter 1: Bowen Hills

3   'Dear Greg, please let me reintroduce myself ...': Hedley Thomas, 'Lyn', email to Greg Simms, 27 October 2017

4   'Lyn has a brother, Greg Simms ...': Hedley Thomas, in conversation with Michael McKenna, 27 October 2017

Chapter 2: Newspaper Stories

13   'Newspapers, after all, are the first drafts ...': Jack Shafer, 'Who Said it First?', *Slate*, 30 August 2010

14   'Our liberty depends on the freedom ...': Library of Congress, 'Selected Quotations from the Thomas Jefferson Papers', loc.gov/collections/ thomas-jefferson-papers/articles-and-essays/selected-quotations- from-the-thomas-jefferson-papers

14   'Police have stepped up the hunt ...': Charles Miranda, 'Police Widen Hunt for Woman's Body', *The Daily Telegraph*, 2 March 2001

16   'There was not a spare seat ...': Charles Miranda, 'League Star, His Student and the Missing Wife', *The Daily Telegraph*, 1 March 2001

17   I started with an online property ownership search ...: Hedley Thomas, reporter's notebook March 2001

18   'I happened to pick up a copy ...': Susan, emailed letter to *The Courier-Mail* letters page, 1 March 2001

18   'I had Chris Dawson in Year 8 ...': Susan, telephone interview with Hedley Thomas, reporter's notebook early March 2001

19   'We are a Christian school ...': St Ursula's School, 'The St Ursula's Story', printed by the author, early March 2001, www.stursulas.qld.edu.au

19   'I am sickened by the fact . . .': Nancileigh, faxed letter to *The Couri-er-Mail* letters page, 1 March 2001

20   'The sister of the first wife . . .': Detective Senior Constable Damian Loone, telephone conversation with Hedley Thomas, reporter's notebook early March 2001

20   'There's a Jeremy Irons movie with twin brothers . . .': Charles Miranda, telephone conversation with Hedley Thomas, reporter's notebook early March 2001

21   'I have two darling nieces . . .': Pat Jenkins, telephone conversation with Hedley Thomas, reporter's notebook early March 2001

23   'That all sounds good but all I want . . .': A woman believed to be Susan Dawson, telephone conversation with Hedley Thomas, reporter's notebook early March 2001

24   'The position of teacher is a position of trust . . .': Denise, letter to *The Courier-Mail* letters page, early March 2001

Chapter 3: Northern Beaches
27   'I'm a twin myself . . .': Damian Loone, conversation with Hedley Thomas, reporter's notebook 5 March 2001

28   'Detective LOONE has caused certain areas . . .': Detective Senior Constable Matt Fordham, 10-page summary of Lyn Dawson case, reporter's notebook 5 March 2001

29   'I am a divorced woman . . .': Jenny Carlson, statement to police, 18 September 1998, reporter's notebook 5 March 2001

Chapter 4: Terrible Twins
42   'He got all the money . . .': Barbara Cruise, transcript of an interview with Damian Loone, 12 August 1998, reporter's notebook 5 March 2001

43   '. . . supposed to be a sexy celebration . . .': Chris Dawson, transcript of an interview with Detective Sergeant Paul Mayger and Detective Senior Constable Stuart Wilkins, 15 January 1991, reporter's notebook 5 March 2001

43   'One female student has stated . . .': Damian Loone, police statement, 17 October 1999, reporter's notebook 5 March 2001

44   'Paul would organise for me to go . . .': Former Forest High student, pseudonym 'Alice', statement, 17 September 1998, reporter's notebook 5 March 2001

59 'Such a strong result . . .': Pat Jenkins, 'Coronial Inquiry', email to Hedley Thomas, 3 March 2003

Chapter 7: Rebecca

61 'We are still unable to get . . .': Greg Simms, 'Lyn Dawson Case', email to Hedley Thomas, 15 August 2011

62 'I don't believe that information . . .': Hedley Thomas, 'Lyn Dawson Case', email to Greg Simms, 16 August 2011

63 'I am a writer researching a book . . .': Rebecca Hazel, 'Inquiry from the investigations web site', email to Hedley Thomas, 30 April 2012

64 'I think your book is a very . . .': Hedley Thomas, 'Thanks for the chat', email to Rebecca Hazel, 1 May 2012

66 'When I first wrote about Lyn . . .': Hedley Thomas, 'Thanks for the chat', email to Rebecca Hazel, 27 October 2017

66 'I really couldn't put it down . . .': Hedley Thomas, text message exchange with Rebecca Hazel, 21 November 2017

67 'Good morning Hedley . . .': Greg Simms, email to Hedley Thomas, 28 October 2017

67 'I have spoken to my brother Phil . . .': Greg Simms, 'Lyn', email to Hedley Thomas, 30 October 2017

Chapter 8: Alexander's Ladder

72 'Dad, why are you going . . .': Alexander Thomas, in conversation with Hedley Thomas, November 2017

74 '. . . a seminal work and examination . . .': Penguin Random House, 'About *The Journalist and the Murderer*', penguinrandomhouse.com

74 'Every journalist who is not too stupid . . .: Janet Malcolm, *The Journalist and the Murderer*, Alfred A. Knopf / Random House, 1990

76 Bizarre conduct and strange decision making . . .: 'The Volkers Case: Examining the Conduct of the Police and Prosecution', Crime and Misconduct Commission, 2003

76 First, a hard-hitting series of stories . . .: Janet Fife-Yeomans, 'Vile – They Left a Woman to Die a Gruesome Death but Will Never Have to Face Court', *The Daily Telegraph*, 3 February 2016

76 Next, a searing ABC *4 Corners* investigation . . .: Caro Meldrum-Hanna, 'Callous Disregard', ABC *4 Corners*, 9 May 2016

76 'The NSW DPP has formally declined . . .': Caro Meldrum-Hanna and Clay Hichens, 'Lynette Daley's Death: NSW DPP Under Scrutiny Over

Unprosecuted Killing', ABC online, 9 May 2016, abc.net.au/news/2016-05-09/nsw-dpp-under-scrutiny-over-lynette-daleys-unprosecuted-killing/7393368

77   'Two men have been found guilty . . .: Mazoe Ford and Dom Vukovic, 'Lynette Daley: Adrian Attwater, Paul Maris Found Guilty Over 2011 Camping Trip Death', ABC online, 6 September 2017, https://www.abc.net.au/news/2017-09-06/lynette-daley-trial-delivers-guilty-verdicts/8878848

77   'The question of whether there are reasonable . . .': 'Lynette Daley Death: Adrian Attwater and Paul Maris Jailed for Brutal Attack', ABC online, 8 December 2017, abc.net.au/news/2017-12-08/lynette-daley-justice-with-attwater-and-maris-sentenced-to-jail/9239312

80   'There is no story or book . . .': Peter Dawson, email to Rebecca Hazel, 23 May 2014

80   'I think we might be able . . .': Rebecca Hazel, text message exchange with Hedley Thomas, 2 November 2017

Chapter 9: Greg and Merilyn

82   'At the time I had two children . . .': Julie Andrew, statement to police, 2 May 1999, brief of evidence

85   'Had a file on Lyn . . .': Greg Simms, text message exchange with Hedley Thomas, 17 November 2017

104   'Reporter Robin Hughes talks with two sets of twins . . .': 'Strange Double Life of Twins', *Sydney Morning Herald*, October 1975

104   '. . . in the matter of my sister Lynette DAWSON . . .': Greg Simms, memo to Detective Stuart Wilkins, 15 October 1993

Chapter 11: The Murder Book

111   'She idolised her two children . . .': Barbara Cruise, transcript of an interview with Damian Loone, 12 August 1998, brief of evidence

Chapter 12: Bib and Bub

124   'V sad. Nonetheless, the police should . . .': Rebecca Hazel, text message exchange with Hedley Thomas, 26 November 2017

124   'I'm going to get a telephone jack . . .': Hedley Thomas, text message exchange with Rebecca Hazel, 27 November 2017

125   '. . . in these disturbing accounts . . .': Neddy Smith, *Catch and Kill Your Own*, Pan Macmillan, Sydney, 1995

126   'My sister Lyn Dawson, a married Sydney mother . . .': Greg Simms,

'Heckle and Jeckle', email to the ABC's archives section, 30 November 2017

126 'I was hoping to merely read . . .': Hedley Thomas, email to Kazeline Dawson, Coroners Court, 9 January 2018

127 'In an unsolved homicide and missing persons matters . . .': Acting court registrar Kazeline Dawson, 'Relations of Lyn Dawson', 10 January 2018

Chapter 13: Schoolgirls

130 'Hi, my name is Kate Erwin . . .': Kate Erwin, Looking for Lyn Facebook page, now defunct, 7 October 2016

133 'I can't remember exact things I did . . .': Don Burke, Nine Network, *A Current Affair*, Sydney, 27 November 2017

137 'I vaguely remember getting a lift . . .:' Former Forest High student, pseudonym 'Alice', statement, 17 September 1998, brief of evidence

Chapter 14: Sex, Lies and Videotape

148 '. . . some guy erecting our shed or something . . .': Chris Dawson, transcript of an interview with Detective Paul Mayger, 15 January 1991, brief of evidence

154 'He described a murderer's two biggest risks . . .': Hedley Thomas, text message exchange with Rebecca Hazel, 3 December 2017

Chapter 15: Cops and Smacka

156 'He volunteered that their good name . . .': Hedley Thomas, text message exchange with Rebecca Hazel, 3 December 2017

158 '. . . deep-seated corruption and criminality . . .': 'Royal Commission into the New South Wales Police Service', Justice James Wood, Sydney, 1994–97

160 'His fellow police will remember him . . .': 'Still Talking', newsletter of the Laryngectomee Association of New South Wales, October 2015

160 'They never had much time . . .': Northern Beaches police officer, statement to police, 30 September 1998

161 'I'm going to try to contact . . .': Hedley Thomas, text message exchange with Rebecca Hazel, 3 December 2017

161 'With all due respect, I don't talk . . .': Former Northern Beaches police officer, Facebook Messenger exchange with Hedley Thomas, 3 December 2017

Chapter 16: Pat Jenkins

Chapter 19: The Long Driveway

Chapter 20: Lost Files

Chapter 22: Carl Milovanovich

Chapter 25: Chequerboard

Chapter 26: Shanelle

Chapter 27: Are You There, Chris?

266 In late May 2003, a few months after the second inquest . . .: Kara Lawrence, 'I Did Not Kill my Wife', *The Daily Telegraph*, 28 May 2003

267 'Probably shouldn't have watched this . . .': Shanelle Dawson, text exchange with Hedley Thomas, 26 March 2018

268 'There's a chance we can resolve . . .': Hedley Thomas, text exchange with Shanelle Dawson, 27 March 2018

269 '. . . an overdue opportunity to solve this case . . .': Hedley Thomas, '*The Australian* podcast series on disappearance of Lynette Dawson', email to Paul Whittaker, 29 January 2018

276 'First, we have the generally grubby stuff . . .': John-Paul Cashen, email to Hedley Thomas, 25 March 2018

Chapter 28: Sue

283 'Thousands of sensitive files including secret . . .': Hedley Thomas and Emma Hart, 'CMC Blunder Exposes Secret Dossiers', *The Australian*, 6 March 2013

284 'The particular file we are seeking . . .': Hedley Thomas, email to Jenny Sloggett, NSW State Archives, 24 April 2018

284 'NSW State Archives holds a file . . .': Jenny Sloggett, NSW State Archives, email to Hedley Thomas, 27 April 2018

286 'Dear Sir, it is three years since my friend . . .': Sue Browett (Strath), letter to the NSW Ombudsman, 5 February 1985

288 'There was a slight possibility of contact . . .': Chris Dawson, antecedent report to police, 17 August 1982

292 'This is a bit of a sensitive . . .': Sue Thompson, file note in Ombudsman's office, 22 March 1985

295 'My daughter had become uptight . . .': Helena Simms, letter to police, 21 August 1982

Chapter 29: A Pack of Male Teachers

299 'This podcast is part investigation, part storytelling . . .': Paul Whittaker, 'The Teacher's Pet: The Unsolved Murder of Lyn Dawson', *The Australian*, 24 May 2018

300 'At the school during the period . . .': Robyn Wheeler, 'Chris Dawson et al', email to Hedley Thomas, 21 May 2018

Chapter 30: Cromer High

304 'Don't stress, you're kicking arse . . .': Shanelle Dawson, text message to Hedley Thomas, 29 May 2018

309 'He was a very fine man . . .': Pat Jenkins, 'Assorted', email to Hedley
     Thomas, 21 April 2019

Chapter 31: The Mint

315 'We were informed of this . . .': Greg Simms, text exchange with Daniel
     Poole, 6 July 2018

315 'I've never seen that handwritten . . .': Damian Loone, text exchange
     with Hedley Thomas, 6 July 2018

322 'You're getting closer and closer . . .': Ben Fordham, text exchange with
     Hedley Thomas, 30 June 2018

328 'The man started by saying . . .': Pat Jenkins, 'The Facebook entries',
     email exchange with Hedley Thomas, 9 July 2018

Chapter 32: The Commissioner

331 'There is no justice system when people who . . .': Wendy Jennings,
     'Unsolved murder (1982) of Lynette Joy Dawson – 1982', 5 July 2018

332 'I am sorry for your loss . . .': Scott Cook, letter from Commander
     Cook to Wendy Jennings, 9 July 1982

332 'What a debacle! We feel incensed . . .': Merilyn and Greg Simms,
     'What a debacle', letter to NSW police and Office of DPP, 6 July 2018

333 'Let me stress that I'm not . . .': Hedley Thomas, 'Dawson case', email
     to Commissioner Mick Fuller, 13 July 2018

333 'In light of the enormous interest . . .': Commissioner Mick Fuller,
     'Dawson case', email to Hedley Thomas, 13 July 2018

334 'Hey Hedley, had a call . . .': Greg Simms, text exchange with Hedley
     Thomas, 17 July 2018

334 'But you knew that already . . .': Hedley Thomas, text exchange with
     Greg Simms, 17 July 2018

Chapter 33: Terry's Balancing Act

339 '. . . my dad's getting hounded . . .': Sally Coates, 'It's a Witch-Hunt',
     Gold Coast Bulletin, 8 July 2018

340 'When I realised the truth . . .': Shanelle Dawson, text exchange with
     Hedley Thomas, 8 September 2018

342 'It has made me realise . . .': Michelle Gunn, 'mothers group', email to
     Hedley Thomas, 11 August 2018

343 'The podcast has generated overwhelming bias . . .': Terry Martin,
     email to Hedley Thomas, 2018

348 'I played rugby league and had contact . . .': Lloyd Babb, statement, 'DPP – Dawson case', email via Anna Cooper to Hedley Thomas, 3 August 2018

348 '[Lyn's family] say they have been treated abysmally . . .': Hedley Thomas, 'Further questions for DPP Lloyd Babb SC', email to Lloyd Babb, 6 August 2018

349 'I have found it necessary not to play . . .': Lloyd Babb, letter to NSW Attorney-General Greg Smith, 14 October 2011

349 'I note that you have sought . . .': Chris Maxwell, Acting Deputy Director of Public Prosecutions, 'Disappearance of Lynette Joy Dawson', letter from the Office of the NSW DPP to Pat Jenkins, 5 August 2011

Chapter 34: Helena

352 'I spent the time thinking . . .': Ruth Mathewson, text message exchange with Hedley Thomas, 8 August 2018

352 'Dad would have been absolutely riveted by it . . .': Hedley Thomas, text message exchange with Ruth Mathewson, 8 August 2018

354 'The 16-year-old boy that she turned . . .': Archie Butterfly, 'The Ocean is Deep and Wide', 5 July 2022, peterprofit.com/the-teachers-pet-trial-the-ocean-is-deep-and-wide-and-filled-with-storiesthat-you-just-couldnt-make-make-up-if-you-tried/?amp=1

354 'Police are searching for a woman . . .': 'Clothes Find: Woman Sought', *Sydney Morning Herald*, 5 October 1956

355 'I know how hard you're working . . .': Ruth Mathewson, text message exchange with Hedley Thomas, 10 August 2018

356 'Is he in jail yet?': Slade Gibson, text message exchange with Hedley Thomas, 18 May 2018

356 'During the stay, he would often go . . .': Jenny Carlson's mother, statement to NSW police, 8 September 1998

357 'And she told me point blank . . .': Jenny Carlson's father, interview with NSW police, 19 August 1998

358 'Jenny there too, Lyn shopping . . .': Helena Simms, diary entry, 6 October 1981

358 'Lyn not going to tennis – upset . . .': Helena Simms, diary entry, 8 October 1981

359 'Dear Pat and Ron . . .': Helena Simms, letter, 21 January 1982

359 'Mummy is lost! Daddy has Jenny now . . .': Helena Simms, diary entry, January 1982

359 'James found it!' Gemma Jones, text message exchange with Hedley Thomas, 1 August 2018

360 'Lyn, I love you. We all miss you . . .': *The Daily Telegraph*, classified advertisement, 27 March 1982

360 'What a sad birthday. No ring from Lyn . . .': Helena Simms, diary entry, 1 February 1982

360 'To footy. Shocking day. Chris brought Jenny . . .': Helena Simms, diary entry, 7 March 1982

360 'Dear Chris, it grieves and saddens . . .': Helena Simms, letter to Chris Dawson, 20 August 1984

361 'I truly believe Chris hated Lyn . . .': Pat Jenkins, 'podcast', email to Hedley Thomas, 16 June 2018

363 'I do know that all these years later . . .': Lulu Wilkinson, 'Thank you', to Hedley Thomas, 10 August 2018

Chapter 35: Hedley, You're a Fucking Wanker

371 'Do you recall whether Chris . . .': Hedley Thomas, 'Counselling', email to Greg Simms and Pat Jenkins, 26 July 2018

372 'Hedley Thomas has set himself up . . .': Chris, Paul and Gary Dawson, and a tradesman, NSW police, exhibit 35, transcripts of intercepted phone calls, 9–10 September 2018

375 'Were you at the dig today? . . .': John-Paul Cashen, text message exchange with Hedley Thomas, 12 September 2018

375 'Fingers and toes crossed . . .': Sue Strath, 'Lynette Dawson', email to Hedley Thomas, 12 September 2018.

Chapter 36: Digging

379 'I was so exhausted last night . . .': Pat Jenkins, 'A disappointing result', email to Hedley Thomas, 18 September 2018

Chapter 37: Arrested

385 'We were a very ordinary family . . .': Pat Jenkins, 'phone call', email to Hedley Thomas, 2 December 2018

Chapter 38: Best Defence is Offence

389 'Paul Dawson, twin brother of Chris Dawson . . .': Louis Bourke, 'Paul Dawson Arrests Self to be With Brother Chris', 12 December 2018, betootaadvocate.com/uncategorized/paul-dawson-arrests-self-to-be-with-brother-chris/

390 '. . . feeling quite strong . . .': Shanelle Dawson, text exchange with Hedley Thomas, 6 December 2018

390 'Greetings from 36,000 feet over China . . .': Hedley Thomas, 'Hi Shanelle – some of the Oz story', email to Shanelle Dawson, 17 December 2018

Chapter 39: Black Blotting Pens

399 'Mr Walsh told Sydney's Downing Centre Local Court . . .': AAP, 'Dawson Material May Have Been Shredded, Court Told', *9News*, 9 May 2019, 9news.com.au/national/teachers-pet-podcast-chris-dawson-case-back-in-court-over-hedley-thomas-evidence/2a01eef0-b829-4ec0-b33c-c09d86b978ff

401 'Chris Dawson's lawyer is distorting the truth . . .': *The Australian* and Hedley Thomas, statement, 9 May 2019

402 'Our job is to help guide you through . . .': John-Paul Cashen, 'Teacher's Pet', email to Hedley Thomas, 6 June 2019

404 'It involves careful consideration of each obligation . . .': John-Paul Cashen, 'Teacher's Pet', email to Hedley Thomas, 6 June 2019

408 'There seems little point in responding . . .': John-Paul Cashen, 'Chris Dawson hearing today', email to Hedley Thomas, 20 June 2019

Chapter 40: Podcast on Trial

430 'Christopher Dawson will avoid facing trial . . .': Emily Ritchie, draft article for *The Australian*, 10 September 2020